A History of Lancaster

New edition

Stephen Constantine
Nigel Dalziel
Michael Mullett
David Shotter
Alan Warde
Andrew White
Michael Winstanley

Edited by Andrew White

Edinburgh University Press

© Stephen Constantine, Nigel Dalziel, Michael Mullett, David Shotter, Alan Warde, Andrew White, Michael Winstanley, 2001

Edinburgh University Press Ltd

22 George Square, Edinburgh

Typeset in Janson Text
by Carnegie Publishing Ltd, Chatsworth Road, Lancaster, and
printed and bound in Great Britain by The Cromwell Press

A CIP Record for this book is available from the British Library

ISBN 0 7486 1466 4 (paperback)

The right of Stephen Constantine, Nigel Dalziel, Michael Mullett, David Shotter, Alan Warde, Andrew White and Michael Winstanley to be identified as authors of this work has been asserted in accordance with the Copyright, Designs and Patents Act 1988.

Contents

Picture Acknowledgments   iv

Introduction   1

1. Roman Lancaster: Site and Settlement   3
   DAVID SHOTTER

2. Continuity, Charter, Castle and County Town, 400–1500   33
   ANDREW WHITE

3. Reformation and Renewal, 1450–1690   73
   MICHAEL MULLETT

4. Trade and Transition, 1690–1815   117
   NIGEL DALZIEL

5. The Town Transformed, 1815–1914   173
   MICHAEL WINSTANLEY

6. Challenge and Change in a New Century   229
   STEPHEN CONSTANTINE *and* ALAN WARDE

Select Bibliography   276

Index   280

Picture Acknowledgments

The Editor gratefully acknowledges sources of illustrations as follows: pages 9, 19, 25, 39, 42–3, 47, 51–2, 60, 67, 137, 143, 152, 269, maps drawn by Peter Lee; page 58, Foundation charter of Lancaster Priory, Harleian MS 3764, fii, by permission of the British Library; page 93, Public Record Office DL 31/112; page 105, Andrew White; pages 141, 175, 178, 186–7, 198–9, 216–8, Lancaster Central Library; pages 188, 191, 212, Michael Winstanley; page 219, copyright © Ian Beesley; page 233, King's Own Regimental Museum; page 247, Marks & Spencer plc; page 250, John Jennings, 1971, by permission of *Urban Studies*; pages 6, 18, 26 David Shotter. All the remainder are courtesy of Lancaster City Museums.

Introduction

An earlier version of this book appeared in 1993 to mark the 800th anniversary of Lancaster's first borough charter. The work was very popular and quickly sold out, showing the need that existed for a detailed and up-to-date history. There are several nineteenth-century histories of the town and an excellent economic history by Schofield, but there had been until then no full-length history published in the twentieth century. This new edition contains a new first chapter to take the story back to the first century AD and Lancaster's Roman origins. Chapter 2 has been revised to accommodate it, and the final chapter has brought the story as far as possible up to date. The middle chapters have been updated but left in the main as they were.

The establishment of Lancaster University in 1963 and S. Martin's College (initially solely for teacher-training) in 1964 have led to a growing number of staff and student research projects. Many details of the archaeology, architecture, housing, industry, living standards and lives of ordinary inhabitants have been revealed by study in recent years, the results of which mainly appear in articles and unpublished dissertations and theses.

Notable inroads into the publication of local history have been made by the Centre for North-West Regional Studies at Lancaster University and by Lancaster City Museums, as well as by other local societies and groups, and so it is appropriate that members of staff of the two institutions have co-operated in the writing of this volume. Dr Andrew White is Head of Museums and Dr Nigel Dalziel is Curator of Maritime History with the City Museums, while Dr David Shotter, Dr Michael Mullett, Dr Michael Winstanley and Dr Stephen Constantine are Senior Lecturers in History at Lancaster University. Dr Alan Warde was formerly Senior Lecturer in Sociology at Lancaster University, but is now Professor of Sociology at Manchester University.

Because of the long period being studied the sources are very varied. They range from the results of archaeological excavations and artefact studies to original documents and secondary sources. Documents are particularly lacking until the eleventh century and even then Lancaster is surprisingly poor in medieval manuscripts. The very rich source of the borough records does not start until the sixteenth century and is not plentiful until the seventeenth, with the exception of the fine charter series. Much of Lancaster's medieval archive must have been destroyed or dispersed during the Scottish raids or in the turmoil of the Civil War. For the later periods there is an embarrassment of sources.

The authors would like to thank the people of Lancaster for manufacturing more history than can be consumed locally. They would also like to thank all those in the community who have helped to make this book possible, some of whose names appear in the bibliography, Peter Lee who drew the maps and the staff at Ryburn/Keele University Press who first let it see the light of day and the staff of Edinburgh University Press who have produced this revised edition.

CHAPTER ONE

Roman Lancaster:
Site and Settlement

David Shotter

We are not aware of any Roman military settlement in Lancaster other than that on Castle Hill; the siting of this will presumably have been prompted by its command of the Lune crossing and its elevated position in a marshy environment. Successive Roman structures on Castle Hill have affected the subsequent townscape – not least because of the 'normal' relationship between the late Roman fort and the medieval Castle. Outside the fort, the civilian settlement and the road system provided the ancestry for Penny Street and Church Street, as well as for the lanes (Anchor Lane and Chancery Lane) which later linked Church Street with Market Street. Further, four lines of entry into, and exit from, the Roman site have survived

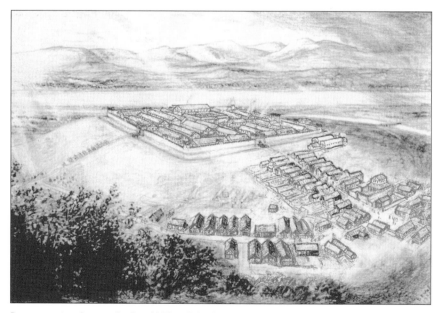

Reconstruction drawing, by David Vale, of the fort and settlement on and adjacent to Castle Hill.

in the lines of the A6 (north and south of the City), as well as those south of the river Lune (through Caton and Brookhouse and through Quernmore). Thus, the influence on the present townscape of the Roman site and elements of its infrastructure, whilst not total, is considerable.

The Early Years

The late prehistory of Lancashire is notoriously under-represented in the archaeological record;[1] considerable difficulties are experienced in attempting to separate the Iron Age from the Bronze Age and, away from Roman centres, it is equally difficult to distinguish between the late pre-Roman Iron Age and the Romano-British Iron Age. Further, agricultural conditions in Lancashire are not generally conducive to the achieving of useful results through aerial photography.[2] However, it is not conceivable that the complex landscapes seen in fragmentary form in the middle and upper Lune valley do not contain features which date from the late pre-Roman Iron Age and from the Romano-British period.[3] This is sufficient to demonstrate that the Iron-Age *lacuna* is more a product of invisibility than of non-existence, and to suggest that the agricultural landscape in the Lancaster area and its hinterland was probably well-developed.

Little help is available from the classical sources on the political geography of north Lancashire on the eve of the Roman occupation, although the existence of hill-forts, such as Skelmore Heads, Warton Crag and Ingleborough, points to the likelihood of some form of hierarchical organisation – based perhaps upon the agricultural and economic success of 'the few'. The Roman historian, Cornelius Tacitus,[4] indicates that much of northern England formed the tribal territory of the Brigantes – the name means 'upland people' – and that this tribe was the most populous in Britain, itself an observation of some significance. Several other tribal names are known to us from various sources, evidently occupying land either within or adjacent to Brigantian territory; those known in the west are the Setantii and the Carvetii.[5] The Carvetii evidently held land in the Solway Plain and in the valleys of the rivers Eden and Lune, whilst the Setantii, who have traditionally been thought of as a group in the Lancashire Fylde, may possibly have held territory around the northern flank of Morecambe Bay. It remains unclear whether the Lancaster area fell into the tribal territory of either of these two, or was simply a 'part of Brigantia'. In any case, it is hardly credible that the agricultural land of the lower Lune valley did not allow some to acquire wealth and, through it, to dominate others. This would suggest the existence of some form of hierarchy local to the Lancaster area.

In the accounts of the classical writers, the north of England appears to have been dominated at the time of the Roman invasion by two people – Cartimandua and Venutius; the latter is described as a warlord second only to the southern leader, Caratacus.[6] Rome decided to put her weight behind Cartimandua as tribal leader,[7] and perhaps insisted on the marriage of the two leaders in an effort to calm factional tension. Whilst there is no clear indication of the locations of their seats of power, it seems reasonable to suppose that Cartimandua's might have been in or to the east of the Pennines, whilst Venutius's was in the west.[8]

The Romans' principal concern was to secure peace and stability amongst the Brigantes, and thus to prevent disruptive attacks on their own advance into the north Midlands and Wales. Plainly, they did not succeed in this – or, at least, succeeded only intermittently; Tacitus's account of Brigantian affairs is imprecise, although it appears that there were outbreaks of trouble within the tribe, evidently during the 50s and 60s. These required Roman military intervention – but only on a temporary basis, since in AD 69 further trouble led to Venutius's emergence as tribal leader, leaving the Romans to rescue the eclipsed Cartimandua,[9] and initiate a new policy.

Tacitus's account offers no basis for a precise understanding of these events – either in chronology or in geography. There are, however, grounds for believing that the Roman tactic, prior to AD 69, was to launch 'search-and-destroy' missions into the north-west, both by land and sea,[10] though stopping short, at this stage, of permanent occupation. In all likelihood, troops were marched overland from bases in the north-west Midlands (such as Wroxeter) to meet up with colleagues who had been conveyed by transport-ships from the Dee estuary and disembarked into the north-west's major river estuaries (such as the Lune). It is likely that the Lancaster area figured in this activity not only because of its position on the estuary of the Lune, but also because it lay at the head of 'King Street', a road-route from the north-west Midlands, which ran through Middlewich, Wilderspool and Walton-le-Dale.[11] The evidence of Roman coins[12] found in and around Lancaster makes such a hypothesis feasible, although it has to said that, to date, no structural evidence in the form of a fort or a campaign-camp that could relate to such an early date has been located in the Lancaster area.

Conquest and Consolidation

Venutius's victory over Cartimandua in AD 69 clearly required immediate action on Rome's part: with the removal of their 'client-monarch', Rome had little option but to bring Venutius 'to book', and to annexe the territory of the Brigantes into the province. It seems likely that this task was shouldered by the incumbent governor, Marcus Vettius Bolanus, who, although regarded as 'light-weight' by Tacitus, was evidently well-thought-of in the Flavian period.[13] It is indeed not impossible that Bolanus reached into Scotland, though again detail is entirely lacking.

Bolanus was succeeded in AD 71 by a high-profile appointment in the person of Quintus Petillius Cerialis, the son-in-law of the new emperor,

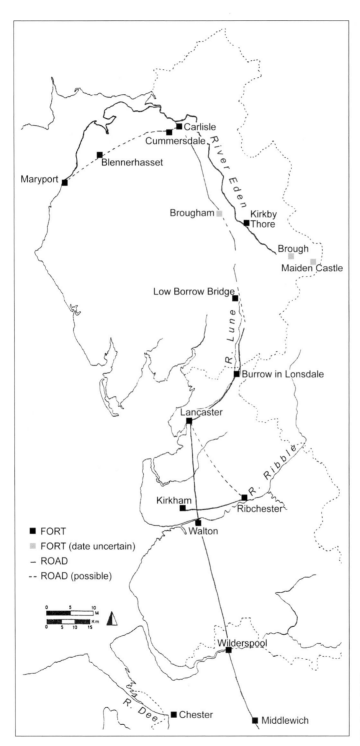

North West
England: military
advances of the
early Flavian
period.

Vespasian.[14] It may be reasonably supposed that, amongst his early policy-decisions, Vespasian had opted for a forward thrust in Britain.

In the past, it has been difficult for historians to separate the military work of the various Roman governors of Britain in the 70s and 80s; a great deal – probably too much – has tended to be associated with Tacitus's father-in-law, Gnaeus Julius Agricola (AD 77–83).[15] It is now clear that the work of other governors, both before and after Agricola, has been seriously undervalued.[16] Recently, however, it has become obvious that the role of Petillius Cerialis, in particular, was much more important than was previously supposed,[17] and that he penetrated deeply into Scotland – perhaps even as far north as the river Tay.

It is evident from Tacitus's description that Cerialis divided the available troops into two main battle-groups, and that Agricola, who was at that time commander (*legatus*) of legion XX at Wroxeter, took control of the western 'arm'.[18] It seems likely that Agricola approached the north-west by the two routes which reiterated earlier approaches: some went by sea, probably from Chester, to make landfalls in the large river-estuaries (including, again, the Lune), whilst others came from their bases in the north-west Midlands, probably penetrating the north-west along the line of 'King Street'. It was probably no coincidence that Cerialis had brought with him to Britain a new legion (II *Adiutrix*) whose soldiers had recently received promotion from the Ravenna fleet and who had deserted from Vitellius to Vespasian at a crucial moment in the civil war of AD 69. To have placed at least a group (*vexillatio*) of these at Chester would appear to have been a dynamic way of utilising their naval experience.[19]

Unfortunately, dating evidence from the earliest permanent Roman fort on Castle Hill at Lancaster is not particularly ample, and there is no input from dendrochronology; however, the chronological pattern of coin-loss would not be inconsistent with a foundation as early as the period of Cerialis's governorship. Indeed, Lancaster may have been an important rendezvous-point for sea-borne and land-based troops before they proceeded along the Lune and Eden valleys to Carlisle, where the presence of Cerialis's troops is now accepted as beyond reasonable doubt.[20]

The nature of this first fort on Castle Hill cannot be described with certainty, unless it is the one whose features have from time to time been located – and ascribed to Agricola who, on present evidence, may have used and possibly refurbished it, rather than having initiated it.[21] Elements of the defences of an early fort, constructed of turf and timber, have been noted in three separate locations: part of the western defensive rampart and two external ditches were found in 1971 in the western Vicarage Field, whilst the site of the east gate and parts of the eastern rampart and ditches were located at the southern end of the Mitre Yard in 1973. A portion of the northern defences, including an exceptionally well-preserved rampart of clay and turf was found in 1975 adjacent to the eastern side of the Old Vicarage. The presence of the Castle and its continued use as a prison have, however,

precluded any examination of the southern half of this fort, although such is
the symmetry normally associated with Roman forts that the full outline can
be projected with reasonable confidence; such a fort would have covered
approximately 5.5 acres. Little is known of the internal arrangements of this
fort, although the burnt remains of timber structures located inside the north
rampart were interpreted as probably relating to barrack accommodation,
which may also have been the source of the substantial re-used timbers which
were incorporated into the structure of the well found near to the site of the
east gate.[22] It is evident from the configuration of the fort that its main gate
lay on its eastern side, so that the line of Church Street represented the chief
route of access into the fort.

Since it is now known that the Lake District forts were not built before
c. AD 90,[23] it is possible that the river Lune did not, at first at least, have a
major crossing at Lancaster. This is not, however, to deny the river's significance; for it was noted during the excavations of 1973 that immediately
outside the east gate another road diverged from the principal 'eastern access'
route and appeared to swing down towards the river, possibly heading for an
anchorage site.[24] It also seems reasonable to suppose that 'through traffic' did
not have to pass through the fort, but used a 'by-pass', which is now marked
by the line of Penny Street.

Although little is known about the history of the early fort at Lancaster,
it is assumed that it remained in working order during the 70s and 80s and
into the 90s, although it may have required refurbishment during that period;
the supposed 'barracks' displayed at least two structural phases, and recent

Clay-and-turf defensive rampart of the earliest Roman fort on Castle Hill.

Forts on Castle Hill, first to third centuries.

evidence from the 'neighbouring' timber fort at Ribchester suggests a complex early structural history.[25] At Lancaster, the coin-evidence suggests that there may even have been a short break in occupation in the later years of the first century AD; flexibility in fort usage is likely at a time of change in frontier development in the province and is, in any case, clearly implied in some of the documents found at *Vindolanda*.[26]

At some stage, the fort on Castle Hill was extended – prior (it appears) to its rebuilding in stone early in the second century, and probably after the short abandonment (suggested above). The enlargement was substantial; the northern rampart was pushed to the north and, if the southern rampart was similarly extended, it will have yielded an almost-square fort, covering between nine and ten acres. Although the details of this enlargement are far from clear, it is possible that it was connected with the building of large forts on the Stanegate frontier, evidently to accommodate the very large numbers of troops who were being evacuated from Scotland in the late AD 80s. It is possible, too, that the enlargement could have involved re-orientation; the fact that the Lake District was receiving forts and garrisons from the early 90s may have persuaded the authorities of the need for a crossing of the Lune (by ford or bridge) at Lancaster. In such circumstances, the north may have become the principal gate; this will have involved a major rebuilding of the fort's interior.

That the fort was, however, rebuilt in stone in c. AD 102 is clear from a fragment of a building-inscription, found in 1863, beneath the Priory Church.[27] Evidence from the northern rampart suggests that this fort was equipped with a stone wall of some six feet in thickness, which was set on to a bevelled plinth-course. Only a few fragments of evidence have given any indication of internal structures, although these did prove sufficient during the excavations of 1973 on the Mitre Yard to facilitate the location of the fort's north-east corner. Further, the earthworks in the western Vicarage Field, though of medieval origin, have been shown to overlie their Roman predecessors precisely, thus proving the location of the north-west

Part of an inscription (*RIB* 604) indicating building-operations on the fort in Trajan's reign.

corner. The only structural feature to emerge was a palisade of timber stakes evidently associated with the fort-ditches at the east gate.

Only two further inferences regarding the occupation of the fort can be drawn from the surviving evidence: first, the coin-loss evidence is strongly suggestive of a loss of garrison (in part or whole) during the period of the Antonine re-occupation of Scotland (*c.* AD 140–165).[28] The second piece of evidence comes in the form of an inscription recording rebuilding-work on the bath-house and *basilica* in the mid-third century.[29] The *basilica* may well have been an example of a *basilica equestris exercitatoria*, a drill-hall attached to the headquarters of cavalry-forts – as has recently been revealed in excavations at the fort at Birdoswald, on Hadrian's Wall.[30] The use in the inscription of the formula, 'collapsed through old age', might indicate a period of demilitarisation and neglect preceding the rebuilding; alternatively, the formula might represent a euphemism for hostile action. In this case, since the inscription was evidently dedicated to the rebel-emperor, Postumus, the need for rebuilding might have arisen from damage resulting from fighting between rebels and 'loyalists' at the time of the establishment of the breakaway *Imperium Galliarum* ('Independent Empire of the Gauls': AD 260–273). Thus, the Roman period may have seen Lancaster involved in the tribulations of civil war in the third century AD, a war which, to judge from the erasure of Postumus's name from the inscription, left bitter feelings in the area.

Other than this, nothing else is known of the fabric of the Roman fort on Castle Hill until its complete remodelling on a different alignment in the fourth century (see below).

Garrisons and Individuals: the Role of Lancaster

Although the Lancaster area has not yielded a large collection of Roman inscriptions, those that we have are of considerable interest, if measured by the information which they give regarding fort-garrisons and some individuals at Lancaster.

The fort, in common with others, may have been constructed by legionaries,[31] but its permanent garrison appears to have been provided by units of auxiliary cavalry, composed of five hundred men each (*ala quingenaria*). Two such units are associated with the area: a tombstone of a cavalryman, Lucius Julius Apollinaris,[32] who came from Trier (on the Rhine), was found in Pudding Lane (Cheapside) in 1772, but has since been lost; it is now known only through a contemporary drawing. This has been reconstructed to show that Apollinaris was a trooper in an *Ala Augusta*; a number of cavalry-units were allowed to entitle themselves *Augusta*, after the emperor, to show their devotion to him. There is no way, however, of determining which of them was appropriate in this case. The tombstone is not dated, but usages on it would suggest that it was not much later than the late first century, and that, therefore, an *Ala Augusta*, if indeed the stone has not been transported from elsewhere, should be placed early in the garrison-sequence. In any case, the presence of a *basilica* and the fact that the timber-lined well contained a considerable amount of horse-dung[33] should leave little doubt that the Lancaster fort was long associated with cavalry. This, of course, raises the question of how far the human and equine populations of the area could be supported by cereal crops grown locally.

The unit of the army that, however, has supplied the most ample evidence of its presence is the *Ala Gallorum Sebosiana*; it is named (as *Sebussiana*) on the bath-house inscription of the early AD 260s, and it appears in a number of relief-stamps and incusions on bricks and tiles, both from Lancaster itself and from the associated tileries at Quernmore.[34] All of these[35] give the name in an abbreviated form – either *Sebusia* or *ALSB*; most other references to the unit that we have give it its 'proper' name.

The *Ala Sebosiana* was on the Rhine and in Italy until AD 69–70,[36] and may, therefore, have come to Britain with Petillius Cerialis in AD 71, and it was certainly in the army of Agricola in Carlisle.[37] However, none of the tile-fragments from sites in Lancaster comes from a datable context, whilst the Quernmore kilns, which began operations in *c.* AD 80, may have still been manufacturing products at the turn of the second and third centuries. In view of the fact that the *Ala Augusta* cannot be identified precisely, we have no evidence for the date of the arrival of the *Ala Sebosiana* at Lancaster; the most likely occasions are, however, the reorganisations which followed either Marcus Aurelius's withdrawal from the Antonine Wall in *c.* AD 165 or Septimius Severus' successful bid for power in AD 197. Thus, the bath-house inscription provides the only secure chronological context for

Inscription (*RIB* 605) recording rebuilding-work on the Bath-house and *Basilica* in AD 262.

Lead sealing of the *Ala Sebosiana*.

Dedication to the god Mars, made by soldiers of the Numerus Barcariorum (*RIB* 601).

the unit at Lancaster, though it might be supposed that the sheer volume of material relating to it suggests a long stay.

The only other unit associated with the Lancaster area is a *Numerus Barcariorum*;[38] the unit is recorded on an altar dedicated to Mars, found in 1794 in Halton churchyard. The unit's name description (*numerus*) shows that it was of the irregular kind, presumably with specialist skills. In this case, a unit of men, equipped with shallow-draughted barges (*barcae*) will have been of particular value in the estuarine conditions of Morecambe Bay, perhaps acting as lightermen for deeper-draughted vessels which could not easily come up the river to Lancaster. It should be noted, however, that these men were soldiers (*milites*) first, and lightermen after that. Logic would suggest that such a unit would have been associated with Lancaster when the remodelled fort of the fourth century, with its maritime associations, was in operation. However, the fine quality of lettering on the altar would be persuasive of a rather earlier date; nor, given the size of the fort at Lancaster, would it be unreasonable to suppose that the *barcarii* may have been barracked at Lancaster alongside a regular auxiliary unit. The unit's lighterage capability suggests that, rather like Ambleside at the north end of Windermere,[39] Lancaster served as a reception-point for men and commodities that were to be transported further inland.

The names of a number of individuals figure on inscriptions found locally: besides the cavalry trooper, Lucius Julius Apollinaris (mentioned above), we have an altar dedicated to Jalonus Contrebis, perhaps the tutelary deity of the river Lune, by Julius Januarius, a retired senior non-commissioned officer (*decurio*). This altar, which was found in 1802 at Bolton-le-Sands (approximately one mile north of the fort site), evidently represents a dedication made, in the hope of favourable agricultural conditions, by a former soldier on the land allocated to him after his demobilisation. The altar is not explicitly dated, but its style would suggest that it should be placed at about the turn of the second and third centuries AD. Although there is no indication of Januarius's province of origin, the fact that he evidently stayed close to his place of service is indicative of the ties which he (and others like him) had formed and points to a growing 'cosmopolitanism' in the hinterland of forts.

Two further names are of unit commanders: Flavius Ammausius was prefect of cavalry in the early 260s, whilst Sabinus – (not to be confused with the provincial governor, Octavius Sabinus) – was in charge of the bargemen. A further commander of the *Ala Sebosiana* appears on an altar from Bollihope Common (Co. Durham);[40] this altar, which carries a dedication to the god, Silvanus, following a successful boar-hunt, was set up by Gaius Tetius Veturius Micianus, *praefectus* of the *Ala Sebosiana*, evidently during the third century. A further piece of evidence may 'conceal' a name:[41] a lead sealing, found in the western Vicarage Field, carries on the obverse *ALS* (*Ala Sebosiana*), whilst on the reverse it has *IPD*, which could represent a name and a rank – for example, *Julius Primus, Decurio*.

One further name mentioned is potentially the most interesting: an altar records a dedication to the Romano-Celtic deity, Mars Cocidius, by Lucius Vibenius,[42] a high-ranking official of a type familiar in the third century, known as a *Beneficiarius consularis* (an 'aide' to the provincial governor, seconded from the army, whose duties appear to have included oversight of customs posts).[43] It is obvious that there will have been a role for such an official at Lancaster, with commercial traffic entering and leaving the province by means of the river Lune, and a consequent need to collect the appropriate dues. It is tempting to connect an official of this status with the substantial courtyard building located immediately to the north of the fort's northern defences.[44] Although the bulk of this building was tested archaeologically under adverse conditions in 1958, more recent excavations have shown it to have had its own bath suite, which was approached through an impressive columnated entrance-way. Such a building is extremely unlikely to have been a private residence; indeed, the only other explanation of it which is in any way consistent with the available evidence is that it was a *mansio* (or 'rest-house' for travelling officials).

Admittedly, much of the evidence for an assessment of Lancaster's role is circumstantial in nature; nor is there a great deal of it over the first three centuries AD. What there is, however, contains indications that the fort was significant. From the outset, it was large and, in its extended form, probably very large for an auxiliary fort at between nine and ten acres. The size certainly suggests a capability of housing a large (presumably double or augmented) garrison; the epigraphic evidence supplies some support for this in indicating that, in the third century, the *Ala Sebosiana* and the *Numerus Barcariorum* may have shared the fort.

As we have seen, the Lune estuary and a fort at Lancaster held a long-term significance for conquest and occupation: the value in the pre-Flavian (and pre-conquest) period was that the area could be approached by both land and sea, thus allowing men who had marched overland from further south to be supplied and reinforced from the sea. The Lune valley also facilitated a deep penetration into Brigantian territory. Once the conquest had been completed (probably by Petillius Cerialis), a permanent fort housed a cavalry garrison which could readily patrol the fort's hinterland and, because of its physical requirements, offer opportunities for local farmers and craftsmen to benefit economically. This will have been enhanced by the bridging (or perhaps initially fording) of the river, which will have permitted patrolling to be easily extended north of the river in the direction of what may have been the heart of Setantian territory on the north side of Morecambe Bay. Such a role will have been emphasised if the fort's main gate was switched from the east to the north side of the fort.

As the occupation established itself, so could the potential of the riverside siting be realised; in particular, men and supplies could be brought into port, and taken further up the Lune valley or northwards towards the Lake District. The presence of the unit of 'lightermen' serves to underscore such a role. In this way, both for security in the area and for development towards prosperity, the role of a Roman fort at Lancaster was vital.

The Civilian Settlement and the Hinterland

Contrary to popular belief, local hostility probably did not long outlast the conquest of the area; even the Roman objects found on Warton Crag, and sometimes cited as evidence of brigandage, do not point unequivocally in that direction. Rather, if the area was less wooded than is sometimes supposed, agriculture will have already developed and populations have become more settled; frequent Roman patrolling in the area will surely, in any case, have served to deter even the more audacious. In short, there is every reason to suppose that people rapidly came to appreciate what was to be gained by co-operation and, like the German tribesmen on the Rhine in the time of Augustus Caesar, 'they grew accustomed to hold markets ... and became different without knowing it.'[45]

An obvious sign of this 'process' was the development, in common with most Roman fort sites, of a civilian settlement outside the fort's walls. However, the evidence from Lancaster's civilian settlement is not abundant; Roman law forbade the burial of the dead inside settlements and, at Lancaster, evidence for burials has been noted in Stonewell, in the upper portion of Penny Street, and at Westfield Memorial Village. This would suggest that the civilian settlement was not extensive, and perhaps concentrated on what is now China Street, Penny Street and the area between Church Street and the river which, in the Roman period, came much closer to the area presently occupied by the bus station. Excavation has taken place on a few sites in Church Street, and a great deal of Roman material was noted in this area when the present properties were being built in the eighteenth century[46] and mains services laid in the nineteenth century.[47]

The evidence of excavation in Church Street suggests that, in common with other settlements of this type, street-frontage space was at a premium; the typical 'unit' consisted of a long, narrow, building, with its gable end facing on to the street and possibly providing a shop on the street-frontage, with living accommodation behind, and perhaps a yard or work area behind that.[48] Although we have no direct evidence from Lancaster of trades that

Dedication to Jalonus, probably the deity of the river Lune (*RIB* 600).

were practised in the civilian settlement, we may, on the analogy of other such sites, be reasonably certain that there will have been potters, a range of metal-workers, manufacturers of religious objects,[49] producers and sellers of food, some of it to satisfy a 'take-away' market, processors of hides and craftsmen in leather goods, as well as those who sold on products that had been brought in by itinerant traders. Such a range of activities will have led to a town which was cramped, busy, noisy and smelly: a town which, perhaps, combined the attributes of a garrison town and one in the pioneering days of the American West. Most of such properties will have been built of timber initially, though some were undoubtedly converted to stone construction over time.

In addition, such towns will have had a range of temples and shrines, which reflected the religious preoccupations of both soldiers and civilians. Lancaster has produced no inscriptions specifically referring to temples in the civilian settlement, although some clues suggest the possibility: two altars are dedicated to Mars, one in the 'local' form, *Mars Cocidius*;[50] the Roman war-god would naturally attract attention in such a military-orientated community, although the fact that Cocidius appears to have had his centre at Bewcastle (in north Cumbria) suggests that the dedicator, Lucius Vibenius, may have had previous connections with Hadrian's Wall. A rather different divinity who received a dedication from the retired soldier, Julius Januarius, was *Jalonus Contrebis*;[51] it is possible that *Jalonus* was a deity connected with the river Lune, and it would not have been unreasonable if the river's importance to the area were marked by worship of its 'presiding deity'. Such worship would presumably have been centred on a temple of the type known as 'Romano-Celtic'. It is likely, too, that other deities would have attracted attention because of their tutelary role with regard to certain trades and to the 'trade guilds' which may have been associated with them; it would not be surprising if Vulcan (metal-workers), Mercury (salespeople) and Apollo (musicians) were represented.

There are, however, two tantalising clues which point to possible religious centres: excavation in Church Street in 1992 recovered a portion of a face-mask, evidently associated with the wine-god, Dionysus (Bacchus); there may have been a temple nearby; secondly, a group of statuary was

Dedication to Mars Cocidius by Lucius Vibenius (*RIB* 602).

recovered in 1794, to the south of Lancaster, evidently from a spot where it had been concealed. The origin and implications of this group have been much discussed,[52] but it was possibly Mithraic in significance: one figure is wearing what appears to be a 'Phrygian cap', whilst another statue has evidently been decapitated – a common fate suffered by Mithraic figures at the hands of Christians. Conversely, there is virtually no direct evidence of Christianity itself: a pottery lamp, bearing a 'christogram', has allegedly been found, though the original provenances of such objects are notoriously suspect.

For the rest, space will have been devoted to the relaxation of soldiers – for example, in the form of bars, brothels and gambling establishments; further, although Roman soldiers were not, until the early third century AD at least, legally permitted to marry whilst on service, unofficial liaisons were overlooked, and many soldiers will have had 'wives' and 'families' living near to the fort and will probably have been able to live with them for some of the time at least. Once discharged from service, a soldier was free to marry whomever he wished, and many may have elected to spend their retirements with their families close to their place of service.

Although the evidence is negative rather than positive, as far as is known, such civilian settlements as Lancaster's were not normally permitted any independence of organisation and administration – except, perhaps, for religious purposes: the settlement will have been under the jurisdiction of the fort commander. There were, therefore, none of the public buildings connected with administration which are normally found in the major towns of Roman Britain. We have, however, noted the large courtyard building to the north of the fort on Castle Hill, with the suggestion that this may have been the residence of an important official. The other building of public significance which has been recognised at Lancaster is the bath-house,[53] which will presumably have been used by both soldiers and civilians. We have already noticed the inscription which refers to the substantial rebuilding of this establishment in the third century; it was situated outside the eastern wall of the fort, and a considerable amount of it evidently underlies the Mitre House office development on the north eastern flank of Castle Hill. This will have represented a major leisure and social facility.

We have noted that burials have been recognised at a number of sites in and around the city: Roman law forbade the burial of the dead *within* settlements. On the other hand, unless such a settlement as Lancaster enjoyed special status (for example, as a veteran settlement), for which there is no evidence, it will not have been permitted walls or other defences. The burials, therefore, will have been located in areas along the access roads, as the settlement 'tailed off' into a kind of 'rural suburbia'.

Although there has been too little excavation in the civilian settlement to

Part ('*Tepidarium*') of the small bath-house attached to the 'Courtyard House'.

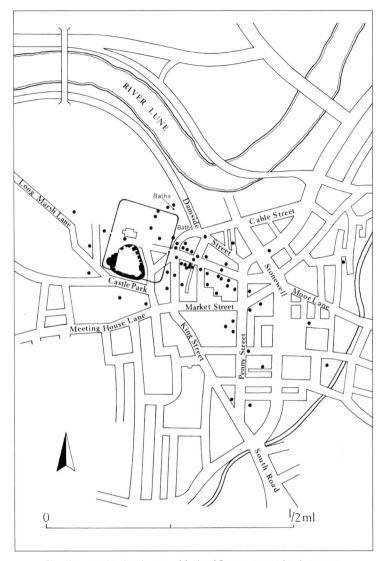

Plan showing the distribution of finds of Roman material in Lancaster.

be certain of its chronology, it appears likely that it started to develop soon after the establishment of the fort – that is, in the last quarter of the first century AD. Whether it then enjoyed unbroken activity cannot be definitely ascertained; as will have been seen, it is at least possible that there were some breaks in the military occupation, and it is unclear whether the economic relationship between the civilian settlement and the rural hinterland alone would have been sufficiently vibrant to sustain economic activity in the absence of the fort's garrison. Thus, if the garrison was moved away, even if only temporarily, many of the civilians may have elected to follow them. A further uncertainty in the archaeological evidence is caused by the fact that most of the present properties in the heart of Lancaster have substantial cellars, which have truncated most medieval and late Roman survival. There is, however, some evidence to suggest that the civilian settlement did not generally outlast the middle of the fourth century. Since this appears approximately to have coincided with the complete redesigning, re-orientation and rebuilding of the fort on Castle Hill, it is possible that soldiers and civilians were from that point both housed within this new fort (see below).

A system of major roads,[54] constructed initially for military purposes, radiated from Lancaster. It is reasonably certain that, from the south, Lancaster was approached from two directions – from Walton-le-Dale and from Ribchester – and that these roads converged in the vicinity of Galgate, and proceeded to Lancaster by way of Highland Brow, Burrow Heights and Ripley Heights, and then by-passing Castle Hill along the line now represented by Penny Street. Two third-century milestones, which evidently stood on this route, were recovered in 1811 and 1834.[55] The road, which left by the fort's east gate, evidently ran by way of the line of Church Street, and headed along Moorgate in the direction of Quernmore, whilst the 'Penny Street route' crossed this road in Stonewell and then ran along the south bank of the river Lune[56] towards Burrow-in-Lonsdale, where it converged with the 'north-south' route from Chester to Carlisle. That the Lune was crossed to the north of Castle Hill cannot be in doubt, and it is conjectured that the crossing may have opened into three routes – one on the north bank of the river Lune, another to Watercrook (Kendal), whilst a third may have crossed the Sands to Furness, by way of Bolton-le-Sands. In a lot of particulars, however, these routes are conjectural. It is equally reasonable to assume that these major routes were the starting points for a network of minor roads and tracks which gave access on to the major road system and Lancaster itself for farmers and others in the hinterland.

The most significant sites in Lancaster's hinterland which are currently known are those in the area of Quernmore.[57] The two known sites, at Lythe Brow and Low Pleasant, have produced evidence of the manufacture of bricks, tiles and pottery, the latter of which produced one example (on a *mortarium*) of a maker's name – Tritus. Different types of kiln have been found, and the two sites appear to be linked by their proximity to the source of raw material. In view of the fact that a major brickworks still operates in the area (at Claughton), it seems likely that other, older, sites of manufacture await discovery. It appears that there were two chief periods of manufacturing activity – from the late first to the mid-second century AD, and again in the early third; it is assumed that the sites perhaps were initially operated under a military aegis, but were later leased to civilians. It is worth noting that hollow voussoir tiles, found amongst the debris associated with the fort bath-house at Lancaster, were shown to have derived from a quite different (and currently unknown) source.[58] This presumably reflects changes that had occurred in the supply pattern of building materials to Roman forts in the north west. There was also some evidence of (presumably Roman) iron-working adjacent to the kiln sites at Low Pleasant. Such local supplying of Roman garrisons, especially in the earlier years of occupation, can be paralleled at a number of other fort sites in north west England.

The other substantial earthwork known in the area is at Burrow Heights (to the south of Lancaster); much uncertainty has surrounded the nature of this site, and because of the fact that it is adjacent to the road from Walton-le-Dale to Lancaster, it has been suggested, on the basis of the group of statuary evidently found close to it (see above), that it might have been a roadside mausoleum. If so, it would appear to have belonged to an owner of substantial means.[59] However, the discovery of a number of Roman coins in its vicinity suggests that the site may have been of military origin – perhaps a watchtower beside the road.[60]

Although the area does boast some raw materials – coal, iron, gritstone – its chief resource was agricultural. There is no evidence that coal was used in this area during the Roman occupation; gritstone, however, was obviously of use for millstones, and it was clearly employed for such monumental purposes as altars and inscriptions. The masons and sculptors presumably did their work in the civilian settlement, but probably had contracts with others for the supply of suitable stone. As we have seen, Quermore (Low

Group of possibly Mithraic statuary found at Burrow Heights.

Pleasant site) has produced a little evidence for iron-roasting, although no tests were undertaken on the slags to determine the origin of the ore; most likely, it was shipped across Morecambe Bay from Furness, as this means of transport would have been preferable to a journey by road.

Agricultural activity will, therefore, have been a principal mode of livelihood for most, and such evidence as there is suggests that a considerable degree of woodland clearance had taken place even before the Roman conquest of the area. As we have seen, there are areas of the Lune Valley such as Eller Beck and Leck Beck, which allow us still a glimpse of such a landscape.[61] Subsequent agricultural activity, however, has done much to damage such ancient landscapes.

We do not, of course, know in detail the views on land tenure put into practice in the area by the Roman occupiers; we may, however, be sure that they had needs for which arrangements had to be made. For example, some land was presumably set aside for veteran settlement; the dedication of the retired decurion, Julius Januarius, shows that this did indeed happen in the Lune Valley and, although there is no indication of the exact location of Januarius's farm, we may reasonably assume that the better and more accessible land was used for this purpose. Presumably, this will have included land freshly reclaimed from forestation and land that had been 'confiscated' from previous owners. It was perhaps leased out until it was needed for settlement. Some land, too, must have been left in the hands of local people, either as owners or tenants; this may have been land that was agriculturally more marginal – perhaps up from the valley-floor.

A considerable number of individual farm sites is known in the Lancaster area, some of them sub-rectangular in type and some sub-circular.[62] There is, however, no way of knowing, without excavation, their chronological patterns of occupation nor the nature of their owners/tenants. Nor can we tell what were their principal strengths, though many may have relied for income on a diversity of activities. Obviously, local farmers were able to supply a range of foodstuffs, and may have had clear indications of what the 'market' required;[63] documentary evidence from the site of *Vindolanda* certainly suggests that requirements were often quite specific. Animals may have been slaughtered and wool woven on the farms themselves, though it is equally possible that animals were taken 'on the hoof' into the civilian settlement for slaughter, and wool taken to be woven there. As the fort at Lancaster housed a cavalry unit, it must have been necessary for considerable areas to be turned over to grass to supply the required hay. Such 'organised' supplies of agricultural produce were presumably supplemented by meat, fowl and fish from individual 'hunters'. It is reasonable to imagine, too, that if the fort also housed a naval unit, then regular supplies of timber will have been required for the building and repair of ships which were presumably carried out on sites adjacent to the river. Such activities also presuppose some level of woodland management to ensure continued supplies of the 'right' timber.

Timber-lined well.

Thus, whilst it is unlikely that local farmers could have produced sufficient crops or stock to supply all of the needs of a large garrison and settlement of civilians and, as a consequence, that some such produce will have had to be 'imported' from further afield, the evidence that we have, albeit patchy in nature, suggests a thriving and mutually beneficial intercourse between fort, civilian settlement and the wider hinterland.

The Later Years

The Roman empire in the third and fourth centuries AD became increasingly embattled by internal and external problems. Lancaster appears to have suffered both the hyperinflation and the civil discord that characterised the middle years of the third century. It is known, too, that the eastern coast of England suffered from raiding and perhaps saw the arrival on a more permanent basis of Germanic settlers, resulting in the walling of major towns and the construction of a new series of forts on the 'Saxon Shore' from the Wash to Southampton Water. Nor did the west coast escape problems of this kind: the Scotti (from Ireland) were amongst the new enemies of Roman Britain emerging in the later third century, and the settlement of such raiders may have been undertaken in Wales.[64]

Clearly, the problems were sufficiently acute to prompt the development in the west of the new kind of fort architecture which was already appearing in the east – at Cardiff, Caernarfon, Caer Gybi (Holyhead) and Lancaster. The evidence for such a fort at Lancaster has long been to hand, since a small portion of it – the Wery Wall – has never been lost to view. Further, it is evident that in the eighteenth century, at least, more of it was visible

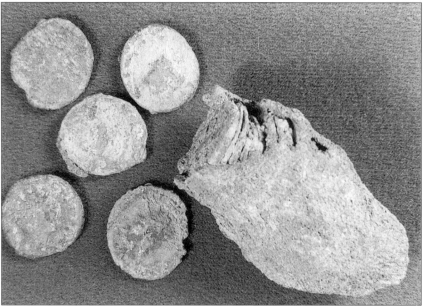

Two Roman coin-hoards from Lancaster:
Top Eight coins of the late Republican and early imperial periods, which survive from a hoard of about 100 coins found on Castle Hill in the nineteenth century.
Bottom Coins of the third century, found in the 1980s near to St George's Quay: the coins were 'contained' in a linen wrapper, part of which survives.

than is the case now.[65] Although the Wery Wall has been much discussed, it was not until excavations in 1973 that it was finally established that the structure was of late Roman origin,[66] and that it was related to a wall, some nine feet thick, which ran up Castle Hill (from north east to south west)

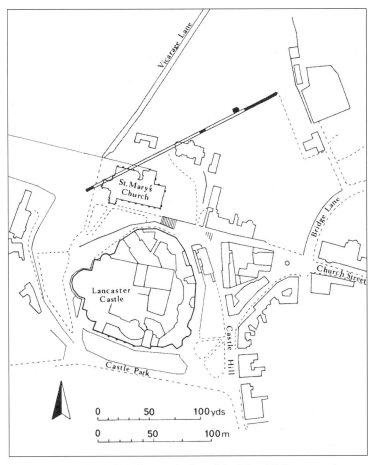

Castle Hill, showing the line of the 'Wery Wall'.

and evidently beneath the Priory Church. The portion which has remained exposed to the present day is now known to have been the core of a bastion, situated either at the north angle of the fort or as an interval structure on the wall. Such bastions were evidently used as mounts for pieces of heavy artillery. The philosophy which lay behind this new type of fort clearly resided in the need to provide protection against attackers for a community defending itself inside; in other words, the Roman fort, which had originally been conceived as a kind of police station, was now being transformed into the precursor of the medieval castle, with high, thick, walls and bastions, and a small number of massively built, but relatively narrow, entrance-ways.

This new fort was evidently an urgent requirement, as its one known wall and outer defences were built across the demolished remains of the bath-house that had been part of the large courtyard house to the north of the original fort (see above). The alignment of the new fort was different, too, and must have required the demolition also of a considerable part of the original fort and its defences. There is no information regarding a particular emergency which may have prompted its construction, evidently in the AD 330s; however, it is worth recording that around AD 315 the emperor, Constantine, appears to have assumed the title *Britannicus Maximus*, and that it must have been some kind of emergency which brought his son, Constans, to Britain in the winter of AD 342–3 together with a portion of a mobile field army;[67] such a journey, involving, of course, a sea-crossing, would not in normal circumstances have been made in the middle of winter.

There is a great deal that is not properly understood about this new fort at Lancaster: besides the line of the wall, already mentioned, the only other structural remain to have been recovered is what appears to have been a massive gateway structure, located close to the east gate of the original fort (and therefore close to Covell's Cross). It is assumed that, if indeed this structure was a gateway and was part of the new fort, then it would have been the south gate. Nor can the overall shape of the new fort be determined; assuming that the medieval castle may have been constructed in a corner of a still-existing wall circuit (as happened in the cases of some of the Saxon Shore forts), then this new fort would appear to have formed an irregular quadrilateral shape. Of course, it may even be too big an assumption to regard it as having had four sides; an alternative reconstruction would see it as part of a three-sided enclosure around an embarkation point on the riverside.

No information has been recovered regarding the internal structures of this fort; indeed, it may be that the imposing walls enclosed a space taken

Castle Hill: fragment of the 'Wery Wall' incorporated into later structures. (These have now been removed, leaving just the Roman work.)

up mostly by sheds and tents. This raises the major question of who lived in this new fort: there is no documentary or archaeological evidence which sheds any substantial light on this. It is known that the manning of Roman forts may have been extremely flexible in numerical terms in the fourth century. Although at one time it seemed reasonable to connect the *Numerus Barcariorum* with the late fort, it is now recognised that the high quality of the lettering on the altar set up by them raises great difficulties regarding this idea. It is tempting, however, to see two statuettes set up by Roman soldiers to the god, Mars Nodons (or Nodens), and found on Cockersand Moss, as late in date,[68] because of the large shrine to this god established at Lydney (on the Severn estuary) in the fourth century.[69] Further, a connection between Lydney and Lancaster might have been of a specifically maritime nature. No certainty, however, can be attached to these questions, particularly since the statuettes are not now available for study.

The only other tentative 'clue' is offered by the fact that some excavations in the civilian settlement, together with the evidence of casual finds, suggest that the occupation of sites in the settlement may have been coming to an end towards the middle of the fourth century. It is possible that security could no longer be guaranteed outside the fort and that, therefore, civilians were being moved into the safety of the new, walled, enclosure. In this way, the new fort will have itself been acting more as a kind of town or village, in which the community defended itself and worked for its own welfare, with the added advantage of having access to sea-borne trade. This kind of semi-independence or self-help in the later years of the fourth century AD and into the fifth seems to be in line with what is being deduced from evidence at other northern fort sites.[70] It should, however, be added that the damage done to archaeological deposits by eighteenth-century cellaring could have removed some evidence of later occupation in the civilian settlement, although recent work on a 'cellar free' site in Church Street appears (provisionally) to confirm the general picture.

The evidence of pottery and coins from Castle Hill suggests that the fort site, at least, remained active into the early fifth century, though what happened subsequently is the object of only the most tantalising of glimpses.[71] Some fragments of pottery and some coins suggest a continuing connection with the outside world (that is, of Europe and the Mediterranean). These may indicate that a 'sub-Roman' community remained intact on Castle Hill, subject to a variety of commercial and cultural influences. Further, the discovery of sections of cross-shaft and of Northumbrian coins from the ninth century may point to the development of a monastic community and suggest that, as had happened at the beginning of the Roman occupation, so at the end, the inhabitants of the Lancaster area became 'different without knowing it'.

Notes

1. C. Haselgrove, 'The Iron Age', 61–73 in R. Newman (ed.), *The Archaeology of Lancashire*, Lancaster University Archaeology Unit, 1996; N. J. Higham, *The Northern Counties to A.D. 1000*, Longman, 1986, 117–49.

2. N. J. Higham, 'Native Settlements west of the Pennines', 41–7 in K. Branigan (ed.), *Rome and the Brigantes*, Sheffield University, 1980.

3. R. A. Lowndes, '"Celtic" fields, farmsteads and burial mounds in the Lune Valley', *Transactions of the Cumberland and Westmorland Antiquarian and Archaeological Society* (2nd series), LXIII, 1963, 77–95; also 'Excavation of a Romano-British Farmstead at Eller Beck', *Transactions of the Cumberland and Westmorland Antiquarian and Archaeological Society* (2nd series), LXIV, 1964, 6–13; N. J. Higham and G. D. B. Jones, *The Carvetii*, Alan Sutton, 1985, 68ff.

4. *Life of Agricola* 17, 1.

5. Ptolemy, *Geographia* 11.3,2 (Setantii); *Journal of Roman Studies*, LV, 1965, 224 and *RIB* 933 (Carvetii).

6. *Annals* XII. 31–40; for the comment on Venutius, see XII. 40, 2–3.

7. See D. C. A. Shotter, 'Rome and the Brigantes: Early Hostilities', *Transactions of the Cumberland and Westmorland Antiquarian and Archaeological Society* (2nd series), XCIV, 1994, 21–34.

8. E. g. I. A. Richmond, 'Queen Cartimandua', *Journal of Roman Studies*, XLIV, 1954, 43–52; B. R. Hartley and L. Fitts, *The Brigantes*, Alan Sutton, 1988; P. Carrington, 'The Roman Advance into the North Western Midlands before A. D. 71', *Chester Arch. Journal*, LXVIII, 1985, 5–22.

9. Tacitus, *Histories* III.45.

10. For such tactics, see W. S. Hanson, *Agricola and the Conquest of the North*, Batsford, 1987, 175.

11. See I. Rogers, 'The Conquest of Brigantia and the Development of the Roman Road-system in the North-west', *Britannia* XXVII, 1996, 365–8; D. C. A. Shotter, 'Roman North-west England: the Process of Annexation', *Transactions of the Historic Society of Lancashire and Cheshire*, CXLVIII, 1998, 1–26.

12. D. C. A. Shotter, 'Coin-loss and the Roman Occupation of Northwest England', *British Numismatic Journal*, LXIII, 1993, 1–19.

13. Tacitus, *Life of Agricola* 8, 1 and 16,5; Statius, *Silvae* V. 2, 143–9.

14. For Cerialis, see A. R. Birley, 'Petillius Cerialis and the Conquest of Brigantia', *Britannia*, IV, 1973, 179–90. (Birley discusses in some detail the likely reasons for the evident antipathy between Tacitus and Cerialis.)

15. See W. S. Hanson, *op. cit.*

16. D. C. A. Shotter, *Romans and Britons in North-West England* (2nd edn), Lancaster University, 1997; the need for revision of traditional views was noted by G. D. B. Jones, 'The Romans in the North-West', *Northern History*, III, 1968, 1–26. Tacitus's rather uninformative comment is to be found in *Life of Agricola* 17,1.

17. See D. C. A. Shotter, 'Petillius Cerialis in Northern Britain', *Northern History*, XXXVI, 2000, 189–98.

18. *Life of Agricola* 8,2.

19. See D. C. A. Shotter, 'Early Roman Occupation at Chester', forthcoming.

20. M. R. McCarthy, *Carlisle: History and Guide*, Alan Sutton, 1993, 3.

21. For an account of the relevant excavations in 1971, 1973 and 1975–6, see

G. D. B. Jones and D. C. A. Shotter (eds), *Roman Lancaster*, Manchester University (Brigantia Monographs 1), 1988, 26–58.

22. See the account of the timber-lined well by W. S. Hanson, 179–83 in G. D. B. Jones and D. C. A. Shotter (eds), *Roman Lancaster* (as cited in note 21).

23. For the chronology of Watercrook and the forts of the Lake District, see T. W. Potter, *Romans in North-West England*, Cumberland and Westmorland Antiquarian and Archaeological Society, Research Series 1, 1979, 139ff and 356–8.

24. D. C. A. Shotter and A. J. White, *Roman Fort and Town of Lancaster*, Lancaster University, 1990, 19ff.

25. K. M. Buxton and C. L. E. Howard-Davis, *Bremetenacum: Excavations at Roman Ribchester, 1980, 1989–90*, Lancaster University Archaeology Unit (Lancaster Imprints 9), 2000.

26. See, for example, G. D. B. Jones, 'The Emergence of the Tyne/Solway frontier', 98–107 in V. A. Maxfield and M. J. Dobson (eds), *Roman Frontier Studies, 1989*, Exeter University, 1990; for the writing-tablets from Vindolanda, see E. B. Birley, R. Birley and A. R. Birley, *Vindolanda Research Reports, II: The Early Wooden Forts*, The Vindolanda Trust, 1993.

27. *RIB* 604.

28. D. C. A. Shotter, *Roman Coins from North-West England*, Lancaster University, 1990, 18; it has been suggested that a fragment of an inscription, found on St George's Quay in 1976, may have come from a building-inscription of the reign of Caracalla (AD 211–217; *Britannia*, XVII, 1986, 436).

29. *RIB* 605; the inscription is discussed in G. D. B. Jones and D. C. A. Shotter (eds), *op. cit.*, 208–11; for the dating of the inscription to *c.* AD 262, see E. B. Birley, 'A Roman Altar from Bankshead': *CIL* VII. 802, *Transactions of the Cumberland and Westmorland Antiquarian and Archaeological Society* (Second Series), XXXVI, 1936, 1–7.

30. T. Wilmott, *Birdoswald: Excavations of a Roman Fort on Hadrian's Wall*, English Heritage, 1997, 95–8.

31. A fragmentary brick-stamp, reading -FEC ('made') was recovered in the excavations of 1973 (G. D. B. Jones and D. C. A. Shotter (eds), *op. cit.*, 186); such a formula may be associated with legionary work. Alternatively, the stamp may be that of a private contractor, working on the courtyard-house (see below and *RIB* 2489.56A).

32. *RIB* 606; for a discussion, see B. J. N. Edwards, 'Roman Finds from Contrebis', *Transactions of the Cumberland and Westmorland Antiquarian and Archaeological Society* (Second Series), LXXI, 1971, 23–5.

33. G. D. B. Jones and D. C. A. Shotter (eds), *op. cit.*, 170–8.

34. G. D. B. Jones and D. C. A. Shotter (eds), *op. cit.*, 186–8; see also pp. 85–92 for the Quernmore kilns; also W. T. Watkin, *Roman Lancashire*, Liverpool, 1883, 175–7 for the earlier discoveries of stamped tiles.

35. *RIB* 2465. 1–2.

36. *ILS* 2533; Tacitus, *Histories* III.6,2.

37. *Tab. Luguval. 44*; see R. S. O. Tomlin, 'Roman Manuscripts from Carlisle: The Ink-written Tablets', *Britannia*, XXIX, 1998, 74f.

38. *RIB* 601; D. C. A. Shotter, '*Numeri Barcariorum*: A Note on *RIB* 601', *Britannia*, IV, 1973, 206–9.

39. See D. C. A. Shotter, *Romans and Britons in North-West England* (2nd edn),

Lancaster University, 1997; 'Romans in South Cumbria', *Transactions of the Cumberland and Westmorland Antiquarian and Archaeological Society* (2nd series), XCV, 1995, 73–7.

40. *RIB* 1041.

41. *RIB* 2411.88.

42. *RIB* 602.

43. See P. Salway, *Roman Britain*, Oxford University Press, 1981, 521ff; D. J. Breeze, *The Northern Frontiers of Roman Britain*, Batsford, 1982, 86. In view of the fact that the centre of the worship of Cocidius was evidently at Bewcastle (Cumbria), it is not impossible that this official had seen service also on Hadrian's Wall.

44. See G. D. B. Jones and D. C. A. Shotter (eds), *op. cit.*, 61–71.

45. Dio Cassius, *Roman History* LVI. 18, 2–3.

46. See W. T. Watkin, *Roman Lancashire*, Liverpool, 1883, 171f.

47. See *Contrebis*, V, 1977, 23–6.

48. See, for example, G. D. B. Jones and D. C. A. Shotter (eds), *op. cit.*, 77–9.

49. It has been argued that the inscription published as *RIB* 608 is one such, though it is thought that it originated from a workshop in Cologne (see B. J. N. Edwards, 'Roman Finds from Contrebis', *Transactions of the Cumberland and Westmorland Antiquarian and Archaeological Society* (2nd series), LXXI, 1971, 25–7).

50. The cult of Cocidius seems to have had its 'central place' at Bewcastle (*Fanum Cocidi*), north of Hadrian's Wall (see P. S. Austen, *Bewcastle and Old Penrith*, Cumberland and Westmorland Antiquarian and Archaeological Society, Research Series 6, 1991). One wonders, therefore, whether the dedicator, Lucius Vibenius (see above), had some previous connection with the area.

51. See D. C. A. Shotter, 'Roads, Maps and Placenames', 1–11 in P. Graystone, *Walking Roman Roads in East Cumbria*, Lancaster University, 1994; D. C. A. Shotter and A. J. White, *The Romans in Lunesdale*, Lancaster University, 1995, 69–70.

52. See B. J. N. Edwards, *art. cit.*, 27–32.

53. See G. D. B. Jones and D. C. A. Shotter (eds), *op. cit.*, 72–6.

54. See P. Graystone, *Walking Roman Roads in the Fylde and the Ribble Valley*, Lancaster University, 1996; D. C. A. Shotter and A. J. White, *The Romans in Lunesdale*, Lancaster University, 1995; D. C. A. Shotter and A. J. White, *The Roman Fort and Town of Lancaster*, Lancaster University, 1990. The identification of the Roman name for Lancaster remains controversial, although it may have been GALACUM; for the arguments, see D. C. A. Shotter, 'Roads, Maps and Place-names', 1–11 in P. Graystone, *Walking Roman Roads in East Cumbria*, Lancaster University, 1994; cf. I. G. Smith, 'Some Roman Place-names in Lancashire and Cumbria', *Britannia*, XXVIII, 1997, 372–83; also *Contrebis*, XXIII, 1998, 9–10 and Shotter and White, *Roman Fort and Town*, 12–15.

55. *RIB* 2270 and 2271; another probable (and earlier) milestone stands at Forton Hall. B. J. N. Edwards, 'Lancashire Archaeological Notes: Prehistoric and Roman', *Transactions of the Historic Society of Lancashire and Cheshire*, CXXI, 1969, 106.

56. A Hadrianic milestone (*RIB* 2272) was found near Caton in 1803.

57. G. D. B. Jones and D. C. A. Shotter (eds), *op. cit.*, 85–93.

58. D. C. A. Shotter and A. R. Wellburn, 'Roman Tile Fabrics from Quernmore

and Lancaster', *Contrebis*, III, 1975, 50–2; D. C. A. Shotter, 'A Note on Tiles found on the Mitre Yard, Lancaster', *Britannia*, XIV, 1983, 270–1.

59. B. J. N. Edwards, *art. cit.* (1971), 27–32.
60. For the coins, see D. C. A. Shotter, 'Recent Finds of Roman Coins in Lancashire: Third Report', *Transactions of the Historic Society of Lancashire and Cheshire*, CXLV, 1995, 201.
61. See R. A. C. Lowndes (as cited in note 3).
62. For example, see D. C. A. Shotter and A. J. White, *The Romans in Lunesdale*, Lancaster University, 1995, 69–76; D. C. A. Shotter, *Romans and Britons in North-West England* (2nd edn), Lancaster University, 1997, 84–91.
63. For this, see G. D. B. Jones, 'The North-western Interface', 93–106 in P. J. Fowler (ed.), *Recent Work on Rural Archaeology*, Bradford-upon-Avon, 1975.
64. In general, see A. S. Johnson, *Later Roman Britain*, Batsford, 1980.
65. Descriptions are reproduced in W. T. Watkin, *Roman Lancashire*, Liverpool, 1883, 167–9.
66. G. D. B. Jones and D. C. A. Shotter (eds), *op. cit.*, 80–4.
67. Julius Firmicus Maternus, *De Errore Profanarum Religionum* 28,6 (See P. Salway, *Roman Britain*, Oxford University Press, 1981, 349).
68. *RIB* 616 and 617; for a discussion, see D. C. A. Shotter and A. J. White, *The Romans in Lunesdale*, Lancaster University, 1995, 97–8.
69. See A. Woodward, *Shrines and Sacrifice*, Batsford/English Heritage, 1992, 113ff.
70. For example, at Birdoswald; see T. Wilmott, *Birdoswald: Excavations of a Roman Fort on Hadrian's Wall*, English Heritage, 1997, 408–10.
71. G. D. B. Jones and D. C. A. Shotter (eds), *op. cit.*, 223–4.

CHAPTER TWO

Continuity, Charter, Castle and County Town, 400–1500

Andrew White

Lancaster's Roman settlement seems to have had a large influence on the later topography of the town. As we have seen, the placing of the prominent group of buildings on the crest of the Castle Hill, the Castle and Priory Church, is due to the position of the Roman fort. Church Street, Lower Church Street and perhaps its continuation Moor Lane owe their alignment to the Roman road leaving the east gate of the fort, while Penny Street and perhaps Cheapside have the same origin.[1] The same influences may even extend to some property divisions, according to evidence found during excavations at Mitchell's Brewery site in Church Street.[2] In this Lancaster differs markedly from its neighbours to north and south, Kendal and Preston, whose plans developed purely from the needs and constraints of medieval market towns.[3]

If Roman streets and boundaries were influential in the Middle Ages there must be a presumption that some Roman buildings survived very late. Indeed we do know from the foundation charter of the Priory in 1094 that part of the wall of the late Roman fort was then still standing high enough to be used as a boundary. This charter – in Latin – refers to *a veteri muro* or 'from the old wall'.[4] Some stone buildings in the *vicus* are likely to have remained as ruins long enough to have determined where the streets of the medieval town ran.

As to the six or seven hundred years which intervened between organised Roman military activity and the start of medieval documents in the late eleventh century we know next to nothing. It is likely that some sort of settlement continued here, although its character is very doubtful. Probably the ruins of the fort on the hilltop maintained some vestige of local authority under the occupation of a chieftain. A long sub-Roman period may have ensued for two centuries or more, in the vacuum between the collapse of Roman power and the first appearance of Anglian colonists in the late sixth century. Archaeology has as little evidence to offer us as history for the period in question. With the possible exception of a small crude pottery vessel found in excavations on the Market Hall site in 1994 no pottery of any kind helps to fill the gap.

It is not until the eighth or ninth century that we start to gain significant archaeological evidence. A series of fragments from carved stone crosses, found in 1903 when the north wall of the Priory Church was demolished,[5] gives us the first clear evidence of Christianity on the site and also material whose date and cultural connections can be assessed. A hoard of small Northumbrian bronze coins or 'stycas', found in 1914[6] in the same general area support the theory that a monastery occupied this site. Other similar coins have since been found in the vicinity.[7] The coins all date from the early ninth century. Although they belong to the kingdom of Northumbria, whose epicentre lay on the other side of the Pennines, Lancaster was quite close to the northern border of Mercia, and may have fallen under the influence of each in succession. The great age of monastic growth was in the seventh century, and it is quite likely that Lancaster is one of the numerous un-named monasteries founded under St Wilfrid.

In Domesday Book of 1086,[8] its first documentary mention, Lancaster appears as two settlements, 'Loncastre' and 'Chercaloncastre'. These were

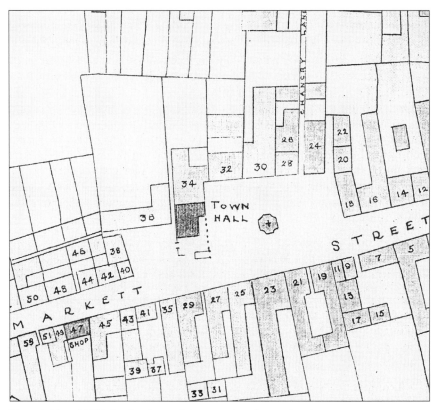

Docton's Map of 1684 showing the much larger market place at that date.

not necessarily two geographically discrete places – Domesday Book is about property ownership, not geography – and may merely have represented the division of the Castle Hill between secular and religious ownership. However, some have read into this a two-focussed town and equated it with Camden's theory of an 'Old Lancaster' burned by the Scots in 1322. There seems to be no evidence to support this theory, as we shall see later on.

We do not know what the character of the place was in the late eleventh century. Was it merely a village or had it started to develop an urban character? Historians differ over the effect of charters. Some see them as effectively creating towns, while others see them as merely acknowledging an existing state of affairs.[9] In Lancaster's case the new factor after the granting of the first borough charter in 1193 may well have been the establishment of Market Street and the market place. There had been no need of a market place prior to the granting of market rights. Market Street is first named in monastic charters of *c.*1225, but we should beware of the argument from silence. Documents are few at this period and absence of mention is not necessarily significant. The market place may originally have been much larger than the present Market Square. There is some evidence from old maps that the present Old Town Hall (City Museum) site is an encroachment into a larger open space which once extended both east and west of it.[10]

The First Borough Charter

In 1193 Lancaster received its first charter, which gave it the status of a borough.[11] By this John of Mortain, later to be King John, gave his tenants in Lancaster a new status and freedom from many of the irksome services they had been bound to provide formerly. The charter is so important that it is worth quoting at length. The original is in Latin, on a piece of vellum 203 × 146 mm in size.

> John, count of Mortain, to all his men and friends of France and England, present and future, greetings. Know that I have granted, and confirm by this my charter, that my burgesses of Lancaster shall have the liberties which I granted to the burgesses of Bristol.
>
> Moreover, I free the same burgesses from the suit of my mill and from ploughing and from other servile customs which they used to perform, so that they shall not mow at my need as hitherto they were accustomed to do.
>
> I have granted to the same burgesses, and by this my charter confirm, that they may pasture their animals in my forest as far from the town of Lancaster as they may go and return in a single day.
>
> I have granted them as much dead wood in my forest as they have

need of for burning, and as much other wood as they need for building, under the supervision of my foresters.

[Witnesses]

[Given at] Dorchester on the morrow of St Barnabas' Day [i.e. 12th June] in the fourth year of our lord King Richard [1193]

What was the effect of Lancaster's first borough charter? It would help us to provide a better answer if only there were more records surviving from before 1193. However, it is possible to speculate. First of all Lancaster was not a new town. Its street pattern had built up over a period of centuries and no doubt its urban character had long been decided. Indeed, it could even be argued that John's charter indicates that burgesses, and therefore a borough, already existed. This argument would be difficult to sustain in the absence of documentary evidence.

The charter is characteristically brief and is more significant for what it implies than for what it says. Indeed, the burgesses would soon find themselves having to defend new liberties which they believed were implicit in the charter against hostile interpretations by the Crown. Essentially the charter commuted agricultural services of tenants for a money rent and removed the requirement for tenants to grind their corn at the Duchy mill. This allowed the townspeople to diversify their interests away from agriculture and laid the groundwork for independence from the Crown and its officers. These may seem very minor benefits, but to a town which had aspirations they were an important starting-point. Other benefits, like the rights of pasture in the Royal Forest, were to lead to disputes with the people of Quernmore at a later date.

The liberties of Bristol were concerned with freedom from toll throughout England and in Dublin, especially valuable to the prospective merchants among the new burgesses, while all of them saw the advantages of market rights. Although these rights are not spelt out in the charter they were thought to be implied and still form the basis of Lancaster's rights to hold a market, following a royal judgement of 1302.[12]

Too much should not be read into royal challenges to established rights, which were particularly common in the reign of Edward I; they were a standard method by which the Crown raised money. The challenge would be made, the burgesses would show their evidence, and then usually end up paying for a confirmation charter, in order to make certain of retaining their rights in future.

One right which their charter certainly did not give them, but which the burgesses nonetheless exercised, was that of executing people! In or before 1247 they did just this to one unfortunate – poor Hulle de Ellel – for what crime we do not know.[13]

Lancaster's first borough charter of 1193. Its seventeenth-century wrapping reads:
'This Grant was thus defaced and the seale pul'd of when as the Towne of Lancaster
was burned the xviii th day of March 1642' [i.e. 1643 by modern reckoning].

Lancaster's second borough charter, issued in 1199.

Mayor and Corporation

Lancaster's first mayor was created in 1337, almost certainly as a result of the Guild Merchant charter of that year.[14] The original charter does not survive but copies of it were made when it was confirmed on later occasions. Before that, and at least from 1246, there had been a reeve as Lancaster's first citizen. Since 1337 there has been a continuous line of mayors down to the present day – over 430 names are recorded, but there are many gaps. Early mayors had very long terms of office, probably as a result of the oligarchic nature of the town's government. If the office has survived, however, the role has transformed dramatically over the centuries. The mayor of those days combined the civic and ceremonial roles that still exist today with an executive function now carried out by paid full-time staff.[15]

There was not much democracy evident in the selection of a mayor. He was selected from the small number of burgesses who themselves were

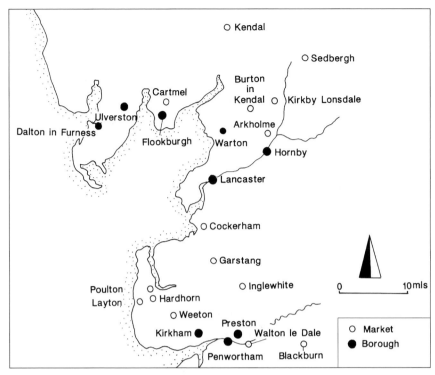

Boroughs, markets and fairs in medieval north Lancashire and south Cumbria.

freemen. Effectively this kept the mayoralty within a small group of powerful citizens. By the time of the Statute Merchant charter of 1432, the corporation consisted of a mayor, bailiffs, burgesses and commonalty, introducing two ranks of burgesses, capital burgesses and burgesses of the commonalty. In later practice each of these groups elected one of the two bailiffs.

By 1504 there were twelve head or capital burgesses, perhaps only reflecting in words a division which had long existed in fact.[16]

Freedom of the borough was jealously guarded and could only be obtained by a few people; those who were sons of freemen, those who served an apprenticeship to freemen, those who bought the freedom, or those who had the freedom as a present from the mayor or bailiffs. Privileges included a share of pasture in the common fields, the Moor and the Marsh, and freedom from tolls, both in Lancaster and throughout the kingdom. Voting rights were also included and were to become especially valuable, and a great bone of contention, in the later Middle Ages.

Liberty of any sort was a fragile commodity in the Middle Ages. Usually the threat came from the Crown, querying established rights and grudgingly confirming them in return for a bribe or fine. In the fifteenth century a greater risk emerged from the unruly gentry and their even more unruly followers. In

1480 Edward IV sent a revealing letter to the mayor and burgesses. In it he refers to the difficulties they had had at their last elections because of the mob

> of various strangers amongst you there as of others, being of the livery and retainers of certain gentlemen of your neighbouring country-side.[17]

He orders them to hold elections and to take note of no liveries but his own, offering his royal protection.[18] It is not clear what the gentry had to gain in this particular case, but they probably wished to influence the result of the election in favour of their own supporters and to legitimise their own power through civic office.

Freemen alone had the vote and for centuries they were the target of bribery and coercion by neighbouring gentry. At all events the picture of Lancaster which it conjures up is one like the setting of Shakespeare's 'Romeo and Juliet' with rival gangs of armed thugs, protected by powerful masters, patrolling the streets and terrifying the law-abiding citizens.

Boundaries

Lancaster's boundaries are very ancient. Until 1974 the borough boundaries were recognizably those established in the Middle Ages, if somewhat truncated on the east by the enclosure of Lancaster Moor, and of Quernmore Moor in 1809. On the north the limit was formed by the waters of the river Lune, while the western edge was drawn across the rather featureless Marsh in which the freemen pastured their cattle. To the south and east the boundary followed the division of fields between Haverbreaks and Aldcliffe and between Bowerham and the Greaves, ending with a broad tongue of common land extending into Quernmore and Littledale, returning north-wards towards the river. This eastern extension may have followed the route to the higher ground, used in summer by the people of Lancaster driving their cattle up to new pastures on Lancaster Moor. This was to be a source of constant friction between them and the men of Quernmore and resulted from the rather vague terms of the 1193 charter. The large rural parish of Scotforth also hemmed Lancaster in to the south east.[19]

From the seventeenth century the borough records give us an almost unbroken series of accounts of the septennial Boundary Ridings which were used to define and reinforce the boundaries of the borough and its associated common lands. Enclosure of these common lands in the early nineteenth century considerably reduced the extent of Lancaster to the south and east.

These boundaries were all lost or rather submerged in the reorganization of local government in 1974 when effectively the area of Lancaster itself was merged with that of the old Hundred of Lonsdale South of the Sands, to become the new City of Lancaster. It has recently been argued that the Hundred boundaries in the north of Lancashire reflect post-Conquest property considerations and so are presumably of eleventh- or early twelfth-century date. If so then the post-1974 city boundary has at least the merit of fossilizing an eight- or nine-centuries-old division.[20]

The borough boundary does not tell us the full story, however. From the earliest times the townships of Aldcliffe to the south west and Newton to the north east were closely associated with the borough. The boundary on the Aldcliffe side was always ill-defined, but between Lancaster and Newton it was formed by a beck which is usually anonymous but which in 1684 was called the 'Jelle Beck',[21] perhaps after William Jelly who held land in the same area at that date. It is significant that St Leonard's Hospital – for lepers – lay just over the borough boundary, in Newton township. The line of both beck and boundary are marked today by Factory Hill, where the nineteenth-century Albion Mill stood.

It is clear that the medieval borough was quite small and was hemmed in to both east and west by its common fields and grazing land. Much of the Marsh remains open ground and the area towards Aldcliffe has only recently filled in. It is the area to the east which became built up earliest, but that is a story for a later chapter.

It is appropriate at this point to look at a myth created in the sixteenth century by Camden and perpetuated since by numerous other historians. Camden states (in the English version of Philemon Holland);[22]

> ... yet for proofe of Romane antiquity they find otherwhiles peeces of the Emperours coine, especially where the Friery stood: for there, they say was the plot upon which the ancient City was planted, which the Scots ... in ... 1322 set on fire and burnt. Since which time they have begunne to build nearer unto a greene hill by the river side ...

The myth is this; that originally the settlement of Lancaster lay to the east, in the area of the Dominican Friary (i.e. in the vicinity of the present Dalton Square) but that following the Scottish attack of 1322 it was rebuilt nearer to, and in the protection of, the Castle. Thereafter, according to the embellishments to Camden, the former area was known as 'Old Lancaster'.

There certainly was an area known as 'Old Lancaster' in the medieval period, though it lay in Bowerham rather than near the Friary.[23] Whatever the basis for the name its relationship with the borough was not temporal or locational; there are numerous instances where 'Old' and 'New' place-names lie in antithesis without there being any satisfactory reason – certainly not the obvious one. As we shall see from the evidence of street-names, Lancaster had many or most of its present central streets by the end of the thirteenth century and some of them may well be pre-Conquest. It is hardly credible that the town should move its focus completely in historic times and carefully rename its streets to match the old pattern. No, this is undoubtedly a case for the use of Occam's Razor, to trim away unnecessary hypotheses. Lancaster's centre lies where it lay in the twelfth century; it has not moved and 'Old Lancaster' is an intriguing, but irrelevant, side-issue.

Despite its urban aspirations there is no doubt that medieval Lancaster would strike us as a very rural place. Townsfolk were dependent on rights in the fields and pastures which ringed the town, and kept a jealous watch on their privileges in the Marsh to the west and on the fringes of the royal forest to the east. Town and country at that time were not opposites, but differing facets of the same economy.

The Castle

The town lay in the shadow of the Lancaster Castle, which sometimes brought it unwelcome attention. The Castle is the largest, oldest and arguably the most important building in Lancaster, and as such it is rather odd to find that its early history is still quite vague and that much of it remains in the realms of conjecture. An important factor in this has been the continued use of the Castle as a prison. This has effectively kept most of it from the public gaze and denied access for analysis of the fabric of the building and for archaeological excavations, both of which have proved to be powerful tools for our understanding of date, function and sequence in such buildings. At the time of writing this is just starting to be rectified.

The Norman, Roger of Poitou, acquired the lordship of Lancaster at some

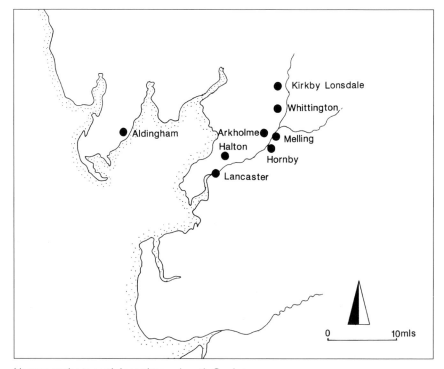

Norman castles in north Lancashire and south Cumbria.

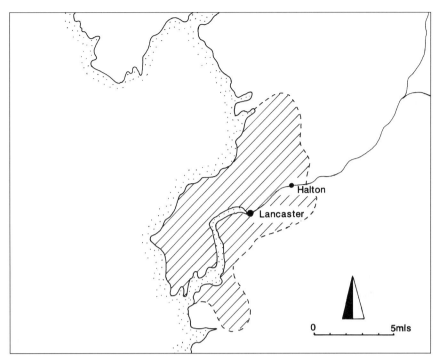

The Manor of Halton, 1086, from Domesday Book.

time between 1086 and 1094, and it soon became the centre of an Honour, based on the villages of the Lune valley and of parts of Furness.[24] Before that the settlement or vill of Lancaster had been in royal hands, as part of the manor of Halton.

This extraordinary state of affairs requires some explanation. Halton is named as the head of the manor in Domesday Book but there is no evidence as to how long it had been so. Halton has an early church, fragments of important Anglo-Saxon and Anglo-Norse stone crosses and a motte and bailey castle of Norman origin to which no precise date can yet be assigned. It can never have compared with Lancaster in strategic importance, access or location, and it is most likely that Lancaster's eclipse and subjugation to Halton was of recent occurrence and of short duration. Perhaps it had suffered some unrecorded disaster during the confusion which prevailed at the time of Tosti's rebellion or after 1069 when Norman armies harried the land. Indeed, as the property of a remote and non-resident landlord (the King) after reversion from a rebellious subject (Tosti), it lay in a power-vacuum where the exact seat of the manor was of little importance.

If Roger built a castle here it is not recorded in any documents. He was banished in 1102 for supporting the rebellion of Robert of Normandy against Henry I,[25] and the King soon afterwards granted the Honour of Lancaster to Stephen of Blois.[26] During the confused years of the Anarchy it fell briefly into Scottish hands, and then passed to William, Count of Mortain, who died in 1164. Eventually it came to Richard I and he almost immediately gave it to his brother John, as Count of Mortain. Whatever his stock in the rest of the country John did nothing but good as far as Lancaster was concerned. It is as King himself that John appears in the official documents spending money on Lancaster Castle, the first such expenditure of which record survives.

The purpose of this swift overview is to consider who is likely to have commenced building work on the Castle. Earlier histories are almost unanimous in pointing to Roger as the founder, but it is certain that he was not responsible for any of the stone buildings, in particular the keep which is usually attributed to him. It is most likely that in his tenure of the Honour earthworks were contrived within the ruins of the Roman fort. Whether these took the form of a motte-and-bailey castle, or a ringwork, or some less easily categorised structure dependent upon the massive ruined Roman walls, is not clear. No part of the Castle is of Roman construction and eighteenth-century attributions to Hadrian and Constantius Chlorus are wholly fanciful, though the myth is extremely tenacious.[27] No evidence survives today for a motte and the roughly circular shape of the pre-1800 Castle argues rather for a ringwork, with timber palisades and a strong timber gatehouse. This might easily be resolved by limited archaeological excavations.

In the mid-twelfth century the whole of the area of modern Lancashire north of the Ribble briefly formed part of Scotland, in the right of Henry, son of King David. It has been suggested that King David of Scotland could have had the time and the motive to fortify one of his new possessions, in which case it was a frontier fortress facing south rather than north as we have always assumed.[28] This is quite possible but as yet there is no clear evidence for building work in the mid-twelfth century, except perhaps for the Keep, known as the Lungess Tower. This massive structure is undoubtedly the earliest surviving part of the Castle, but offers us little diagnostic evidence for assigning a close date to it. An indication of its date can, however, be gained from the fact that in 1202–3 it needed repairs. The Pipe Rolls record:[29]

> et in emendatione domorum Regis in castello de Lancaster iiiim. et in emendatione turris viis. [and in repairs to the King's lodgings in the castle of Lancaster 4 marks and in repairs to the tower 7s.]

Since the accounts do not specify a particular tower, we can probably assume that there was only one at this time.

It seems fairly clear that the work on the remainder of the stone defences must have been conceived in the reign of King John since he spent over £630 in total on Lancaster Castle.[30] The earliest recorded expenditure was in 1193, when £25 was paid for strengthening the Castle, but relatively small amounts were involved until 1209–10 and 1210–11, when £352 and £180 respectively were incurred, and 1215 when costs totalled nearly £34.[31] Was this expenditare sufficient to build a stone castle, or does this merely cover alterations and additions to an existing structure? Comparisons with other castles suggest that work at Lancaster was done piecemeal and that the circuit of walls with its complement of round flanking towers and square lodging towers was not complete until perhaps the end of the thirteenth century.

In 1199 the Castle was besieged by Hubert de Burgh. Substantial repairs and improvements followed this, but the outer defences were apparently still only earthworks. A writ of 1208 instructed Ranulf, Earl of Chester, and Robert de Gresley and others to provide men to cut ditches and build ramparts. The heavy expenditure of 1209–11 covered this work and probably the building of a great hall, part of the curtain wall, and the so-called 'Adrian's Tower'.

During the reign of Henry III building work went on.[32] In 1243–44 the Sheriff spent £128 on the gate, bridges and the stockade (the curtain wall must still have been incomplete at this time) and £68 on lead for the roof of the tower (probably the keep), while in 1254 £257 was spent on the curtain wall itself and the gateway. It is inconceivable that the castle had been utterly without a gatehouse before this date; probably rebuilding or strengthening of some earlier structure was involved. Anomalies within the existing gate passage suggest that the fifteenth-century gatehouse incorporates part of its predecessor, while a thirteenth-century stair turret certainly survives at the north west corner.

In 1267 the Honour of Lancaster passed to Edmund, first Earl of Lancaster, along with other huge estates. From that date until the Dukedom of Lancaster was united with the Crown in 1399, little further work was done on the Castle except that in 1377 260 oaks were brought here from the royal forest in Quernmore, a formidable quantity of timber for works of which there is no other record.[33] Following the Scottish attack on the town in 1322[34] a carpenter was paid £5 14s.

> for making the prison and bridge at the entry to the castle of Lancaster burnt by the Scots.

It is difficult to visualise a timber prison outside the castle walls, but presumably the bridge crossed the moat from the gatehouse, the sort of outwork which was vulnerable to attack but expendable.

Henry IV, who combined the Duchy of Lancaster with the Crown, issued an order to the Duchy's Receiver in Lancashire to spend 200 marks (£133) annually on the Castle.[35] This policy was continued by Henry V, his son, and the consequence was that over a period of some twenty years more than £2,500 was spent on the Castle. The most obvious result of this spending was the well-known gatehouse, usually and erroneously known as 'John O' Gaunt's Gateway'. This splendid structure fulfilled many of the functions which the keep had served two centuries earlier, and represents the latest in tactical thinking, but more particularly a desire to dominate and overawe, which was a commonplace in patrician fifteenth-century secular architecture. John O' Gaunt himself had been dead several years when this was constructed. Other work carried out at this time has left little trace. An inspection in 1476 by the Duchy Council referred to;

> ... a Towre begonne of old tyme on the north part of the castell and ...
> not passing x fete above grownde ...

which might be unfinished work of the 1402 campaign or something much earlier. The north side was somewhat thinly defended by only the curtain wall and this area might well have been a candidate for strengthening; since the tower is known to have been round, however, it probably belonged to the thirteenth-century work.

Although the Castle survived to withstand sieges in the Civil War, the main reasons for its continued use and repair by the Duchy were as a centre for local estates, housing the Receiver and his documents, as a prison, and as a court.[36] The last two functions have continued to the present day.

At its peak, and before the addition of new court and prison accommodation after 1788,[37] the Castle's topography was as follows. Starting at the gatehouse and proceeding left (clockwise) there was a stretch of curtain wall followed by the 'Dungeon Tower', a rectangular tower projecting well beyond the wall face. This was set at an angle to the curtain wall on either side of it, suggesting that perhaps the tower was an addition and that the wall was built in phases, of which this represents a junction. Further on was the round tower called 'Adrian's Tower'. Attached to this was the great hall which ran along the inner face of the curtain wall to another round tower, parts of which survived into the eighteenth century; its remains now lie under the Shire Hall. Next to this, and with two sides projecting beyond the curtain, was the Lungess Tower, the great Norman keep, with access from inside the walls by external steps to first floor level. There may have been a forebuilding to protect these steps, but if so then it has left no trace. Beyond the Lungess Tower was a long stretch of curtain wall, forming two angles. Here, on the north side, was the unfinished tower noted in 1476. Next, on the east side, came the Well Tower, another square tower, which contained one of the Castle wells and also perhaps prison accommodation in its stone-vaulted basement. Finally a short stretch of curtain wall returned to the gatehouse. In the interior there were undoubtedly other necessary buildings such as stables, barns, smithy and so on.

The names by which we know most of the towers of the Castle are not particularly ancient. Clearly the name of the Lungess Tower ('Longens Tower' in 1531–3)[38] is of great antiquity, and indeed the significance of the name is unknown. Of the others the Dungeon Tower is so named in a document of 1663,[39] but the names of neither the Well Tower nor Adrian's Tower seem to go back beyond the eighteenth century. Instead we have mentions of the Sheriff's Tower (1511–13), the Receiver's Tower (1476) and the Prisoners' Tower (1555–6). Some of these may be synonymous, and in all probability the Sheriff's Tower is Adrian's Tower, and the Prisoners' Tower is the same as the Dungeon Tower. The Receiver may have had his lodgings in the gatehouse or possibly in the Well Tower. The ancient documents are not sufficiently specific.

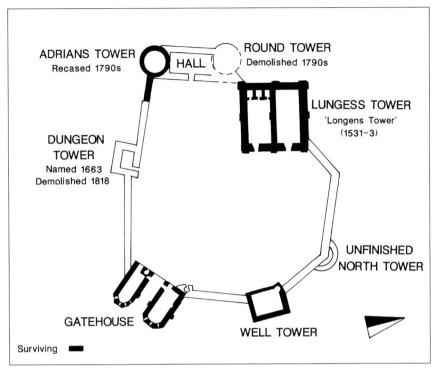

Plan of the Castle prior to 1788, showing names of towers.

The River Crossing

Inherited from Lancaster's Roman origins were two important factors; its strategic hilltop fortress site and the crossing of the river Lune. Whether the Romans built a bridge here or not is at present unknown, but it is very likely that the crossing-point itself persisted. The Lune is not particularly deep and at low tide it may be forded in many places; it is the tidal range of up to 10 metres which causes the problems, and this itself makes it very probable that a bridge has long been in existence here.

Downstream of the present St George's Quay the river made two streams around an island known as Salt Ayre (now reclaimed). At the eastern end of the island the river was once shallow enough to be fordable. An eighteenth-century plan[40] shows the southern approach as Priestford (Priest Wath, an ancient name which appears in the Priory foundation charter of 1094), and the northern side as Scale Ford. Perhaps the two had really always been synonymous.

The more direct route and narrower crossing was that using the ancient bridge, which in the Middle Ages and up until the early nineteenth century lay at the point where the millstream rejoined the river, just below the Castle

Hill. Running down to its south end was Bridge Lane, the line of which was almost wholly eradicated in 1938, when the new bus station was built. Its north end was on the Skerton bank of the river but was oddly unrelated to the village. Its line can still be made out as an access point from the river, running under the end of Greyhound Bridge and continued by Lune Street. A new pedestrian bridge is currently taking shape near to this point.

It is impossible to give an exact date for the bridge; the first mention is in 1215 [41] when a grant to the monks of Furness of timber for the repair of their fishery 'at the bridge of Lancaster' is proof that it already existed. Later grants of timber for the bridge itself, such as in 1251–2,[42] demonstrate that at this date it was either wholly or substantially of timber (large quantities of timber were, of course, needed for starlings or for piles even in a masonry bridge).

Pontage – a toll collected on passing goods and put to repairs of a bridge – was granted on numerous occasions and for varied periods, such as in 1291 (five years), 1324 (three years), 1327 (three years), 1330 and 1379. In 1373 'six score oaks' were supplied to the works from Wyresdale Forest. The burgesses of Lancaster seem to have been responsible for the actual repairs up to the early fourteenth century but by the 1370s the Duchy of Lancaster was in charge. In the mid-fifteenth century no lesser personages than the Duke of Suffolk and the Chancellor of the Duchy were here to view the bridge.[43] It is tempting to envisage the 'Old Bridge', which we know from illustrations, as a product of this visit; it was plainly of late-medieval design and must have replaced the earlier timber bridge. The hand of the Duchy

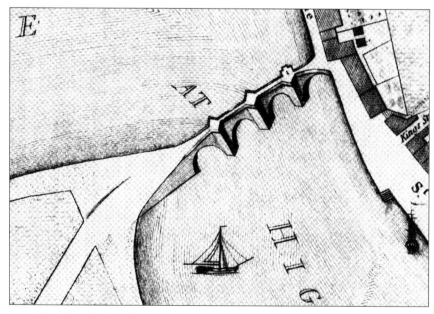

Detail from Mackreth's map of 1778, showing the late medieval bridge still standing.

of Lancaster on a bridge which was beginning to carry much heavy regional traffic – the road was after all the principal west-coast link with Carlisle and the borders – makes considerable sense.

Many views of this bridge survive from the sixteenth century onwards,[44] charting the gradual process of decay and final abandonment in favour of a wholly new bridging-point further upriver at Skerton. Stephen Mackreth's map of 1778 shows it as a four-arched structure with angled cutwaters and refuges for pedestrians, that on the east side of the southernmost pier being squared off and containing a pillar, possibly part of a cross.

Houses

Medieval Lancaster was a town of timber and thatch. That much is clear from the descriptions of building materials required for the more substantial houses. Lesser houses have left little evidence of any kind but it would make little sense to assume that they were any different. What is quite surprising is that, with the exception of parts of the castle and the Priory church, nothing substantial remains of any medieval buildings.

There are several reasons for this. Firstly we know that during the late seventeenth and early eighteenth centuries there was an almost complete rebuilding in stone, so that even earlier seventeenth-century buildings survive only in the form of a few reused timbers. Secondly a predominantly timber and thatch town such as Lancaster was especially prone to destructive fires. These might start by accident but on at least two occasions in the Middle Ages visits by Scots armies led to immense destruction. The principal occasion was in 1322 in the turmoil of Edward II's reign, but there was a repeat in 1389 after the Battle of Otterburn. These were compounded by intentional burning in 1643 of a large part of Penny Street during the Civil War and, by accident, of some thirty houses in Church Street in 1698.

Some direct evidence for the nature of buildings in medieval Lancaster comes from documentary sources. A rental of the lands of Thomas, Earl of Lancaster, dated 1314, records the expenses in building a new house for Sir Robert de Holand in Lancaster.[45] (Sir Robert was a favourite who himself fell from grace in 1328, six years after Earl Thomas.)

The carpentry work totalled £18 16*s.* 8*d.* (£18.83) and included roofing. First the site was cleared, then a waggon belonging to the Abbot of Furness, with two waggoners, was hired for twenty-eight weeks to fetch timber and roofing for the house. Expenses for the carpenters and others totalled over £41, so perhaps it was prefabricated elsewhere and set up on site as a separate job. Then came the 'cruck-rearing', if this is the correct interpretation of the Latin '*levatio*', when gangs of men pulled the prefabricated sections into place with ropes and secured them. Next special nails were required for the roofing, which was of shingles rather than thatch. Clearly this was a grand house and quite different in scale from those of ordinary townsfolk. It may have stood on the site of the Judges' Lodging, the roof of which contains timbers from a medieval house of some pretensions.[46] However, it is interesting to see that in what we think of as a traditional stone area, a grand medieval house could still be wholly timber-framed.

In 1338 Stephen Lemeyngs and his wife Emma were obliged, according to the terms of a lease, to build a house with a solar, a garderobe and a chamber of new timber on a burgage in St Mary's Street.[47]

There are various other records which show the legal or illegal use of oak from the Royal Forest for building projects – in 1297, for instance, ten green oaks went into building a solar for the warden of Cockersand Abbey[48] – but all seem to indicate that the town was predominantly of timber construction during the Middle Ages. Of course our knowledge is biased by the presence of the royal forest; we know much more about the use of timber from the associated fines than we do about any use of stone.

We should no doubt be surprised by the town's small size as well as its appearance. There are no maps earlier than that of Speed in 1610, nor are the estimates of population very reliable. Throughout the Middle Ages the parish of Lancaster was very large and we should be careful to distinguish between the population of the parish and of the town itself. It is doubtful whether the population of the town ever exceeded 1,500 during the Middle Ages. Speed's map, though comparatively late in date, seems to reflect a town which had seen little recent change. The street pattern, for example, contains no streets which are not recorded in medieval documents. The layout consists in general of ranges of buildings lining the street frontages with nothing but gardens behind. Our impression would be of a very small, quiet place with an agricultural aspect and a low density of buildings.

Development of the Street Pattern

The town centre contains a small number of streets, the names of which which are all recorded at quite an early date.[49] They form a characteristic pattern that eight centuries of change has done little to obliterate.

As we have seen, Church Street has a very ancient line, fossilizing the eastern approach to the Roman fort. In the Middle Ages it was known as St Marygate, a name now confined to its western end, from China Street to the Priory steps, but recorded as early as 1220.[50] Parallel to this runs Market Street, 'Markahastrete' in a document of 1200–40. That name seems to contain some corrupt reference to a market hall, for which there would be no occasion prior to the granting of the first charter in 1193 or its confirmation in 1199.[51] As 'vico fori' the street is first named in 1225–35.

The eastward extension of Market Street, St Nicholas Street, was a victim of the redevelopment of this area in 1967–71, even its line being lost. It first appears as 'vico sci nich.' in a rental of the Priory in 1360,[52] but may be earlier. Linking Church Street with these was Pudding Lane, later Butcher

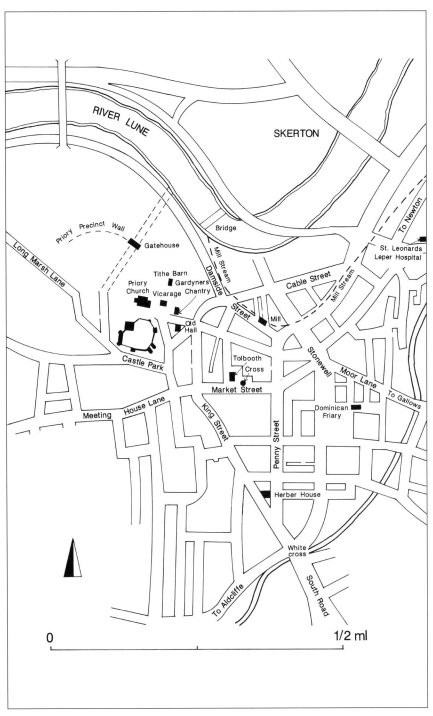

The medieval topography of Lancaster.

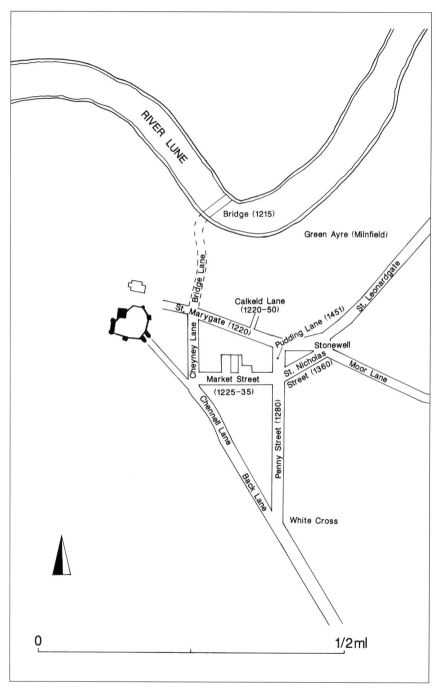

Medieval street-names of Lancaster.

Street and now Cheapside; it is not mentioned until 1451 [53] but is almost certainly as old as the streets it links.

Penny Street, like Church Street, seems to have a Roman antecedent but is first referred to in *c.* 1280.[54] Its property boundaries are text-book examples of burgage plots, long narrow strips running back from the street frontage; on Mackreth's map of 1778 the precinct wall of the Blackfriars' house respects the rear of these plots and clearly demonstrates that they were already in existence when it was built, probably in the late thirteenth or early years of the fourteenth century.

Calkeld Lane, leading from Church Street on to the Green Ayre, bears a very ancient name.[55] It is composed of two Norse words meaning 'cold spring', and in fact there is a spring in one of the adjoining basements, which was at one time used in brewing. Unfortunately we cannot closely date the naming of the lane because Anglo-Scandinavian dialects may have been in regular use as late as the thirteenth century, when it first appears in a document. However its position giving access to the Lune Mill, there from at least the late twelfth century, gives us a context for its creation.

On the west side of the town, towards the Castle, the present line of King Street, China Street and Bridge Lane looks ancient, but this is a case of looks belying the evidence. While Bridge Lane in its pre-1938 layout must be roughly as old as the bridge to which it gave access, China Lane does not seem to be so old. Until it was widened in 1894 China Street was excessively narrow and furthermore, according to a plan of 1684, the burgage plots did not run at right angles to it but rather to Church Street and Market Street.[56] So, though it looks like a through route to the north, earlier evidence makes it appear more like a track between burgage plots, subsequently upgraded.

King Street may appear under the Latin guise of *'regiam viam'* in the Cockersand Chartulary as early as 1225–40,[57] but this phrase is also regularly used to mean 'the King's Highway' in a very general way. It could, therefore, be applied to many of the older streets in Lancaster. In 1610 King Street was known as 'Chennell Lane', and its medieval form is unknown.

It is not known when the Roman road layout into Lancaster from the south broke down. This would have involved a road well to the west of King Street, aiming at the south gate of the Roman fort. A road roughly on the line of Penny Street may have acted as a 'bypass', avoiding the fort and serving the settlement outside its walls. We have seen that the Romans had an enduring influence on elements in the town plan. When the Castle and Priory church were built they may well have diverted road traffic from its previous line, creating King Street and Castle Hill as a through route to Long Marsh lane and the ford of Priestwath, or later to Bridge Lane and the bridge. China Lane would be a logical development of this, cutting through between the burgage plots and avoiding the high ground on the shoulder of the Castle Hill.[58]

Water Mills

Lancaster had at least two water corn-mills in the Middle Ages and their history is complicated. The oldest recorded mill lay on the crescent of open land in the bend of the river known as the Green Ayre. It was fed by a millstream which left the Lune at Newton, well above Skerton Bridge, and returned into the river at the start of the modern St George's Quay. This stream is remembered in the name of Damside Street and water still continues to flow through the culvert under the roadway which in general preserves its line. In Roman times the line of this millstream had probably been the course of the river itself, which over the centuries had cut another channel further to the north.[59] The mill stood across the stream, roughly opposite the lower end of Calkeld Lane. Known as 'Lune Mill', this is first referred to in the borough charter of 1193 when the burgesses were freed from 'suit of my mill' by John, Earl of Mortain.[60]

Despite its location in the town this mill had little to do with it, remaining Duchy of Lancaster property throughout most of its existence, though it was usually leased out to some local person. It gave its name to various features in the medieval topography, including 'Milne Feld' (1236–49) and 'Milne Fleet' (1216–22),[61] which we can probably equate with the Green Ayre and the millstream itself. The farm of 'Lone mill' and 'Brokmyln' is recorded in a rental of 1314 as £13 6s. 8d. (£13.33)[62] (Brokmyln was a fulling-mill, used for the fulling of cloth), while in 1464 King Edward IV gave four marks from the profits of Lune Mill to an old soldier injured at the Battle of Wakefield. The grant refers to;

> … our milne, sette in oure water of Lowne, in oure parish of Lancaster called Lownismylne, to our duchie of Lancaster belongyng …[63]

which causes certain problems of identification. This mill certainly did not stand in the water of Lune, as we have already seen, but Edward's scribe may not have been concerned with local topographical exactitude.

In the thirteenth century St Leonard's Hospital also had a watermill, but nothing further is heard of it, or its location.[64]

Lune Mill was demolished as late as 1769 by the borough, having probably been acquired before 1574 along with the mill at Newton. A few years earlier in 1755[65] a survey of the mill for HM Surveyor General had indicated the extent of dilapidation; a small sketch of the mill building attached to the survey is the only illustration that survives of this ancient structure.

Lancaster's other medieval water-mill lay at the upper end of the same millstream, in the township of Newton, at or near a place called Brerebutts,[66] which has been identified with Briery Field.

The mill at Newton is described as 'newly-built' in 1460, when it belonged to Syon Abbey,[67] but it may represent an older site, perhaps once belonging to the leper hospital; John Gardyner was the lessee and from its profits he endowed a chantry and his Free School. It seems to have come into the hands of the borough as trustee of Gardyner's will in the late fifteenth century and was leased to Robert Dalton of Thurnham in 1574.[68] By the eighteenth century even its exact site had become a matter for conjecture.

The Priory

The Priory church occupies a prominent position on the summit of the Castle Hill, next to the Castle – medieval church and state stand manifestly hand-in-hand. It was never a large house; at most it contained some half-dozen monks, some of whom were probably sent from the mother-house of Seez in Normandy. Its function was, as in the case of so many other 'alien priories', to collect revenues from the English possessions and send them home to Normandy. In the early days fifty marks (£33.33) were transmitted in this way each year.[69] It is hardly to be expected that a small house of this nature would carry out all the religious obligations assumed by larger monasteries, but the evidence still points to some degree of communal religious life.

The Priory church stood on the same site as its present-day successor, but little is left of the original structure because after it passed into the hands of the nuns of Syon in the early fifteenth century they rebuilt it as a parish church.[70] The new work, principally of the 1430s, but occupying a long building period, replaced all but the west wall and south door of the older church, although some of the old stone seems to have been reused, especially on the north side where a number of carved stone crosses of Anglo-Saxon and Viking date were found in 1903.[71] It is possible that the north wall of the nave was left largely untouched from Norman times until the building of the King's Own Memorial Chapel in 1903.

In 1911 the reflooring of the chancel allowed an opportunity for the architect Hubert Austin to carry out some investigations.[72] He found walls aligned east and west which may have been Roman and, more particularly, the remains of an apse underlying the first bay of the chancel, slightly offset to the north of the modern line. In all probability this represents the apsidal presbytery of the Norman priory church; if the surviving masonry at the west end represents a contemporary wall then we have a church of some ninety feet in length overall. Its later form (there is some evidence that alterations and enlargement took place before the end of the fourteenth century) is not known. To this period, however, belongs the set of beautifully ornate choir-stalls dating from around 1345 which are the glory of the church today.[73] Tradition has it that they were brought from Cockersand Abbey at the Dissolution, but while they would just physically fit the long aisleless choir that excavations have revealed there,[74] the backs could not have been seen – and they were clearly intended to be visible – so the story is therefore implausible. As original fittings of the Priory church while it was still monastic, these stalls offer us evidence for a wide and spacious choir so the Norman church must have been enlarged before the fourteenth century.

Domestic buildings for the priory do not survive. There is no room for them on the usual, southern, side of the church but many smaller alien priories dispensed with the formal arrangement seen in larger houses and adapted their layout to available spaces, or built them to the north instead. Here it would seem that the north side was the logical place, an area now occupied by the King's Own Memorial Chapel and the garden of the vicarage. Indeed, when we look at the plan of the Norman apse against the later form of the church it seems very likely that the southward expansion of the church was determined by the pre-existence of domestic buildings immediately to the north. These would have denied any northward movement without great complications, including total rebuilding.

There is also some evidence that the priory had its own precinct with a wall and gatehouse.[75] Leland, writing in c.1535, says:

> The old waul of the Circuite of the priory cummith almost to Lune bridge. Sum have thereby supposid that it was a peace of a waul of the toune. But yn deade I espiyd in no place that the toune was ever waulid.

and again:

> The ruines of old walles about the bridg were onely of the suppressid priory.[76]

Excavations in 1928 revealed part of 'a room or turret' next to Vicarage Lane, containing charcoal, roofing slabs and medieval pottery.[77] Interestingly Speed shows a gatehouse-like building in this vicinity on his plan of 1610, although his topography at this point is somewhat distorted. Aligned with this gatehouse is one of the linear earthworks in the adjacent Vicarage Field, which was examined in 1971[78] and which appears to be the remains of a precinct wall or bank, revetted with stone. On balance the evidence points to the priory having a precinct wall and gatehouse, controlling one access route from the medieval bridge. What went on towards the south, where the Castle stood, is quite unknown.

The priory had long held a parochial role as well as a monastic one; indeed its nave had acted as the church for a huge parish. As the wars of the fourteenth and fifteenth century with France drove a wedge between the alien priories and their French mother-houses, a political solution became necessary. Revenues formerly sent to France were now farmed out to laymen or taken by the Crown. In 1414 Henry V gave the revenues of Lancaster to his newly-founded Bridgettine nunnery of Syon; later, after the death of the last Prior, he gave them the priory itself.[79] The nuns had to wait until 1428 to gain physical possession of the buildings but in 1430 the church became wholly dedicated to parochial uses, with the exception of a chamber and stable for the use of visiting officers of Syon, and since that time there has been a vicar of Lancaster.

Associated with these changes was an ambitious programme of rebuilding, which resulted in the removal of most traces of the original monastic function, apart from the south doorway of *c.*1200 and the west wall. The church we see today is mostly a creation of the fifteenth century, beginning at the west end and working eastwards. The exterior is constructed of very large blocks of newly-quarried sandstone, contrasting with the rubble walling of the older parts and interior surfaces which were not intended to be seen, but which were probably always whitewashed. The easternmost bays of the two chancel aisles formed chantry chapels. When completed (and we do not know how long the process took) the interior must have seemed exceptionally tall, light and airy with its lofty arcades and clerestorey. It took later generations to fill the large windows with stained glass and the interior with pews.

A new tithe barn was also built in about 1430 to the north east of the church; remains of this were encountered in the course of archaeological excavations in 1975.

Foundation Charter

The earliest surviving document specific to Lancaster is the foundation charter of the Priory, dated 1094.[80] It comes from the Priory Chartulary, a small medieval manuscript volume recording the possessions of the Priory, which is held in the British Library. In it the founder, Roger, Earl of Poitou lists his initial gifts to the monastery of St Martin of Seez in Normandy, which was to be the 'mother house' of Lancaster until the wars with France parted them.[81] It was quite common practice for the first generation of Norman landlords to make gifts of English properties to monasteries in their homelands, often in thanks for the success of the Conquest. Where the English properties included or led to the founding of a monastery this was usually referred to as an 'alien priory', and its revenues tended to be appropriated by the mother house. Lancaster was no exception.

Interestingly the charter refers to the gift of 'the church of St Mary of Lancaster, with all things pertaining to it …', which indicates that the church was already in existence, but was not, up to this point, a monastery. We have already seen that Domesday Book records in 1086[82] a vill of 'Chercaloncastre' which implies, though it does not specify, a church. Other evidence, in the form of Anglo-Saxon stone crosses, suggests that there had been a church on this site from at least the eighth or ninth century and in all probability that this was monastic[83] since monastic workshops seem to have been the main centres of production. It probably fell victim to the advent of pagan Norse Viking settlers but was refounded as a parish church before 1066. Unfortunately the scribe of Domesday regularly substituted 'ch' for 'k' in placenames which we know included the Scandinavian form 'kirk' for 'church', but we can perhaps safely set the naming of 'Chercaloncastre' into a period of Norse or Norse-influenced speech, and hence the date of the church likewise.

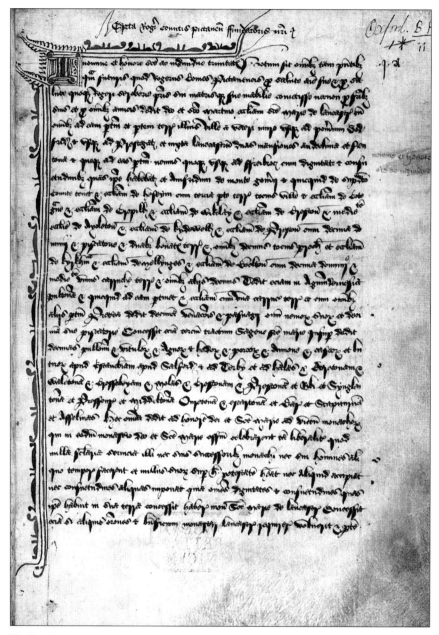

The foundation charter of Lancaster Priory, given 1094, survives in this fifteenth-century copy. It is the oldest detailed documentary source for Lancaster.

As well as the church this first grant included;[84]

> ... part of the land of that vill, from the old wall [*a veteri muro*] as far as Godfrey's orchard, and as far as Prestgat; and near to Lancaster two mansions, Aldcliffe and Newton ...

These topographical details of nine centuries ago call for some explanation. We have already discussed Aldcliffe and Newton. Until nineteenth-century workers' houses and the twentieth-century suburban growth of Lancaster spilt over the boundary, Newton was almost wholly unpopulated, apart from the little hamlet of Bulk (which stands near the present motorway junction no. 34).

Godfrey was Earl Roger's sheriff (*vicecomes*) at the time of the charter, to which he was a witness. It is recorded that on hearing of the Earl's gifts he added 'whatsoever he had in Lancaster, houses and orchard'. The exact position of his orchard is not recorded. We have already seen that 'the old wall' is a reference to the late-Roman fort wall, still standing. Prestgat sounds like the name of a road, but later documents show that this was in fact 'Priest Wath', the latter word being the dialect word for shallows or a ford in a river. Priest Wath appears to be synonymous with Scale Ford, crossing the Lune at the island of Salt Ayre. Since Norman-French does not distinguish between the sounds of 'g' and 'w', the form of 'Prestgat' is clearly a scribal confusion.

There seems to be no reasonable doubt that the lands just described included much of what was to become the main piece of glebe-land in the post-medieval period, the Vicarage Fields.[85] This represents a great swathe of land, running northwards from the Priory site and extending in a rough triangle bounded today by St George's Quay, Carlisle Bridge and the old Bridge Lane. Indeed the specific mention of three boundary markers points to a roughly triangular area, in which case we may be justified in placing Godfrey's orchard near St George's Quay, in the area of the old bridge.

Other property is detailed; the wood in Newton as far as Frithbrook (Denny Beck),[86] Amfridus de Montgomery and his holdings, Heysham church, with a third of the vill, and a group of other churches at Cotegrave, Coppull, Wikelay, Croston, half of that at Eccleston, Childwall and Preston. With the latter were tithe of the lordship and the fishery. Other churches at Kirkham, Melling, Bolton-le-Sands and Poulton-le-Fylde complete the tally of possessions granted by Roger, along with extensive gifts of tithes.

One gift, 'the third draft of the seine of St Mary', is problematical on two counts. It looks as if the scribe has omitted a word or two. We know that later references to the rich Lune fishery mention a particular landmark, perhaps a deep place in the river, called 'St Mary's Pot'.[87] This latter word may have been left out. Later on Furness Abbey received the grant of the fishery, presumably the first two drafts of the seine which Roger had tacitly kept to himself. The unspecific nature of the grant to Furness was to lead to two centuries of legal wrangling between the two houses.

The Monasteries

Much of the property in Lancaster for which we have any records belonged
to monastic houses, principally Lancaster Priory and Furness and Cockersand
Abbeys. Monasteries, in their role of great landowning corporations, not
only kept good records but also tended to survive while lay magnates could
lose their heads and their property.

Most of their records were kept in chartularies, usually consisting of bound
manuscript volumes with transactions recorded according to date or to
locality. Even after the Dissolution of the Monasteries in 1535–40 many
documents survived, either because they continued to serve as title-deeds to
land, or from some stirrings of antiquarian sentiment in the new owners.
Consequently we know proportionately more about monastic holdings than
any others.

Monasteries initially acquired property wherever they could. Usually there
was a founder's grant which contained land in the immediate vicinity, as we
have seen in the case of the Priory, but during the twelfth and thirteenth
centuries land fell into monastic hands in a steady stream. We can discern
in many of the better-run establishments a deliberate policy of acquisition
in specific areas, with a pattern of exchange, purchase and influence to

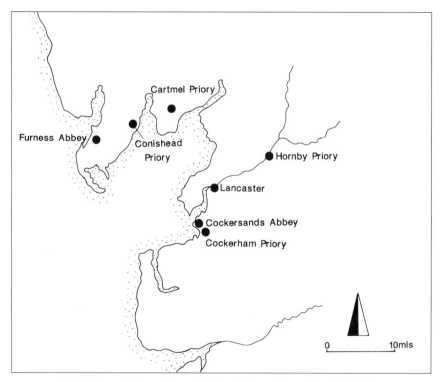

Medieval monasteries and hospitals in north Lancashire and south Cumbria.

consolidate certain holdings. Up to the late thirteenth or fourteenth century land was mostly kept in hand; later falling manpower and changing patterns of agriculture led to the monasteries leasing much of it out on a long-term basis.

All three houses obtained burgage plots in the town and rights in the common fields. As we have seen, Lancaster Priory gained a large tract of land on the north-west side of the town which can still be identified today. Our earliest references to street names come from these sources. Furness Abbey early obtained a concentrated land-holding on the borders of Skerton and Bolton-le-Sands. This it named Beaumont, a Norman-French place-name which does not appear in Domesday, and created there a typical Cistercian grange.[88] A grange was a large farm controlling a more-or-less specialised holding of several hundred acres, but standing outside the manorial system and wholly controlled by the monks. Nearby stood the monks' *bercaria* or sheep ranch of 'Mabildancote',[89] and associated with the grange was the important salmon fishery in the Lune. Beaumont Grange and Beaumont Cote seem to mark the sites of the two former properties.

The fishery is clearly very ancient; elsewhere in the country the existence of fisheries can be shown to antedate the Domesday Survey.[90] Lancaster Priory had a partial grant of it in 1094,[91] while Furness won its rights from Stephen de Blois somewhat later.[92] Since this is all rather confusing it is worth taking a closer look at the right.

Medieval fisheries were a legal entity and usually a physical entity as well. They could be granted or sold. Fishing was carried out in two main ways. The first involved a boat and a seine net; one end of the net stayed on shore while the other was rowed out into the current. When all the net had been paid out the boat brought the free end back to the shore, thus forming a great bag of net. The fishermen pulled this ashore, full of fish if they were lucky. The other method involved building a great weir or baulk out into the river, narrowing and increasing the speed of its flow. Nets suspended across gaps in the weir caught the salmon and sea-trout as they ran upriver.[93]

There is ample evidence that Lancaster Priory used nets and that Furness used both methods. The Priory's right to the third draft with the net implies Furness's right to the first two. Furness also had a great weir or baulk which stuck out into the river roughly where Dalton Dam stands today, although they may have had another nearer to the old bridge. Effectively this created the limit of navigation on the river. An acre of ground nearby no doubt served as their 'fishgarth' where they could dry and repair their nets. Both houses were locked in dispute over the fishing until 1315, when agreement was reached between them. Subsequently the Priory's rights fell into the hands of Syon Abbey, which in 1460 assigned them to the old rival, Furness![94]

As late as 1526–7 the fishery was causing trouble. In a case taken to Star Chamber[95] in the latter year the Abbot accused one William Tunstall and others of menacing his fishermen and damaging his nets and weir. The scene is well conveyed in the plaintiff's words;

... [Tunstall] assemblyd divers riottous and mysruled persons to the
number of 8 and above, whereof some were the manuall servantes of
the seid Tunstall, and them sent in riotous maner to the seid water of
Loyne, where the selerer of the seid monastery in peasyble maner was
beholding the seid abbottes fyschers in the seid free fyschinge, and
there they manysshed [menaced] and thrett the selerer and fyschers
that yf they toke any fysche there they should grevously repent it, and
then forcibly toke the abbottes nette and fished there with the same,
and toke from the selerer all the fysch that had bene takyn by the
abbottes fyschers ...

On a later occasion they;

dystroyed 200 stakes of the same were; and ... they and dyvers other
persons came to the said water of Loyne with arrowes in there bowes
redy to have schotte the same fyschers, who withdrewe, feringe for
there lyffes, and never since darre fysche there ...

This fishery was extremely valuable; in 1314 it was claimed that the Prior's
fishermen had unlawfully taken as much as £300 worth of fish.[96] Even
allowing for an inflated claim, this is impressive. No doubt the value
accounted for the endless litigation. 'Beaumont Fishing' outlived its monastic
owners and survived as a distinct right in the river Lune until about 1900.

It is clear that the early rush of piety demonstrated by gifts to monasteries
was not sustained. Many lay people stood back aghast at the flow of valuable
property into monastic hands and their view received official backing by the
Statute of Mortmain in 1279. Denied opportunities to give land to monasteries for the good of their souls, many townspeople turned their attention
and generosity to the friars, who corporately owned little land, were
personally destitute, and lived mainly by alms. Wealthy people sought burial
in the friars' churches, much to the chagrin of parish priests, who could
thereby lose the fees.

Chantries

The later Middle Ages saw the creation of many chantries – private chapels
within churches and friaries where priests prayed for the souls of the founder
and his family. One at least of these was in the Dominican Friary, while the
Priory church had several more. Associated with one of these, originally
perhaps as the chantry priests' house, was Herber House.[97] This building,
of 'timber, thatch and daub' stood, as we know from a reference of 1650,
at the south end of Penny Street.[98] In 1504 a certain John Standish leased
the lands belonging to it and in payment he had to maintain a priest to
serve St Patrick's Chapel in the Priory church, keep up the fabric of Herber
House for twenty years and to give vestments, altar cloths, 'a boke called

myssall' and 'a chales of silver'. We must hope that he found the deal worthwhile!

The Dominican Friary

The Dominican Friary or Blackfriars lay to the east of the town with entrances to the south, from what is now South Road, and from the north in Moor Lane. The Friars settled here[99] in about 1260 and by 1312 they had already obtained a grant to extend their house. A further extension of their property by two acres, in 1319, probably shows their popularity with the townsfolk. Ultimately they held twelve acres in their precinct, and sundry other property.

A number of local landowners were buried in their church. In 1513 Brian Tunstal of Thurland Castle and in 1523 Edward Stanley, Lord Monteagle, left money in their wills for masses to be said for their souls or sermons provided. The Friary was dedicated to the Holy Trinity and in its latter days contained a chantry with a similar dedication; in whose memory this was endowed we do not know.

The Friars were the stormtroops of the medieval church and as such, tend to remain somewhat anonymous. However, three Priors are recorded by name. In 1410 John of Lancaster, DD, was elected provincial of the English Dominicans. In 1523 Richard Beverley, DD, was Prior, and in 1533 the name of Galfrid Hesketh is given.[100] It is not surprising to find Doctors of Divinity as Priors since the Dominicans were always noted as being among the most learned of the Friars.

Of the Friary buildings nothing survives. On the Dissolution of the monasteries, in 1539, the site was sold off to Sir Thomas Holcroft and successively passed into the hands of the Rigmaiden, Carus, and Dalton families. A house was built here, known as 'the Friers' or 'the Frierage'. probably incorporating parts of the conventual buildings. A grant of the Friary Lands in 1556 includes '. . . church, bell tower and cemetery' as well as land at Edenbreck and at Friars' Moss in Quernmore.[101] The greater part of the precinct no doubt contained orchards and gardens, at the centre of which stood the Friary church with its cloisters and other domestic buildings.

In March 1801, when Sulyard Street was under construction, remains of buildings were discovered. Mr Edward Batty measured the remains of what he called 'cells' and found them to be 7½ feet by 6½. Fragments of several large columns and a quantity of human remains were also found.[102] These facts suggest that the discovery was not of 'the Friars' cells' as Batty thought but perhaps of the south transept of the church, containing a series of small chapels, as we know from a number of other friaries.

Some years before 1852 when a drain was made through the same street a considerable space was found to be covered with 'tiles, bearing various devices, in a rough character, but evidently formed to be joined, and thus make one large pattern'.[103]

In 1873 the rebuilding of the Wesleyan Chapel in Sulyard Street led to the discovery of four pier bases, one at the south-east corner still retaining its plinth. From the position of the piers it was suggested that they carried the tower and that the presbytery had been narrow but the nave had aisles.[104] This accords well with what we know of friars' churches which had a long narrow choir for the friars themselves, a tower with a 'walking space' beneath it, and a large public preaching nave to the west. On this and subsequent occasions fragments of sculpture, including part of an effigy of a knight, window mouldings and floor-tiles, were found.

If the church itself lay under and to the north of Sulyard Street then it is likely that the conventual buildings lay to the south, in the area marked now by the Borough Club, nos 4–5 Dalton Square and their respective garden areas. Limited excavations in 1980–1 on two sites, at the Sulyard Street Chapel and to the south of 5 Dalton Square, failed to produce any structural evidence other that a fragmentary wall at the latter site, and some ninety-four fragments of floor-tiles.[105]

On Binns' map of 1821 can be seen the outline of the Frierage property, which almost certainly corresponds to the friary precinct. Binns marks three surviving sections of the precinct wall; just to the south of George Street, just to the north-west of Gage Street, and to the east of Bulk Street. In 1840 Simpson records two surviving fragments which correspond to the former two noted by Binns.

> [The walls] have a kind of projecting coping raised on flags; the building is of a very rough character, but the mortar by which the stones are cemented is very hard.[106]

The shape of the precinct can still be made out on the ground, fossilized as it is by later development of the estate. The odd projections to the north and east are probably explicable as the extensions made in 1312 and 1319. When the Scots army came to Lancaster in 1322 the Blackfriars and the Priory were the only properties not damaged, probably because both had precinct walls.

The cemetery, which no doubt contained the bodies of many townsfolk as well as the friars themselves, lay to the north of the church, between Sulyard Street and Moor Lane. In 1793 two skeletons were found on Messrs Hadwens property, near Dalton Square, and the same area has produced bones from time to time ever since. The better-off citizens would have been buried in the friary church itself, which, as in other places, became a serious rival to the parish church.

The Leper Hospital

Just outside the bounds of the borough, marked by a small beck, and in the township of Newton, stood the leper hospital of St Leonard. The reason for its isolation was very simple. The disease of leprosy was much feared and misunderstood in the Middle Ages. Sufferers were cast out from society and had to make their living as best they could, avoiding human contact but relying on gifts of food etc. A limited number were fortunate enough to gain places in leper hospitals, provided by generous founders and administered by the church. It was once thought that the disease was brought back from the Holy Land, where it was endemic, by returning Crusaders, but now pathological evidence for leprosy in this country as early as the Roman period has been discovered, so the issue is clearly much more complex.

St Leonard's Hospital gave its name to St Leonardgate, at the far end of which it stood. Its founder was probably John, Earl of Mortain (1189–94).[107] As such it was the second oldest religious foundation in the town. It had a chapel, a lazar house (where the lepers themselves lived) and we may reasonably add a warden's house and various outbuildings to our mental picture of it. Nothing now remains, though part of the chapel survived late into the nineteenth century and a tombstone and numerous burials were found in 1811 when the area was redeveloped.[108] The chapel was served by a priest and the hospital held nine inmates. Its support came from gifts made by its founder including free pasture for its animals in Lunesdale and the right to take timber for both building and firewood free of charge in the same area.

Poor as it was, the Hospital still had many problems to deal with, not least the jealousy of the Priory, annoyed at the loss of tithes.[109] At least two legal disputes took place between them. The king's forester of Lunesdale, too, exacted payment from it for pasture and refused to allow the free taking of timber. The Hospital was by no means a rich prize but was still watched closely by those who saw profit in it for themselves. In the confusion following the fall of Thomas, Earl of Lancaster, William de Dalton acquired the wardenship and promptly ejected several of the lepers and other poor inmates! This was in 1323. By then leprosy had begun to be much less common and within a few years it seems to have virtually died out in England.

Medieval hospitals were relatively weak and very easily subverted to wrongful purposes. The richer ones became retirement homes for former civil servants. The poorer found their revenues being misappropriated.[110] In 1356 Henry, Duke of Lancaster, gave the Hospital to the desperately poor nunnery of Seton in west Cumbria, largely at the insistence of Sir Robert Lawrence of Ashton, who happened to be related to the prioress.[111] The nuns had little interest in the Hospital. It was far away and all that they wanted was its revenue. Consequently the Hospital fell gradually into decay and though it had been agreed that the nuns should establish a chantry at the Priory to replace the chapel and priest there is no evidence that they ever did so.

The Hospital's property consisted of one ploughland in Skerton and a manor and a mill in Lancaster. It is by no means clear which mill this was. Five burgages and sixteen acres of land known as the 'Nuns' Fields' were sold by the Crown in 1557.[112] The latter lay to the east of St Leonardgate. These seem to represent the original property of the Hospital.

The Scottish Raid of 1322

One of the greatest disasters ever to befall Lancaster occurred in 1322 when two victorious Scottish armies swept southward unchecked. Holinshed, the chronicler, takes up the tale;[113]

> Passing from thence they came to Lancaster, which town they also burnt, save onlie the priorie of blacke moonks, and a house of preaching friers; heare came to them the Earle of Murrey and the Lord James Dowglasse with an other armie.

It is apparent that of the two Scottish armies which were involved, one came south over Shap Fell while the other followed the Cumbrian coast through Furness and then crossed the sands of Morecambe Bay. Lancaster was unfortunate in being at their natural meeting place.[114]

There is no direct account of what the Scots did in the town but as it was built principally of timber and thatch it was highly susceptible to fire. Other than the two religious buildings which were protected either by their precinct walls, by the piety of the attackers, or by bribery, the only stone building was the castle. There is no evidence that this fell to the attackers. Probably the Scots left it alone, knowing they would outnumber the garrison if it sallied forth, but having insufficient time for a siege.

The consequences of the attack are apparent when we look at the rental of Lancaster taken in 1323, a year after the event.[115] Again and again we come across burgages with a rental value of nil or far below its previous level. Two examples will suffice.

> Agnes de Baldreston holds 1 burgage and was wont to render yearly at Easter and Michaelmas 2s. and by reason of the burning of the Scots she now renders at the same terms only 18d.

> ... of the issues of the site of the castle he does not answer because it was altogether burnt by the Scots ...

In the latter case it is not the castle itself which was burnt, but the herbiage of the ditch and so on. The prison and the bridge at the entrance to the castle had also to be repaired at a cost of £5 14s. (£5.70) as a result of the attack, which suggests that at least the outworks were taken.

A further note indicates in rather more detail what went on.

> ... the said toft was burnt by the Scots ... and despoiled by them through their being there for 4 days within the quindene of the feast of St John the Baptist ...

Skerton also suffered its share of damage. Goods were stolen and corn trampled by the horses and beasts, suggesting that the armies' picket lines and cattle rustled on the way were kept there temporarily. A large army of several thousand men could hardly have been billeted on a town which they

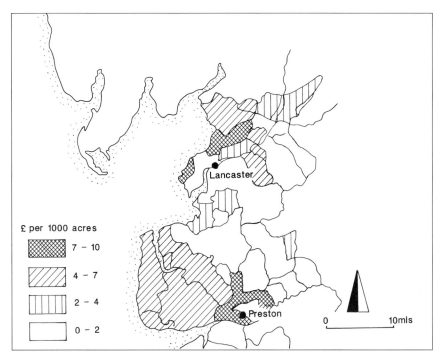

Wealth in north Lancashire, 1334 (after Glasscock).

had just burned; it is more likely that the leaders would commandeer some of the better houses (and thus save them from the initial burning) while the rank and file lay encamped in fields on the Skerton side of the bridge.

Perhaps we can see further effects of the Scots' attack in the figures for the Lay Subsidy of 1334. This tax has been analysed both to reconstruct the population figures and to estimate wealth. Glasscock[116] analyses the figures for Lancashire by dividing them into five bands, based on £s per 1,000 acres. Lancaster parish fits into the very lowest band of £0–2 per 1,000 acres, which seems very low indeed for a royal borough and a county town. It may be that the large size of the parish, with a high content of low-valued and thinly-populated countryside, may mask a local concentration of wealth in the town, or we may have real evidence for the economic effects of the disaster.

The Black Death

The town, which had been badly damaged by the four-day stay of the Scots army in 1322, can hardly have begun to revive before there was another blow. The Black Death, a bubonic plague of unheard-of virulence, ravaged the whole of western Europe during the late 1340s. Nowhere was safe, though the crowded towns and cities were more at risk than the countryside.[117]

Obtaining figures for the scale of the plague is difficult; medieval statistics are usually suspect and in this case so great was the catastrophe that many people thought that the end of the world was at hand, so records are more than usually bad. However a dispute over certain fees in the Deanery of Amounderness gives us unusually firm statistics for the number of deaths in this area, though the jury that was empanelled for the purpose accepted only one quarter of the figure claimed. It was said that in the period between 8 September 1349 and 11 January 1350 (presumably the period of highest mortality) Lancaster parish lost no less than 3,000 people.[118]

It would help if we knew the total population of the parish at that time. The parish was very large, including many places which are now parishes in their own right and also a number of detached fragments as much as twenty miles away.[119] However the population centre of this parish was quite clearly the borough itself, and the mortality rate may have been as high as one in three. If the jury was correct that the actual deaths were about 750, this ratio would put the population at about 2,250. But it would have been odd if anyone had claimed a death rate higher than the total population, even in the not very statistics-conscious Middle Ages!

These cold statistics do not do justice to the horror of the situation. In all probability no family escaped without the death of one or more members and some must have been totally wiped out.

Opinion has moved away from the view that many rural settlements were deserted at this time; indeed, it is relatively hard to find any examples of this happening at all, though some marginal hamlets may have been nudged into a process of gradual decay. However, mortality on this scale must have struck at the very roots of civilisation, and social structures will have taken a very long time to rebuild.

Sometimes the deaths of officials while in office give us some useful clues. Certainly 1349 brought to an end the long mayoralty of John de Bolron and he was succeeded in 1350 by John de Catherton, but whether it was as a result of the former's death we cannot now tell.

At the end of the Middle Ages Lancaster had suffered a number of economic blows which threatened to stifle the growth of the town. Its county town status, its strategic importance and its market helped it to survive in the face of difficulties and focused Crown and Duchy attention on it, for better or worse. We shall find this a recurring theme in Lancaster's history.

Notes

1. D. Shotter and A. White, *Roman Fort and Town of Lancaster*, Centre for North-West Regional Studies, University of Lancaster, 1990.
2. J. Williams and R. Newman, 'Excavations on the Mitchell's Brewery Site, Lancaster, 1988', *Contrebis*, XV, 1989, 65–7.
3. M. Beresford and H. P. R. Finberg, *English Medieval Boroughs: A Handlist*, David & Charles, 1973, 132–3, 176.

4. W. O. Roper, *Materials for the History of the Church of Lancaster*, Chetham Society, vol. 1, 1892, 8–12.

5. W. G. Collingwood, *Northumbrian Crosses of the Pre-Norman Age*, Faber & Gwyer, 1927; R. N. Bailey, *Viking Age Sculpture*, Collins, 1980, 82, 264.

6. N. Heywood, 'A Find of Anglo-Saxon Stycas at Lancaster', *British Numismatic Journal*, ser. 2, vol. 1, 1914, 1–2.

7. A. J. White, 'Anglo-Saxon Coins from Lancaster', *Contrebis*, 11, 1983–84, 46–9.

8. P. Morgan (ed.), *Domesday Book: Vol. 26, Cheshire*, Phillimore, 1978.

9. M. Bailey, 'Trade and Towns in Medieval England: new insights from familiar sources', *The Local Historian*, vol. 29, no. 4, 1999, 194–211; A. White, 'Medieval Towns', in R. Newman (ed.), *The Archaeology of Lancashire; Present State and Future Priorities*, 1996, 125–38.

10. Especially the Towneley Hall plan of 1684, found as rough survey sheets in 1952, and redrawn. K. H. Docton, 'Lancaster 1684', *Historic Society of Lancashire and Cheshire*, 109, 1957, 125–42; M. R. G. Conzen, 'The use of town plans in the study of urban history', in H. J. Dyos (ed.), *The Study of Urban History*, 1968.

11. T. Pape, *The Charters of the City of Lancaster*, 1952; Beresford and Finberg, *Medieval Boroughs*; W. O. Roper, *Materials for a History of Lancaster*, 1907.

12. Rev. R. Simpson, *The History and Antiquities of the Town of Lancaster*, T. Edmondson, 1852, 271–3.

13. J. Parker (ed.), *Calendar of Lancashire Assize Rolls*, Record Society of Lancashire and Cheshire, 47, 1904, 113 (30 Hen. III).

14. Pape, *Charters.*

15. Roper, *Materials*, 1907, 363; W. Farrer, 'Early Mayors of Lancaster', *Historic Society of Lancashire and Cheshire*, LXIII, 1912, 174–7; LXIV; 1913, 324; LXVII, 1916, 166–7.

16. Pape, *Charters.*

17. R. C. Richardson and T. B. James (eds), *The Urban Experience – A Source Book. English, Scottish and Welsh Towns, 1450–1700*, Manchester University Press, 1983, 65–6.

18. J. Brownbill and J. R. Nuttall, *A Calendar of Charters and Records Belonging to the Corporation of Lancaster*, Lancaster Corporation, 1929, 16.

19. R. Cunliffe Shaw, *The Royal Forest of Lancaster*, Guardian Press, 1956.

20. D. Kenyon, *The Origins of Lancashire*, Manchester University Press, 1991.

21. Docton, 'Lancaster 1684'.

22. W. Camden, *Britannia* (Philemon Holland's English edition), 1610, 754.

23. W. Farrer (ed.), *The Chartulary of Cockersand Abbey of the Premonstratensian Order*, Vol. III, pt. I, Chetham Society, Vol. 56, 1905, 821.

24. Kenyon, *Origins.*

25. Kenyon, *Origins*, 152–6.

26. I. J. Sanders, *English Baronies 1086–1327*, Oxford University Press, 1963, 126–7.

27. C. Clark, *An Historical and Descriptive Account of the Town of Lancaster*, C. Clark, 1807, 16–18.

28. A. Grant, *Lancaster Castle in the Middle Ages*, University of Lancaster, 1985.

29. W. Farrer, *The Lancashire Pipe Rolls* (s.d. 1202–3), 1902.

30. R. A. Brown, 'Royal Castle-Building in England, 1154–1216,' *English Historical Review*, 70, 1955, 353–98.

31. K. Docton, *On Lancaster*, 1971; Farrer, *Pipe Rolls.*

32. R. A. Brown, H. M. Colvin and A. J. Taylor (eds), *The History of the King's Works. 2. The Middle Ages*, HMSO, 1963, 692–3.

33. Cunliffe Shaw, *Royal Forest*, 68.

34. W. Farrer, *Lancashire Inquests, Extents and Feudal Aids*, Pt. II, Lancashire and Cheshire Record Society, 54, 1907, 175.

35. Brown *et al.*, *King's Works*, 693.

36. H. M. Colvin, D. R. Ransome and J. Summerson (eds), *The History of the King's Works*, 3, Pt. I, 1485–1660, HMSO, 1975, 178–9.

37. E. W. Cox, 'Lancaster Castle', *Historic Society of Lancashire and Cheshire*, XLVIII, 1896, 95–122.

38. Colvin *et al.*, *King's Works*, 260–1.

39. Roper, *Materials*, 248–51.

40. Lancashire Record Office, copy in Lancaster City Museum.

41. E. Jervoise, *The Ancient Bridges of the North of England*, The Architectural Press, 1931, 132–3.

42. Docton, *On Lancaster*.

43. R. Somerville, *History of the Duchy of Lancaster, I, 1265–1603*, The Chancellor and the Council of the Duchy of Lancaster, 1953, 193.

44. PRO, MR15.

45. Farrer, *Lancashire Inquests*, II, 27.

46. S. H. Penney, *Lancaster: the Evolution of its Townscape to 1800*, Centre for North-West Regional Studies, University of Lancaster, Occasional Paper no. 9, 1981, 20.

47. Chetham's Library, Manchester; Kuerden Fol. MS 246.

48. Cunliffe Shaw, *Royal Forest*, 140.

49. Penney, *Lancaster Evolution*, 14–19.

50. W. Farrer, *The Chartulary of Cockersand Abbey of the Premonstratensian Order*, III, pt. III, Chetham Society, 64, 1909, 823.

51. Farrer, *Cockersand Chartulary*, 825.

52. PRO, DL SC12/9/78.

53. Farrer, *Cockersand Chartulary*, 1284.

54. J. Brownbill, *The Coucher Book of Furness Abbey*, II, pt. I, Chetham Society, 74, 1915, 203.

55. D. Mills, *The Place Names of Lancashire*, Batsford, 1976, 29; Brownbill, *Furness Coucher*, 198–9.

56. Penney, *Lancaster Evolution*, 18.

57. Farrer, *Cockersand Chartulary*, 823.

58. Penney, *Lancaster Evolution*, 18.

59. Shotter and White, *Roman Fort and Town*, 16, 27.

60. Pape, *Charters*.

61. Brownbill, *Furness Coucher*, 199.

62. W. Farrer, *Lancashire Inquests, Extents and Feudal Aids*, pt. I, Lancashire and Cheshire Record Series, 48, 1903, 126; Farrer, *Lancashire Inquests*, II, 23.

63. Simpson, *History and Antiquities*, 291.

64. Cunliffe Shaw, *Royal Forest*, 364.

65. PRO, MPD 179.

66. Brownbill, *Furness Coucher*, 222.

67. E. Baines, *The History of the County Palatine and Duchy of Lancaster*, 3rd edn, 1892, 467, 489.

68. Roper, *Materials, 292;* Lancaster Central Library MS 5221.
69. W. Farrer and J. Brownbill, *The Victoria County History; Lancashire*, vol. 2, 1908, 170.
70. N. Pevsner, *The Buildings of England; Lancashire, 2, The Rural North*, Penguin Books, 1969, 153–4; J. Champness, *Lancashire's Architectural Heritage*, Lancashire County Council, 1988, 25–6.
71. Collingwood, *Northumbrian Crosses*, 36.
72. H. J. Austin, 'Notes on the discovery of an apse at St Mary's Church, Lancaster in 1911, and of other discoveries,' *Transactions of the Lancashire and Cheshire Antiquarian Society*, XXXI, 1913, 1–6.
73. J. Alexander and P. Binski (eds), *The Age of Chivalry. Art in Plantagenet England 1200–1400*, Royal Academy/Weidenfeld & Nicholson, 1987, 427–8.
74. J. Swarbrick, 'The Abbey of St Mary-of-the-Marsh at Cockersand', *Transactions of the Lancashire and Cheshire Antiquarian Society*, XL, 1925, 163–93.
75. A. White, 'Did Lancaster Priory have a Precinct Wall?', *Contrebis*, XIV, 1988, 8–12.
76. L. Toulmin Smith (ed.), *The Itinerary of John Leland in or about the years 1535–1543*, 1910 (reprinted Centaur Press Ltd, 1964), vol. IV, 11.
77. J. P. Droop and R. Newstead, 'Excavations at Lancaster, 1928', *Liverpool Annals of Archaeology and Anthropology*, XVI, 1929, 27.
78. G. D. B. Jones and D. C. A. Shotter (eds), *Roman Lancaster; Rescue Archaeology in an Historic City 1970–75*, Brigantia Monographs, no. 1, 1988, 30.
79. Farrer and Brownbill, *VCH Lancashire*, 171.
80. Roper, *Church of Lancaster*, 8–12.
81. E. M. Grafton, 'Notes on the Benedictine Abbey of Seez: Its English Lands and Charters', *Historic Society of Lancashire and Cheshire*, n.s. 23, 1907, 119–31.
82. Morgan, *Domesday*, 301d.
83. Collingwood, *Northumbrian Crosses*, 36.
84. Roper, *Church of Lancaster*, 8–12.
85. Farrer, *Pipe Rolls*, 292.
86. Cunliffe Shaw, *Royal Forest*, 154.
87. Brownbill, *Furness Coucher*, 217.
88. Brownbill, *Furness Coucher*, 181; C. Platt, *The Monastic Grange in Medieval England*, Macmillan, 1969, 125–6.
89. Brownbill, *Furness Coucher*, 129.
90. M. Aston (ed.), *Medieval Fish, Fisheries and Fishponds in England*, British Archaeological Reports, 182, 1988.
91. Roper, *Church of Lancaster*, 10.
92. J. C. Atkinson (ed.), *The Furness Coucher Book*, I, pt. I, Chetham Society, n.s. 9, 1886, 122–3.
93. Aston, *Medieval Fish*; J. G. Jenkins, *Nets and Coracles*, David & Charles, 1974, 223–62.
94. Brownbill, *Furness Coucher*, 180, 217, 219.
95. R. Stewart-Brown (ed.), *Lancashire and Cheshire Cases in the Court of Star Chamber*, pt. I, Record Society of Lancashire and Cheshire, 71, 1916, 98.
96. Simpson, *History and Antiquities*, 238.
97. Lancaster Central Library, MS 5553.
98. Lancaster Borough Records, Copies of Charters, Grants etc., f282, headed 'A list of several old papers', '2 A Lease from the Corporation to Clement Toulnson

of Stakes for a Houstead where formerly stood Harberhouse &c. at the South end of Penny Street AD 1650'. This site clearly became that of Toulnson's Almshouses, in turn demolished in 1811.

99. Farrer and Brownbill, *VCH Lancashire*, 161–2.

100. W. Gumbley, 'Provincial Priors and Vicars of the English Dominicans 1221–1916', *English Historical Review*, 33, 1918, 246.

101. *Cal. Pat. R.*, 3 Philip & Mary (1556) 61.

102. Clark, *Historical and Descriptive Accuunt*, 1807, 30.

103. Simpson, *History and Antiqutities*, 242.

104. *Lancaster Guardian*, 16/8/1873, 30/8/1873.

105. S. H. Penney, 'Lancaster Friary Excavation, 1981; An Interim Report', *Contrebis*, 9, 1982, 15–17; S. H. Penney, 'Excavations at Lancaster Friary 1980–81', *Contrebis*, 10, 1982, 1–13.

106. Simpson, *History and Antiquities*, 242; the 'Fryers Wall' also appears as a property boundary to houses in Penny Street in 1749: see LCC Deeds 171a.

107. Farrer and Brownbill, *VCH Lancashire*, 165.

108. Simpson, *History and Antiquities*, 245; 'Cross Fleury', *Time-Honoured Lancaster*, Eaton & Bulfield, 1891, 49–51.

109. Farrer and Brownbill, *VCH Lancashire*, 165.

110. R. M. Clay, *The Medieval Hospitals of England*, Methuen, 1909 (2nd edn, Cassells, 1966).

111. Farrer and Brownbill, *VCH Lancashire*, 165.

112. *Cal.Pat.R.*, 4–5 Philip & Mary (1557), 282–3. A marker, known as 'Nuns' Stone', still stands near Ridge Lane bridge.

113. *Holinshed's Chronicles of England, Scotland and Ireland in Six Volumes*, J. Johnson et al., 1808 (reprinted AMS Press Inc., 1965), V, 355.

114. Roper, *Materials*, 7.

115. Farrer, *Lancashire Inquests*, II, 115ff.

116. R. E. Glasscock (ed.), 'The Lay Subsidy of 1334', *Records of Social and Economic History*, 1975; M. Morris, *Medieval Manchester*, vol. 1, The Archaeology of Greater Manchester, Greater Manchester Archaeological Unit, 1983, 23–4.

117. P. Ziegler, *The Black Death*, Penguin Books, 1970, 191–2 + fn.

118. W. Farrer and J. Brownbill, *The Victoria County History; Lancashire*, vol. 8, 1914, 12; A. G. Little, 'The Black Death in Lancashire', *English Historical Review*, V, 1890, 526, 528.

119. Farrer and Brownbill, *VCH Lancashire*, 8, 4.

CHAPTER THREE

Reformation and Renewal, 1450–1690

Michael Mullett

For the whole of the period covered in this chapter, the life of Lancaster was strongly influenced by the Castle and the Priory church, the two majestic buildings dominating the hill-top site above the town.[1] The Castle, the quintessential expression of Lancaster's strategic significance, frequently conferred on the borough a national importance and involved it, at times damagingly, in national struggles. The history of the Priory church in our period forms an accurate microcosm of the nation's religious history in the period before, during and after the Reformation.

Lancaster emerged as a port for Ireland (under Chester's supervision) in the fifteenth century – though that period has also been described as 'a period of decay at Lancaster', in fact the opening of a long-term recession in the town's life lasting until the later seventeenth century. The Tudor antiquary John Leland (c. 1506–52) regarded Lancaster as a kind of large agricultural village, referring to its soil – 'very fair' – and 'plentiful ... wood, pasture, meadow and corn'.[2] In the sixteenth and seventeenth centuries, the Castle and the activities going on inside it – especially its judicial functions – were to play a key compensatory role in the life and economy of a town whose commercial and industrial base, compared with the expanding towns of south Lancashire, would remain weak until the end of our period. However, the Castle's actual military function was in fact to remain minimal until the mid-seventeenth century. The fifteenth-century dynastic Wars of the Roses 'seem to have passed [Lancaster] by', and the statement by the romantic-minded historian of Lancaster, 'Cross Fleury', that Lancaster lay on the path of Lambert Simnel's force aimed against the first Tudor king, King Henry VII, in 1487 has recently been described as 'a rather dubious tradition': landing near Ulverston, Simnel's army would have crossed the Sands at Hest Bank and then probably have advanced towards pro-Richard III centres at Hornby Castle and into Wensleydale, approaching Lancaster no nearer than Carnforth.[3]

Although the economic outlook for the town was not bright – and even Lancaster's strategic significance would be down-graded – Lancaster's late medieval religious life was full of vitality. Indeed, the town took a full part in the dramatic upsurge, described by the historian Haigh, in Catholic piety in Lancashire in the late Middle Ages.[4] As we shall see, Lancaster evolved a long tradition of civic Christian philanthropy reflected in pious charitable foundations. The earliest expression of this tradition in the town was the Hospital of St Leonard, founded probably in the late twelfth century. However, by the end of the Middle Ages this was a run-down institution, the church and other buildings dilapidated and, allegedly, no alms were dispensed between about 1470 and 1530.[5] The preaching order of St Dominic had one of its numerous urban bases in Lancaster. The town also evolved a rich devotional life characteristic of the late Middle Ages and centred on chantries and fraternities (religious institutions set up to pray for the deliverance from Purgatory of the souls of the faithful departed).[6] However, far and away the most important single religious institution in late medieval Lancaster was the Priory church; it was one of Lancashire's most influential and powerful parish churches, with dependencies as far afield as Toxteth and Fulwood, and was described as controlling 'many parochial chappells, hamlets, and forests belonging to Lancaster, and far distant from their Mother Church'.[7] Developments at the Priory at the end of the Middle Ages vividly reflect the positive as well as the negative aspects of the state of religious life in England.

The Priory Church

In the course of the fifteenth century, the status of the Priory as a local parish church rather than as a monastic foundation became more clearly defined. The new proprietor of the church (from 1415 and from 1431), the Bridgettine Abbey of Syon in Middlesex, tended to delegate its economic interests in the area to local lay people. A 1492 survey of local Syon properties, with their cash values, includes 'Adcliff' (£20) and Newton (also £20); other lands included 'Asheton', 'Bere' (Bare), 'Pulton', 'Torresholme', 'Balk' (Bulk), 'Osclif', 'Catton', 'Scotfield' (Scotforth) and 'Skyrton'. On the occasion of its total transfer to Syon in 1431, the archdeacon of Richmond established a vicar at Lancaster who was in turn to maintain an impressive clerical presence of six chaplains, three of them for dependent chapels.[8]

Lancaster's first vicar, and indeed his immediate successors too, evinced many of the deficiencies of the late medieval Catholic clergy: careerism, pluralism (holding two or more benefices simultaneously), consequent absenteeism, obsession with money, and litigiousness. A royal chaplain and Henry VI's agent for Eton College, vicar Richard Chester (who served 1431–66) has been described as one whose 'interest in Lancaster was mainly financial'.[9] Chester was a papally licensed pluralist on a large scale, collecting benefices all over England and Ireland, and a regular visitor to centres of ecclesiastical power on the Continent. His biographer says, with elegant irony, 'he may even have spent some time' in Lancaster, in about 1455. Chester was also involved in long-running financial dispute with the abbess of Syon (her 'thorn in the flesh'), drawing up in 1440 a lengthy schedule of his expenses; though much of this document looks like special pleading in his dispute, it does indicate the large and expensive scale of Lancaster Priory's activities as a parish church and as the centre of religious life and worship in Lancaster's hinterland.[10]

Chester's successor, Richard Burton (served 1466–84) was out of the same mould. Like Chester, Burton was closely linked with King Henry VI's pet project, Eton College, where Burton had acted as clerk of the works. This connection with Henry VI through the Eton project certainly strengthens the speculation that these men were appointed to Lancaster by Syon through pressure brought to bear by the crown, which continued to maintain a close patronal relationship with the abbey. At the same time, as Mr Johnston pointed out, it was helpful to have a building expert as a vicar at a time when the Priory was undergoing major re-building. Burton's surviving writings show a man with some, though not much, interest in religion and, apparently, a marked preference for astrology. An intriguing mixture of hard-headed realist and credulous star-gazer, Burton, who was by his own admission *cupidus* (greedy, avaricious), was quarrelsome and locked in dispute with Syon over revenues; he was also money-mad and basically cynical about the Catholic Church which he served. Along with a successor, William Green (served 1525–40), he has been identified as one of a series of well-educated royal administrators and pluralists appointed to Lancaster – men who were priests in only the most formal sense of the word.[11]

So how could Lancaster's religious needs be catered for by such uninspiring clerics? The answer is, adequately, or more than adequately. The incumbent of a wealthy medieval church such as Lancaster's was often more like a senior non-executive director of a firm than a modern serving minister of religion. Under absentee parochial vicars, the town and its neighbourhood were served by the six resident chaplains. And regardless of the negligence or absenteeism so often found amongst its senior clergy in the period, this was a golden age in the Priory church's building history, as much of the fabric that we know today dates from the decades before the Reformation. The records show that it was the townspeople and not the distant patron Syon Abbey who poured out their money, their piety and their civic pride on the magnificent new aisle in 1479.[12]

Although Syon's control of distant Lancaster was, as Johnston pointed out, remarkably close given the conditions of the troubled fifteenth century, relations between Lancaster and Syon seem also to have been cordial; possible tensions between the town and the proprietor of its church were assuaged, as at a court held in Aldcliffe in 1510 when church repairs and the always controversial issue of enclosures at Quernmore were negotiated; the abbesses have been described as generous towards the town.

One particular expression of this harmony was the set of financial and spiritual agreements made between John Gardyner ('of Ellel') and Syon. Gardyner's leasing contracts with the abbey can be seen as part of a long-term process of devolution of financial assets in which Syon gradually turned over the exploitation of its Lancashire properties to local lay clients; in one sense, the process can be seen as culminating at the Dissolution of the Monasteries in the enforced transfer of the Priory estate to Robert Dalton of Bispham. John Gardyner, leasing Syon lands in Lonsdale and Amounderness, typified this process of transfer of resources or of their management. But Gardyner was a friend and indeed a devotee of Syon as well as the abbey's client and business partner, and his pious benefactions, in part made possible by his profitability as a lessee, included the sponsorship of endowed prayers at Lancaster for the welfare of the abbess and abbey of Syon. In 1469 the abbess granted Gardyner a corn mill on the Lune at a low rent in consideration of his intention of establishing a chantry with a school attached. Gardyner's will was drawn up in 1472 and proved in 1485. It contained three distinct eleemosynary provisions: a chantry chapel (which would be dissolved when the doctrine of Purgatory was officially attacked in the Reformation under Edward VI), an almshouse (intended for four poor people) and a school.[13]

The Free School

As it turned out, this separation of the chantry from the other two provisions in the Gardyner will allowed the school and almshouse or hospital to survive the closure of the chantry in 1547. Typical of the grammar school founda-tions of its age, the school was to concern itself with morals and Latin; the teacher was to be 'abull [competent to teach] in sciens [learning] and conversacion [behavior] ... a profund gramarian keping a Fre Scole, teching and informing the children unto their most profette, *nothing taking therefor*' [my emphasis in the quotation]. The author of the relevant section of the *Victoria County History* was absolutely right to insist that Gardyner's intention, re-stated posthumously for him in 1500, was to set up completely free tuition in what is now Lancaster Royal Grammar School. Further regulations of 1500 also set out the school's daily timetable: 6–8 a.m., 10 a.m.–12 noon, 2–6 p.m. – eight widely separated teaching hours.[14]

    Although the school, as a distinct charitable foundation, was able to survive the Edwardine closure of the chantries, the free school was not immune from financial stringencies, especially the results of the neglect of the mill, the profits of which Gardyner had earmarked for the school, by its purchaser Robert Dalton. We shall see later in this chapter how, supported by continued private donations and by the borough corporation, Lancaster's free school survived and prospered, to the end of our period.[15]

The old Grammar School, founded in the fifteenth century, rebuilt in 1682 and finally moved to East Road in 1851. From a lithograph by Bedford after Fielding.

Livery and Maintenance

At the time of the original foundation, in the year of the inception of the Tudor dynasty, 1485, John Gardyner's will was submitted for royal approval. Perhaps this might have been taken as an appropriate indication that Lancaster – which through the Duchy of Lancaster had a kind of double relationship with the crown – would now have to deal with a highly activist, authoritarian and interventionist central government under the Tudor kings and queens. The impact of Tudor rule and imperiousness was felt, at Lancaster and elsewhere, most dramatically in the Reformation and the Dissolution of the Monasteries, but in fact from the beginning Lancaster was to know the full effects of the Tudors' determination fully to rule their realm. Like their Yorkist and Lancastrian predecessors, one particular problem the Tudor sovereigns faced in controlling and policing the kingdom arose over 'livery and maintenance', the keeping of what were in effect private armies of heavies under the control of nobles and gentry; these forces were employed to intimidate juries, carry on vendettas and inter-family feuds, and generally perpetuate a kind of aristocratic anarchy. Close to a number of centres of gentry and noble power, such as Hornby Castle, Lancaster was particularly prey to these kinds of aristocratic gangsterism: in 1535, for instance, Lord Monteagle's cook 'sore bete and struck' a Lancastrian. In the face of disorder and violence spawned by noble faction, Tudor royal orders like that of Henry VII (undated but repeated by Philip and Mary in 1557) instructing Lancaster men not to accept livery from nobles may well have found a sympathetic echo amongst townspeople. Similarly, Henry VII's masterfulness towards the 'overmighty' baronage had clear benefits for a town like Lancaster: in 1488 the king ordered the powerful Lord Strange, son of the Earl of Derby, and other magnates to go to the help of Lancaster officials in their attempts to levy bridge tolls. Ten years later came even more tangible royal concessions to Lancaster: a royal confirmation of the town's various historic privileges, which included the highly valuable (for local trade) monopoly of assizes and other courts in the county and the trading privileges of the ancient 'Statute Merchant' of Acton Burnell (1285). For such concessions there was always a price to pay, especially under the acquisitive Henry VII: forty marks (about £27). In a wider sense, too Lancaster under the Tudors was perceptibly favoured by the crown, but the political price does seem to have been one of considerable subjugation, particularly in the parliamentary arena, with the town giving up its electoral independence to the crown in its persona as the Duchy of Lancaster.[16]

The Tudors issued a series of charters and similar documents to Lancaster: a confirmation of privileges by Henry VIII (1509–10) enforcing Lancaster tolls but freeing Lancastrians from tolls elsewhere; a further confirmation by Henry VIII (1511) of Henry VI's grant of 1430; a confirmation by Edward VI (1552); a further confirmation by Philip and Mary (1556–7); a grant by Elizabeth I (1563); and a codification of borough customs (1572). Three issues in particular can be detected as being dealt with in these grants: Lancaster's status as a main or exclusive centre for courts of justice in the county; the commercial privileges which Lancaster and Lancastrian merchants enjoyed; and Lancaster's claims over Quernmore.[17]

The Assizes, Charters and Privileges

The town's historic primacy as the county's judicial capital is unmistakable. One incidental reflection of this administrative and judicial leadership is the fact that all the standard weights and measures for the county were kept at Lancaster. In 1362 the crown ordered county sessions always to be held in Lancaster. In the medieval period, the twice-yearly assizes for the county were normally held in the town, though an outbreak of plague in 1466 sent them to Preston. As late as 1688, when the eddies of commercial prosperity were starting to lap round the town, a biannual 'great exodus' of lawyers and their clerks from Preston, where the assize business was prepared in law offices, must have done wonders for the catering trade in the county town. So the fact that by custom, prescription and royal order the courts must come to Lancaster was a considerable fillip to the local economy, all the

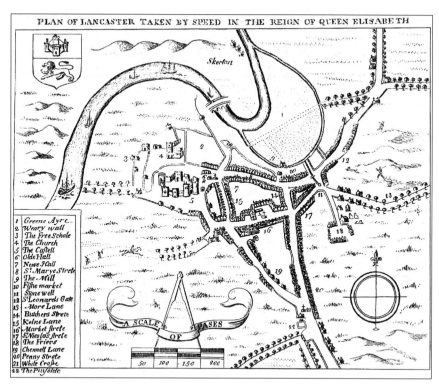

PLAN OF LANCASTER TAKEN BY SPEED IN THE REIGN OF QUEEN ELISABETH

Skerton

1 Greene Ayre
2 Weary wall
3 The Free Schole
4 The Church
5 The Castell
6 Olde Hall
7 Newe Hall
8 S.t Marye Strete
9 The Mill
10 Fishe market
11 Stone well
12 S.t Leonards Gate
13 More Lane
14 Buthers Strete
15 Kelne Lane
16 Market strete
17 S. Nicolos strete
18 The Friers
19 Chennell Lane
20 Penny Strete
21 White Croße
22 The Pinfolde

A SCALE OF PASES

50   100   150   200

Speed's map of Lancaster, 1610, which appears in the corner of his county map of Lancashire. It is the earliest plan of Lancaster.

more so in the sixteenth century, and for much of the seventeenth, when that economy was in the doldrums.[18]

Not only the topographers and the tourists but the crown and parliament in official papers, agreed that the town's economy was in a bad way in the post-medieval period – with the clear implication that a state-supported shot in the arm in the shape of a monopoly of at least the higher courts of law, was in order. An Act of Parliament under Henry VIII (35 Hen. VIII, c. 4, 1544) painted a melancholy picture of a town in which 'divers beautiful houses of habitation have been ... which are now fallen down, decayed'; the Chancellor of the Duchy in 1553 heard that Lancaster was 'very ruinous and in great decay'; and a precept of Philip and Mary depicted 'our town of Lancaster' lying 'in great ruin' – though on this occasion the crown put the dilapidation down to the continued vice of livery and maintenance. However, even though Lancaster seemed to need to keep as much court business as it could, the crown sometimes pursued conflicting policies in this regard, certainly with respect to courts lower than the assizes.

The rising towns of south Lancashire were increasingly side-tracking Lancaster's monopoly and under Henry VIII, in 1546, the crown endorsed this development by setting up five quarter sessions centres in the county. In 1552 Edward VI's government issued a confirmation of Lancaster's privileges, but the town was given only two, not four, quarter sessions. However, a settlement highly favourable to Lancaster was arrived at under Philip and Mary. Following a petition presented by Thomas Carus, frequently member of parliament for the town, which cited the privileges granted by Edward III in 1362, the crown allowed that all courts in Lancashire, including quarter sessions, must be held in Lancaster. Elizabeth's grant of 1563 followed this up by ordering the holding of all 'Pleas and Sessions' in the county town. Given the notorious difficulty of communication in sixteenth-century Lancashire, decisions such as that taken under Philip and Mary can hardly be seen as practical-minded, and did not stand the test of time, but such measures certainly provide striking confirmation of the crown's continued favour towards the town.[19]

As well as its hold over the judicial process in the region, Lancaster enjoyed by royal favour a number of commercial privileges. Taken together, these implied a somewhat contradictory combination of a highly controlled economy locally and freedom of trade elsewhere. The first town charter, with its frequent confirmations, included the grant of a weekly market and two annual fairs. Further, a charter of 1410 granted Lancastrian merchants freedom from tolls throughout England and Ireland and, as we shall see, such commercial privileges were lovingly remembered and cited in favour of Lancaster merchants in the second half of the seventeenth century, as the borough's trade expanded. The contradiction was that Lancastrians were inclined to claim market freedoms in England and Ireland as a free trade area while at the same time the town insisted on its own chartered rights to impose restraints on commerce: by virtue of the (non-extant) charter of Henry VIII (1509–10), the town insisted both on its entitlement to impose local tolls (for instance, a levy demanded by the Lancaster bailiff in 1529–30 from a drover taking cattle from Lancaster market to Leicester) and also on the freedom of its merchants from tolls elsewhere – a right endorsed by Edward VI in 1552 and cited in individual test cases in the seventeenth century.

To resolve any apparent paradox here, we need only be aware that a medieval and early modern English borough tended to see itself as a kind of guild which existed primarily to seek the best interests of its commercial members, with claims based on precedent and grant and regardless of whatever degree of double-think was thereby involved.[20]

The same principal – that a town and its government fought like a lion for its own economic advantage – guided Lancaster's attitude to Quernmore and its valuable resources. Given Lancaster's character in the Tudor and Stuart periods as an 'agricultural town' – 'well manured, lying open, fresh and fair, …' (Leland) – access to exploitation of the Quernmore area, of both its grazing and its mineral resources, was highly desirable from the town's point of view. Traditionally, Lancaster paid the crown, in return for its chartered liberties, an annual 'fee farm rent' of £13 6s. 8d., but in 1511 the town paid an extra £2 10*s.* in rent for 80 acres taken out of Quernmore forest. In 1541, in line with an already well-established policy of fining individuals for allegedly illicit grazing, the corporation impounded livestock said to be grazed illegally at Quernmore: on that occasion, the matter was referred to a government enquiry, which entered a non-committal report. A royal 'Inspeximus' patent of 1570 confirmed the boundaries of Lancaster and Quernmore. However, one problem arising from Lancaster's insistence on its rights and privileges over Quernmore was that this insistence might threaten to open up a breach, which was detectable as early as the reign of Henry VII, with a rival claimant, the Duchy of Lancaster itself. This matter came to a head in the seventeenth century, as the crown, under Charles I, applied itself relentlessly to the exploitation of its own real estate and complaint was entered in the Duchy chamber against Lancastrians, in effect for trespassing on the Duchy's territorial claim over Quernmore. However, in the Tudor period friction between Lancaster and the Duchy seems to have been minimised. Generally speaking, the crown, 'owner' of the Duchy, looked favourably on Lancaster and seems even to have understood the town's problems. In fact, in the course of the sixteenth century, the Duchy became the single most important patronal influence over the town, over-taking that of the Monteagles of Hornby. This can be seen with particular clarity over the question of parliamentary representation.[21]

Parliamentary Representation

Lancaster sent burgesses (members) to Parliament between 1295 and 1331. The town was not entered on a list of parliamentary constituencies drawn up in 1512 and in fact did not regain its representation until 1523. On that occasion, the influence of the Stanley-Monteagle connection – they held property within Lancaster as well as the Hornby base only eight miles away – still seems to have been predominant, and the representation may have been re-gained through collusion between Edward Stanley, first Lord Monteagle, sheriff of Lancashire, and his deputy sheriff, Lawrence Starkey, mayor of Lancaster and himself possibly one of the two MPs of 1523. However, as a result of an overall expansion of Duchy influence under the first Earl of Southampton, Duchy chancellor from 1529 to 1542, the Duchy won effective control of Lancaster's parliamentary representation. The relevant volume of the *History of Parliament* explains the order by Philip and Mary proscribing liveries as a measure intended to exclude all rivals for patronal influence over the town, apart from the crown through the Duchy: there were to be no assemblies 'but only by our commission under the seal of the Duchy of Lancaster or of our chancellor'. A string of Lancaster MPs directly linked to the Duchy and the crown followed from about the middle of the sixteenth century: Sir Walter Mildmay, Duchy auditor, selected for, though not returned by Lancaster in 1553; Thomas Carus, a Duchy official, returned in the two parliaments of 1553 and again in 1555; Sir Thomas Tresham (October 1553), a Catholic protégé of Queen Mary Tudor; and the members John Heywood, George Felton and Richard Weston, all returned in 1554 and all personally connected to the Duchy chancellor Sir Robert Rochester. The social cohesion of the group of Lancaster MPs and their close links as professional lawyers with the Duchy and its legal activities are evident in the fact that seven out of 18 Lancaster members from the restoration of representation to 1558 were lawyers of the Middle Temple.[22]

This same pattern was repeated in the reign of Elizabeth I. Of the members for 1559, Sir Thomas Benger was an associate of Duchy Chancellor Sir Anthony Cave, and his fellow member William Fleetwood (also member in 1563) became a Duchy official. The other member of 1563, John Hale I, was connected, through the Court of Chancery, with a leading Duchy official, Sir Ralph Sadler; the latter, with the return of his sons Henry (1571, 1584, 1586) and Thomas (1572), seems to have been well on the way to turning Lancaster into a family pocket borough as well as a Duchy parliamentary dependency. In 1584, alongside Henry Sadler and also by means of family nomination, Duchy Vice-chancellor Sir Gilbert Gerard secured his son Thomas's return, and was probably behind the return of John Audley II and John Preston, both in 1593. Other MPs for Lancaster closely connected to the Duchy were Roger Dalton (1589), linked through the espionage service to Duchy Chancellor Sir Francis Walsingham; Thomas Hesketh (1597), Vice-chancellor of the Duchy of Lancaster; and Edward Hubberd (1597), who was possibly returned through the influence of a Duchy attorney. It may be that the electoral influence of the Duchy of Lancaster reached its height under the Tudors, from the 1540s to the 1590s. As well as being a Duchy parliamentary dependency and a berth for lawyers, Lancaster was as a consequence largely a carpet-bag constituency, with an estimated thirteen out of eighteen members between 1523 and 1558 not of Lancashire and only three with dwellings in the town. And it is all the more remarkable that Lancaster should have become in effect a nomination borough (of the crown) when its franchise was an open one, vested in the mayor, bailiffs, burgesses and 'commonalty' or perhaps in the mayor, bailiffs, burgesses and all 'older men'.[23]

Religion

If the crown's involvement with Lancaster reached a particularly high point over the town's parliamentary representation, the effect of the Tudor dynasty's measures on the town's religious life was vastly more dramatic. The Duchy's control over the town's representation in Parliament was subtle, ramified, partly concealed; and, arguably, the town's franchise was effectively handed over to the Duchy because, for the broad mass of Lancastrians entitled to vote Parliament was an institution geographically and conceptually remote from their lives, an affair for lawyers and gentry. In contrast, religion, and the Tudor state's revolutionary intervention in its patterns, affected the lives and consciousness of every Lancastrian, as of every Tudor English man and woman, in the most intimate ways. Indeed, it is difficult for us, in our largely post-Christian society to imagine how inextricably life and religion were enmeshed in late medieval and early modern England: in the way that the Christian Church controlled education; that the seasons of the year were mapped out in feasts and fasts; that the life of the individual was marked and measured in a sequence of sacramental 'rites of passage' from birth to death; that the physical appearance of a town of low-rise dwellings could be dominated by the majesty of a church such as Lancaster Priory; and the way that the community and the neighbourhood were constantly brought together and sacralised in religious worship. Thus the abrupt changes wrought by Tudor governments in the nation's religious life under Henry VIII (especially in the 1530s), under Edward VI (1547–53) and under Elizabeth I (1558–1603, but particularly in and immediately after 1559) had a profoundly unsettling effect. This was especially so in parts of the country away from the progressive-minded South-East and in areas like Lancaster and Lancashire which had witnessed a genuine revival of Catholic piety in the decades before the Reformation.

Lancashire's resistance, either active or passive, to the Tudor Reformation has been well documented, especially by Haigh. As the implications of Henry VIII's attack on the papal headship of the Church and his statements in Parliament of his own supremacy in religion became ever clearer, murmurs of treasonable dissent were heard in this area; in 1536, for instance, Henry Salley was imprisoned at Lancaster for saying, in his cups, that no 'secular knave' (common layman) could be head of the Church. Then, in the same year, northern resistance to sweeping government changes in religion – to the abrogation of the pope's headship of the Church and, even more, to the state's attacks on the monasteries – exploded in the rising known as the Pilgrimage of Grace. Most of the North Country had a strong attachment to the monasteries which, in this relatively under-developed zone, still played a vital social as well as religious role. Lancaster, ringed round with monastic houses such as Cockersands and Cartmel, also had its own traditional links with the religious orders through the Priory church and the Dominican Priory.[24]

It is, therefore, a reasonable speculation that when the Northern Catholic rebels in the Pilgrimage of Grace advanced on Lancaster in 1536, they were expecting, to say the least, passive sympathy. A much less serious rising against Tudor rule, the Lambert Simnel movement, had, as we saw, by-passed Lancaster. But the Pilgrimage of Grace, the most serious protest that Tudor government had to face, threatening as it did a secession of the North, took full account of the town's strategic as well as symbolic importance. The rebels came down from Kendal and the Lakes, via their muster on Kellet Moor, late in 1536. In his report to the crown, the Tudor policeman of the

North-West, the Earl of Derby, whilst vague about the number of his
opponents (between three and six thousand), was clear about their favourable
reception locally, not least amongst Lancaster's common people: the rebels,
Derby reported, met no opposition in Lancaster; the townspeople took the
'pilgrim's oath' of solidarity, and they pressured the mayor to back the rising
– a hint here that the town's rulers, dependent as they were on the goodwill
of central government, took a more prudential view of events than did the
common people.[25]

At the end of 1536 Henry VIII's government was still in no position to
crush the pilgrim-rebels, so it acted as if it were, and pardoned them. In
March 1537 the town of Lancaster was designated the centre to which the
men of Lonsdale were to come and take the oath of allegiance to Henry
VIII. And Lancaster was now about to begin its gruesome career as a place
of slaughter for political and religious dissidents; the melancholy processions
to the Moor, the gallows, the screams, the death reek and the gore, the
obscene mutilations and displays of human flesh were to represent the price
the town was to pay for its carefully guarded status as judicial centre of its
region. Following the crushing of the Pilgrimage, a group of leading
Lancashire monastics, including Abbott Paslew of Whalley Abbey, who had
been implicated in the rising, was selected for execution at Lancaster.[26]

The policies, especially the attack on the abbeys, that the Pilgrimage had
tried to halt, were resumed, quite literally with a vengeance, by Henry VIII's
government. Lancaster's own religious structure now felt the more direct
impact of government policy. In 1538 Bishop Richard Devereux, agent to
Henry VIII's minister for religion, Thomas Cromwell, identified Lancaster's
Dominican Priory as one of twenty places where friaries 'yet ... be stondeyng
in the north parte ...', but the house was surrendered, probably in 1539,
and sold to a courtier, Thomas Holcroft, for £126 10s. Lancaster settled
down again after the rising and seems, at least on the surface, to have accepted
the further packages of religious change that Henry VIII, his son Edward
VI and his younger daughter Elizabeth had in store. There is certainly
evidence of external compliance in the town: in October 1559 the visitors
sent by Elizabeth's government to secure adhesion to the new and distinctly
Protestant religious settlement met with complete conformity at Lancaster.
There is also, though, evidence of a more passive and more covert conservative dissent: in complete defiance of official Protestant norms, as late as
1564 a candle burned in honour of St Nicholas in the Priory church.[27]

None of this account of active and passive resistance to Reformation takes
note of growing popular support for Protestantism in Lancaster. Despite the
entirely correct emphasis of historians on the persistence of Catholicism in
Lancashire, the region, and especially the south-east and the area around
Manchester in particular, was open to Protestant influence from a relatively
early date. An outstanding early Protestant leader was George Marsh from
Dean, a retired farmer and widower who took up what the contemporary
historian of the English Reformation, John Foxe, called 'godly studies' and

who was ordained as a Protestant minister in 1552. Shortly afterwards, during the Catholic reaction under Queen Mary, Marsh was arrested and sent to Lancaster Castle for imprisonment, as part of a sustained attempt to win him back to Catholicism. However, his incarceration in the town had the unlooked for result (from the authorities' point of view) of disseminating his Protestant views from their south-Lancashire (and Cambridge) points of origin to the far north of the county – though Haigh speculates that Lancaster's political links as a county town with London also helped introduce Protestant influences there. But Foxe, concerned as he was with heroes and with dramas, stressed the personal contribution that Marsh made to the Protestantisation of Lancaster, recruiting to his Protestant cause the mayor – 'a favourer of the gospel' – and the schoolmaster. The delightful story told by Marsh himself of his evangelising at the window of Lancaster Castle is worth repeating:[28]

> The truth is, I and my prison-fellow Warburton, every day kneeling on our knees, did read morning and evening prayer, with the English Litany every day twice, both before noon and after, with other prayers more, and also read every day certain chapters of the Bible, commonly towards night: and we read all these things with so high and loud voice, that the people without in the streets might hear us, and would often-times, namely in the evenings, come and sit down in our sights under the windows, and hear us read ...

The 'Dean martyr' George Marsh may be seen as the first in an heroic procession of prisoners of conscience at Lancaster in the sixteenth and seventeenth centuries. Early modern English prisons were indeed in themselves death-traps, insanitary and often over-crowded. So some of those who died in Lancaster Castle for their beliefs died of imprisonment itself, as did the Catholic priest Richard Halton (*c.* 1586) and the Catholic laymen Richard Blundell of Little Crosby and Richard Worthington of Blainsclough (1592), both of whom were arrested by the Earl of Derby as Catholic recusants (refusing to attend Church of England worship). However, as well as witnessing the deaths of religious dissidents as a fortuitous effect of their imprisonment, Lancaster saw the trials and deliberate executions of a long line of Catholics.

Persecution

The town was as we have seen, the great centre of justice of the County Palatine. And justice in pre-modern England, hopelessly inadequate when it came to policing, relied for crime prevention on terror, through the systematic use of 'exemplary' punishments which were intended by their carefully constructed barbarity to intimidate potential offenders into avoiding crime. There was no crime more serious than high treason, the offence, as of 1585, that Catholic priests ordained abroad were deemed to have committed. For this offence the most unimaginably brutal punishment was conceived – consisting of partial strangulation by hanging, emasculation and disembowelling of a body while still alive, decapitation and quartering up of the body. These horrors were to take place – of necessity in public – in London and in key provincial centres, market towns and nuclei of law and administration, where large crowds congregated, taking the lessons of exemplary punishment into their hearts and back with them to recount in their native places.[29]

For more than a century Lancaster, chief town of the county that emerged in the Elizabethan period as England's most Catholic shire, was to watch the ghastly executions of monks in the wake of the Pilgrimage of Grace and then the death of James Layburne, in 1583, for declaring Queen Elizabeth to be deposed; James Bell, an Oxford-educated priest who had once become an Anglican and was re-converted to Catholicism, was executed in 1584; the layman John Finch, a farmer from Eccleston who was accused of harbouring priests, was also put to death in 1584; the Dominican friar Robert Nutter from Burnley and Edward Thwing (or Thweng), a priest from Heworth in Yorkshire, both died in 1600; two other Yorkshiremen were sentenced in the following year – Thurstan Hunt from Leeds and a Jesuit from York, Robert Middleton; in 1604 a Lancashire miller, Lawrence Bailey, was hanged for rescuing a priest; in 1616 John Thules or Thewles, a priest from Whalley, was executed, and in the same year Roger Wrenno, from Chorley, another layman, was hanged for succouring priests; in 1628 Edmund Arrowsmith, a Jesuit from Haydock, was hanged, drawn and quartered; in the same year the layman Richard Herst (Hurst or Hayhurst), from Broughton, was hanged on a murder charge; in 1641 the Benedictine monk Ambrose, or Edward, Barlow from Manchester suffered at Lancaster, and on the same bloody day in 1646 the priest Edward Bamber of Carleton, the Franciscan friar John Woodcock from Clayton-le-Woods and another priest, Thomas Whitaker (alias Starkie) from Burnley, were all executed.[29]

These executions were well-publicised events; the sentences were delivered with all the majestic ritual of English law and carried out near town, probably opposite what is now the Quernmore Road entrance to Williamson Park. In almost all cases, the victims were patently dying for sincerely-held religious beliefs rather than for political subversion or for 'crimes' other than their faith. Though the priests among them were trained abroad, they were not Spaniards or Frenchmen – foreigners deeply repugnant to the xenophobic early modern English; they were northerners, and for the most part Lancashire men, with Lancashire names – Haydock, Hayhurst, Bamber, Woodcock, and the rest – and Lancashire accents. Sixteen executions for Catholic faith took place over a period of sixty years, an approximate average of one major public killing every four years – though some of these judicial deaths were arranged in clusters in certain years. In any case, no Lancastrian who wished to do so in the period between the Spanish Armada and the

Civil Wars need have missed seeing the execution of at least one Catholic martyr during his or her lifetime. In addition even for those who did not actually see them, these executions, we may be sure, would have been fully discussed in the streets and alehouses, and were also well publicised for a mass audience in Catholic martyrological productions such as the ballad 'songe of four preistes that suffered death at Lancaster ...' (*c.* 1615).[30]

So is it possible for us to conjecture what might have been the attitude of local people to the steady succession of officially sanctioned slaughters carried out on the open moor above a quiet town? Were locals callous, inured, hardened to these repeated atrocities, or were they appalled at the apparently endless run of slaughters in this period? We are fortunate in having eyewitness evidence from that time of horrors which suggests that in fact the attitude of seventeenth-century Lancastrians towards state torture and judicial savagery was much like ours today. The contemporary report – an account of the deaths of the two Catholics, Arrowsmith the priest and Herst or Hayhurst the layman, executed in 1628 – may be regarded as biased insofar as it is distinctly pro-Catholic. Nevertheless, the narrative carries an unmistakable ring of authenticity and of factual reportage:

> The behaviour of the Town of LANCASTER was very remarkable on this Occasion:

(the author wrote of the death of St Edmund Arrowsmith)

> to shew their Detestation of this Murther, no Man could be prevailed upon to undertake the Execution, except a Butcher, who tho' ashamed of doing the Job himself, engaged for five pound, that his servant should dispatch him.

However the servant absconded and was replaced by an army deserter who immediately came to be 'detested by the good people of LANCASTER ...'[31]

Apparently fearing disorder, the judge planned a low-profile execution at an inconvenient time but in fact the event 'unpeopled LANCASTER'. Did people go out to see and even revel in a horror show? The evidence is that many there at the gallows were in fact Lancashire Catholics who came 'to be edified'. In addition, though, our author assesses the crowd reactions from the more uncommitted spectators who were treated to the sight of 'his Head, agreeable to the Sentence, ... set upon a Pole, among the Pinnacles of the Castle, and his Quarters hanged on four several Corners thereof'. Reactions varied – from admiration of the martyrs' heroism and 'Detestation of this bloody Act' to a rather modern-sounding amazement that anyone should go as far as Arrowsmith in defence of religious beliefs. Of public callousness, still less of relish in these barbarities, there is no trace in what comes across as a carefully observed report.[32] Lancastrians, then, may well have been evincing considerable 'detestation' at some of the melancholy and ghastly implications of their town's stature as a primary place of judgement and punishment.

Witchcraft

Lancaster's role as a legal centre introduced the town to other instalments of human tragedy apart from the trials and executions of Catholics. The sixteenth and seventeenth centuries form the age of what has been called the 'witch craze', a collective hysteria which left few parts of Europe unscathed and which slaughtered thousands, chiefly women, before it expired around the end of the seventeenth century. The craze seems to have particularly affected poor and upland regions, in which scarcity of resources fostered suspicious and hostile relations between neighbours. Additionally, the witchcraft malaise may have been prevalent in areas of uncertain religious allegiance, borderlands in the contemporary struggle between Catholicism and Protestantism. Certainly, these features – the poverty of an upland zone on or near a frontier between antipathetic variants of Christianity – could be said to have characterised the Pendle district in east Lancashire in the early seventeenth century. It was from this area that 15 women and five men were brought to trial at Lancaster in 1612. The majority of the victims were indeed poor, ignorant and old women – perhaps the kind of women who at an earlier stage of social and religious development could have relied more on the Christian charity of their neighbours. By the earlier seventeenth century, in contrast, a more critical attitude to 'indiscriminate' charity and a greater emphasis on self-reliance and self-help seem to have been denying casual relief to indigent old women. Thwarted in their pleas for alms, such women were often free with curses against their niggardly better-off neighbours. Not infrequently, the bitter imprecations of beggars denied hand-outs must have seemed to come true: any household disaster, major or minor, and the beggar woman's curse would be recalled and seen as causing the misadventure: a witch had been discovered. As a sceptical contemporary put it, reconstructing a typical scenario and chain of accusation:

> She [the alleged witch] was at my house of late, she would have a pot of milke, she departed in a chafe because she had it not, she railed, she curssed, she mumbled and whispered, and finallie she said she would be even with me: and soone after my child, my cow, my pullet died, or was strangelie taken.[33]

This mind-set, then, provides us with some understanding of the background to the Lancaster witch-trials of 1612. The county and county town were certainly no strangers to witchcraft allegations and trials: even the shire's unquestionably dominant family, the Stanley clan of the Earl of Derby, were embroiled in 1594. Then in 1597 one Edmund Hartley was hanged at Lancaster for the alleged offence of bewitching members of the family of Starkie of Cleworth. Nor did the Lancaster witch scare of 1612 burn out the craze in the county: fresh trials took place in 1630, again involving a leading family of the county, that of Ralph Assheton of Middleton, whose son Richard was allegedly bewitched by one Utley who was tried and hanged

THE
WONDERFVLL
DISCOVERIE OF
WITCHES IN THE COVN-
TIE OF LAN-
CASTER.

With the Arraignement and Triall of
Nineteene notorious WITCHES, at the Assizes and
generall Gaole deliuerie, holden at the Castle of
LANCASTER, *vpon Munday, the se-*
uenteenth of August last,
1612.

Before Sir IAMES ALTHAM, and
Sir EDWARD BROMLEY, Knights; BARONS of his
Maiesties Court of EXCHEQVER: And Iustices
of Assize, Oyer *and* Terminor, *and generall*
Gaole deliuerie in the circuit of the
North Parts.

Together with the Arraignement and Triall of IENNET
PRESTON, *at the Assizes holden at the Castle of Yorke,*
the seuen and twentieth day of Iulie last past,
with her Execution for the murther
of Master LISTER
by Witchcraft.

Published and set forth by commandement of his Maiesties
Iustices of Assize in the North Parts.

By THOMAS POTTS *Esquier.*

LONDON,
Printed by *W. Stansby* for *Iohn Barnes,* dwelling neare
Holborne Conduit. 1613.

The title-page from Potts' *Wonderfull Discoverie of Witches in the Countie of Lancaster.*

at Lancaster. Other Lancaster trials were held in 1633, when seventeen were reprieved, followed by an actual execution in 1634; enquiries were conducted by the Bishop of Chester in 1635, two executions may have been carried out in 1654 or 1655 and a final hanging, that of Isabel Rigby of Hindley, took place in 1666.[34] However, without any doubt the most sensational trials – and executions – of accused witches were those held at Lancaster in 1612.

At the beginning of the seventeenth century two desperately poor and very old women lived with their families in the Forest of Pendle: Elizabeth Southerns, alias 'Old Demdike', and Ann Whittle, alias 'Old Chattox'. They were reputed witches, and indeed competed for business, dealing in spells, love potions, charms, cures, amulets and the rest in their area. From the point of view of the authorities in church and state, both nationally and regionally, pockets of witchery like those represented by Chattox and Demdike were part of Lancashire's distinctive and ramified social problem. Prone to 'popery', Lancashire was also identified as one of the most notorious 'dark corners of the land', places where folk superstition, economic backwardness, indolence, poverty and ignorance reigned. Belief in the power of witches was indeed thought likely to abound in such areas, but magistrates like Roger Nowel of Read themselves took witchcraft very seriously, as an objective fact, seeing it as the fulcrum of an all-too-real diabolic plot to destroy the Christian community both spiritually and materially. As the best current wisdom – certainly wholeheartedly endorsed by King James I (1603–25) – had it, witches, sexually voracious old women unable to attract human lovers, had carnal knowledge of Satan himself and did his bidding to achieve the ruin of Christian society. For men like Nowel, witchcraft was neither myth nor joke: it posed the greatest imaginable threat to Christendom, and all the resources of the legal process had to be applied to counter it. Thus in April 1612, Nowel brought Demdike, Chattox and two associates, Alizon Device and Anne Redfern, up to Lancaster to stand trial. In reply to this attack, it was alleged, the sect of witches in the Pendle country convened – on Good Friday 1612 – so as to plan the destruction of Lancaster Castle and the murder of its gaoler, Covell.

In the witch craze, children were regularly called up as witnesses to testify against their elders, and in the Pendle case nine-year-old Jennet Device, Demdike's granddaughter, lodged accusations about the malign convention in Pendle. Now that proof positive of a demonic conspiracy seemed to be to hand, the net was thrown wide to trawl in 'witches' from the Pendle district: Demdike's son and daughter, James and Elizabeth Device; a lady of some rank and fortune, Alice Nutter; along with John and Jane Bulcock, Katherine Hewitt and others. The trials began and were carefully recorded in *THE WONDERFVLL DISCOVERIE OF WITCHES IN THE COVNTIE OF LANCASTER. With the Arraignement and Trial of Nineteene notorious WITCHES, at the Assizes and generall Gaole deliverie, holden at the Castle of LANCASTER.* [August 1612], a work compiled by the enterprising clerk of the court, Thomas Potts.[35]

The very full transcripts of the Lancaster trial of 1612 provide us with unique insights into the dynamics of the witch craze in seventeenth-century England. We encounter, for instance, – and in a society in which disease prevention was rudimentary and infant mortality horrific – the reflex assumption that the deaths of children were induced diabolically through witchcraft. We read sensational accounts of congress with diabolic creatures:

> ... The said three Women and this Examinate danced, every one of them with one of the blacke things aforesaid, and after their dancing the said black things did pull downe three Woman, and did abuse their bodies, ...

We become aware of the connections that were made in the dominant culture between what were widely believed to be Lancashire's linked problems of witchery and popery:

> Thus at one time may you behold Witches of all sorts from many places in this Countie of Lancaster which now may lawfully be said to abound as much in Witches of divers kindes as Seminaries [seminary-trained Catholic priests], Jesuites, and Papists.

We discover a society convinced of the material effects of words, spells and curses and of the very tangible and malign efficacy of malediction:

> ... *John Law* the Pedler, before his unfortunate meeting with this witch, was a verie able sufficient stout man of Bodie, and a goodly man of Stature. But by this Devillish art of *Witch-craft* his head is drawne awrie, his Eyes and face deformed, His speech not well to bee understood; ...

The court and the jury thought they had heard enough. Old Demdike died in prison but sentence of death by hanging was passed and carried out on eight women and two men at Lancaster in August 1612.[36] The prosecution was, of course, completely without foundation, even though some of the 'witches' may indeed have thought that that was what they were. But credulity, paranoia, bigotry and cruelty were clearly notching up further victories in the assizes at Lancaster.

Other Prisoners

Alongside the high drama of the trials of witches, priests and lay recusants, Lancaster Castle also continued to serve as a working prison. It hosted the odd distinguished inmate, such as the leading critic of the royal Court, Henry Burton, in 1637. It must have been with Burton in mind that the author of the strongly pro-Parliamentarian *A Discourse of the Warr in Lancashire* recalled the pre-Civil War use of the Castle which

> The King's part [party] ... made use of to imprison many honest men who would not comply to do what they thought ...

The Castle also contained humbler malefactors such as the Daniel West of Burnley who was in gaol in the Castle in 1630 'for sunderie great crymes, as shooting gunes, keepinge of grayhoundes, trasing or killing of hares, . . .'. A report of 1683 disclosed that the Castle in its capacity as a prison contained forty-four debtors, six felons, two priests, five inmates reprieved or to be transported, six coin clippers, eight Quakers (under writs of excommunication) and eight 'papist recusants' – seventy-nine prisoners in all. A worrying submission to the Mayor and Corporation on that occasion revealed

> that the Judges are dissatisfied to keep the Assizes at Lancaster, in respect of the ruines of the castle of Lancaster, conceiving some danger to sitt there untill the same be repaired.

Assuming that the role of sole host for the county assizes was still important to Lancaster's economy and service trades, this was a warning to cause alarm, and the JPs ordered repairs to be carried out.[37]

The Castle also continued to possess strategic importance or potential. In Tudor times, Leland had described the Castle as 'strongly builded and well repaired', though a repair survey was carried out in 1578. The Castle's military value was certainly appreciated in the crisis-laden 1580s, the decade of the Armada, and major work was undertaken in 1586. In the same year the town of Lancaster received a commission from Queen Elizabeth for a muster of the county's forces to take part there, and in October 1587 Lancaster was one of six venues for mustering the trained bands of the militia. In the long years of peace following the end of war with Spain under James I, the Castle's military significance was lost sight of, and, as we have seen, it took on the primary roles of court of law and place of sentence and detention. Then, with the outbreak of Civil War in 1642, the ancient position of Lancaster and its Castle as a key fortress came to be realised once more.[38]

The Civil War

Yet Lancaster's role in the Civil War, however eventful, was a passive rather than an active one. The town and townspeople did not themselves take any major recorded initiative in the conflict and did not win for themselves any clearly etched partisan reputation as did people in other Lancashire towns, like the puritan Parliamentarians of Bolton or the much vaunted (after 1660) Royalism of Preston and Wigan. Lancaster, its Castle once more its burden, was a victim rather than an actor in the Civil Wars. And we should make no mistake about the real brutality and sufferings of those wars, not least in Lancashire in that decade of the 1640s when, it was said, 'England turned Germany' – that is to say, the country caught more than a glimpse of the long agony suffered by central Europe in the terrible Thirty Years War (1618–48). Lancaster endured an ample measure of that wartime misery and came to know the casual brutality of the armies of both sides. The attitude

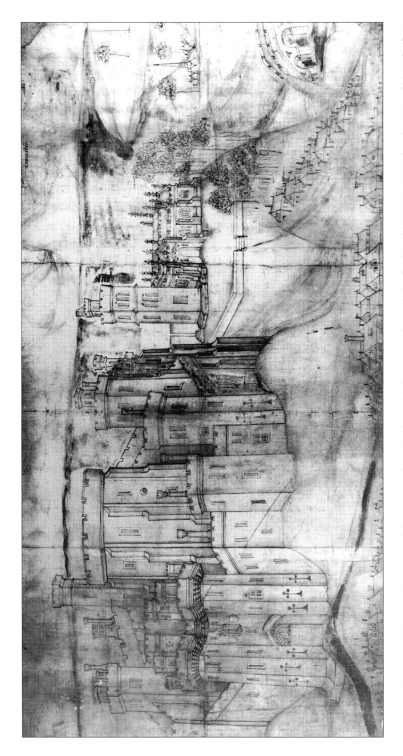

Lancaster Castle in 1562, one of a series of drawings made probably to familiarise members of the Duchy of Lancaster council with some of their far-flung responsibilities.

induced as a consequence in the minds of townspeople and their local rulers may well have amounted to a preference for peace above partisanship and an equal coolness towards both warring factions.

In 1640, what is perhaps the most decisive parliament in English history – the Long Parliament (1640–60) – met, in an atmosphere of intense bitterness, especially amongst the ruling and tax-paying classes and amongst serious-minded Protestants. In the course of the 1630s, the government of King Charles I had seemed, simultaneously, to be bent on reversing the Protestant Reformation in Britain and re-introducing Catholicism through the back door, as well as centralising government, imposing taxes without parliament-ary consent and, apparently, planning a royal despotism based on military force. Lancaster had petitioned against features of the king's government, but as far as voting patterns are concerned, the constituency expressed none of the political anger against the Court which surrounded the convening of the Long Parliament. Continuing the earlier tradition of Duchy influence, the borough's two Long Parliament MPs were Royalist.

True, the town's member Thomas Fanshaw was a discreet partisan – only nominally' a Royalist – but his colleague, the strongly Royalist Sir John Harrison of Beaumont, 'a prominent financier and custom official of London', was deeply implicated in schemes whereby the crown had hoped to bolster its finances by means of monopolistic deals with members of the business community. Harrison in fact 'voluntarily forebore' to take his seat in view of a parliamentary order barring monopolists from sitting.[39]

If the town's political position on the eve of the Civil War was quiescent or ambivalent, its military and strategic value was evident for all to see. When we consider the 'English Civil War' as it ought to be regarded – as a *British* civil war involving three kingdoms and a principality – we will see, by looking at the map of the British Isles, just how central and critical Lancaster's geographic positioning was. The port faced nearby Ireland, where a Royalist Catholic uprising had broken out in 1641. Then, with the entry of the Scots into the Civil War on the Parliament's side in 1643, Lancashire as a whole became once more part of a crucial debatable land between the two kingdoms, with its county town and main fortress a potential cynosure of military operations, commanding a vital north–south road and river crossing over the Lune. The historian of the Civil War in Lancashire rightly regards Lancaster (along with Preston, Wigan, Blackburn and Bolton) as one of the principal foci around which the 'real struggle' of the Civil War in the county would be fought out. But we could go further than that: in war, certain targets – historical places, political and religious centres – have a symbolic value beyond purely and objectively military calculations. Particularly in the opening moves of a conflict, when jockeying for territory is all-important and morale-raising victories are sought, such sites magnetise military operations. During the first nine months of the Civil War first the Parliamentarians, then the Royalists showed their determination to possess Lancaster.[40]

Yet given the high value of Lancaster in the chess game of civil war, it seems a little odd that the Castle was not well invested by the Royalists in possession in 1642: these 'did not Garrison it neither the towne of Lancaster'.[41] Thus, in the early months of 1643, Lancaster's Castle presented few obstacles to a resolute and determined, though relatively low-key, Parliamentarian bid.

In February, a sergeant-major (Birch) and a company were sent up from Preston and took the surrender from the royalist commanders Sir John Girlington and Roger Kirkby with no difficulty, leaving Captain William Shuttleworth in command. It was at this point that an extraordinary subsidiary event intervened. A well-armed Spanish vessel, bound with a squadron of troops for the Spanish war-effort in the Netherlands, was cast up near Rossal Point. Its valuable 'Ordenance' (guns) were trans-shipped

> downe [sic] Loyne [the Lune estuary] to Lancaster and there they were laid up in the Castle Guard where they were kept and preserved ...

It was, according to one interpretation, these guns that drew Lancashire's principal Royalist commander, the seventh Earl of Derby, to Lancaster. Be that as it may, surely some advantage greater than the relatively short-term calculation of acquiring the ordnance stored at the Castle must have dictated the scale of Derby's assault on Lancaster in March 1643. Early in that year, Parliament held north Lancashire in a tight grip and it was reported that

> Lancaster, Preston, the Ship Ordenance, with the whole Country round about [were] in the Parliaments power ...

But militant Royalism was still very much on the offensive in 1643, and the outcome of the national struggle still a long way off a final decision. Thus it may well be that Derby, intending to make up for the Royalist complacency that had recently allowed Parliamentarians to pick off Lancaster with so little difficulty, rightly saw the town and Castle as the key to the war in the North-West and decided to try to break Parliament's stranglehold in north Lancashire by re-taking Lancaster. Issuing a blanket conscription in the areas under his control, on 13 March Derby left Wigan with an impressive force of 600 foot and 400 cavalry, adding to his numbers as he marched through the Royalist Fylde and joined by the Royalist chieftains Sir John Girlington and the Catholic Thomas Tyldesley.[42]

It has traditionally, but inaccurately, been assumed that in the Civil War all Catholics were automatically active Royalists, a belief certainly encouraged at the time by the kind of Parliamentarian propaganda which cultivated the image of a Papist-Royalist crusade against Protestantism and liberty:

> The Earl of Derby advanced towards us [at Lancaster], the papists rising wholly with him.

Certainly Derby's force would have been consolidated numerically by a Catholic element, whether or not north Lancashire Catholics rose 'wholly' in support of him. His army was certainly large enough to deter pursuit by the capable but prudent Parliamentarian leader Colonel Ralph Assheton. On 18 March Derby called on Lancaster to capitulate, offering the alternatives of prompt surrender to be followed by 'fair usage', or refusal and forcible seizure resulting in the application of the 'law of Warre' – a seventeenth-century euphemism for unleashed military barbarism as punishment for keeping an attacking force at bay.

The Parliamentarian garrison, under their commanders Holcroft and Sparrow, was sizeable, but Derby had a stiffening of cavalry plus the recruits he had collected between Wigan and Lancaster. There was an engagement, in which the Parliamentarian Captain William Shuttleworth was killed, but the garrison's defence of the town was distinctly lack-lustre:

> Upon Fryday the … [18 March] they [Derby's force] entered the Towne of Lancaster several waies, there being very few souldiers if any, to resist them save those that kept the Castle …

It is some tribute to the state of repair and maintenance of Lancaster Castle at this time that 'the Castle they [Derby's Cavaliers] could not enter …'. The garrison was clearly determined to look to its own security and simply retreated into 'the safety of the castle', where, according to a Parliamentarian report, they evinced 'heartinesse' and enjoyed 'comfortable provision'. The town was thereby abandoned to Derby and the 'law of warre': plunder, sack, arson, and wanton destruction.[43]

In more Royalist parts of Lancashire, the memory of the seventh Earl after his execution in 1651 became that of a political martyr, second only to his royal master Charles I. That attitude to Derby can hardly have been widespread in Lancaster in or after 1643, given the perception that 'all the crueltie arises from the Earl of Derby …'. Derby had been cheated of a vital strategic prize whose control might have dictated the whole course of the war in Lancashire. Even from the admittedly loaded Parliamentarian account of the time, the impression of the Earl's blind, frustrated wrath, directed against innocent civilians, is quite unmistakable:

> Such was their cruelty that they set fyre upon the towne in several parts of it, having none to withstand them. In the hart of the Towne they burned divers of the most eminent houses. That long street from the Whit croft [Penny Street, from White Cross] all was burned Dwelling houses barnes corne hay cattel in their stalls. The Club men [term here used to indicate Cavalier irregulars] plundered unmercifully carrying great packets home with them.[44]

Apart from the vivid and clearly partisan reportage of *A Discourse*, there are other sources for the damage done to Lancaster in 1643, surely a particularly low point in the town's long history. After claiming that 3,000 Lancastrians had come out to welcome Derby, the Royalist *Mercurius Aulicus* reported, with a kind of laconic callousness, that

Hearing that help was coming to the town from Preston, the Earl set fire to Lancaster.

Other reactions, though, reveal the depths of Lancaster's misery in 1643. Colonel Assheton was reported to be 'moved … to greef' at the

pitifull rewings … with the clamour of the people for it and their plunderings by the souldiers.

In truth, there existed a kind of unspoken conspiracy of the military in wartime in early modern Europe, as if it were understood by combatants that whereas to attack each other overmuch was unprofitable and could be dangerous, to agree to target civilians was both safe and rewarding. Lancaster in 1643 provides us with a particularly clear instance of this kind of professional solidarity of soldiers ostensibly from opposite sides: while the Royalist marauders ran amok in the town, the Parliamentarian defence force remained safely holed up in the Castle, its 'heartinesse' and 'comfortable provision' undented by the sufferings going on in the street below the grey walls.[45] Parliament's resolutions echo the reality of the damage done to Lancaster, not least to its housing stock, with an estimated loss of ninety premises. Perhaps feeling some guilt at the abject failure of the Parliamentarian garrison to protect the town, on 7 January 1645 Parliament made a grant of £8,000 compensation 'for the Burning of the Said Towne. The Amount to be equally divided amongst the Inhabitants'. Though this award provides us with official confirmation of the scale of the damage done by Derby's men, there were strings attached to it and serious delays and difficulties in its collection. It was targetted only at 'Inhabitants themselves being noe delinquents [active Cavaliers]', and it had to be collected by the fire victims themselves, who were supposed to raise the proceeds out of 'the papists & delinquents Estates within the County of Lancaster as were att the burning …'. The sum was not to exceed £2,000 in 1647, when the compensation seems to have been re-awarded.[46]

As if Derby's atrocities were not enough, the Castle subsequently became a base for an exceptionally predatory band of Parliamentarian troopers. Even the Parliamentarian *Discourse of the Warr* admitted that these men presented a particularly serious problem: the Castle, the *Discourse* recalled, was garrisoned by

a rude company of Yorkshire Troopers … the cruellest persons that ever this Country was pestered with. They were an unmeasured torment to the Hundreds of Lansdaile and Amonderness …[47]

England as a whole suffered acutely from the Civil Wars, and what has been identified as an 'anti-army ideology' was bred or confirmed in the 1640s and '50s, when the country was first harassed and then ruled by soldiers. It seems likely that many Lancastrians, living below an army fort and having experienced the worst of treatment from both sides in the civil conflict, would have developed an advanced form of that anti-military ideology.

Lancaster's experiences in the 1640s, especially Derby's raid and the occupation by the Yorkshire Roundheads, confirmed the belief in some quarters that the Castle was a source of instability and, indeed, of potential misery in the town and its neighbourhood. Strongly influenced, according to the author of the *Discourse of the Warr*, by the experience of the Yorkshire garrison, leading Parliamentarians in the county decided on major demolitions at the Castle, in effect de-militarising it and taking it back to its recent and pre-Civil War primary usage as a prison:

> ... eminent men in the County [the *Discourse* reported] ... taking notice of the inconvenience and losses it would be dayly put unto, if the Castle should continue long to be guarded by such rude men [as the Yorkshire troops], therefore thought that if it could be obtained of the Parliament that the Castle might be so farr demolished as that it would not be tenable for a Garrison to shelter in, though it might retaine the Prisoners for the County, proposed to the Parliament the same, who gave way that all the Walls about it should be thrown downe, only the Gate House, the buildings upon the West and South sides, with the Towers, retained; ... the workmen were set on who threw downe all the Walls of the Quadrangle, and so the Guard was gone, being taken off.

Essentially, the reductions formed part of a Parliamentarian plan for pacifying the country through the 'slighting' of ancient fortresses and meant the destruction of all Castle fabric beyond that needed to house the law courts and the county gaol. The damage must have been extensive, since in 1664 when plans were afoot to restore the Castle's military capacity, the bill for repairs, including re-roofing, was just short of £2,000.[48]

As we have seen, Parliament in the 1640s had at least shown a willingness to compensate Lancastrians for war damage. In addition, Parliament's demolition orders were clearly designed in part to rid Lancaster and its region of the Castle as a source of disorder and violence. Clearly, then, insofar as the Parliament that emerged victorious out of the Civil Wars had any policy towards Lancaster, it was one of some benevolence. This belief is also borne out by the continuation on the part of Parliament of an earlier royal policy of upholding Lancaster's claim to retain the law courts, as ordered in the 1649 *Act for the Sessions of Assizes to be held and kept in the Castle of Lancaster* .... Arguably, such a measure, renewed by the Long Parliament towards the very end of its long life, in 1659, showed Parliament offering a boost to a war-damaged urban economy, while at the same time Parliament favoured the county town at the expense of Preston, with its Royalist image.[49]

Parliament's tight hold over Lancaster during the Civil War period undoubtedly increased the influence locally of the strongly etched English Protestantism that we know as puritanism. Partly because of acute polarisations between Catholicism and advanced Protestantism, squeezing out centrist or 'Anglican' options, much of Lancashire had shown a distinctly puritan streak in its Protestantism since the reign of Elizabeth. But until the Civil War this puritan orientation was generally contained within the established Church, as at Lancaster where a puritan tradition was nourished at the parish church by a succession of relatively radical-minded vicars. Throughout the county following the outbreak of civil war, Puritanism emerged fully and freely, in an organised institutional 'Presbyterian' form which was highly developed in Lancashire during the 1640s. Lancaster was designated one of the county's nine centres of Presbyterian '*classes*', and the overwhelming Presbyterian commitment of the area's ministers is expressed in their assent from thirteen parishes in Lancaster's immediate area to the Presbyterian talisman, the Solemn League and Covenant, in 1647. A leading custodian of the puritan tradition at Lancaster itself was William Marshall (1621–83), a Yorkshireman and author of *Answers upon several heads in Philosophy* (1670). He was vicar from 1650 until deposed following the re-introduction of the Church of England at the Restoration in 1660. As we shall see, the Presbyterianism that had become institutionalised in Lancaster and its area during the Parliamentarian ascendancy went underground after 1660, to resurface again from the late 1680s.[50]

Quakers

Meanwhile a form of Puritanism far more radical than Marshall's Calvinism was to hit Lancaster in 1652. The Puritanism that was such a marked feature of Protestant Christianity in seventeenth-century Lancashire insisted strongly on the doctrine of the sixteenth-century reformer John Calvin (1509–64) that only a fixed proportion of sinful humanity was singled out in advance by God for salvation, the rest being marked for certain damnation. The Quaker founder George Fox (1624–91) brought a different interpretation: a hopeful view of 'that of God' in every man and every woman, a lessened emphasis on human sin and guilt and a depreciation of the Calvinist dogma of 'election' or 'predestination'. In early the 1650s, Fox, a Leicestershire man who had himself undergone and overcome a protracted spiritual agony, was evangelising the Midlands and Yorkshire and then, in 1652, entered Lancashire from the direction of Pendle Hill. From there he moved towards Kendal and into Furness and only later came to Lancaster. George Fox had a strong sense of Christian social justice and equity, and used the occasions of fairs and markets to point out the need for fairness and honesty in pricing and dealing. This he did on his arrival in 1652 – a dramatic, hectoring, powerful personality at Lancaster's ancient weekly market:

> On market day I went to Lancaster and I spoke in the market at the
> cross in the dreadful power of God and declared the day of the Lord

to them and against their deceitful merchandise, and preached righteous-
ness and Truth ...

He evoked a positive response amongst some townspeople and indeed was
himself responsible for the founding of Lancaster's Quaker community:

> Several people came to my lodging and many were convinced [converted]
> and stand to this day. And a meeting there was settled in the power
> of God.[51]

The Sunday following the market day, Fox held an open meeting address-
ing local people and soldiers from the garrison: his pacifism had already
become well established and may have found an echo in a war-weary town,
as well as amongst disillusioned troopers. Then in the afternoon following
his Sunday morning open-air service, Fox invaded the Priory church with
his challenging message, directly confronting the highly articulate spokesman
for the 'orthodox' Calvinist mainstream, William Marshall. To read now in
cold print about Fox's abrupt entry into the Priory church in 1652 leaves
little impression on us, unless we can imagine some of the indignation of a
worshipping congregation roused by the rude and noisy interruption of their
service:

> And in the afternoon I went up to the steeplehouse [parish church] at
> Lancaster, and when I had declared the Truth to both Priest and people
> and showed them the deceits they lived in and the power and spirit of
> God that they wanted, they haled me out and stoned me along the
> streets till I came to John Lawson's house.[52]

Fox's disruptive behaviour in the Priory church had fairly predictable
results: he had lambasted the Calvinist doctrines and worship upheld at the
time in the parish church, and an incensed congregation chased him off.
However, the hue and cry had a positive outcome: it brought Fox to the
home, near the site of the medieval leper hospital in St Leonardgate, of
John Lawson. He was a convert who was soon to emerge as the first of a
succession of Quaker entrepreneurs who were to help re-make Lancaster's
commercial fortunes in the seventeenth and eighteenth centuries.

By the autumn of 1652 Fox's sense of kinship with the divine had provided
a basis for the compilation of a set of exaggerated charges of blasphemy
against him, allegations which he was to answer at the Quarter Sessions at
Lancaster. The event was one of the most dramatic trials ever to take place
even at Lancaster Castle which in previous decades had witnessed powerful
forensic tragedies, including the trials of the Lancaster 'witches' and of
Edmund Arrowsmith and other martyrs. But on this occasion Fox was not
to be ranged with the victims of repression. According to his own account,
he had lined up against him forty clerics led by William Marshall of the
Priory. On the other hand he had a sympathiser in justice Thomas Fell, an
influential Puritan politician and a man in part attuned to Fox's brand of

spirituality. With the support of Fell and of other sympathetic lay magistrates, and above all aided by his own supreme self-assurance, Fox turned the October 1652 Lancaster sessions into a forum for proclaiming his beliefs, a personal triumph and an opportunity for further conversions, including that of Thomas Rippon, Lancaster's mayor in 1653 and 1654: '... the Quakers had got the day', it was reported in Lancaster's taverns and streets, 'and the priests were fallen'.[53]

When Fox won his court-room victory at Lancaster in 1652, the political climate was relatively benign towards his kind of charismatic piety. George Fox's next judicial appearance at Lancaster took place in much altered circumstances, those of the crackdown against religious radicals after the Restoration of the Stuart monarchy in 1660. In June of that year Fox was imprisoned at Lancaster in particularly harsh conditions as a 'disturber of the peace of the nation', and, although he was set free in October of the same year, he was brought before the Lancaster sessions again in 1664 for refusing the oaths of allegiance and supremacy and again imprisoned. This was one of a string of incarcerations Fox underwent during the reign of Charles II (1660–85).[54]

By this time, the Lancaster Quaker community, despite persecution, had expanded considerably since its establishment by Fox in 1652. Fox's convert John Lawson established Lancaster's sugar refinery, a significant contribution to the town's exploitation of its Atlantic trading potential, and was, briefly and illegally, a member of the town council. By the mid-1670s Fox was reflecting on the gratifying growth of the local Quaker community with its 'very full, large and peaceable men's and women's meetings'. The Friends built their first meeting house in 1677, replacing it in 1708, and in the early 1690s they established their school. One of the most distinctive features of Lancaster's richly varied religious life, a relatively large and influential Quaker community, had been firmly established before the end of the seventeenth century.[55]

Restoration of the Monarchy

The Restoration of the monarchy in 1660 presented both challenges and opportunities to Lancaster institutionally and politically. Some individuals in local government, such as mayor Henry Porter, Fox's persecutor, were heavily compromised by their strong attachment to the Parliamentarian and Cromwellian regimes of the Civil War and post-Civil War periods, and the Earl of Derby, son and successor of the architect of the 1643 atrocities, sought a wholesale ejection from the corporation of 'all who had ever been against the King, or given no testimony of loyalty before the Restoration ...'. On the other hand the Restoration presented opportunities for the borough to readjust itself to central government and to clarify and even improve upon its institutional status. There were certainly no insuperable obstacles to

Lancaster's successfully adapting itself to the restored royal government in and after 1660. Charles II had himself been proclaimed king at Lancaster in 1651, and in 1660 the corporation, loyally returning to the crown the 'poor mite' of its annual fee farm rent of £13 6s. 8d., waived under the Commonwealth in 1650, made a series of impeccably royalist honorary appointments to the burgess body, including the Earl of Derby. These measures can be seen as preparing the way for an application for a renewal of Lancaster's charter, so as to put the town's relations with the crown once more on a clear and, for the town, advantageous, foundation.[56]

We saw earlier that the Tudors had favoured Lancaster with a series of charters and confirmations of liberties, and in 1604 James I issued a ratification of old charters and a grant of significant new privileges. This grant represented a full incorporation of the borough, with a mayor (to act as a JP and coroner) assisted by two bailiffs and twenty-four capital burgesses, the incorporated whole to have the use of a common seal. Following the James I charter, the period 1604–63 saw the emergence of an aldermanic system with six 'benchers in seniority' from whom the mayor was chosen. In June 1663 the mayor and burgesses successfully applied for royal ratification of the town's now mature corporate structure endorsed by the James I grant. In this first charter of Charles II, Lancaster was recognised as an ancient borough and county town and was awarded three JPs of its own, the mayor, his predecessor and the recorder. Despite some signs of disorder, and of discontent and disillusionment with regard to the restored monarchy, the town of Lancaster was now institutionally equipped to respond to the opportunities of a national economy ready to expand after years of political instability and disorder.[57]

Trade

The key to Lancaster's take-off was the Atlantic and the whole long-range and massive shift taking place in the seventeenth and eighteenth centuries away from the traditional European and Mediterranean focus of the British economy in favour of an orientation towards the New World. From the mid-seventeenth century onwards, Lancaster, along with a necklace of fellow west-coast ports from Glasgow to Bristol and beyond, were suddenly poised, by their very location, to take advantage of the glittering opportunities of trade around the Atlantic rim.

All the evidence before the mid-seventeenth century indicates that Lancaster's economy remained dominated by the immediate locality, marketing and agriculture: Camden had observed that 'all the inhabitants ... are given to husbandry', and it will be recalled that the tally of losses in the Penny Street fire of 1643 included mostly agricultural premises, produce and livestock: '... barnes corne hay cattell in their stalls'. An important feature of this agricultural orientation of the town's economy was concentration on livestock marketing, linking England, and ultimately London, with Scottish livestock production. It was not an unprofitable trade: in 1638, for instance, a trader sold 100 'weathers' – 'well coloured mutton' – at £7 a score in Lancaster, having paid £4 10*s.* a score for them in Dumfries. It may be significant that the main road through Lancaster traced in 1603 looks rather like a drovers' road finishing up in the capital, a voracious consumer of meat: the route went: Cockermouth – 'Kyswyck' – 'Grocenner' [Grasmere] – Kendal – Burton – Lancaster – Preston – Wigan – Warrington – Newcastle [Under Lyme] – 'Lychfield' – Coventry – London. Horse trading was even more important than the cattle business, Lancaster having emerged as a nationally known mart. *One* explanation for the horse-shoe laid in the pavement at Horse Shoe Corner is that the placing of a shoe there was a traditional way of announcing a forthcoming horse fair. At a transitional

William Stout, Quaker merchant and autobiographer, a shrewd and uncompromising observer of his times.

phase in the development of the town's economy, on the eve of the take-off of Atlantic commerce, the local trader Henry Coward, the Quaker William Stout's first boss, a horse dealer, is himself a reminder of the town's established role as a place for the marketing of horseflesh.[58]

Signs of the alteration in the orientation, capacity and reach of Lancaster's economy begin to be apparent after the Restoration, with the 1680s arguably the vital decade in the economic lift-off. Some of the signs of change are elusive, anecdotal, rather than firmly statistical, and concern particular individuals: a woman is indentured for service in Virginia, John Lawson opens his sugar house, a tobacconist puts in an appearance in town records. As far as tobacco is concerned, the one individual who epitomised the first phase of change in the borough economy was John Hodgson, four times mayor, and bankrupt, the 'greatest and most repuitable merchant' in Lancaster, importer of colonial exotica, tobacco and fine Canary wines, expansive, a social climber and an over-reacher. But Hodgson fell from a high ledge in a town economy with more storeys to it than that of the pre-Restoration agricultural market borough. All of a sudden, Lancaster was becoming linked not so much with 'Kyswyck' and 'Grocenner' (though its Westmorland sister, Kendal, was also now on the brink of an Atlantic-led trade boom) but with Virginia and the Caribbean. In 1654 Parliament had authorised a weekly parcel post between Lancaster and Carlisle, but by 1683 Lancaster was ready to take its place, alongside the rising stars of the Lancashire economy, in an ambitious banking consortium designed to under-pin commerce: '... an office ... is intended to be shortly established in Liverpool, Lancaster and Manchester, called the Corporation Credit, or a Bank of Credit, the use of which will certainly be of great advantage to the advancement of trade'.[59]

It was some time before the shift in the Lancaster economy would show through in the town's physical appearance or the way it presented itself to visitors. At around the time of the Revolution of 1688–89, Captain Thomas Bellingham was still treating Lancaster as a picturesque tourist spot to be visited and viewed. The usually acute Celia Fiennes, as late as 1698, was still writing in the spirit of Leland and Camden:

> Lancaster town is old and much decayed ... The town seems not to be much in trade as some others, but the great store of fish makes them live plentifully ...

– though Fiennes did admit 'there are trades of all sorts'. Perhaps what Celia Fiennes had in mind, though, when she wrote of 'trades' was the highly organised structure of six trade guilds which, as late as 1688, the assize judges allowed to be set up: medieval and pre-capitalist in character, this was a protective framework for small-scale artisans, including shoemakers, tailors, carpenters and weavers, producing for a local market, rather than a slipway from which globally-minded venture entrepreneurs would sail into the buffeting Atlantic winds of challenge and opportunity. Essentially medieval institutional structures of chartered privilege and protection in fact formed

Every effort was taken to make tradesmen's tokens resemble coins, including adorning them with emblematic devices such as the large bird or bird-like creatures on William Prockter's 1671 halfpenny token.

John Lawson was a local retailer known to William Stout, who crowed rather when in about 1690 Lawson, or his business, or both, 'broke in a crazed [confused] condition so that he never recovered his creddit or right capacety'. His crudely die-struck undated farthing almost resembles a medieval coin with the ancient symbol of the 'Lamb and Flag' or *Agnus Dei*.

In a period when the English silver coinage was over-valued and an adequate base-metal coinage did not exist, leading English urban merchants adopted the custom of issuing tokens for the lowest value coins so as to lubricate local trade. The small farthing (¼ of a penny) token of Lancaster's controversial Presbyterian mayor of 1688, John Greenwood, has a lion motif on its obverse.

The Stallenge Rolls of Lancaster represent a snapshot of the old local, protected retail economy on the eve of the town's take-off into a global and Atlantic commercial market. 'Stallengers' paid an annual payment for the privilege of keeping a stall in the weekly market. Their names in 1685 include some familiar from the pages of William Stout's *Autobiography* (Henry Coward, John Hodgson), as well as surnames still familiar in Lancaster and its area today (Kellett, Dixon, Hodgson, Patchett, etc.). Three women feature as stallholders. (Corporation Minute Book B, 1676–1702.)

the shelter from which Lancastrian merchants took their first steps into the uncharted waters of financial and commercial capitalism. In 1682, the year before the ambitious, modern-minded and progressive-sounding scheme for a banking link-up with Manchester and Liverpool, two major local credit transactions were registered by the corporation under the provisions of the ancient 'Statute Merchant' of Acton Burnell as applied to Lancaster through its 1432 charter of Henry VI. And between 1656 and 1665 and between 1676 and 1693 respectively the Lancaster merchants William Yates and John Hodgson claimed special commercial privileges under a charter of Henry VI on the basis of the particular commercial benefits that Lancaster derived on the model of the Northampton charter of 1199 (copied 1391). At the same time, the corporation itself continued to impose a traditional regulative system, including strict checks on new buildings.[60]

A major determinant of economic growth, in Lancaster and in England at large after 1660, was political stability and social peace. Civil wars seldom really end with the making of a formal peace: their passions and recriminations may poison a nation's atmosphere for generations after their cessation. Post-Restoration England remained an edgy, frightened and bitter land, the baseless fantasies of anti-popery continuing to infect the air. A particularly jumpy phase, during decades when the country's attainment of prosperity was still being impeded by political clamour and insecurity, was the Popish Plot hysteria of 1678, followed by a protracted campaign, which threatened a renewal of civil war, to bar from the throne the heir presumptive, the Catholic James Duke of York. As itself a constituency and also the voting centre for county elections, Lancaster experienced at first hand the country's over-dose of politics and the de-stabilising effects of the Popish Plot and Exclusion Crisis, with an estimated 30,000 in town for a general election in 1679 and consequent fatalities. There were fresh executions of priests and Catholic laymen (though not at Lancaster) following the Popish Plot, and in January 1679 a large trawl of recusants was indicted at Lancaster assizes, with a strong suspicion that this needless witch-hunting was clogging the proper business of the courts. In May 1680 the Lonsdale justices had their time taken up with the prosecution of recusants. In a country still far too taken up for its own good with the politics of fear, the steady pursuit by towns like Lancaster of their own commercial business and prosperity was inevitably distracted by these political, electoral and judicial turbulences, as was Lancaster's civilian progress still threatened by its military functions: in 1685, during the renewed disturbances occasioned by the Monmouth uprising in the West Country, army movements were ordered to Lancaster and a local innkeeper who refused to declare the Duke of Monmouth a traitor was imprisoned.[61]

Politics

England after 1660 was still continuing to suffer from a surfeit of excessively confrontationary politics, of political violence, actual or threatened, and of unreconciled religious division, all the bitter legacy of civil war. Was there a way out? The letters and speeches of King Charles II suggest that he had a kind of vision of national development in which people might attain peace and growth, through handing over responsibility for government to their betters, each thereupon attending only to his own business and thereby to the common good. This was the hierarchical and authoritarian solution to the country's problems, and it was given a try in England after the mania of the Popish Plot died down in 1681. Lancaster was to know the effects of this experiment in stability through firm government.

Within Lancaster's municipal government, after 1681 Whig supporters of the exclusion of the Duke of York from the succession were systematically purged from the corporation, and a ruling Tory group, linked to the customs service and with a stake in the town's commercial growth, jockeyed itself into power. Lancaster's first Charles II charter was surrendered to the King's representative, the high Tory Lord Chief Justice Jeffreys, and a new charter was granted in 1684. This confirmed the Tory group in power, ratified existing privileges, awarded the borough mines in Quernmore and introduced new mechanisms for crown control of appointments to the corporation. With its new charter, one-party rule and a good working relationship with central government, the town of Lancaster might have been considered by some to be in a position to enjoy the political tranquillity necessary for economic growth.[62]

The problem with this authoritarian scenario is that not only did it alienate many of the town's freemen from the town government and narrow the political base of local administration, but it also carried a heavy price in religious repression. The period known as the Tory Reaction following 1681 involved a heavy crackdown on Protestant Dissenters, partly because in Tory ideology Nonconformity carried the stigma of responsibility for the Civil War, and partly because, more recently, they had overwhelmingly given their support to the Whigs.

In Lancaster in 1684 the High Churchman James Fenton succeeded as vicar and repression reigned supreme in the town, with 'seveir execution of the laws against conventicles' [Dissenting meetings for worship], as the Quaker William Stout observed. The Quakers themselves, an industrious and peaceable community within the community, had their meeting house locked up (meeting instead in Meeting House Lane), and numbers of Friends were, once again, imprisoned in the Castle. A leading citizen, John Greenwood, who held a 'Presbyterian conventicle in his house', with his son faced a massive fine of £20 in 1683. And this whole wave of repression in the Tory Reaction was particularly unfortunate in a town like Lancaster which had a significant Dissenter presence, Presbyterian and Quaker, made up of

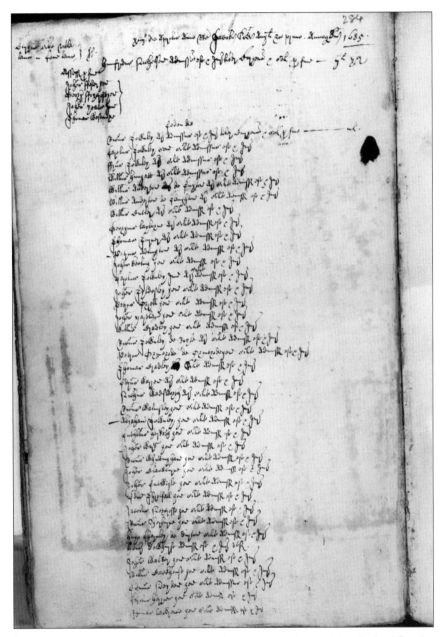

In 1685 in a blatant act of vote-rigging to head off a general election victory by Lord Brandon Gerrard, a Whig popular with Lancaster's indigenous freemen, a huge raft of spurious freemen was sworn in, dependants and servants of the county's Tory gentry obtaining the borough freedom at twopence a head; 'two peny free men' (Stout). Each of the 192 entrants is recorded as '*Admissus est* + *Jurat*' (was admitted and sworn). (Corporation Minute Book B, 1676–1702, f.284)

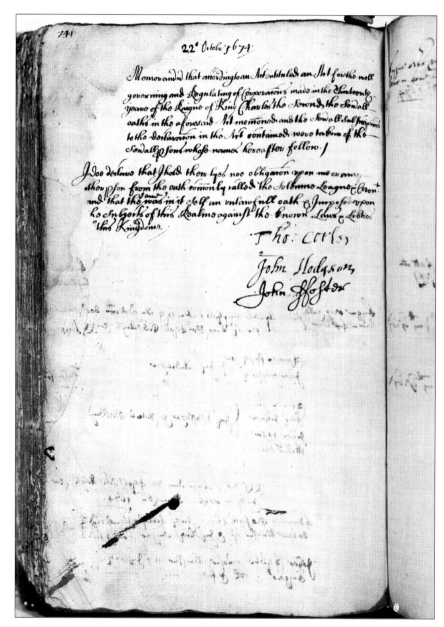

In common with all other English and Welsh municipal corporations, Lancaster and its corporation members were obliged to comply with the anti-Nonconformist 1661 Corporation Act. Here three members, Thomas Corles, John Hodgson and John Foster, declare, as required by the Act, against the 1643 Solemn League and Covenant of the Presbyterians – 'an unlawful oath imposed upon the subjects of this Realme against the known Laws and Liberties of this Kingdome'. (Corporation Minute Book A, 1664–76, f.741)

hardworking people who, left untroubled, were likely to make a substantial contribution to the town's growth.[63]

However, within two years of his accession in 1685, the former Duke of York, now king as James II, set about demolishing the apparatus of Tory–Anglican repression that had been built up since 1681. As a Catholic who was committed to find a place for his co-religionists in national life, James seems also to have been a convinced believer in religious toleration for all peacable Christians. Lancaster and its government, with its population in and near the town of Dissenters and Catholics, was spectacularly affected by the reversal in government policy under James: in 1687 Mass was celebrated in the Free School and attended by a senior Catholic judge; complimentary visits were paid by the likes of the Bishop of Chester to the legendary 'Catholic virgins', the Dalton ladies of Aldcliffe who had nurtured their faith through darker days; and at Aldcliffe itself and at Thurnham in 1688 large numbers of Catholic confirmations took place. The Presbyterians also shared in the sudden and extraordinary emancipation of 1687–8. John Greenwood, hounded and vilified at the height of the Tory Reaction, now in 1688 headed a corporation (on to which Catholics had been drafted) and as mayor attended 'the Presbiterian place of worship' with the full panoply of civic office.[64]

The king was going too far, too fast, too unconstitutionally. The idea of a tolerant, plural society was only slowly taking root and many Anglicans, particularly among the ruling class of nobility and gentry, were alarmed at the apparent undermining of the special position of the Church of England in the national life. In Lancaster in 1688 the political atmosphere heated up once more. The mayor and an alderman were involved in a riotous altercation; there were rumours that Irish cavalry had landed at Piel Island and were moving on Lancaster; half of Colonel Rigby's regiment was ordered to the town, and to add to the general mayhem, the prisoners in the castle rioted and locked out their gaolers. In December King James fled and in 1689 a peaceful revolution put the Protestant William and Mary, James's son-in-law and daughter, on the throne. One more attempt was to be made to bring peace to this troubled isle – a 'Revolution Settlement'.[65]

Toleration

A key ingredient in this settlement, bringing a belated peace to England's strife-torn religious life, was an Act of Toleration giving freedom of worship to Protestant Nonconformists. Lancaster, with its diverse denominational patchwork, was an immediate beneficiary. 'A house in Lancaster' appeared at the top of a list of Quaker places of worship in the county, and Presbyterian worship was registered in 'An upper chamber over a Warehouse in Moor Lane'. The Catholics were excluded from the terms of the Toleration Act, but they too felt some of the benefits of the somewhat more tolerant attitudes that had helped engender the Act. By the time of the Revolution, Lancaster had not seen the execution of a Catholic for his Catholicism for over forty years, and it seems indicative of the improving atmosphere that the eight recusants supposedly incarcerated in the Castle in 1683 were actually lodged, casually enough, in the town. In the early eighteenth century the Catholic squire Thomas Tyldesley, grandson of the Cavalier assailant of the Castle, although denied the political rights and duties normal with his class, had no difficulty in getting to Mass at the Dalton properties at Bulk, Aldcliffe and Thurnham.[66]

Lancaster at the end of the seventeenth century was a much less tense and divided community than it had been, probably since the end of the Middle Ages. Actual religious persecution was effectively at an end, and the pall of recurrent and barbarous judicial murder for religious belief was at last lifted from the town's shoulders. Although there would continue to be emergencies and invasions, the Castle was no longer an inevitable target for insurgents and warring factions. Lancaster was poised on the edge of an age – the Georgian eighteenth century – when the English could be described, with some exaggeration, as 'a polite and commercial people', a more stable, peaceful, secular and in many ways more civilised society, bent on enrichment.

Benefactions

The town had not lost its tradition, going back to John Gardyner and beyond, of charitable provisions. The school had been a particular beneficiary of this tradition throughout the seventeenth century. In 1615 Randall Carter of Southwark left an annuity of £10 to provide for a school 'usher' (an assistant teacher). The school seems to have prospered through the disturbed middle decades of the seventeenth century and drew on a wide catchment area, including Tunstall and Sedbergh. In the 1680s, with the town's prosperity starting to climb, the town council, which from the beginning was intended to take a major share in overseeing the school's fortunes, provided for building repairs and extensions 'for the credit of the Towne'. By this time boys were going up to Cambridge in significant numbers. True to the traditions of John Gardyner, in 1700 a local merchant, Giles Heysham, left £100 'to augment the Usher's salary'. Also within that tradition of civic benefaction, in 1668 Sir John Harrison assigned revenues from his Beaumont fishing reach to build a new town hall, an early anticipation of the architectural transformation of Lancaster in the eighteenth century.

Notes

1. For the Castle, see John Champness, *Lancaster Castle: A Brief History*, Lancaster County Books, 1993; for the Church, M. McClintock, *Lancaster Priory: the Church of Blessed Mary of Lancaster*, Pitkin, 1980.

2. W. Farrer and J. Brownbill (eds), *The Victoria History of the County of Lancaster* 8 vols, Constable, 1906–19 (hereafter *VCH Lancs*), vol. 8, Pt. 1, 11–3; S. H. Penney, *Notes on the Topography of Medieval Lancaster*, Lancaster Museum Monographs, 1979, 1–10; S. H. Penney, *Lancaster: The Evolution of its Townscape to 1800*, University of Lancaster, Centre for North-West Regional Studies, Occasional Paper no. 9, 1981, 14–21.

3. 'Cross Fleury', *Time-Honoured Lancaster*, Eaton & Bulfield, 1891, 38; M. Bennett, *Lambert Simnel and the Battle of Stoke*, Alan Sutton, 1987, 33, 72–3. It is possible that the rebels tried to obtain supplies from Lancaster.

4. For the background of popular piety, see C. Harper-Bill, *The Pre-Reformation Church in England 1400–1530*, Longman Seminar Studies in History, 1989, esp. ch. 7; C. Haigh, *Reformation and Resistance in Tudor Lancashire*, Cambridge University Press, 1975, ch. 5.

5. *VCH Lancs*, vol. 2, 165.

6. R. N. Billington and J. Brownbill, *St Peter's Lancaster a History*, Sands & Co., 1910, 9–11; Penney, *Lancaster Townscape*, 19–20.

7. *Historical Manuscripts Commission. The Manuscripts of Lord Kenyon*, HMSO, 1894 (hereafter *HMC Kenyon*), 8.

8. E. R. Johnston, 'The Lancashire Lands of Syon Abbey', *Transactions of the Historic Society of Lancashire and Cheshire* (hereafter *THSLC*), CVII, 1956, 43–4.

9. Johnston, 'Lancashire Lands of Syon', 45.

10. Johnston, 'Lancashire Lands of Syon', 45–7; Billington and Brownbill, *St Peter's, Lancaster*, 197–9.

11. E. R. Johnston, 'Richard Burton, Vicar of Lancaster, 1466–84', *THSLC*, CIV, 1952, 163–7; Johnston, 'Lancashire Lands of Syon', 47–8.

12. Johnston, 'Richard Burton', 47; R. Dunning, 'The Muniments of Syon Abbey; their Administration and Migration in the Fifteenth and Sixteenth Centuries', *Bulletin of the Institute of Historical Research*, XXXVII, 1964, 110.

13. Johnston, 'Lancashire Lands of Syon', 50.

14. *VCH Lancs*, vol. 2, 166, 171–2, 561–4; Johnston, 'Lancashire Lands of Syon', 48. Original documents relating to John Gardyner's bequest are in Lancaster Central Library, Mss. 6541–6544. For the school's history see A. L. Murray, *The Royal Grammar School Lancaster: A History*, Heffer, 1952.

15. See below, 87.

16. *VCH Lancs*, vol. 2, 217; J. Brownbill and J. Nuttall, *A Calendar of Charters and Records Belonging to the Corporation of Lancaster*, Lancaster Corporation, 1929, 16–17; T. Pape, *The Charters of the City of Lancaster*, Lancaster City Council, 1952, 42.

17. Brownbill and Nuttall, *A Calendar of Charters*, 10.

18. M. Dalton, *The Country Justice . . .* (1635), cited in P. M. Turner and S. Horrocks (eds), *Lancashire History; Historical Period Stuart. A Contribution towards a Lancashire Bibliography*, vol. 8, Joint Committee on the Lancashire Bibliography, 1976, 18; *VCH Lancs*, vol. 8, Pt. 1, 11; A. Hewitson (ed.), *Social Life and National Movements in the 17th Century Diary of Thomas Bellingham An Officer under William III*, Geo. Toulmin, 1908, 10.

19. Pape, *The Charters*, 45–7; Brownbill and Nuttall, *A Calendar of Charters*, 10; Penney, *Lancaster Townscape*, 22.

20. S. T. Bindoff, *The History of Parliament; The House of Commons 1509–1558; Appendices, Constituencies, Members A–C*, Secker & Warburg for the History of

Parliament Trust, 1982, 120; Pape, *The Charters*, 42–3, 75–7: another charter, of Edward VI, to tenants of the Duchy, granted them freedom from tolls throughout the kingdom; see Pape, *The Charters*, 45–6; *VCH Lancs*, vol. 2, 293.

21. Leland, quoted in *VCH Lancs* vol. 8, Pt. 1, 13; Bindoff, *House of Commons*, 120; Pape, *The Charters*, 43–4; *VCH Lancs*, vol. 2, 292, 447: the area of Quernmore continued to be a valued asset to Lancaster into the seventeenth century – in 1675 the corporation reported that the 'slate delfe [quarry] at Claughaw' was within the borough limits; see Brownbill and Nuttall, *A Calendar*, 25.

22. *VCH Lancs*, vol. 8, Pt. 1, 12; Bindoff, *House of Commons*, 120.

23. P. W. Hasler, *The History of Parliament; The House of Commons 1558–1603; Introductory Survey, Appendices, Constituencies, Members A–C*, HMSO, for the History of Parliament Trust, 1989, 188 (and for list of members); Bindoff, *House of Commons*, 121 (and for list of members).

24. For the background of some popular reactions to Protestantisation, see J. J. Scarisbrick, *The Reformation and the English People*, Basil Blackwell, 1984; for Lancashire's opposition to Reformation and for Lancaster and the Pilgrimage of Grace, see Haigh, *Reformation and Resistance*, especially 131 and 134; *VCH Lancs*, vol. 2, 124.

25. Haigh, *Reformation and Resistance*, 131–2.

26. Haigh, *Reformation and Resistance*, 134–5; *VCH Lancs* vol. vol. 2, 43–4; G. Baskerville, *English Monks and the Suppression of the Monasteries*, Jonathan Cape, 1937; paperback edn, 1965, 166–7. J. B. McGovern, in a learned paper delivered to the Lancashire and Cheshire Antiquarian Society (*Transactions*, XL, 1922–23, 213–14), reviewed the evidence as to whether Abbot Paslew was executed at Whalley or Lancaster and came down in favour of Whalley.

27. T. Wright (ed.), *Three Chapters of Letters Relating to the Suppression of the Monasteries*, Camden Soc., 1st Ser., 28, 1843, 191–3; *VCH Lancs*, vol. 2, 161, 49–50; Haigh, *Reformation and Resistance*, 114.

28. Haigh, *Reformation and Resistance*, 166, 169, 173, 176, 183–5; G. Townsend (ed.), *The Acts and Monuments of John Foxe:* ... 7 vols, Seeley, Burnside & Seeley, 1846, VII, 46–7.

29. *VCH Lancs*, vol. 8, Pt. 1, 14; E O. Blundell, *Old Catholic Lancashire*, 2 vols, Burns, Oates & Washbourne, 1925, I, 27, 33; Billington and Brownbill, *St Peter's Lancaster* 34: Squire Blundell was imprisoned for illegally aiding a priest ordained abroad. For the background of post-Reformation Catholicism, see M. A. Mullett, *Catholics in Britain and Ireland, 1558–1829*, Macmillan, 1998; for the Catholic community in Lancashire, see J. A. Hilton, *Catholic Lancashire From Reformation to Renewal 1559–1991*, Phillimore, 1994, and Norman Gardiner (ed.), *Lancashire Quarter Sessions Records: Registers of Recusants, 1678, 1679*, 2 vols, North West Catholic Record Society, 1998; for Lancaster Catholics, see Sharon Lambert, *Monks, Martyrs and Mayors: The History of Lancaster's Roman Catholic Community and Cathedral 1094–1991*, Lancaster Cathedral Bookshop, 1991.

30. For the ballad, see M. Mullett and L. Warren, *Martyrs of the Diocese of Lancaster Beatified November 22nd 1987*, Diocese of Lancaster, 1987, 52–3.

31. R. Herst, *A True and Exact Relation of the Death of Two Catholics who Suffered for their Religion at the Summer Assizes, held at Lancaster in the Year 1628* (reprinted 1737), 18–26.

32. Herst, *True Relation*, 18–26. The Lancaster Martyrs are now commemorated

in a memorial erected on the field opposite the gate of Williamson Park, Quernmore Road, Lancaster.

33. J. Crossley (ed.) and intro., *Potts's Discovery of Witches in the County of Lancaster* Chetham Soc., VI, 1845 intro., xv. For the Lancashire witches, see Jonathan Lumby, *The Lancashire Witch Craze: Jennet Preston and the Lancashire Witches, 1612*, Carnegie Publishing, 1995, and Rachel A. C. Hasted, *The Pendle Witch-Trial, 1612*, Lancashire County Council Library and Leisure Committee, 1987.

34. *Potts's Discovery*, notes, 51; *VCH Lancs*, vol. 8, Pt. 1, 16.

35. *Potts's Discovery*, intro., xlix, liii.

36. *Potts's Discovery*, L3, M3, L2, T2, S.

37. *VCH Lancs*, vol. 8, Pt. 1, 16; Anon. (F. Beaumont, ed.,) *A Discourse of the Warr in Lancashire; A Trew and impartial Relation of some of that unhappie Intestine Warr ... such as Happened ... within the countie Palaintine of Lancaster*, Chetham Soc., vol. LXII, 1864, 20.

38. *VCH Lancs*, vol. 8, Pt. 1, 1, 6, 8, 13, 266–7. For the background to the Civil War, see, for example, R. Ashton, The *English Civil War, Conservatism and Revolution 1603–1649*, Weidenfield & Nicolson, 1978.

39. Lancaster Central Library, Ms. 3472; F. Broxap, *The Great Civil War in Lancashire 1642–1651*, Manchester University Press, 1910, 30–1; D. Brunton and D. H. Pennington, *Members of the Long Parliament*, George Allen & Unwin, 1954, 56–7.

40. Broxap, *Great Civil War*, 67.

41. *A Discourse of the Warr*, 20.

42. Broxap, *Great Civil War*, 71–4; *A Discourse of the Warr*, 25–7.

43. 'Cross Fleury', *Time Honoured Lancaster*, 144; Broxap, *Great Civil War*, 71–5.

44. *A Discourse of the Warr*, 28.

45. *Mercurius Aulicus*, quoted in T. Bulmer & Co., *History, Topography and Directory of Lancaster and District*, Bulmer & Co, 1913, 19; *A Discourse of the Warr*, 30.

46. Lancaster Central Library, MS. 5935: *Orders of the Houses of Parliament ...*, *1645, 1647*.

47. Broxap, *Great Civil War*, 75, 87.

48. *A Discourse of the Warr*, 63; *VCH Lancs*, vol. 8, Pt. 1, 6–8.

49. Turner and Horrocks (eds), *The Lancashire Bibliography*, 8, 104.

50. *VCH Lancs*, vol. 2, 64; Lancaster Central Library, PT160: *The Harmonious Consent of the Ministers of the Province within the County Palatine of Lancaster with ... the Ministers of London, ... and to our solemn league and covenant* (1648); for Marshall, see A. Gordon (ed.), *Freedom after Ejection; A Review (1690–1692) of Presbyterian and Congregational Nonconformity in England and Wales*, Publications of the Manchester Historical Series, No. XXX, Longmans Green for Manchester University Press, 1917, 299.

51. J. L. Nickall (ed.), *The Journal of George Fox*, Cambridge University Press, 1952, 119–20.

52. *Journal of George Fox*, 120.

53. *Journal of George Fox*, 133–7.

54. *Journal of George Fox*, 378–9, 391, 461, 463, 469.

55. N. Morgan, 'The Social and Political Relations of the Lancaster Quaker Community', in M. Mullett (ed.), *Early Lancaster Friends*, University of Lancaster, Centre for North-West Regional Studies, 1978, 22; R. Dove and Helen Sedgebarth, *A History of the Friends Meeting House Lancaster*, Lancaster Univer-

sity, 1991: see also David M. Butler, *The Quaker Meeting Houses of Britain*, Friends Historical Society, 1999; R. Randles, '"Faithful Friends and Well Qualified": The Early Years of the Friends School Lancaster', in Mullett (ed.), *Early Lancaster Friends*, 33–42; N. J. Morgan, *Lancashire Quakers and the Establishment, 1660–1730*, Ryburn Academic Publishing, 1993.

56. For Porter, see *Journal of George Fox*, 375 ff.; M. A. Mullett, 'Conflict, Politics and Elections in Lancaster, 1660–1688', *Northern History*, XIX, 1983, 64–7; Brownbill and Nuttall, *A Calendar of the Charters*, 12, 18–19.

57. Hasler, *The House of Commons 1558–1603*, 120; Bindoff, *The House of Commons 1509–1558*, 120–1; Brownbill and Nuttall, *A Calendar of Charters*, 11; M. Beloff, *Public Order and Popular Disturbances 1660–1714*, Frank Cass, 1963, 36.

58. Camden, quoted in *VCH Lancs*, vol. 8, Pt. 1, 14; *HMC Kenyon*, 57; G. Scott Thomson, 'Roads in England and Wales in 1603', *English Historical Review*, XXXIII, 1918, 234–43; Pape, *The Charters*, 25.

59. Brownbill and Nuttall, *A Calendar of Charters*, 33; Mullett, 'Conflict, Politics and Elections', 72; *HMC Kenyon*, 160.

60. Diary of Thomas Bellingham, 10; M. M. Schofield, *Outlines of an Economic History of Lancaster from 1680 to 1860. Part 1, Lancaster from 1680–1800*, Lancaster Branch, Historical Association, 1946, 7–12, 35–6; K. Docton, 'Lancaster 1684', *THSLC*, CIX, 1958, 125–7; Celia Fiennes, quoted in *VCH Lancs*, vol. 8, Pt. 1, 18; Pape, *The Charters*, 27–31, 33–5; Brownbill and Nuttall, *A Calendar of Charters*, 24.

61. Mullett, 'Conflict, Politics and Elections', 68; *HMC Kenyon*, 109–10, 119–21; Lancaster Central Library, MS. 6576–6572; E. Kennerley, 'Men of Lancaster', Lancaster Central Library, MS. 8782.

62. Mullett, 'Conflict, Politics and Elections', 70–6.

63. Mullett, 'Conflict, Politics and Elections', 62–3, 72.

64. Mullett, 'Conflict, Politics and Elections', 78–9.

65. Mullett, 'Conflict, Politics and Elections', 83–4; *HMC, Kenyon*, 202.

66. *HMC Kenyon*, 230, 159–60; J. Gillow and A. Hewitson (eds), *The Tyldesley Diary. Personal Records of Thomas Tyldesley ... During the Years 1712–13–14*, A. Hewitson, 1873, 1, 15, 38, 42, 44, 69.

CHAPTER FOUR

Trade and Transition, 1690–1815

Nigel Dalziel

In the eighteenth century Lancaster was transformed. In 1690 the town was an inherent part of the rural fabric and essentially unchanged in form and function from the medieval period. By 1815 it was a fully urbanised society, having experienced a period of rapid economic development and population growth. In common with many other towns, Lancaster had emerged from a highly independent and parochial development to an existence profoundly influenced by the outside world at the start of the industrial age.

To the casual observer the most notable feature of the period to 1800 was the development of a thriving international commerce within a wider economic prosperity – the period usually termed Lancaster's 'Golden Age'. The economic metamorphosis resulted from the expansion of the home economy and the empire which the Navigation Acts and protectionist legislation ensured was serviced predominantly by British shipping. Lancaster, like Liverpool, Bristol, Glasgow and Whitehaven, was favourably situated on the West coast to take advantage of the reorientation of trade towards America and the West Indies, involving the import of largely primary tropical products and the export of the new manufactured goods in demand in colonial markets. The prosperity derived from her role as a centre of exchange and as entrepot for the Morecambe Bay region was fundamental to the social and political changes which took place.

Trade and Manufacture

Lancaster's role as a market town continued to be important and the fortunes of agriculture underlay her prosperity. When Celia Fiennes visited in 1698 she was impressed by 'the great plenty of all provisions', including fish from the River Lune.[1] The fertile coastal plain and Lune Valley produced plentiful quantities of oats, cattle, barley and rye. Agricultural productivity probably improved throughout the period but, consistent with national

trends, particularly from the middle of the eighteenth century. In 1759 the
Bristol merchant, John Crofts, on his journey from Garstang to Lancaster,
took a particularly jaundiced view of local agriculture, referring to

> the badness of the soil, and the husbandry through all this side of
> Lancashire; a great number of what they call mosses, producing nothing
> but peat and turf for firing.[2]

Subsequently, however, mosses at nearby Heysham, Cockerham and Carnforth were drained to provide additional rich agricultural land.

Other travellers had different views. An anonymous visitor journeying
from Scotland to Nottinghamshire in c.1764, described the area between
Burton and Lancaster as 'a fine cultivated and fruitful country', and, to the
south, 'a large tract of cornfield and meadows ... the country beautifully
cultivated with fruit and corn; on our left hand Ellen Crag and Wiersdale
mountains, adorned with abundance of wheat and barley'.[3] The parliamentary
enclosure movement led to the reclamation and colonisation of vast areas
of upland moor and rough grassland beginning at Ellel, to the south, in
1757 and including nearly all the Lonsdale common fields by 1800.[4] Even
Lancaster's grazing land on the Marsh was enclosed, embanked and drained
in 1796. Agricultural improvements on the Duke of Hamilton's estate,
concentrated on Ashton Hall to the south of Lancaster, were pursued on a
wider scale by the Lancaster Agricultural Society, founded in 1799 with the
Duke as patron. As befitted the importance of agriculture to Lancaster, its
annual meetings were held in the Town Hall and patronised by the Mayor
and Corporation.[5]

Agricultural improvement contributed to and supported the large growth
in population which occurred in the countryside between 1740 and 1780,
helping to treble the population of the county to 672,700 between 1690 and
1801.[6] As the market centre, Lancaster benefited from this increased production and demand. At the same time it acted as a conduit for the new
improving ideas and, through the operation of the market, exerted an
economic influence which encouraged agricultural development further. The
traditional markets in the town became busier, leading to an acute shortage
of space. In 1774 the Corporation moved the meat market from Cheapside
to the newly-built Shambles leading off Market Square, where livestock could
also be slaughtered and sold undercover. In 1802 the potato market on
Church Street was moved to the Assembly Room Square on Back Lane
(King Street) together with the butter and egg markets, relocated to the
Cock Pit, which had been forced out of the Town Hall due to the growth
of the grain market.

The workings of the market also became more sophisticated over the
period. Even in 1698 Celia Fiennes noted that Lancaster did not seem 'to
be a lazy town and there are trades of all sorts.'[7] From the late seventeenth
century an increasing number of permanent shops were established clustered
in or near Market Square selling manufactured and increasingly specialised

goods. Wholesale trading and the rise of the middleman developed further, along with systems of credit and new trading networks. With improved transport, merchants travelled further and despatched goods over longer distances to market. As trade became more streamlined, the three annual fairs for cattle, cheese and cloth became less significant, although they remained important throughout the period. The career of the Lancaster Quaker diarist, ironmonger and merchant, William Stout, illustrates these trends. He started his retail, and later wholesale, business in a shop near the market in 1688, travelled with other Lancaster traders to obtain stock in London, Bristol, Sheffield and elsewhere, and made good use of trade contacts among his co-religionists to amass assets of £1,100 (plus £220 owed) during his first nine years in business.[8]

Increased wealth in the town provided money for investing in maritime trade and goods for shipment along the coast and abroad. Lancaster's situation on the Lune gave her a vital transportation advantage. The diversion of surplus wealth into shipping, maritime commerce and associated merchandising of goods in bulk greatly multiplied this prosperity. Daniel Defoe's remarks on the absence of seaborne trade and shipping at Lancaster in the 1720s are not entirely consistent with the picture provided by Stout and other evidence, although there is no doubt that both were still limited in scale. It is entirely possible that his opinion was based on information that was out of date.[9] In contrast, the Reverend Thomas Coxe was able to describe Lancaster in 1720 as 'at present very prosperous, and a thriving Corporation, and a convenient port'. By 1747 the early promise had begun to be realised: James Ray of Whitehaven testified to 'a populous, thriving Corporation, trading to the West Indies with Hardware and woollen Manufactures, and in return imports sugars, Rum, cotton etc', a trade apparently inaugurated with the voyage of the 50-ton *Lambe* to Jamaica in 1687.[10]

We know that a large number of small local tradesmen and shopkeepers in the town, like Stout, were prominent investors in maritime trade, attracted by the prospect of high rewards. Similar trends were evident in other ports by the early eighteenth century. Two local merchants in particular, John Hodgson and Robert Lawson, showed the way. Hodgson, a grocer and apothecary, formed a partnership with his brother-in-law, a merchant at York and Hull, and they were responsible for the first shipment of tobacco from Virginia to Lancaster in the 1670s. On a subsequent voyage, because of the scarcity of tobacco in 1689 at the start of the War of the League of Augsburg, he made a profit of £1,500. Unfortunately, his extravagance and business reverses, remarked on by Stout, led to bankruptcy and he died in the debtors' prison in Lancaster Castle.[11] Robert Lawson, similarly involved in the plantation trade and in importing wine and brandy from Bordeaux, prospered over a long period (although his nephew, also Robert, failed in trade in 1728 owing £14,000). The potential for wealth was apparent.[12]

The more cautious Stout was tempted into overseas trade in the more settled conditions between the war of 1689–97 and the War of the Spanish

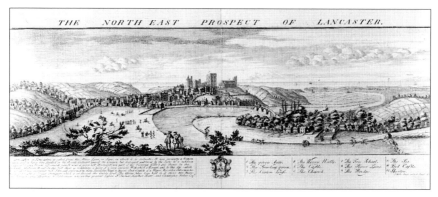

Engraved view of Lancaster from the north east by S. & N. Buck, 1728, before the large-scale rebuilding and development of the eighteenth century. Ships engaged in foreign trade lie in the river beyond Skerton (right). The earliest known quay – Lawson's – was possibly the square walled enclosure on Green Ayre (left), although it is described in the legend as a bowling green at this date.

Succession, 1702–13, investing in the voyages of the *Imployment* and others to Virginia, the West Indian islands and, finally, Riga in 1730.[13] He found coastal trade more profitable and less risky. Many others were drawn into successful foreign trade, however, such as Robert Gillow, founder in 1729 of the famous Lancaster cabinetmaking firm. From the 1730s he was heavily involved in selling a wide range of goods in the West Indies, North America, the Iberian Peninsula, Holland, Russia and the Baltic states in return for local products.[14] As the century progressed, a large number of merchant groups became established whose profits and continued investment came increasingly from success in overseas trade. The most important was the Dilworth-Rawlinson grouping, already very active in the 1730s, and by the end of the century the Rawlinsons were Lancaster's most prominent merchants.[15]

The extent of the town's investment in maritime commerce is reflected in the figures for shipping tonnage belonging to the port of Lancaster, which grew from 1,000 tons in 1709, to 2,300 tons in 1751 and 10,700 tons in 1792.[16] Ships engaged in foreign trade from the 1670s were few in number. The Customs referred to four vessels in 1692 and all the evidence suggests a very minor involvement, plantation trade being supplemented by isolated voyages to Archangel and the Baltic from the 1690s. More regular voyages occurred from the 1730s involving a handful of vessels in search of wood, tar, flax, hemp and Swedish iron, in strong demand in the shipbuilding and repair industries which accompanied the growth of the plantation trade. A small number of ships also voyaged to southern Europe. Altogether, a total of ten vessels were stated to have arrived in Lancaster from foreign ports in 1722.[17]

From that date the growth of foreign trade quickened. West Indies trade grew solidly to the extent that the average of four to six vessels per annum arriving at Lancaster in the 1720s increased to thirty ships entered in the Port Commission registers in 1750. The Bristol merchant, John Crofts, was very impressed with maritime activity at Lancaster in 1759, stating that

> more than 40 ships are employed in their trade to the West Indies Africa, Portugal, Dublin etc.[18]

Arthur Young was equally impressed in 1771:

> Lancaster is a flourishing town, well situated for trade, of which it carries on a pretty brisk one; possessing about one hundred sail of ships, some of them a good burthen, for the African and American trades.[19]

Normally, the West Indies trade employed over half the number of Lancaster ships engaged in foreign trade, returning great quantities of rum, sugar, molasses, ginger, mahogany, dyewoods and other commodities to Lancaster quaysides. The numbers involved in the West Indies trade normally remained over 30 and peaked at 57 ships in 1799–1800.[20] The comparative number at Liverpool was between three and four times that figure during the 1790s but it made Lancaster the fourth most significant West Indies port at the end of the century, with about eight per cent of all shipping trading to the Caribbean islands.[21] The total number of ships paying tonnage dues at Lancaster from all foreign ports rose from thirty-six in 1759 (3,588 tons) to seventy-eight (15,539 tons) in 1800. The total number from all ports (including home ports) grew during the same period from 122 in 1760 to 364 in 1799.[22] Lancaster's shipping interests were therefore considerable, over 400 individual vessels being identified in colonial trade from Lancaster alone during the period 1744–86. In 1799 one observer estimated the outward West Indies cargoes – 11,669 tons in 90,000 packages – to be worth £2½ million.[23]

Many traders were tempted to break into the established merchant elite by way of the potentially lucrative slave trade, inaugurated at Lancaster by the *Prince Frederick* in 1736. Success in the triangular trade – a commercial system whose viability has been re-emphasised by Kay – brought both wealth and useful commercial contacts across the Atlantic. One committed early investor in the trade was the grocer, apothecary and rope-maker, William Butterfield, who was also engaged in Baltic trade. Thomas Hinde and Miles Barber were also heavily involved. All of them were sometime mayors of Lancaster. The most active period was between 1750 and 1775 when as much as twenty per cent of the Atlantic fleet arriving at Lancaster was involved in slaving, primarily from the Gambia and the Windward coast of West Africa. In 1760 the 100-ton Lancaster ship *Cato* alone carried 560 slaves to Barbados. Over the whole period at least 180 slaving voyages were made to America and the West Indies, making Lancaster the country's fourth most significant slaving port, although some way behind Liverpool, London and Bristol. The Lancaster economy and merchant wealth were heavily dependent on the plantation economy – including directly-owned plantations

Portrait of Dodshon Foster (1730-93), one of the most prominent of Lancaster's slave merchants and ship owners in the third quarter of the eighteenth century. He prospered in general West Indies and American trade and was associated by marriage with the successful Birket and Rawlinson group of established merchants.

belonging to the Rawlinsons, Hargreaves and others. Records and local graves testify to many dozens of blacks who arrived in Lancaster as servants to returning ships' captains, factors and plantation owners. Lancaster joined Liverpool at the turn of the century in strongly opposing Parliamentary moves against the slave trade.[24]

The long-established trade along the North West coast and around the Irish Sea also benefited from the general increase in prosperity, the dispersal of the increasing volume of overseas imports and concentration of goods for export. There was a particularly vigorous trade with Ireland in the early 1700s involving linen, wool, tallow and soap in return for colonial goods, manufactures and coal.[25] An accurate impression of early coastal trade is difficult to obtain, but by 1760 there is no understating the amount of shipping involved. In that year 118 vessels (totalling 4,016 tons) paid tonnage duties at Lancaster, which rose to a peak of 273 (13,322 tons) in 1800.[26] Most of this trade was carried on with ports in the Irish Sea, primarily the coast between Whitehaven and Liverpool. A growing proportion of the coastal shipping came from Liverpool during the period, as the port began to extend its economic power and influence along the North West coast. It forwarded a great variety of goods to Lancaster, including tropical produce (tobacco declined as a direct Lancaster import), while cotton and other goods were despatched in return. Henry Escricke of Bolton and the Touchets of Manchester made sizeable purchases of cotton at Lancaster in the early eighteenth century and it remained important to the town.[27] The areas bordering Morecambe Bay were rich in cargoes for Lancaster shipping, and assisted in the growth of local maritime trade. The Furness and South Lakes area to the north produced large quantities of iron ore, slate, woodland products and foodstuffs which developed strongly through the eighteenth century.[28]

Lancaster also benefited from the associated industrial development encouraged by foreign trade which provided additional goods for export. Other branches of retailing and production were able to benefit from the new economic activity, providing services for shipping and the increasingly large and wealthy merchant community. Maritime trade became the dynamic sector in the local economy, stimulating the general growth of Lancaster and its hinterland, although its dependence on foreign trade made the town extremely vulnerable to rapid economic change at the end of the century.

Late seventeenth-century Lancaster possessed the usual trades of any market town – saddlers, shoemakers, butchers and tailors – but no significant larger-scale manufacturing activity. The first noticeable change occurred in the area of shipbuilding and repair. In 1713 Thomas Tyldesley of Myerscough Hall referred to the building of a sixty-ton ship by a 'mariner', Richard Brekell, and some carpenters. In 1720 Stout noted ships being built at Sunderland Point downstream; and, in 1743, near the Old Bridge in Lancaster, he talked to 'some carpenters of my acquaintance [who] were fitting out a ship intended for the Jamaica trade' moments before being run down and seriously injured by a galloping horse.[29] Although 'fitting out' may suggest preparative rather than construction work, the Colonial Naval Officers List for Barbados records Sunderland Point and Lancaster-built ships trading to the island between 1715–30.[30] There were certainly a number of 'ship carpenters' operating in Lancaster in the early eighteenth century, such as Thomas Wakefield, who occasionally ventured into shipbuilding. Recently, new evidence in the form of a shipbuilder's daybook of 1722–7 attributed to Edward Barrow (1682–1727), with its references to the building and repair of 13 ships plus smaller vessels at Lancaster and Sunderland Point, has allowed us to identify shipbuilding as a significant Lancaster industry much earlier than originally supposed. George Brockbank, however, a qualified sailmaker and ship carpenter from 1738–39, was responsible for establishing the first recognisable shipyard on Green Ayre.[31] He moved to a house there around 1730, possibly to take advantage of a waterfront site for repair, and here he began building around mid-century. The first known Brockbank-built ship was the eighty-ton brigantine *Olive Branch* of 1763. Another was building shortly afterwards, witnessed by a traveller in *c.*1764, who

> entered the town by a bridge of four arches over the Lune; near which are the harbor and key [sic], where we saw about fourteen sail of merchantmen from 60 to 200 tons burthen. A new ship was building to carry 300.[32]

New research has identified, with varying degrees of certainty, 134 ships built at Brockbank's on Green Ayre and below the Old Bridge near the Pot House downstream. This site was brought into use during the firm's busiest period. In July 1792, David Cragg, a Quaker farmer from Over Wyresdale, was visiting Lancaster and

> went down to the Pothouse to see a ship launched, 'The Clarendon of London' ... but not being properly launched, it set off, got into the water ... and ran aground, broke the tiller, and as it set off, the mate, who *threw a bottle of rum* in its face, ... broke his thumb; the ship could not be got off before next spring tides.[33]

Most were built for the West Indies trade and grew considerably in size over the period, from around 100 tons to 551 tons in the case of the *Minerva*, built in 1804 for the Jamaica-Clyde trade of W. Ritchie & Co., Greenock. It made launching ships even more difficult and ultimately contributed to the decline of the industry at Lancaster.

Brockbank's benefited, however, from the American War of Independence, supplying ships to replace those captured and destroyed. After 1782, production peaked as a result of the Navigation Acts which eliminated American competition. This is reflected in the figures for the decades:

1760s	1770s	1780s	1790s	1800s	1810s
4	11	45	36	28	10

(Canal boats excluded.) [34]

Production continued strongly, slowing with economic crisis in the mid-1790s but continuing again until a steady decline set in from 1801. The demand was such that by 1791 another shipbuilder, James Smith (made a Freeman 1784–5), established another yard on the north bank of the river just below the Old Bridge, probably where Stout had come to grief. In 1802 the yard passed to Worthington & Ashburner. In all, twenty-five ships are known to have been built between 1791 and 1816. Although ownership of many vessels is unknown, considerably over half of Brockbanks' ships were supplied to Lancaster merchants. The Suarts and their partners bought at least eight between 1785–1800; Messrs Edward Salisbury & Co. at least seven between 1779–1800; and the Burrows, who came to concentrate their affairs in Liverpool, another eight from 1793–1809. The Rawlinsons, Worswicks, Masons and other purchasers act as a roll-call of Lancaster's merchant elite.[35] From the available information, approximately thirty ships were sold to Greenock, Glasgow, Whitehaven and Liverpool, where the firm had its strongest market. At least three were sold to the Lancaster (later Liverpool) firm of Thomas Hinde & Sons for the Jamaica trade, including the thirty-gun *Jane* (1801).

Both yards built and converted merchantmen as privateers – vessels licensed by Admiralty Letters of Marque to attack and capture enemy merchant ships – in the American and French wars. It was an enthusiasm remarked on by *Williamson's Liverpool Advertiser* in 1781 which noted seven ships being armed and fitted out at Lancaster.[36] The town's first involvement in privateering came in the Seven Years War (1756–63) in which thirteen vessels took up Letters of Marque. This increased to thirty during the American War of Independence (1775–83), sixty-two between 1793–1801 and thirty-three between 1803–15.[37] Although the majority of ships used their licences purely for opportunist attacks on enemy shipping and for defensive purposes, others were engaged in marauding campaigns against enemy vessels. The *Kidnapper* of Lancaster moved to the Channel approaches and was successful, according to the *Newcastle Courant*, in landing 'three more prizes' at Falmouth in 1781, although she was herself kidnapped and taken into Brest by two French cutters in 1782.[38]

At the start of the American war a former slaving captain, Thomas Weeton, was engaged by the Rawlinsons as master of a privateer. According to his daughter he had 'been most successful in taking prizes and ... realized a fortune of 10 or 11 thousand pounds'. His wish to retire, however,

> was overruled by his employers ... For some months glowing accounts came of my father's valour and success; so much so that songs were composed by some Lancaster poets in his honour, and sung in the streets, accompanied by bands of music; and stopping opposite my father's house at the top of Church Street, gave repeated cheers.

News eventually arrived of his death at the hands of an American ship apparently commanded by a former school friend. Her mother took his death very badly,

> for she not only lost a kind husband, but was defrauded out of the whole of his prize money and other property gained by his voyages by the Rawlinsons, who never would deliver any account, or shew the books.[39]

It is hardly surprising that the scale of financial reward both tempted and corrupted many.

There is no doubt that the extra work and employment had important economic advantages in the port, but whether the overall balance of loss and benefit was favourable to the town remains to be decided. Losses of ships, men and cargoes appear to have seriously disrupted trade. After a successful duel with the French privateer *Bonaparte* off Barbados in 1804, for example, Captain Charnley of the Lancaster ship *Thetis* reported two killed and nine wounded, and the ship 'much shattered in our Hull, Sails and Rigging'.[40] Many others were captured and condemned or ransomed. In a public meeting at the Town Hall in 1795, merchants petitioned against impressment at sea of men for the Royal Navy because of the disruption and danger it caused.[41] Nevertheless, ships such as the French *Paragon*, captured en route from New Orleans to Marseilles and brought into Lancaster in 1803, were less common than the losses suffered. In 1783 *Williamson's Liverpool Advertiser* remarked that at Lancaster in the course of the late war a greater number of vessels were taken by the enemy or lost than at present belong to it, and a much greater number (in proportion) than were lost by any other Port in the Kingdom.[42]

Even so, the recovery through the rest of the century was remarkable in both shipping and trade. Individual commercial loss was perhaps counter-balanced by a wider commercial gain.[43]

By 1792 shipbuilding, together with cabinetmaking, was recognised by Oldfield as Lancaster's most important industry. The shipyards employed a large number of people directly and indirectly, including anchorsmiths and blockmakers who were established in Lancaster by at least the 1720s. They joined rope and sail makers whose products were sent along the coast and abroad.[44] Cabinetmaking developed into a major industry encouraged by the import of cheap tropical hardwoods, particularly mahogany which was used in the manufacture of fashionable and fashion-setting furniture by Robert and Richard Gillow, established in workshops in the narrow streets on Castle Hill. Thomas Pennant wrote in 1772:

> the inhabitants are also fortunate in having some very ingenious cabinet-makers settled here, who fabricate most excellent and neat goods at remarkably cheap rates, which they export to London and the planta-tions. Mr Gillow's warehouse of these manufactures merits a visit.[45]

Gillows were not the only producers. The previous year Arthur Young noted that:

> the only manufactory in the town is that of cabinet ware: here are many cabinet-makers, who work up the mahogany brought home in their own ships, and re-export it to the West Indies, &c &c.[46]

In 1794 there were at least eleven cabinetmaking workshops in the town.[47] Other industries which developed included candle and soap-making, based on tallow imports from the Baltic; tobacco and snuff manufacture; dye-making, using tropical woods; and sugar refining, all based on direct and indirect imports from, and trade with, the West Indies.[48]

Visitors to Lancaster in the late eighteenth century often failed to identify a characteristic manufacture although they often remarked on the flourishing state of maritime commerce. Crofts, in 1759, for example, omitted cabinet-making but mentioned maritime-related industries and

> a particular manufactory of silk carried on by a Mr Noble; in which he employs sometimes 200 hands, in working up the waste, that comes from dressing and twisting mills, into women's laces, ordinary stockings and sewing silk.[49]

The absence of a distinctive manufacture is due partly to the scope of trades present in Lancaster and the surrounding country areas. Technological improvements in textile production from the 1770s, combined with available water power in the Lune Valley and Bowland Fells, led to the establishment of a number of new spinning and later weaving mills. In 1801 sixteen mills were working cotton, silk, wool and linen in the area, particularly at Caton, Halton, Galgate, Bentham and Dolphinholme. Low Mill at Caton, established in 1784, and Willow Mill around 1790, grew to be sizeable cotton spinning establishments.[50]

All of these industries helped Lancaster's trade, including commerce with Scandinavia and the Baltic. Flax imports through Lancaster boosted the domestic spinning industry and linen production at Yealand Conyers, Priest Hutton, Galgate and Leck.[51] From 1785, Hornbys of Kirkham (in the Fylde) imported flax and hemp at Lancaster for their mill at Bentham and for sale in the town. Their spun yarn was also sent down to Kirkham.[52] Iron production also developed as part of the important Morecambe Bay region in which Lancaster Quaker merchants, particularly the Rawlinsons, had a significant involvement. Around 1752 the Halton Iron Company established a furnace by the Lune upstream at Halton to supply a forge at Caton on the Artle Beck (1727–96) and, subsequently, two others at Halton.[53] In 1755 it took over the Leighton charcoal furnace from the Backbarrow Company, which itself sent pig iron by sloop from Backbarrow near Newby Bridge, to the north of Morecambe Bay, for refining at Caton. It also stored and sold iron in Lancaster. The Halton Iron Company itself had a warehouse on the Quay by 1807, probably associated with the shipment of their firegrates, ranges, and tools.[54] This development is matched by other industries in the district: mills for papermaking were established at Oakenclough (1775) and Beetham (before 1788); and snuff at Ashton-with-Stodday, downstream from Lancaster.

Thus Lancaster was at the centre of a strong regional web of agricultural development, commerce and industry during the eighteenth century. Maritime trade encouraged and benefited from its development and the port grew to service its needs. If the general cause of Lancaster's growth can be considered to be the workings of wider, impersonal, immutable economic forces, it was the ability and actions of individuals which determined her success. Lancaster's merchants and mariners were undoubtedly dynamic and enterprising but as the century advanced this was increasingly based more on joint creativity and developed institutional structures than on virtuosic brilliance. It was reflected in joint endeavour in business and port organisation and to a certain extent in civic affairs. Nevertheless, the business elite operated very much on the basis of personal relationship and acquaintance heavily based on family groupings and ties of marriage. There developed a sophisticated business community of impressive self-reliance. It was confident, expansive and increasingly influenced by the outside world.

Wealth, Representation and Religion

The Hodgson and Lawson family groups dominated the early foreign trade of Lancaster. They were successful partly because of their family connections and the wider contacts they were able to establish. Foreign trade was extremely risky. It could be affected by severe market fluctuations, wartime disruption, loss of ships, shortages of crew, bad debts, and difficulties obtaining cargo in the plantations. The honesty and ability of captains and supercargoes responsible for buying and selling cargoes in the colonies was often a gamble. All of these risks occurred in the context of normal commercial competition. Spreading the risk was essential and reduced the initial capital outlay. But personal contacts in commerce at home and abroad were also important in providing a bond of trust to facilitate the finance and organisation of trade; to establish credit arrangements and speed the flow of goods.

The Quakers successfully developed their religious and commercial network through marriage. From 1716 the Lawson family became connected with Isaac Moss, a Manchester hosier, an arrangement which led to contacts with another Manchester textile firm, Thomas Touchet & Sons. Moss jointly owned a number of Lancaster ships, starting with the Lancaster-built *Sunderland* in 1717, involving the Robert Lawsons (junior and senior) plus the Touchets, Thomas Hutton Rawlinson (with Furness iron connections), Miles Townson and John Dilworth who 'inherited the importance and perhaps even the trading connections of the Lawsons of Lancaster and Sunderland Point'.[55] The grouping was stable over a long period and later expanded to include younger members of the various families, sometimes employed as factors and agents in foreign ports, and ensuring its domination of Lancaster trade in the eighteenth century.[56] By 1765 Thomas Hutton Rawlinson established the Rawlinson & Chorley partnership in Liverpool, which had extensive West Indies connections.[57]

This powerful, sophisticated, wealthy group of merchants and mariners sought to articulate their interests in a variety of ways. The Corporation of Lancaster was the obvious channel for their views. In 1721 they successfully petitioned the Corporation for a buoy on the Shoulder of Lune (at the mouth of the estuary), half the cost and all the replacement cost to be met by subscription. It attracted seventy-two names – some from Manchester and Ireland – between 1721 and 1729. Other petitions followed, including a number to the Customs Commissioners concerning unfair tobacco duties (1722) and requesting new legal quays (1731 and, successfully, in 1738) to keep pace with growing trade. From 1734 they agreed to voluntary duties on goods entering the port, the funds supervised by three 'Buoy Masters' elected annually by the merchants and shipowners who were anxious to improve the trade of the port. This organisation possibly acted as an embryo chamber of commerce, paying for two petitions to government in 1747. It also prepared the ground for the important new Lancaster Port Commission authorised by Act of Parliament in 1749.[58]

Pen and wash drawing by Gideon Yates, c.1790, showing the Old Bridge and St George's Quay –
the centre of Lancaster's maritime trade – with its warehouses and porticoed Custom House (1764).
Smith's shipyard can be seen below the Old Bridge (extreme left).

The Commission, established in 1750, was a more formal and powerful body sought by the business community to undertake the new improvements demanded by growing trade. The commissioners themselves were elected from merchants and mariners owning at least one sixteenth of a Lancaster ship of 50 tons or more, which spread the franchise widely and perhaps indicates the number of small merchants involved in maritime trade. The finances they were permitted to raise funded the new stone-built St George's Quay below the Old Bridge from 1750, the purchase of land behind (sold off in 'Lotts' about twenty feet wide in the 1750s and 1781) primarily for warehousing, manufacturing, commercial and associated domestic use. In 1759, Crofts enthusiastically noted that 'ships of 300 tons burthen are navigable up the Lun [sic]', arriving at 'a complete quay wall of 200 yards length, with wharfs'.[59] In 1764, Richard Gillow's Palladian-style Custom House was completed for the Port Commission and was described by a contemporary visitor as

> a very handsome new building with a neat portico facing the river supported by four plain pillars, each formed of a single stone, beautifully veined.[60]

The Custom House, set in the middle of what West described in 1793 as 'a fine quay and noble warehouses', remains a visible reminder of the wealth and confidence of the merchant community.[61]

The commissioners were active through the rest of the century, building the New Quay downstream for larger and deeper-draughted ships (1768);

and Glasson pier (1781–2), and the wet dock (1787) which developed from it, to the designs of Thomas Morris (subsequently dock engineer at Liverpool). The commissioners opened a stone quarry for the purpose at Overton in 1781. They also extended their activities into Morecambe Bay by building a landmark as an aid to navigation at Rossall Point (1766), at modern-day Fleetwood, and a lighthouse on Walney Island near Barrow-in-Furness (1790). They continued to mark and improve the Lune channel, introduce bye-laws, establish an efficient system of cartage, and build and improve roads to Glasson Dock and New Quay. The Commission also acted in the wider interests of maritime trade by, for example, lobbying Parliament on trade matters in 1766 and petitioning the Admiralty for an Atlantic convoy from Cork in 1776.[62] In 1780 it created a committee of trade consisting of seven commissioners empowered to correspond on all public business'.[63] The new committee appears to have been a response to the difficulties of the American war, and to the Trade Tax Committee set up by Lancaster merchants in 1776. This was effectively a chamber of trade, a voluntary body which collected funds to further the commercial interests of the port and arrange meetings on subjects of concern. Its own committee was elected to work in conjunction with the port commissioners.[64]

A separate and independent port authority had important advantages over Corporation control of the port and responsibility for its improvement: no financial loss (or the need to borrow) endangered the Corporation; the Commission's authority could be extended more naturally into other local authority areas; all income could be concentrated on the port and without the danger of being siphoned into other areas of Corporation involvement; and the Port Commission was able to include the important and powerful group of Quaker and Nonconformist merchants who were legally excluded from membership of the Corporation. Indeed, the establishment of the Commission may indicate a limited view of the Corporation's role in contrast with Liverpool where the Corporation played a more active part in stimulating trade.[65] At Lancaster, however, the Mayor and many members of the Corporation were able to pursue the borough's interests as elected commissioners. By law the Mayor was an ex-officio member. The duplication of membership during the eighteenth century reflected the same interests. So did the Corporation's financial contribution to Port Commission activities, such as the cost of building and paving St George's Quay and making a new ship-tracking road down to Aldcliffe Marsh (1757). There was also a close collaboration on new Acts of Parliament associated with the Port Commission's activities, such as the suggested increase in tonnage duties (1788) and the proposed scheme for a new dock at Thornbush (1799), at the mouth of the Lune, connected by canal to Lancaster.[66]

In the eighteenth century the town continued to be run on the basis of traditional custom and ancient rights enshrined, though modified, in the Royal Charter of 1664. The Corporation comprised the Mayor, Recorder, Town Clerk and thirty-three aldermen, bailiffs, capital burgesses and common councilmen at the head of a wider freeman populace. Their numerous officers included moormen, mossmen, hedge-lookers, flesh-lookers, ale-tasters, two sergeants-at-mace, one bellman, beadle and 'three waits or musicians'.[67] There was no democratic franchise, the Mayor and Corporation members effectively forming a self-perpetuating oligarchy, although with little evidence of the corruption present in other towns.

The Corporation was tied very closely to the development of the markets, which required policing and regulation and provided income in tolls and rents. As an incorporated borough Lancaster also had its own court of sessions presided over by the Mayor and Recorder, and was represented by two MPs. The purpose of the Corporation was to preserve these rights and privileges, particularly the freemen's monopoly of trade, and husband the financial resources of the town in their interests. There was little concept of democracy or of the wider responsibility of local government to the citizens of the town (many of whom were excluded from the franchise and town government on the basis of religion), although here things were beginning to change.

In 1688 there was a reversion to Tory control of the Corporation. Although gentry involvement in town politics continued, the influence of rich urban merchant traders – who were independent of gentry interest – in the Corporation increased with economic development. The mayoralty, dominated by wealthy merchants, reflects the increasing representation of those involved in commerce towards the mid-1700s. As required by the 1661 Corporations Act, the mayors and other corporation members were committed adherents of the Church of England and supporters of the Constitution, which was celebrated with fervour on the centenary of the 'Glorious Revolution' in 1788. Even so, until the 1790s the Corporation appeared to have no clear party political allegiance and concentrated instead on the pursuit of the town's commercial interests, an emphasis reflected in the influence – though not the choice – it exercised in the election of the two Members of Parliament for the borough.

The Corporation left the selection of parliamentary representatives largely to the local gentry and aristocracy in the traditional manner.[68] Nevertheless, candidates who had majority Corporation backing invariably won the elections, probably as a result of freeman deference and merchant patronage which were powerful influences in open elections. Many tradesmen and masters of small workshops supplied the West Indies merchants and depended on maritime trade. The power employers had to mobilise votes is reflected in Oldfield's observations of the borough in 1792:

> As shipbuilding and the cabinet business are the only manufactures there, he who has the most ships to build or repair, or he who will lay out a few hundreds of Pounds in mahogany furniture, is most likely to carry his election. The journeymen are at the command of their masters; they get intoxicated during the canvas and having 5s. to eat and drink

on the day of the election, they give a shout and go quietly to work again ...[69]

Candidates improved their chances through commercial patronage: Sir James Lowther apparently ordered ships from the Lancaster yards in the 1780s.[70] The Members of Parliament themselves were normally from the gentry and aristocratic landowning families, such as the Lowthers of Lancashire and Cumberland, the Cavendishes from Cartmel and the Marquis of Douglas of Ashton Hall (heir to the Duke of Hamilton and MP 1802–6). Yet, they were forced to have increasing regard for the interests of the town's trade and the new affluent urban bourgeoisie. This was certainly the case with Sir George Warren (MP 1761–96) and John Dent (MP 1790–1812) Lancashire landowner and London banker, respectively, who strongly represented the West Indies interests of the town in Parliament.

Even so, the town's own merchants took some share in the parliamentary representation. The merchant interest emerged more overtly with the election of Robert Heysham in 1698, and later his brother William, MP until 1729, both Lancaster West Indies merchants operating from London. Later from 1780 to 1790, another West Indies merchant, Abraham Rawlinson, represented the town for the Whigs. Interestingly, other gentry representatives, Edward Marton (1747–61) and Francis Reynolds (1761–73), were subject to merchant concerns as port commissioners.[71] Nevertheless, in terms of parliamentary representation, the Corporation was subject to the typical eighteenth-century power politics of the landed magnates and party groupings for control of the borough's representation. Contests were often fierce. Sir James Lowther sought to add to his parliamentary influence by installing a member at Lancaster in 1784 and 1786, and successfully in 1796 in the person of Richard Penn. The election of 1786 was said to have cost £25,000. Not all elections were contested, however, and in the interests of law and order the Corporation preferred it that way.[72]

The control of the voting system and its corruption – in borough elections and parliamentary town and county elections held at Lancaster – were increasingly challenged later in the century following the development of a nationwide political consciousness and new radical, more democratic ideas adopted among the middling and lower classes. By that time the most important issues of the day were less concerned with religion, which dominated politics at the start of the period, than with social order and class, which were of particular concern in the industrialising towns. Fear of lower class radicalism combined with the patriotic fervour of the French wars to make the Corporation more manifestly Tory, intensely loyal and even more demonstrably patriotic than in previous wars. Yet, despite this Tory profile, there was a tendency towards a political, social and religious rapprochement between the Dissenting merchant and Corporation families and the gentry in local affairs on the basis of a united interest in the established social order.

Nevertheless, the divisions of the seventeenth century took a long time to heal. The Revolution of 1688 and the expulsion of James II in favour of Queen Mary and William of Orange alienated many Protestant Royalists as well as Catholics. Nonconformists and Whigs were generally in favour of the new succession. The town population, and particularly its Nonconformist and Whig elements, was generally in favour of the Revolution and, later, the Hanoverian Protestant Succession, although a relatively high level of Jacobite support remained in the countryside. Catholics, including the numerous Catholic gentry families around Lancaster, were regarded with great suspicion. They formed a large proportion of the Lancashire population and owned as much as thirty-five per cent of land in the county.[73] When Queen Anne died in 1714, and the throne passed to the Hanoverian George I, there were sporadic disturbances. Leaders of a Manchester protest mob were tried at Lancaster and sentenced to the pillories in Market Square, followed by imprisonment. The rising of the Earl of Mar in Scotland and Earl of Derwentwater in Northumberland led to a wider rebellion in 1715 on behalf of the Pretender, James Stuart.[74]

The campaign of 1715 saw the rebel army march via Longtown, Penrith, Appleby, Kendal and Kirkby Lonsdale to arrive at Lancaster on 7 November 1715. The militia retired before them. Derwentwater and roughly 1,400 soldiers, bagpipes playing, entered the town and proclaimed the 'Old Pretender', James II's Catholic son, as King James III at the cross in Market Square. The townsmen had already disposed of all their gunpowder in the public well there, but the rebels seized some arms including six cannons from the ship *Robert* lying at Sunderland Point. They also took some money from the Excise Office and the Postmaster, together with some horses, and released a number of Crown prisoners from the Castle. The soldiers were billeted on the population. As a Quaker, William Stout feared

> that the Scots and Northern rebels would have plundered us; but they were civil, and to most paid for what they had; but I had five of the Mackintosh officers quartered on me two days but I took nothing of them.[75]

The atmosphere contributed to fraternisation. Peter Clarke described how, the day after they arrived,

> the gentlemen soldiers dressed and trimmed themselves up in their best cloathes for to drink a drop of tea with the ladys of this town ... [who] ... apeared in their best riging and had tea tables richly furnished for to entertain their new suitors.[76]

They were joined by around 100 local gentry and their supporters, including the Catholics John Dalton of Thurnham and Albert Hodgson of Leighton. The English, wearing cockades of red and white, and the Scots blue and white, left Lancaster on 9 November and marched to defeat by General Wills at the Battle of Preston five days later.

Many soon returned. According to Stout:

about fower hundred of them were brought to Lancaster Castell, and a regiment of dragoons Dormer's quatred in the town to gard them.

Stout was responsible for supplying provisions and described the prisoners being

laid in straw in the stables, most of them. And in a month time about one hundred of them were conveyed to Liverpoole to be tryed, where they were convicted, and near 40 of them hanged at Manchester, Liverpoole, Wiggan, Preston, Garstang, and Lancaster. And about two hundred of them continued a year.

A total of nine were executed on the Moor above Lancaster, all in 1716.[77] Parish records refer to forty-five prisoners, mostly from the counties of Inverness and Perth, who died in the prison between December 1715 and July 1716.[78] 'The rest', Stout continued

were transported to America, exept the lords and Gentlemen, who were had to London and there convicted and their estates forfeit.[79]

Local confiscations included the estate of Albert Hodgson, sold by public auction in 1722 but later regained, and Halton Hall which belonged to the Catholic Carus family.[80]

A similar tragedy unfolded in another November thirty years later, but proved to be the final resurgence of the old issues in militant form. Prince Charles Edward Stuart landed in Scotland in August, and travelled with an army of under 6,000 from Edinburgh to Carlisle, Kendal and Lancaster. On the 24th the van crossed the river and passed up Bridge Lane and China Street to Market Square to proclaim Charles as Regent for his father, the Old Pretender. The Prince arrived the following day with the main body of troops and a large number of Scottish nobility. He lodged in Church Street overnight and left for Preston the next morning, followed by a rearguard which only stayed long enough to eat some bread and cheese standing in the street. Some zealous citizens captured several stragglers, imprisoned in the Castle, but they were released by the Jacobite army on 13 December following the retreat from Derby. The houses of the most active supporters of the Hanoverian succession were attacked and plundered, including Dr Fenton's vicarage on Castle Hill. The occupants thought it wise to withdraw for the duration. On the fifteenth the Jacobites left, followed by the dragoons of General Oglethorpe's government army. Their commander, the Duke of Cumberland himself, arrived the following day. The Castle was full once more.[81]

The Lancaster response to the rebellion had been less forthcoming than in 1715. The Hanoverians were now fully established and the fall-off in religious persecution since 1715 had helped reconcile Lancashire Catholics to the status quo. The steady growth of commercial prosperity in Lancaster

Pen and wash drawing of the large and imposing vicarage on Castle Hill, just below the parish church of St Mary's, ransacked by the Jacobite forces in 1745. It was built by the Reverend Augustus Wildbore in 1638 and demolished in 1824.

took the edge off discontent and alienation, lessened the appeal of Jacobitism as a vehicle for protest, helped integrate the urban community despite religious differences and cemented widespread attachment to the Whig and Hanoverian system. There was certainly widespread cooperation among merchants of different religious persuasions. Stout consigned trade goods to the Anglican John Bowes in the voyage of the *Love* to Barbados in 1715; and the Quaker grocer Joshua Whalley was in partnership in shipowning and trade with the Catholic Gillow and Anglican saddler and tallow-chandler Edward Suart in the 1740s. There were others.[82] The Nonconformists, as supporters of the established order, were certainly viewed with less hostility in the early eighteenth century. The national trend towards greater toleration was reflected in, and assisted by, legislation – from the 1689 Act of Toleration to the 1778 and 1791 Acts for the relief of Catholics – but it was encouraged in a practical way by the developing prosperity.[83] Economic development helped ameliorate divisions within the local community, and was perhaps reflected in West's description of the inhabitants as 'wealthy, courteous, hospitable and polite'.[84] It perhaps explains the cooler response to the Forty Five.

Townscape and Social Change

Political transformation was matched by changes in society and in the physical, especially the urban, landscape. They were associated with a whole nexus of new enlightened ideas and attitudes which came to the fore in the eighteenth century and, in social terms, were displayed particularly by an element of the social elite termed 'polite society'. Politeness was another aspect of growing toleration and was associated with the use of rational argument and appreciation in understanding both the human condition and the natural world. It was part of a cultural transformation, strongly associated with ideas of improvement – applicable to all fields of human activity – which it facilitated.[85] Assisted by economic success and growing prosperity, the new attitudes were both encouraged and disseminated in the English provincial towns. Greater energy and greater wealth were expended in solving practical problems, 'improving' the environment and developing resources.

Encouraged by the improving society, the face of Lancaster changed dramatically between 1690 and 1815. Part of this change was natural renewal and improvement, but suitably modified by the new styles and requirements. New buildings and facades were created using neat, regular honey-coloured ashlar quarried principally on the Moor above the town. Slate increasingly replaced thatch. Local masons and carpenters adopted the standard elements of eighteenth-century design involving symmetry and regularity of appearance. The changes were noted in 1771 by Arthur Young:

> It is a town that increases in buildings; having many new piles, much superior to the old streets, and handsomely raised of white stone and slate.[86]

In 1793, Thomas West remarked on the many architectural improvements which, he thought,

> add much to the pleasing, or rather striking appearance this town has at a distance, on account of the Castle, Church, and the conspicuous situation of several good stone houses. The new houses are particularly neat and handsome, the streets well-paved and thronged with inhabitants, busied in a prosperous trade.[87]

'Polite' architecture, improved street planning, public amenities and a concentration on the attractive and picturesque were important developments. They satisfied the needs of polite society for public meeting places and developed the town's role as an important service centre.

Lancaster's role as a service centre for the gentry and country population was, of course, traditional. With the right to hold the fortnight-long biannual assizes, the quarter sessions and county elections, the social elite of Lancashire descended on the town at regular intervals. Public entertainment was geared to the social season it created, but there were other advantages generated by the presence of county legal and administrative organisation. Wealth and work supported a host of retailers of ordinary and luxury items, craftsmen such as coachbuilders and cabinetmakers along with doctors, lawyers and architects. This role also assisted the developing financial service sector which was emerging strongly in association with international trade. A great deal of

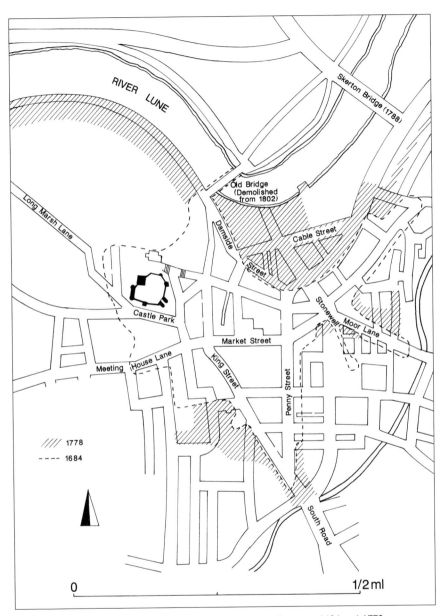

Map showing the physical expansion of Lancaster between 1684 and 1778.

personal borrowing, on bond, took place within the local community, and even the Corporation borrowed from individuals with spare cash. In 1794, however, the Lancaster merchants Robert and Alexander Worswick established the town's first bank. Another was established the same year by Dilworth & Hargreaves.[88] The banking sector was important in recycling the large landed and commercial fortunes of the time.

Lancaster and the New Bridge across the River Lune (1788) from the top of the tree-lined Ladies Walk. The Mill Race is in the foreground. Watercolour by George Pickering, early nineteenth century.

The importance of the Assizes continued until the 1830s at Lancaster and encouraged the mixing of town and country elites, whose members invariably comprised the new polite society. Lancaster became the venue for ostentatious display and for the dissemination of new ideas of fashion, manners and dress. To provide for the needs of polite society during the season a whole new infrastructure was created. The Assembly Room on Back Lane (later King Street) was built in 1759 as a commercial venture by Penny's charity, eager to profit from the demand for elegant social centres mimicking those of Bath and other major towns. Clark recorded in 1807 that even in winter there were

> three substantial concerts. The gentlemen of the musical society perform at the concerts, beside whom some professional musical performers attend from Liverpool and Manchester.[89]

Public walks were also created, where news was transmitted, sociability encouraged and social acceptance achieved. Ladies Walk was laid out between an avenue of trees beside the Mill Race at the northern end of Green Ayre. After walking it with friends in 1798, John Harden described it as 'a nicely planted stretch along the river above 1 ml & half very beautiful'.[90] It was used as a route to Alexander Stevens' and John Rennie's aqueduct carrying the Lancaster Canal across the River Lune, which West was prompted to describe as one of the handsomest bridges of its size in Europe'.[91] Another walk was established at the foot of the Castle walls; and a promenade was laid out by the county magistrates to the west of the Castle, with fine views across Morecambe Bay.[92] The Corporation had already planted and fenced trees on Castle Hill in 1747–48.[93]

The views particularly appealed to the romantically-inclined. In 1759, John Crofts reflected the still prevailing classicism of the earlier eighteenth century in describing the 'awfull aspect of the mountains of Westmorland rising their lofty heads before you'.[94] The growing appreciation of the sublime and scenically spectacular made Lancaster a powerful magnet for visitors, particularly those travelling to the newly fashionable Lake District. The town featured in West's popular guide to the Lakes which, for devotees of the picturesque, described Gray's recommended viewing stations in the Lune Valley from which to appreciate Ingleborough to the east.[95] William Wilberforce advised climbing Castle Hill to see the view, although 'the day was thick' when *he* chose to do so.[96] The Reverend MacRitchie, looking back at the town on the road south, described as 'one of the noblest of prospects' the backdrop of the bay, the Cumbrian mountains, the Isle of Man and Piel Castle.[97] Many other visitors were similarly struck by its location, including Robert Southey, who wrote with admiration during his visit in 1807. Lancaster was firmly on the tourist map. Together with the proximity of the newly-fashionable sea bathing at Sunderland Point and Poulton-le-Sands, the town was a suitable resort for the county elite.

It was made more so by the theatre, the mark of urban arrival. Although theatrical performances had, by Corporation indulgence, taken place in inns and barns in the town as early as the 1760s, the first permanent building was erected in St Leonardgate only in 1781. It was funded by local subscription organised by Joseph Austin and Charles Edward Whitlock (an actor and dentist), managers of a circuit of theatres in Chester, Manchester, Sheffield, Newcastle and Whitehaven. The theatre's first performance took place in time for the races in June 1782. At the opening, the *Cumberland Pacquet* described it as:

> a small but very elegant and commodious theatre ... The Earl of Surrey [MP for Carlisle] honoured it with his presence every evening in the race week; – consequently every person of distinction and taste visited it

although the quality of performance appears to have been marred by the accompanying, unspecified, disorder.[98] In the same summer season the company performed *Hamlet* 'to a very crowded house ... and even the honest Tars in the gallery were all attention'; and the *Belles Stratagem* (sic), for which 'it was the general opinion that it was not possible for 2 plays to be performed so well, with every theatrical etiquette, out of London'.[99] Pantomimes, farces and comic operas were all highly popular, although when MacRitchie visited in 1795 *Macbeth* was doing the rounds; the representation, he thought, 'was very tolerable on the whole', although Sarah Siddons, as Lady MacBeth, was 'poorly supported'. Nevertheless, it was 'a brilliant audience; the Lancashire ladies in all their charms'.[100] Mrs Siddons, the famous actress and sister-in-law of Whitlock, returned to Lancaster in 1799 'and performed five nights to the most crowded and fashionable audiences ever seen in Lancaster'.[101] The theatre prospered, although by 1815 the declining economic fortunes of the town appear to have undermined its significance and profitability.[102]

Horse racing was also an important feature of the social scene. By 1762, royal and aristocratic patronage had encouraged the establishment of seventy-six racecourses in Britain. Lancaster's racecourse, first noted in 1758, was built on the Common Marsh, which John Crofts described in 1759 being 'half a mile below the Quay on the flat offshore'.[103] It was subsidised and promoted by the Corporation, which contributed to the prizes and sought to add to the entertainment and amenities expected of the county town and social season. The gentry and aristocracy, including the Duke of Hamilton and Earl of Derby, raced their horses for enjoyment and sport but also, in the case of Sir James Lowther in the 1780s, to develop their local influence for political ambition. The races lapsed after 1797 with the enclosure of the Marsh but were reinstated with added vigour on the Moor in 1809.[104]

Traditional sporting activities developed and remained popular but were increasingly threatened by the refinement of town society. A Corporation pack of hunting hounds, in the care of green-liveried huntsmen, was kept in kennels on Green Ayre by 1747 and appear to have continued well into the nineteenth century.[105] A number of bowling greens appeared in the 1700s for the more genteel. Cock-throwing, which took place with gentry patronage, was more vulnerable. In 1765 a contest occurred between 'A main of cocks to be fought at Skearton [sic] near Lancaster' for cash prizes between the gentlemen of Westmorland and Lancashire. Another took place on Lancaster Moor in 1774. The following year the *Manchester Mercury* advertised fights 'at the new cockpit in Lancaster' (on Back Lane) between the gentlemen of Preston and Lancaster.[106] The sport declined in the late eighteenth century and appears to have ceased by 1804. Like many such rowdy gatherings, they were felt to be a threat to urban order and frowned upon by magistrates. This coincided with widespread concern for the morals of the labouring classes, notably their drinking, gambling and lack of Sabbath observance. The Mayor had banned the sale of liquor on Sunday mornings as early as 1787, but Evangelical influence in favour of reform met with limited success in the face of the gentry and town elite's enjoyment of traditional pastimes, theatre-going and horse racing.[107] Culturally, the local elite and the lower orders continued to share traditional tastes and habits up to the eve of the Industrial Revolution.[108]

That said, however, the elite of the town were increasingly likely to participate in the more refined pursuits of a new, developing upper class culture increasingly divorced from popular experience. Many joined the new societies which were being established, and the culture of 'visiting' encouraged excursions to local attractions. It became quite normal to take part in an improvement society or charitable committee as well as civic affairs.[109] The Musical Society, for example, included local gentry among its office-holders and members, as well as the school master, the Reverend Watson, as its Vice-President. It was polite, civilised and refined. At the meeting in November 1778 to commemorate St Cecilia's Day, the *Cumberland Pacquet*

A True and Exact L I S T of all the

HORSES, MARES, AND GELDINGS,

That are Entered to Run on

Lancaster Marſh,

On *Monday* the 1ſt, *Tueſday* the 2d, and *Wedneſday* the 3d Days of J U L Y, 1776.

MONDAY, the Noblemen and Gentlemen's Plate of Fifty Pounds, Weight for Age.

Sir James Lowther's Grey Horſe *Sloven*, 5 Y. old, 8ſt. 5lb. W. Inſley Yellow
Sir Walter Vavaſor's Bay Horſe *Silver Heels*, 5 Y. old, 8ſt. 5lb. Len. Jewiſon Straw.
Mr. Gadeſſes's Cheſnut Mare *Miſs Wilkes*, 6 Y. old, 9ſt. W. Armſtrong Red.

TUESDAY, the Members' Plate of Fifty Pounds, Give and Take.

Sir James Lowther's Grey Horſe *Pleader*, 6 Y. old, 14H. 3-8ths In. 8ſt. 1lb. 12oz.
   W. Inſley Yellow
Thomas Clifton, Eſq.'s Grey Horſe *Favorite*, aged, 14H. 1I. 3-8ths. J. Mangle Red.
   9ſt. 2lb. 12oz.
J. Hutton, Eſq.'s Bay Horſe, *Northumberland*, aged, 14H. 7-8ths. W. Ridley Blue.
   8ſt. 13lb. 2oz.
Mr. Rock's Grey Horſe *May Duke*, aged, 14H. 2-8ths In. J. Carter Red.
   8ſt. 8lb. 12oz.

WEDNESDAY, the Town's Plate of Fifty Pounds by 4 Year Olds.

Mr. Hutton's Bay Colt *Veteran*, 8ſt. 10lb. W. Ridley Blue.
Mr. Dawſon's Ch. Colt *Young Fellow*, 8ſt. 10lb. A. Hall Red.

Sir WATTS HORTON *and* ⎫ Stewards.
Sir THOMAS EGERTON, ⎭

All Perſons are deſired to keep their Dogs at Home; and no Perſon whatſoever will be allowed to paſs within the Cord during the Time they are running.

A COCK-MAIN, ORDINARIES, AND ASSEMBLIES, AS USUAL.

Poster advertising horse-racing (and a foot race) at Lancaster over a period of three days in July 1776. It became an important and established part of the town's social season.

reported that various works and songs were performed, including Handel's 'Ode to St Cecilia's Day', and that

> the intervals of conversation and toasting their musical friends and acquaintances of both sexes were filled up with a variety of catches, glees, duets etc. and the whole evening exhibited a most pleasing instance of that perfect harmony and social friendship which first founded, and has hitherto invariably supported, raised and distinguished that respectable association.[110]

The fashionable sporting society, John o'Gaunt's Bowmen, was 'revived' in 1788 with similar – and exclusive – social purposes, and included as members the Rawlinsons and other prominent citizens of town and country.[111]

The town also acted as a centre for news and the transfer of information, vital functions in the development of the polite and improving society. The first public library – the Amicable – was founded in 1768 in Church Street. Somewhat later, in 1815, the Literary & Philosophical Society was established as a means of disseminating information on the many technical and artistic developments and improvements of the period.[112] Bookshops and printers appeared for the first time and Lancaster's first newspaper, the *Lancaster Gazette*, was published in 1801.

The new media, venues and organisations helped both socially and commercially. Inns and hotels continued in this role. The Golden Ball, Sun Inn and King's Arms were popular throughout the period and hosted meetings of the Port Commission, Freemasons, Lancaster Agricultural Society, Musical Society and others. The quintessential eighteenth-century institution, the coffee house, played an important role. A coffee house was established as early as 1716.[113] From 1770 the Merchants' Subscription Coffee Room in Market Square acted as a centre for the exchange of commercial information and meeting place of the merchant interest. Schofield suggests that it may have acted as an insurance broking floor, but it was certainly an auction house for ships and goods from the West Indies well into the nineteenth century.[114] The Philippi Club, founded in 1797, proved an important vehicle for social and business intercourse, comprising the principal members of the civic and commercial elite and the borough's two Members of Parliament. It met every night in favoured inns and in the early nineteenth century settled on the Black Horse, the Corporation inn on Common Garden Street.[115]

While the culture of toleration grew and the sting of religious difference lessened, religion continued to be of fundamental importance. But the popular significance of the established church declined as the shackies of religious repression loosened and a more 'open market' in religion developed. The 1689 Toleration Act was important to Protestant Dissent and lifted much of the burden of repression complained of by Stout in Lancaster, although the Quakers continued to suffer at the hands of clergymen and lawyers.[116] Charles Rigby's legal skills were used in encouraging litigious suits, and espetially in forwarding persecutions against the Quakers for their conscientious refusall of paying tyths and the clergy's demands [117]

and James Fenton, vicar of St Mary's from 1685 to 1714, was

a haughty man and very seveire in exacting his pretended dues, to the imprisonment of sevral.[118]

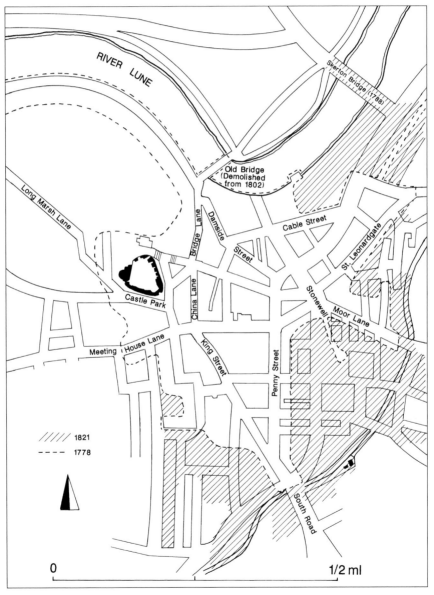

Map showing the physical expansion of Lancaster between 1778 and 1821.

The subsequent preoccupation with tithes – and worldly preferment – appear to have been a feature as common to the large Lancaster parish as anywhere else. Lawsuits between the incumbent and parishioners concerning the commutation of tithes certainly became more common in the early nineteenth century.[119] The church continued to offend many just as enlightened thought was increasingly questioning the theocentric view of the world and militant secularism was advancing. Nevertheless, to the town elite and country gentry the church remained an important bastion of social order, especially in the uncertain times towards the end of the century.

'Politeness' assisted the generation and dissemination of the new enlightened ideas but a major impetus to improvement was financial advantage. It could often reflect a desire for the broader good but was increasingly the product of personal self-interest which was, according to Adam Smith, the means to the general good.[120] The Corporation's view of its limited role in local life was starting to change. There was a growing involvement in town and transportation changes prompted by a local desire to encourage economic improvement and to uphold Lancaster's position as county town and rising commercial port. Lancaster was also an important communications centre on the main road between north and south. A large number of travellers made use of the many hotels, inns and alehouses. The seventeen recorded in the town in the 1690s had risen to sixty-five listed in *Pigot's Commercial Directory* in 1818.[121]

They were encouraged by improved transport. The coaching service developed rapidly towards the end of the century, connecting Lancaster

View of the old King's Arms Hotel (right) at the bottom of Meeting House Lane. It was built in 1625 and became Lancaster's principal hotel. It was demolished in 1879 to make way for the present King's Arms. The later Merchants' News Room, with the oriel window, can be seen on Market Street further down on the right.

directly with Liverpool, Manchester, Carlisle, Whitehaven and significant towns en route. In 1786 the first mail coach from London arrived in Market Square. Carriers' waggons, providing regular national services, and pack-horses became increasingly common with the development of the port and general trade. In 1799 thirteen coastal vessels were listed trading regularly between Lancaster and London, Liverpool, Bristol and Whitehaven.[122] In 1752 an estimated sixty horse-loads of goods were carried by waggon every week from Lancaster to Kendal alone.[123] The town benefited from the passage tolls exacted from travellers and goods through the borough and collected at toll gates on the main routes into town, including St George's Quay.[124]

The Corporation was also involved with arranging turnpike Acts on the highways between Lancaster and Kendal, Garstang and Richmond from 1750.[125] Travellers still complained, although turnpikes – the equivalent of improvement trusts – were a great advance. Within the town a particular effort was made to alleviate the problems caused by the increasing amount of wheeled and other traffic. One traveller in 1764 typically described 'narrow & crowded' streets, whose constraints were progressively alleviated by the creation of new thoroughfares and the widening of others at the behest of the more active Corporation.[126] In 1748, New Street was built to connect the Market Place with the parallel Church Street. The original suggestion to name it Charles Street was considered politically unwise. New Road followed in 1752 to allow better access to Green Ayre and the new St George's Quay.[127] Some buildings were also demolished to allow road widening, such as the old Toll House on Bridge Lane in 1764 and the Custom House steps in 1774.[128]

Streets were increasingly well-paved too. Celia Fiennes in 1698 described some of these as being well pitched and of good size but

> when I came into the town the stones were so slippery crossing some channells that my horse was quite down on his nose.[129]

Later travellers described well-paved streets, laid out largely by the Corporation.[130] Improved access was still hindered by the single, narrow unsafe Old Bridge which was a serious bottleneck. In 1788, Thomas Harrison's new bridge – 549 feet long – was opened upstream to replace it at a cost of £14,000 to the county.[131] It brought Green Ayre into prominence, now on the main north road, allowing visitors such as James Mackenzie to arrive in the town

> by a very handsome bridge of five arches ... and through a very good, handsome wide avenue until we came near our inn which is the King's Arms.

The effect was somewhat spoiled by arriving 'in a very small back yard and being conducted through the kitchen'.[132]

The decision to press for a new bridge and lay out a connecting road

Engraving after Westall, 1829, of 'Lancaster Sessions House and Market' – the Town Hall of 1783. It cost £2,000. The Corporation was sufficiently pleased that it conferred on the architect, Major Thomas Jarrat, the freedom of the borough, suitably recorded on vellum and presented in a silver box. The cupola was a later alteration by Thomas Harrison.

twenty yards wide – Cable Street and Parliament Street – was apparently taken as early as 1770, but in 1783–4, after the American war, the Corporation drew up plans for the development of the area. Twenty-three individual plots were laid out on a regular pattern, based on Cable Street and including the proposed Jamaica, Barbados and Antigua streets leading off to the riverside. The Corporation specified strict building controls and took responsibility for the upkeep and repair of certain new streets and passages, but in Cable Street the new purchasers were required to maintain a gravel footpath with a handsome hewn curb stone.[133] As Gooderson has said, the Corporation desired to combine improvement and profit by specifying uniformity of development, including access at front and rear, for quality housing (probably incorporating warehousing too) to satisfy merchant needs.[134] Although the expected development failed to occur, the new classically-styled toll house was built at the north end (1786) together with various developments nearer the town. These included St John's Chapel (1755), St Mary's attempt to provide for a growing population, which was built on land and with money given by the Corporation.[135]

The Corporation also saw to its own immediate needs. West described the 'new town-hall, or exchange (designed by Major Jarrat) esteemed a handsome building, with a noble portico', completed in 1783.[136] It replaced the inadequate Town Hall of 1671, providing new meeting and court rooms, the town lock-up and an open commercial area on the ground floor. The Corporation was also responsible for continuing minor works, including stables for two of its toll houses in 1804, and buildings for charities of which it was trustee. Whatever the project, the Corporation set a high standard of provision and improvement.

Improvement also involved the development of private housing. Castle Park became a select area. Abraham Rawlinson had a house lower down the hill as early as the 1770s. Fine houses in Church Street and all the main streets were supplemented by development off Meeting House Lane and the newer High Street and Queen Square on the western edge of town, where more land was available. They became more specialised areas of better class housing and marked the shift from the traditional mix of housing and trade premises. The town elite built handsome houses and lived in style, although the outward geographical shift continued, for it became more common to own villas on the edge of town or houses in the country. For others, such as the Brockbanks on Cable Street, a town house was essential for work. New housing schemes to overcome the problem of overpopulation were held up by the American war, but in 1784 John Dalton obtained an Act to develop the Frierage. It was a more considered plan, allowing the eastward extension of the town based on Dalton Square and a network of new streets occupied by a variety of houses, warehouses and workshops. The finer houses in the square took longer to materialise because of the decline in West Indies trade after 1800, which affected similar proposed schemes off Meeting House Lane and St Leonardgate.[137]

The building of the Lancaster Canal was a more obvious response to economic need. Although the idea of a canal connection with south Lancashire was suggested in the 1760s, disagreements over the course of the waterway and economic interruptions had prevented any decision. Patience finally ran out in 1791 when thirty merchants petitioned the Mayor to call a public meeting. They were anxious to develop the town's inland communications, prompted particularly by the growing threat of Liverpool to the port's trade. The petition mentioned the Leeds-Liverpool Canal under construction, giving

> the merchants and traders of ... [Liverpool] ... so decided a superiority in the vend of their imports as greatly to diminish the imports of this town ... unless some means can be found to meet them in the market upon more equal terms.[138]

The meeting in the Town Hall in February 1792 decided on a survey by John Rennie to connect the Leeds-Liverpool with Preston, Lancaster and Kendal. It also obtained immediate promises of £247,000 for the project which soon rose to £370,000. An Act was obtained in 1792 and the first section opened in 1797. It successfully laid the foundations of Lancaster's early industrial development, allowing the supply of cheap coal from the Wigan coalfield to the town's new cotton spinning mills.[139]

The same improving spirit was evident in the decision of the county justices to rebuild Lancaster Castle, the gaol and seat of county government,

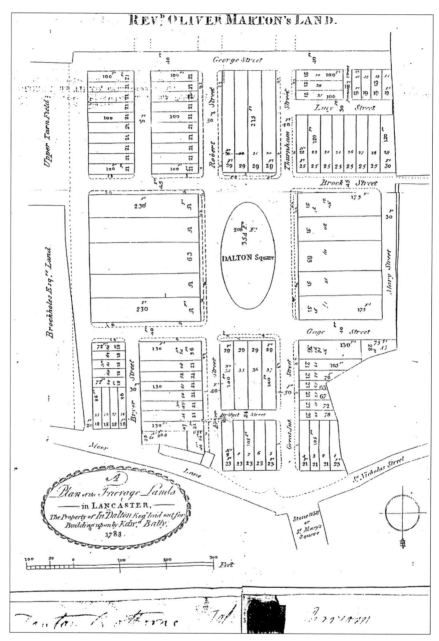

Plan of the proposed Dalton Square development by Edward Batty, 1783. It was Georgian Lancaster's most ambitious piece of urban planning, regrettably never fully realised because of economic decline. The street layout and individual buildings from the period remain.

to provide more adequate accommodation. The growing number of prisoners reflected increasing social problems in the industrial towns and the rise in population. With the loss of the American colonies there was also less transportation, although in 1790 David Cragg noted the transfer of felons from Lancaster to Plymouth for Botany Bay.[140] The number of prisoners rose from eighty-seven in 1774 to 213 (plus five lunatics) in 1809.[141] In line with national prison reform the idea took root of reforming prisoners and improving living conditions at the same time, eliminating typhus (gaol fever), which had killed the prison governor John Higgin in 1783.

Conditions in the castle had been basic for a long time, although an anonymous visitor in 1764 did describe the jail as 'spacious & airy'.[142] In 1774 the prison reformer, John Howard, reported favourably on the state of the prison but made various suggestions. Following an improvement Act obtained by the county in 1778, various buildings were erected, including male and female felons' prisons, secure cells and baths. In 1807 Clark decided that

> the elevated site of the Castle, with the late additional buildings, reservoirs, pumps, drains, and the great attention to cleanliness, render it one of the most commodious and healthy county gaols in this kingdom: and the style of the new parts being all carefully adapted to the old, the whole now forms a group of castle-building, which, perhaps, is not excelled in the empire.[143]

Clark was equally enthusiastic about the new humanitarian regime, separating male and female felons, debtors and lunatics; generally avoiding the use of fetters, 'except for the refractory'; and

> a system of [paid] industry, by which every prisoner capable of labour, is engaged in some useful employment, such as weaving, shoemaking &c,

training prisoners for a trade to take up on their release. Debtors had always been permitted a superior regime which allowed them a skittle-ground and bowling green in the Castle Yard, mock elections at the time of parliamentary campaigns and a choice of accommodation which depended on their ability to pay. The diet of prisoners also improved, to include wheat bread, oatmeal, potatoes plus boiled beef and soup on Sundays. Two 'airy and spacious rooms' were used as a hospital and a surgeon (first recorded in 1777) employed 'for attending the Crown prisoners', with medicines provided by the county.[144] Following the improvements, the Reverend MacRitchie was one of a number of tourists to put the Castle on their itinerary. In 1795 he found it

> as well worth seeing as anything of the kind I have ever seen. The new apartments for the state prisoners lately erected by Harrison on a plan that would highly please the benevolent Howard himself. Sixty-four

'The New Buildings, on the West Front of Lancaster Castle, comprehending the County Hall, Grand Jury Room, John of Gaunt's Tower, etc.', designed by Thomas Harrison as an appropriate seat of law and county government. Drawn by Robert Freebairn and published in 1802.

neat apartments for them, with enclosed ground without for air and exercise.[145]

Prisoner accommodation was only part of the plan. Harrison designed the new complex of courts, county offices and rooms on the west side of the castle, built across the old moat. The Shire Hall (Nisi Prius Court), capable of holding 1,500 persons, was the most impressive of all.[146] The Castle improvements which Clark pronounced 'worthy of the great commercial and opulent county to which they belong', were designed by Thomas Harrison and completed from 1799 by Joseph Gandy.[147] The same cannot be said of the death sentences handed down there. Executions were nothing new, of course. Prisoners were taken through the town by cart or sledge to be hanged (and, in the case of the Jacobites, quartered) on Lancaster Moor. In 1772 the *Gentleman's Magazine* reported that Mary Hilton, convicted of poisoning her husband, was hanged for fifteen minutes, cut down and burned to ashes, possibly while still alive.[148] From 1800, public executions took place north of the Shire Hall, averaging seven per year between 1800 and 1825.[149] The Castle Chaplain (from 1804) and school master, Joseph Rowley, thought public hangings sufficiently edifying to escort boys from the grammar school to witness them.[150]

The architecture of the Castle and other buildings in Lancaster reflected the ideas of the age. In the Palladian-style Custom House (1764) and more severely classical Town Hall (1783), the citizens of Lancaster adapted architectural forms which, in Corfield's words, 'appropriated for the eight-eenth-century towns the antiquity and majesty of a legitimate civic vision'.[151] The style was also appropriate for private use, reflecting a suitably refined element of social display and – in contrast with vernacular styles now under threat – emphasizing social superiority. It also emphasized the growing pressure of outside influence in every aspect of town life. Richard Gillow designed a number of local buildings and some early semi-detached town houses. This widespread adoption shows how quickly the towns, as information centres and setters of fashion, were able to receive the most advanced ideas in polite achitecture and, certainly in the case of Gillow, develop them further in architecture and furniture design. The wealth and potential of Lancaster was also able to attract Thomas Harrison, 'the first professional architect of any standing to settle in the provinces'.[152] He had already studied in Rome and went on to design major buildings in the county town of Chester. At Lancaster Castle he designed in the Gothic style determined by the existing structure but also 'as a symbol of the medieval origin of county government and of Castle Gothic as an expression of security and authority'.[153] It was a style entirely appropriate to traditional society on the verge of the industrial revolution and the new challenges of urban culture.

Social Need and Community Response

The improvements to Lancaster's main buildings and thoroughfares were matched by difficulties endured in all rapidly-growing towns. They provided a challenge in which ideas of improvement were also applied to the condition of the lower orders. The economic success of the port and town drew in migrants from the surrounding region, leading to much of the urban squalor that developed in Lancaster. Migration was also propelled by population growth in the countryside and agricultural changes which provided an element of 'push' to match the economically attractive 'pull' of the town.[154] John Crofts, on his journey to Lancaster in 1759, referred to the attraction of the ports and industry in the region 'draining the country of their hands'.[155] In the 1790s Holt similarly remarked on the flow of rural wealth and family to the towns.[156] The origins of many Lancaster merchants lay in the surrounding region, particularly the south Lakeland area including Lancashire North of the Sands. Migratory demographic expansion was enhanced by a natural increase in the town itself. The borough birth rate was certainly outpacing the death rate by the 1780s, according to the baptism and burial figures at St Mary's.[157] It was probably the case much earlier. In the mid-1700s, in a period of noticeably quickening economic activity, the population of Lancaster was around 4,000–5,000 and it had doubled by the end of the century.[158] In 1784 Clark put the figure at 8,584, and the census

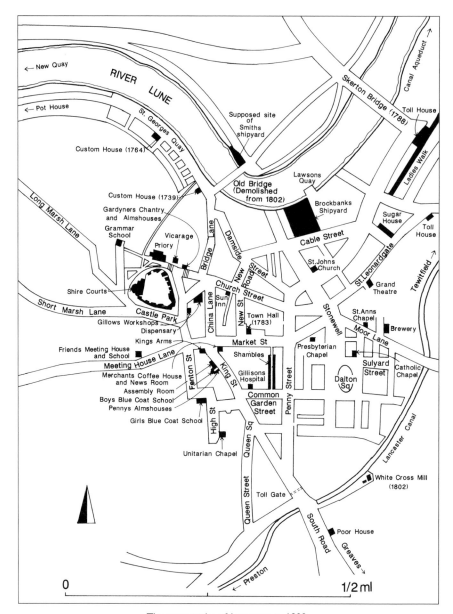

The topography of Lancaster in 1800.

of 1801 recorded 9,030.[159] Seamen were excluded. A period of stagnation followed and the population was only 9,247 in 1811.[160]

Population growth in the centre of Lancaster resulted in a huge increase in the density of population as housing was built on the back gardens of the narrow burgage plots fronting the main streets.[161] The area between Market

Watercolour of the Stonewell area of Lancaster, c.1800, by Gideon Yates. It is a rare view of the poorer housing inhabited by many in the town. Thatched roofing, a particular fire hazard, had yet to be fully replaced with slate.

Street, Church Street and Castle Hill was particularly affected. It gave rise to a network of yards and courts accessed through doors and arches on the main thoroughfare but without any form of servicing – neither the water supplies, sewerage system, nor even the lighting provided on the main streets as early as 1738. The whole centre of town became an agglomeration of fine houses and public buildings, squalid lower class housing, warehouses, shops and workshops. Tan pits on Green Ayre added to the stench of ordure in many streets and alleyways to which the butchers, later concentrated on the Shambles, made their own contribution. Scavengers paid by the Corporation, such as the Beadle Thomas Shires in 1730, were by no means universal and only attended to the main streets.[162] In 1786, the Port Commission hired Bulman, Helme & Co. to sweep and remove rubbish from St George's Quay. They were paid £3 3s. for the year and were allowed to keep all horse manure.[163] At the same time, visitors such as West could state that 'The air of Lancaster is salubrious' and certainly the fresh sea breezes were enjoyed by many.[164] Nevertheless, everyone lived close to the harsher and less pleasant aspects of life.

The urban masses endured the worst conditions. They were also increasingly vulnerable to trade fluctuations, felt keenly in the ports, which left them even more subject to the vicissitudes of an untamed market economy. Increased eighteenth-century employment specialisation left them dependent on the market for the sale of their labour and purchase of food and provisions. In hard times demand for labour declined and prices increased. At the same time they were probably less able to obtain additional food and income from the gardens and smallholdings (apparent on Docton's map of 1684 and even Mackreth's map of 1778) in Lancaster itself. As a small town Lancaster was probably better off than the large industrial cities, but the quality of life of the labouring class was probably worse at the end of the century than at the start. Certainly the great gap between rich and poor in the small, densely-populated town would have been very apparent. The American and French wars from the 1770s both worsened economic conditions and, especially after 1789, gave rise to the spectre of a radicalised urban population. Fear of social insurrection was apparent in Lancaster as it was throughout Britain, and combined with the humanitarian, religious and paternalistic motivations in a more active communal – including civic – response to the distressed urban condition. The town's wealth, especially from the 1770s, provided the means, and civic pride, religious awareness and social concern the essential motives.

Lancashire as a whole had a tradition of charitable endowment in social and educational provision.[165] Good works were a means to salvation. In 1716 William Penny, sometime Mayor and owner of land and property in and around the town, left £700 for the establishment of almshouses for '12 such poor, indigent men, of and within the said town of Lancaster'. In the event of a shortage, women qualified for residence and the quarterly allowance. Some money was to be used to apprentice poor boys. The stone and thatched almshouses, in a courtyard off Back Lane (King Street), were finished in 1720. They were attached to a later chapel whose curate was paid for out of profits from the endowment. The MP William Heysham, who made good in the London West Indies trade, also left an estate in 1727. Stout, who dealt with Heysham as a merchant in Barbados, described him as 'an indolent man, and of noe service. But he left an estate at Greaves, the rent to eight poor freemen, to be named by the mayor, recorder and three of the oldest aldermen; and so succesivly as any die, which is at least five pounds a year each, the estate being above 40l [£] a year'.[166] Gillison's Hospital, off Common Garden Street, was founded in 1790 through a bequest of Anne Gillison, daughter of a Lancaster merchant, and provided for the construction of eight houses for women, who each received £3 and a new gown every year. It was subsequently augmented by a series of legacies and gifts.[167] Following tradition, all these charities were administered by the Mayor and Aldermen. The civic authorities were also trustees of the older Gardyner's Chantry almshouses for four poor persons, rebuilt in 1792.[168]

These charities were only a partial response to need, and they operated on the very personal basis of the recipients being either members of a favoured group or otherwise suitable in the eyes of the trustees. Their private exercise of charitable patronage was distinct from the care of the public poor who were the responsibility of the parish and paid for by the poor rate. Demand was heavy in times of economic distress. In February 1783, at the end of the American war and two years of bad sugar harvests which seriously

Gillison's Hospital, Common Garden Street, completed in 1792 and comprising eight houses for the benefit of unmarried women. It was demolished in the 1960s.

affected the trade of the port, 2,214 people in Lancaster (out of a population of 8,582) were in receipt of poor relief. Relief committees came to be a feature of charitable works in times of crisis. In early 1783 large quantites (163,649 lbs) of oatmeal were distributed with the £1,112 6s. collected by public subscription. The Corporation subsequently took advantage of the permissive legislation of the Poorhouse Act, 1782, to order the building of a new poorhouse on Lancaster Moor in 1787–8.[169]

The earlier parish poorhouse of 1730 had been replaced in 1748 by another at White Cross built at the Corporation's expense on town land and rented to the Poor Law overseers.[170] The Corporation's involvement in 1787–8 developed this further. A large area of the Moor was given for the use of the poorhouse, which Clark described in 1807 as 'large and commodious, but the poor have so much increased that a few years ago an additional wing became necessary'. It also contained fever wards. The land included 10 acres for 'the use of the poor ... [which were] ... now in a state of good cultivation'.[171] Personal charity towards the poor and unfortunate continued strongly, however, and even included the prisoners in the Castle who benefited from numerous bequests.[172]

Health was also a matter of concern to wealthy town dwellers and lay at the heart of much civic improvement. It was of greater significance to the urban poor, however, who naturally suffered higher rates of mortality from epidemics and disease. Referring to the year 1725, Stout wrote that 'The small pox has prevailed this summer, and the measles, of which very many have died in and about Lancaster', although records suggest that 1725 was not itself unusual.[173] The communal response to conditions of health led to the foundation of the Lancaster Dispensary (and an associated lying-in charity in 1807) during the economic distress caused by the Ametican war, and was immediately concerned with the typhus epidemic of 1782–5 in which 500 were infected. According to Gooderson, it was partly due to the Dispensary that only thirty-four died.[174] It was supported, in Clark's words, 'by donations and annual subscriptions. Its objects are poor persons who are incapable of paying for medical or surgical assistance'.[175] In 1805 the Dispensary treated 1,278 patients, the largest number suffering from catarrhal infections (133), fever (101), measles (100), stomach complaints (93), 'cutaneous eruptions' (91) and a host of other complaints including smallpox (67) and 'cow pox by inoculation' (35).[176] Certainly the medical assistance it deployed was impressive. Dr Campbell, for example, the Dispensary's first physician, made a special study of the disease and published his influential observations in 1785.[177] The attraction of the county town to a growing number of medical practitioners was highly advantageous, but the Dispensary itself was available only to sufferers referred by its sponsors. It was highly selective.

Religious movements also contributed directly to health reform. Evangelical Anglicanism was represented in Lancaster by the Reverend Robert Housman (son of the West Indies merchant Thomas Housman), Curate of St John's from 1785 and of St Anne's Chapel from 1795. He founded the Benevolent Society two years later 'to promote financial aid in times of sickness and need for those who attended some place of divine worship'. The small but growing number of Methodists (fifty-three in 1795), whose first minister was appointed in 1792 and whose first chapel was opened in Sulyard Street in 1805, made attempts to visit and assist their co-religionists. Such attempts were obviously limited and non-comprehensive, but part of a growing institutionalisation of health care. Evangelicalism, involving a moral revival, was influential across the religious divide, however, and was even introduced to Lancaster by the Minister of the Independent Chapel in High Street, the Reverend George Burder, 1772–92. It underlined the Christian duty to the poor and, in Lancaster, according to Gooderson, stimulated the traditional paternalism of the town's rulers.[178]

Education also reflected this important but partial response to community need and the demands of the poor. The Grammar School, overseen and supported by the Corporation, was itself increasingly exclusive on the basis of wealth. The principle of free education for the sons of freemen was undermined by the annual gratuity of 'cockpennies' and entry fees paid to the master and usher. From at least 1719 an unpaid writing master was appointed who charged fees to the sons (and daughters) of both freemen and non-freemen for tuition outside the strongly classical curriculum. From 1764 he was provided with a salary by the Corporation and taught maths for the benefit of those entering trade and commerce. By 1809 his teaching responsibilities also included book-keeping, geometry and navigation at an extra cost of five shillings.[179] These fees reflected the course of developing class consciousness which emerged fully by the end of the eighteenth century, helping to exclude the poor in favour of the sons of wealthier tradesmen and merchants.

Charitable gifts and bequests continued to be received by the school and administered by the Corporation. In 1700 Giles Heysham left £100 to augment the Usher's salary. In 1733 Sir Thomas Lowther and Robert Fenwick gifted 10s. 6d. each to the school library, usually able to acquire a dozen books per annum. The Corporation was otherwise well-disposed to the school, building a new porch and upper storey in 1682 and contributing to the salaries of the staff. This remuneration was often inadequate, encouraging the Anglican churchmen to seek curacies and the Castle prison chaplaincy to supplement their income. This further soured relations with the Corporation, apparently concerned that the school's business was being neglected, although other factors often underlay this mutual hostility. Thomas Holme (Master 1708–25), who was twice threatened with suspension or dismissal, wrote in 1718:

> The Council look upon us as depending vassals, not as generous benefactors; and that body consisting chiefly of illiterate petty tradesmen and mechanicks look for so much respect that many are disappointed if we are not obsequious to flattery. We also meet with children who, presuming upon their parents' power, are refractory and bad examples, and to parents who are haughty and vexatious to the master for doing his duty to such children.[180]

As the wealth, social standing and even educational accomplishments of Corporation members increased during the century, the learned schoolmasters were less able to assume an obvious superiority and were better able to reconcile their responsibilities. The problem of inadequate finance was overcome as the Corporation found itself with sufficient income to increase salaries. By 1785 the school was costing the Corporation £100 per annum, double the sum of 1725. Greater interest and concern was reflected in the establishment of a committee in 1802 to provide for the efficient oversight and government of the school. It was soon concerned with falling rolls at a time of economic difficulties.

The Dissenting population of Lancaster also provided for their own educational requirements. The Friends' School was established in 1690 but suffered from official persecution which gradually relaxed in the eighteenth century. It competed for pupils with the Grammar School but also subsisted on the basis of fees and charity. Other children were sent away to school, including the Independents' Academy in Warrington. Few Dissenters were prepared to have their children educated by Anglicans. In the late eighteenth century they also developed a social exclusiveness. Nevertheless, the needs of the poor, regardless of creed, were partly provided for by the Charity (or Blue Coat) Schools for Boys in 1770 (in the Chapel of Penny's Hospital) and Girls in 1772 (on High Street). Instruction was provided in the three 'Rs', although only 450 boys – mostly the sons of craftsmen – received free instruction between 1770 and 1816.[181] The education of the girls was partly paid for by the product of their own labour in knitting, spinning and sewing.[182]Anglican and Dissenting evangelical influence was felt in religious education with the establishment of Sunday Schools in Lancaster from 1787.[183] The Evangelicals and the churches generally were very much on the side of law and order. Housman preached against rebels and the principles of the French Revolution and Radicalism. Education was highly selective on the basis of religion, social position and personal acquaintance, and although reflecting a charitable disposition, it upheld the social order and was used to keep the lower class in its place.

The lower class was not without its own response to its condition. Mutual self-help, provided on a very personal basis, was later supplemented by the Friendly Societies (particularly in the period 1793–1815), which received contributions and paid benefits to its members in need. In 1797 there were eighteen societies in Lancaster, including three female societies (plus the Marine Society from 1792 for the wives and children of normally wealthier Masters and Mates of Lancaster ships).[184] In 1804, at their peak, their membership totalled 3,313, one third of the population, but they declined during the subsequent period of economic hardship, especially in the post-war years from 1815, as migration from Lancaster increased and income declined.[185] The Samaritan Society founded in 1787 continued longer as a sick pay and funeral club for persons aged twenty to thirty. These organisations played an important part in alleviating the worst hardships.[186]

The results of the charitable and philanthropic activities of Lancaster's wealthier classes, and Lancastrian self-help, appear to have been important in reconciling the urban working class to the established order. Merchant paternalism and the personal contacts allowed by the comparatively small size of Lancaster were also important factors in the apparently limited radicalism of the working class. The town's role as a port also appears to have united the population in hostility to the French and the American rebels in wartime. Overall, however, there is a shortage of evidence concerning radical activities. A strong body of opinion was certainly against the radicals and a loyal declaration of 1792 contained over 2,000 signatures in support of the 1688 constitution and existing 'liberties', and expressing opposition to 'seditious' writings and civil disorder. In 1795 a procession of local Friendly Societies, including a band playing 'God Save the King' and 'Rule Britannia', reflected patriotic working-class loyalties in the town.[187] Cragg seems to imply that the gatherings were more concerned with drinking.[188] But there was other evidence of a working class political awareness and organised labour, seen in at least one strike by journeymen at Brockbank's shipyard in 1798 and a petition by journeymen shipwrights in Lancaster against the draconian Combination Acts (outlawing labour organisations and meetings) in 1799.[189] The Chamber of Trade petitioned Parliament in 1779 against 'a combination of masters and vessels in this port'.[190]

Nevertheless, Lancaster did not have a large textile industry and, unlike the South Lancashire towns, it had few hand-loom weavers, a group particularly associated with political agitation. Textile production was concentrated in scattered country villages and largely involved spinning. The Lancaster workshops and early mills were limited in number and size and subject to paternalistic control. As port and market town, as well as manufacturing centre, Lancaster had a very broad occupational base. Household theft, which increased in response to economic hardship, certainly became more common in the 1780s and led the Corporation to open a subscription for a town watch. It was not until 1790, however, that a private watchman was hired by individual subscribers to patrol the main streets, supporting the efforts of two town sergeants and parish constables. The most significant elements in maintaining order, however, were the army and militia. Regular army garrisons were installed in the Castle in times of emergency and supplemented the Lancaster Volunteers (founded in 1795) and Lonsdale Local Militia. One of the most significant reasons for the weakening of working class discontent after 1800, however, was the economic decline at Lancaster which was responsible for much migration to Liverpool and elsewhere.[191]

Decline and Transition

The economic changes from 1800 were of fundamental significance to the development of the town. Transatlantic commerce entered a terminal decline and, in 1802, Lancaster's first industrial textile mill opened. The confidence of her powerful merchant elite, largely responsible for the building of the Lancaster Canal which made industrial development possible, now evaporated and the community gradually dispersed. The favourable conjunction of economic and geographical factors which allowed Lancaster to flourish in the eighteenth century had been steadily eroded. It lacked the populous hinterland and developing industry possessed by Liverpool and South Lancashire. The canal, Glasson Dock and Thornbush were all responses to these factors and the need to maintain and develop trade.

The decline was sharp after 1800. Shipping paying dues at Lancaster reached 29,564 tons in 1799, 29,861 tons in 1800 but fell to only 12,171 tons in 1803 after the Peace of Amiens (1802). It fluctuated and peaked again in 1810, fell at the end of the war in 1815 and only began to recover its former health around 1820. West Indies trade fell from 11,562 tons in 1799 to 1,668 tons in 1802. Between 1804 and 1814 it averaged under 3,800 tons. The difficulties facing Lancaster merchants were legion. Depredations by French privateers, and natural causes, led to a rate of ship loss in the 1790s which Schofield put as high as fifty-three per cent.[192] Commodity price fluctuation was worsened by wartime interruption of supply and demand. Convoys, made compulsory in 1798, operated to and from Liverpool and not only depressed commodity prices when their arrival glutted the market, but also drew Lancaster more into the influence of Liverpool. Lancaster merchants and ships were increasingly based there. The wars also increased costs: insurance premiums were high, the arming of merchant ships decreased the amount of space available for cargo, and larger crews were required to man them. The swings of the 1790s ended in a boom which collapsed following a bumper sugar harvest in 1799, and the disruption of the European market. Liverpool and Lancaster merchants petitioned for, and received, Exchequer Bills to the amount of £500,000 to remain solvent.

The chances of recovery diminished. After 1800 the West Indian sugar isles declined in prosperity and productivity. Soils were exhausted, estates badly run and slavery, the basis of the plantation economy, was undermined and eventually abolished. Profits on the estates virtually vanished by 1807. Lancaster's other major West Indies import, cotton, was increasingly imported via Liverpool and from the American states with which she had little trade. Cotton and sugar from both North and South America were increasingly sold on the European market in competition with British supplies, reducing the re-export trade. Imports of other West Indies goods, such as coffee, declined in proportion. The economic depression at the end of the Napoleonic war led to a final slump in the town's West Indies trade and for a few years continued as a pale shadow of its former self. The Corporation petitioned hopefully for the abolition of the East India Company's monopoly of trade to India in 1815, but it was too late.[193]

Timber imports from Canada increased from 1807, however, to offset reduced supplies from the Baltic which were interrupted by the war and the American embargo on British trade in 1807. Although Canada became Lancaster's largest source of trade by tonnage it was not as extensive or as profitable as the West Indies trade.[194] Furthermore, the local industries which used flax, hemp, timber and tar were not only subject to supply and price fluctuations but found much of Lancaster shipping haemorrhaging to Liverpool, thus reducing the market for ship materials. Between 1800 and 1803 thirty-two Lancaster ships (5,985 tons) were re-registered at Liverpool, over half the average overseas volume of the 1790s.[195] Coastal trade, based on the entrepot role of Lancaster, suffered accordingly. Shipbuilding by Brockbank's staggered on until 1817, and at Worthington & Ashburner's (successors to James and Caleb Smith who moved to Liverpool) until 1827, but supplying merchants predominantly from London and Liverpool rather than Lancaster. War, political disputes and economic change had a disastrous effect on

'Lancaster from the East', by Gideon Yates, 1811. Watercolour. A vessel can be seen in Brockbank's shipyard on Green Ayre, for whose convenience the Old Bridge had begun to be demolished. St George's Quay, beyond, had begun a slow decline from the peak of activity in the 1790s.

Lancaster shipping and related industry. The basis of her eighteenth-century trade vanished.

Lancaster slave merchants, such as Thomas Hinde & Sons, had already transferred their operations to Liverpool (as required by law in 1799). The Rawlinsons had long-established connections there. Members of the Salisbury family moved to Liverpool, as did the Charnleys, Beakbanes, Moores, Willcocks and others, together with manufacturing firms which included two tallow-chandlers and a soap-boiler. Other merchants moved to country estates or family homes in the vicinity, such as Thomas Inman to Silverdale (whose younger brother's family established the Inman Line at Liverpool).[196] Some entered the legal and medical professions and the church. Alexander Worswick & Co. and Burrow & Mason appear to have moved their West Indies ships into the Liverpool–London trade. Merchants in foreign trade who paid the voluntary Lancaster trade tax declined in number and payments ceased altogether in 1810. Others listed in trade directories declined from thirty-four in 1787 to only eighteen in 1809.[197]

Referring to the crises from 1799, Edward Baines (1836) wrote that five 'principal merchant houses were obliged to wind up their affairs under circumstances of extreme embarrassment, and the shock has never since been fully recovered'.[198] These were only a small number of the total merchant population, however, and mostly smaller investors tempted into the trade in the booming 1790s. George Danson, who was bankrupted in 1801, managed to survive in business as an agent for West Indies goods and Danzig wheat imported via Liverpool and died in Jamaica in 1812.[199] Some went out of business for natural reasons. The Rawlinson brothers were both dead by 1803, although their cousin Thomas's firm continued after his death in 1802.[200]

Other West Indies merchants, however, diversified into industrial development. Thomas Hodgson had bought the Low Mill, Caton in 1784, and Thomas Hinde developed the Dolphinholme Mill for worsted yarn spinning. In 1802, George Burrow, son of a West Indies merchant, and Thomas Mason, opened the White Cross Mill in Lancaster which was supplied with coal from the canal alongside. Minor cotton spinning workshops in the streets and yards in the town seem to have declined with textile mill competition and even the mills were not as conveniently situated in Lancaster for supplies of coal and cotton. The town was not able to develop a large industrial base in the early years of the nineteenth century and manufacturing was limited to small-scale handicraft production as before. Now, however, the shipping-related industries declined, together with the candle and soap-making industries which relied on exports to the West Indies. Except for Gillow's, which had extensive commercial contacts and London showrooms, cabinetmakers were also hit by the West Indies decline. Tobacco and snuff manufacturers and dyers survived in their small-scale workshops and imported materials from Liverpool. Metalworking also continued.[201] Only very slowly was Lancaster able to replace its maritime commerce with industrial manufacture.

In the period of transition Lancaster relapsed into a form of polite gentrification associated with her role as a service centre and in the administration of the law. Coincidentally, however, even the role of Lancaster as a county assize town was threatened, placing her even more on the defensive in the early nineteenth century. The growth of population and towns in South Lancashire encouraged demands as early as the 1780s for a more convenient centrally-situated meeting place for the assizes and Court of Common Pleas. In 1798, following disagreements between the Lonsdale magistrates and colleagues in the rest of Lancashire, county business in the General Sessions was adjourned to Preston. It was made permanent by Act of Parliament the same year, against strong Lancaster and Lonsdale opposition which included mobilisation of Lowther and Hamilton interests in Parliament. The Corporation set about fending off any further assault on its position, helped by the already large investment in the county prison and courts at Lancaster Castle (and its role as the county lunatic asylum) which weighed against transfer of business elsewhere. To maintain the asylum in Lancaster the Corporation offered a free site on the Moor for a proposed new building, eventually opened in 1816.[202]

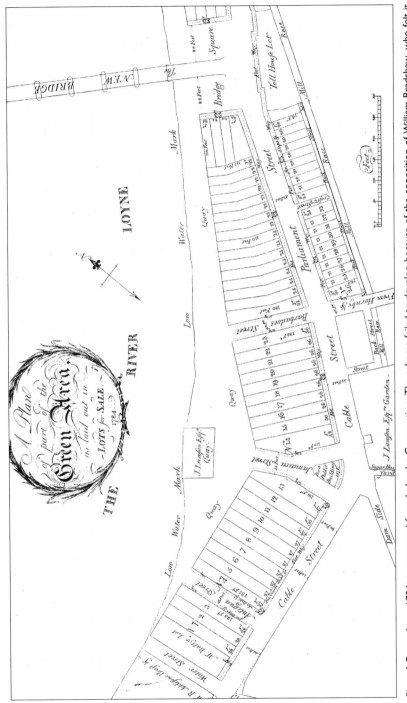

Plan of Green Ayre, 1784, as proposed for sale by the Corporation. The scheme failed to develop because of the opposition of William Bradshaw, who felt it infringed his own property rights, and, like Dalton Square, it fell victim to changed enonomic fortunes at the end of the eighteenth century.

The economic position after 1800 – inflation during the French wars, declining income and the cost of opposing the move of the annual general sessions to Preston – all undermined the financial position of the Corporation. It also suffered administratively due to the departure and unavailability of many leading merchants, and from related inefficiency in the management of its assets which was already apparent in the 1790s. Town improvements virtually came to an end and the initiative passed to private residents who, if they joined forces, were able to press the Corporation to act. In 1813, following a meeting of borough householders, it agreed to pay for a new sewer along Pudding Lane and Calkeld Lane to the Mill Dam, thereby accommodating surface run-off from the three main streets (Church, Market and Penny Streets). It was the only addition to the single sewer running from Stonewell into the Mill Race.[203] Civic inactivity was partly due to the legal challenges to the Corporation's actions by reluctant appointees to office (who could be fined by the Corporation for refusing) and by those who opposed the constitutional exclusivity of the Corporation. The effect was administrative seizure and lack of corporate confidence which was only partly overcome by the new Charter of 1819.

In the early years of the nineteenth century, however, the traditional paternalism of the merchant elite continued – in the absence of improvement commissions – together with a wider concern for the town's interests: what Gooderson calls 'a sense of total responsibility derived from long traditions and unrestricted powers'.[204] Street lighting and improvement, for example, continued to be regarded as its responsibility even though its financial position was weak and its first responsibility was to the freeman body. Even after 1800 the Corporation continued to be dominated by the old merchant elite, who both maintained a strong link with the local gentry and involved themselves in the affairs of the town, often in charitable concerns.[205] They increasingly socialised with the Dissenting community, however, while the rising industrial middle class and tradesmen were beginning to make their presence and involvement felt in town affairs. Nevertheless, in the dog days between the decline of maritime commerce and a more pronounced nineteenth-century industrial development in the town, the old ways continued. Soon they would disappear.

Lancaster suffered a form of relapse after 1800, declining from a position of almost unexpected affluence to a reduced gentility which was perhaps more to be expected. Many of the changes evident in social and religious affairs were mirrored in towns across the country, but the improvements were greatly assisted by the prosperity she experienced. This wealth encouraged the emergence of a responsible, paternalistic, refined urban elite, generally tolerant of diverse opinions – a characteristic often associated with the more cosmopolitan outlook of ports. The new cooperation was reflected in the commercial institutions that emerged, and in the policies of the Corporation which played an increasingly active role in pursuit of the wider interests of the town. The same attitude of improvement was apparent in the field of social welfare. Personal responsibility and Corporation generosity were, however, both undermined after 1800 just when urbanisation and industrial development were demanding sustained involvement. The town was forced to rebuild almost from scratch, but the new institutions were on different lines, responding to the demands of modern urban society.

Notes

1. Celia Fiennes in J. Hillaby (ed.), *The Journeys of Celia Fiennes*, 1983, 219.
2. John Crofts in B. G. Hutton, 'A Lakeland journey, 1759', *Transactions of the Cumberland and Westmorland Antiquarian and Archaeological Society*, LXI, 1961, 289–90.
3. Anonymous diary of a journey from Scotland to Nottingham, c. 1764, M380. Nottinghamshire Archives Office, 74, 78.
4. D. M. Clark, 'The Economic and Social Geography of Rural Lonsdale 1801–1861', unpublished MA dissertation, Department of Geography, University of Liverpool, May 1968, 12.
5. J. H. Sutton, 'The Lancaster Agricultural Society 1799–1977', unpublished typescript in Lancaster Reference Library, MS258, May 1978; J. K. Walton, *Lancashire. A Social History 1558–1939*, Manchester University Press, 1987, 75.
6. Clark, 'The Economic and Social Geography of Rural Lonsdale', 11; Walton *Lancashire*, 78–9; J. D. Marshall, *Lancashire*, 1974, 49.
7. Celia Fiennes in Hillaby (ed.), *The Journeys of Celia Fiennes*, 219.
8. R. Craig and M. M. Schofield, 'The trade of Lancaster in William Stout's time', in J. D. Marshall (ed.), *The Autobiography of William Stout of Lancaster*, Chetham Society, 1967, 24–5; William Stout in Marshall, entry for 1697, 119–20.
9. P. Rogers (ed.), *Daniel Defoe. A Tour Through the Whole Island of Great Britain*, 1989, 8–10; Daniel Defoe in Rogers, 195; Craig and Schofield, 'The trade of Lancaster in William Stout's time', 36.
10. Thomas Coxe quoted in M. M. Schofield, *Outlines of an Economic History of Lancaster from 1680–1860*, I, Lancaster Branch of the Historical Association, 1946, 14; James Ray quoted in Craig and Schofield, 'The trade of Lancaster in William Stout's time', 36.
11. William Stout in Marshall (ed.), *The Autobiography of William Stout*, entries for 1689 and 1703, 95, 144–6; Craig and Schofield, 'The trade of Lancaster in William Stout's time', 26–7.
12. Craig and Schofield, 'The trade of Lancaster in William Stout's time', 27–30; Schofield, *Economic History of Lancaster*, I, 10–11; H. Cunliffe, *The Story of Sunderland Point*, 1984, 5–11; A. M. Kay, 'The Slave Trade and the Economic Development of Eighteenth Century Lancaster', unpublished MLitt thesis, Department of History, University of Lancaster, 1988, 20ff.
13. R. Craig and M. M. Schofield, Appendix A: 'Excerpts from the public records relating to William Stout's shipping ventures', in Marshall (ed.), *The Autobiography of William Stout*, 282–91; William Stout in Marshall (ed.), *The Autobiography of William Stout*, entry for 1730, 206; Schofield, *Economic History of Lancaster*, I, 11; M. M. Schofield, 'The letter book of Benjamin Satterthwaite, 1737–1744', *Transactions of the Historic Society of Lancashire and Cheshire*, 113, 1960, 138.

14. M. E. Burkett, E. Tyson and D. How, *The Furniture of Gillow of Lancaster*, 1977, 6; Craig and Schofield, 'The trade of Lancaster in William Stout's time', 40, 58–9.

15. Schofield, 'The letter book of Benjamin Satterthwaite', 130.

16. P. J. Corfield, *The Impact of English Towns 1700–1800*, 1982, 36, quoting BL Add MSS 11,255 and Add MSS 38,432.

17. Craig and Schofield, 'The trade of Lancaster in William Stout's time', 36–52.

18. John Crofts in Hutton, 'A Lakeland journey, 1759', 290.

19. A. Young, *A Six Months Tour Through the North of England*, III, 1771, 152.

20. List of ship numbers and tonnages trading to Lancaster 1750–1845, compiled at the Tonnage Office, Lancaster, Lancaster City Museums (Maritime Museum). Schofield states that the number peaked at 53 ships in 1800, *Economic History of Lancaster*, I, 25.

21. Schofield, *Economic History of Lancaster*, I, 194, 256.

22. Schofield, *Economic History of Lancaster*, I, 21.

23. John Britton quoted in *Economic History of Lancaster*, 1, 30; M. M. Schofield, 'Shoes, ships and sealing wax: eighteenth century Lancashire exports to the colonies', *Transactions of the Historic Society of Lancashire and Cheshire*, 135, 1985, 61–82.

24. Kay, 'The Slave Trade and the Economic Development of Eighteenth Century Lancaster', 8, 12–3, 26; Schofield, *Economic History of Lancaster*, I, 26–9; M. M. Schofield, 'The slave trade from Lancashire and Cheshire ports outside Liverpool *c.* 1750–*c.* 1790', *Transactions of the Historic Society of Lancashire and Cheshire*, 126, 1977, 30–72. For details of Dodshon Foster see Melinda Elder (née Kay), 'Dodshon Foster of Lancaster and the West Indies 1730–93', *Lancaster Maritime Journal*, 1, 1997, 14–18, Lancaster City Museums.

25. Craig and Schofield, 'The trade of Lancaster in William Stout's time', 39–40; Schofield, *Economic History of Lancaster*, I, 15. Margaret Robinson, '"An Intercourse of Trade": Coastal Shipping in the North West, 1700–1750', in the University of Lancaster *CNWRS Regional Bulletin*, NS, No. 13, Summer 1999, 30–7.

26. Schofield, *Economic History of Lancaster*, I, 31–2.

27. Schofield, 'The letter book of Benjamin Satterthwaite', 135–7.

28. J. D. Marshall, *Furness and the Industrial Revolution*, 1958, 82–96; W. H. Chalenor, 'William Stout and the Backbarrow Iron Company', in Marshall (ed.), *The Autobiography of William Stout*, 295–6; Schofield, *Economic History of Lancaster*, I, 32–3.

29. William Stout in Marshall (ed.), *The Autobiography of William Stout*, entry for 1743, 237.

30. Craig and Schofield, 'The trade of Lancaster in William Stout's time', 46.

31. E. Kennerley, *The Brockbanks of Lancaster – The Story of an 18th Century Shipbuilding Firm*, Lancaster City Museum, 1981, 2–3, 6; Nigel Dalziel, 'A Lancaster Shipbuilder's Daybook 1722–27', *Lancaster Maritime Journal*, 1, 1997, 4–13.

32. Anonymous diary of a journey from Scotland to Nottinghamshire, *c.* 1764, 74.

33. David Cragg quoted in 'Gleanings in Local History', Scrapbook 2, Lancaster Reference Library, 3.

34. Information held on Lancaster ship database TSHIP at Lancaster City Museums (Maritime Museum).

35. Kennerley, *The Brockbanks of Lancaster*, 11, 14.

36. Entry for 18 January 1781 quoted in Kennerley, *The Brockbanks of Lancaster*, 12.

37. D. J. Starkey, *British Privateering Enterprise in the Eighteenth Century*, 1990, 165, 322, 323.

38. Starkey, *British Privateering Enterprise in the Eighteenth Century*, 205, 225; Kennerley, *The Brockbanks of Lancaster*, 12–13.

39. Nelly Weeton in E. Hall (ed.), *Miss Weeton, Journal of a Governess 1807–11*, I, 1936, 7–11.

40. Letter from Captain John Charnley to Suart, Housman & Co., 10 November 1804, quoted in the *Lancaster Gazette*, 22 December 1804, p. 3, c. 4; T. Cann Hughes, *Captain John Charnley of the Thetis, Freeman of Lancaster*, n.d.

41. 'Resolution of shipowners to the effect that when a ship had provided its quota of men for the Navy, it should be exempt from impress, 1795', General Folder 1, Port Commission Records, Lancaster Reference Library.

42. Entry of 5 June 1783 quoted in Kennerley, *The Brockbanks of Lancaster*, 13.

43. D. J. Starkey, 'The economic and military significance of British privateering 1702–83', *Journal of Transport History*, 9, 1, 1988, 50–9; Starkey, *British Privateering Enterprise in the Eighteenth Century*, 268 ff.

44. Schofield, *Economic History of Lancaster*, I, 36, 40.

45. T. Pennant, *Tour in Scotland*, 1772, i, 1726, 23.

46. Young, *A Six Months Tour Through the North of England*, 152.

47. J. W. A. Price, *The Industrial Archaeology of the Lune Valley*, Lancaster University, Centre for North-West Regional Studies, 1983, 56.

48. Schofield, *Economic History of Lancaster*, I, 43; K. H. Docton, 'Lancaster 1684', *Transactions of the Historic Society of Lancashire and Cheshire*, 109, 1957.

49. Quoted in Hutton, 'A Lakeland journey, 1759', 59.

50. Price, *The Industrial Archaeology of the Lune Valley*, 14–30.

51. Price, *The Industrial Archaeology of the Lune Valley*, 14; also, Russian lead bale seals discovered at Yealand Conyers and Lancaster, LM86.16, Lancaster City Museums (Maritime Museum).

52. F. J. Singleton, 'The Flax Merchants of Kirkham', *Transactions of the Historic Society of Lancashire and Cheshire*, 126, 1977; J. Corry, *History of Lancashire*, 2, 1825.

53. J. Price, 'Iron making at Halton', *Contrebis*, 9, 1981, 23.

54. J. Marshall, 'Early local iron industry', *Lancaster Comment*, 67, 3 June 1976, University of Lancaster.

55. Craig and Schofield, 'The trade of Lancaster in William Stout's time', 53–7.

56. Kay, 'The Slave Trade and the Economic Development of Eighteenth Century Lancaster', 19–23.

57. Schofield, 'The letter book of Benjamin Satterthwaite', 130–1, 141; L. Namier and J. Brook, *The House of Commons 1754–1790*, III, 1964, 348.

58. Craig and Schofield, 'The trade of Lancaster in William Stout's time', 61–3.

59. John Crofts in Hutton, 'A Lakeland journey, 1759', 290.

60. Anonymous diary of a journey from Scotland to Nottinghamshire, c. 1764, 72, 74.

61. T. West, *A Guide to the Lakes*, 1772, 23. The Custom House is now occupied by the Lancaster Maritime Museum.

62. J. B. Shaw, 'The construction of Glasson Dock', in *History of the Port of Lancaster*, n.d., articles originally printed in the *Lancaster Observer*, 1926–7.

63. Shaw, 'Introduction to a lighthouse', in *History of the Port of Lancaster*.

64. Schofield, *Economic History of Lancaster*, I, 29, 51.

65. Corfield, *The Impact of English Towns 1700–1800*, 90–3.

66. 'Thornbush' Folders, items 1–3, Port Commission Records, Lancaster Reference Library; Shaw, *History of the Port of Lancaster*.

67. C. Clark, *An Historical and Descriptive Account of the Town of Lancaster*, 1807, 57–8; P. Gooderson, 'The Social and Economic History of Lancaster 1780–1914', unpublished PhD thesis, Department of History, University of Lancaster, 1975, 28, 66.

68. Gooderson, 'The Social and Economic History of Lancaster', 90–1.

69. Quoted in Schofield, *Economic History of Lancaster*, I, 36.

70. Gooderson, 'The Social and Economic History of Lancaster', 88.

71. 'Cross Fleury', *Time Honoured Lancaster*, Lancaster, 1891, 488–91.

72. Gooderson, 'The Social and Economic History of Lancaster', 91.

73. Walton, *Lancashire*, 92.

74. E. Baines, *The History of the County Palatine and Duchy of Lancaster*, I, 1888, 326–34.

75. William Stout in Marshall (ed.), *The Autobiography of William Stout*, entry for 1715, 173.

76. Quoted in W. O. Roper, *Materials for the History of Lancaster*, James Stewart, 1907, 70.

77. 'Cross Fleury', *Time Honoured Lancaster*, 152; Baines, *The History of the County Palatine and Duchy of Lancaster*, 330.

78. W. G. Howson, footnote 210 in Marshall (ed.), *The Autobiography of William Stout*, 270.

79. William Stout in Marshall (ed.), *The Autobiography of William Stout*, entry for 1716, 176.

80. Anon., *Leighton Hall*, Derby, 1989, 3; 'Gleanings in Local History', Scrapbook 2, Lancaster Reference Library.

81. Roper, *Materials for the History of Lancaster*, 86–99; 'Cross Fleury', *Time Honoured Lancaster*, 153–5.

82. Craig and Schofield, 'The trade of Lancaster in William Stout's time', 58–9; William Stout in Marshall (ed.), *The Autobiography of William Stout*, entry for 1715, 172.

83. M. Reed, *The Georgian Triumph (1700–1830)*, 1983, 197.

84. West, *A Guide to the Lakes*, 23.

85. M. Girouard, *The English Town*, 1990, 86; A. White, *The Buildings of Georgian Lancaster*, University of Lancaster, Centre for North-West Regional Studies, 2nd edn, 2000.

86. Young, *A Six Months Tour Through the North of England*, III, 152. This description was echoed by an anonymous ('W. M.') Lake District journal of 1817, Cheshire Record Office, DDX224, 19.

87. West, *A Guide to the Lakes*, 23.

88. 'Cross Fleury', *Time Honoured Lancaster*, 230–2.

89. Clark, *An Historical and Descriptive Account of the Town of Lancaster*, 45.

90. Quoted in D. Foskett, *John Harden of Brathay Hall 1772–1847*, 1974, 6.

91. West, *A Guide to the Lakes*, 24.

92. 'Cross Fleury', *Time Honoured Lancaster*, 5.

93. T. Cann Hughes, *Notes on the County Town of Lancaster in the Eighteenth Century*, 1935, 19–20.
94. Quoted in Hutton, 'A Lakeland journey, 1759', 290.
95. West, *A Guide to the Lakes*, 25. A description of the guide in use can be read in William Monson's diary, 1816, Lincolnshire Archives Office, 15/B/2.
96. William Wilberforce in C. E. Wrangham (ed.), *Journey to the Lake District from Cambridge – A Summer Diary*, 1779, 1983, 44.
97. Rev. W. MacRitchie, *Diary of a Tour Through Great Britain in 1795*, 1897, 35. Piel Castle is near Barrow-in-Furness.
98. *Cumberland Pacquet*, 25 June 1782, p. 2, c. 4, quoted in A. G. Betjemann, *The Grand Theatre, Lancaster: Two Centuries of Entertainment*, Lancaster, 1982, 3.
99. *Cumberland Pacquet*, 20 August 1782, p. 2, c. 4, quoted in Betjemann, *The Grand Theatre*, 6.
100. MacRitchie, *Diary of a Tour Through Great Britain in 1795*, 35.
101. *The Monthly Mirror*, August 1799, quoted in Betjemann, *The Grand Theatre*, 9.
102. Betjemann, *The Grand Theatre*, 1–16; Hughes, *Notes on the County Town of Lancaster*, 8–9.
103. John Crofts in Hutton, 'A Lakeland journey, 1759', 290.
104. Gooderson, 'The Social and Economic History of Lancaster', 59; handbill, 'Lancaster Races, 1816', Scrapbook 1, Lancaster Reference Library, 218.
105. Hughes, *Notes on the County Town of Lancaster*, 20; J. Binns, 'A Map of the Town & Castle of Lancaster, 1821'.
106. Hughes, *Notes on the County Town of Lancaster*, 7, 9.
107. Gooderson, 'The Social and Economic History of Lancaster', 143, 148.
108. Walton, *Lancashire*, 98–9; Reed, *The Georgian Triumph*, 195–6.
109. Corfield, *The Impact of English Towns*, 143.
110. *Cumberland Pacquet*, 1 December 1778, quoted in 'Lancaster 100 Years Ago', Scrapbook 2, Lancaster Reference Library, 33.
111. 'Cross Fleury', *Time Honoured Lancaster*, 457 ff.
112. 'Cross Fleury', *Time Honoured Lancaster*, 222.
113. E. Kennerley, *William Penny and Penny's Almshouses*, Lancaster City Museums, Local Studies, 3.
114. Schofield, *Economic History of Lancaster*, I, 51–2.
115. 'Gleanings in Local History', Scrapbook 2, Lancaster Reference Library, 5.
116. William Stout in Marshall (ed.). *The Autobiography of William Stout*, entry for 1680–81, 77–8; W. G. Howson, Appendix B: 'Distraints suffered by William Stout, 1698–1747', in Marshall (ed.), 292–3.
117. William Stout in Marshall (ed.), *The Autobiography of William Stout*, entry for 1721, 182–3.
118. William Stout in Marshall (ed.), *The Autobiography of William Stout*, entry for 1680–81, 78–9.
119. 'Cross Fleury', *Time Honoured Lancaster*, 40; Clark, *An Historical and Descriptive Account of the Town of Lancaster*, 33–40.
120. Girouard, *The English Town*, 87.
121. E. Kennerley, 'Lancaster inns and alehouses 1600–1730', *The Lancashire Local Historian*, 5, 1990, 50; *Pigot's Commercial Directory*, 1818–20, 184–9.
122. *Universal British Directory*, 1799, 624.
123. J. Satchell, *Kendal on Tenterhooks*, 1984, 31.

124. Hughes, *Notes on the County Town of Lancaster*, 21, 28.
125. Hughes, *Notes on the County Town of Lancaster*, 20.
126. Anonymous diary of a journey from Scotland to Nottingham *c.* 1764, Nottinghamshire Record Office, M380, 78.
127. 'Gleanings in Local History', Scrapbook 2, Lancaster Reference Library, 2.
128. Hughes, *Notes on the County Town of Lancaster*, 28, 30.
129. Celia Fiennes in Hillaby (ed.), *The Journeys of Celia Fiennes*, 219.
130. See George Thornhill of Diddington, diary of a journey from Northamptonshire to Lancashire, 1760, Huntingdonshire Records Office, 148/5/274, 18; West, *A Guide to the Lakes, c.*1772, 23.
131. J. Champness, *Lancashire's Architectural Heritage*, 1989, 86; Hughes, *Notes on the County Town of Lancaster*, 10–11.
132. James Mackenzie, diary of a journey from Scotland to London, 1792, typescript in Lancaster City Museum, 54.
133. Corporation Minutes in Gooderson, 'The Social and Economic History of Lancaster', 101.
134. Gooderson, 'The Social and Economic History of Lancaster', 100–1.
135. Hughes, *Notes on the County Town of Lancaster*, 7; 'Cross Fleury', *Time Honoured Lancaster*, 40.
136. West, *A Guide to the Lakes*, 22–3.
137. Clark, 'A Plan of the Town of Lancaster, 1807', in *An Historical and Descriptive Account of the Town of Lancaster*.
138. Quoted in Schofield, *Outlines of an Economic History of Lancaster*, II, 1951, 50.
139. Schofield, *Economic History of Lancaster*, II, 48–68.
140. G. Fandrey, *The Craggs of Greenbank*, privately printed, Springside, Saskatchewan, 1977, 12; Girouard, *The English Town*, 91–2.
141. Roper, *Materials for the History of Lancaster*, 231.
142. Anonymous diary of a journey from Scotland to Nottinghamshire, *c.* 1764, 76.
143. Clark, *An Historical and Descriptive Account of the Town of Lancaster*, 24.
144. Clark, *An Historical and Descriptive Account of the Town of Lancaster*, 23, 25, 27.
145. MacRitchie, *Diary of a Tour Through Great Britain in 1795*, entry for 3 July, 35.
146. Roper, *Materials for the History of Lancaster*, 242. Roper states the capacity to be 2,000 persons.
147. Clark, *An Historical and Descriptive Account of the Town of Lancaster*, 23; J. Britton, *The Beauties of England and Wales*, IX, 1807, 60–2.
148. 'Gleanings in Local History', Scrapbook 2, Lancaster Reference Library, 1.
149. Roper, *Materials for the History of Lancaster*, 243.
150. A. L. Murray, *The Royal Grammar School Lancaster, A History*, Heffer, 1952, 114.
151. Corfield, *The Impact of English Towns*, 173.
152. Girouard, *The English Town*, 126.
153. Girouard, *The English Town*, 54.
154. Clark, 'The Economic and Social Geography of Rural Lonsdale', 11; Walton, *Lancashire*, 76–7.
155. John Crofts in Hutton, 'A Lakeland journey, 1759', 289–90.
156. J. Holt, *General View of the Agriculture of the County of Lancaster (1795)*, 1969, 13.
157. Clark, *An Historical and Descriptive Account of the Town of Lancaster*, 120.
158. Gooderson, 'The Social and Economic History of Lancaster', 26.

159. Clark, *An Historical and Descriptive Account of the Town of Lancaster*, 56–7, 119–20.
160. 'Cross Fleury', *Time Honoured Lancaster*, 540.
161. S. H. Penney, *Lancaster: The Evolution of its Townscape to 1800*, University of Lancaster, Centre for North-West Regional Studies, 1981, 31.
162. Hughes, *Notes on the County Town of Lancaster*, 16.
163. Agreement with the Port Commission, 'Lancaster' folder 7, Port Commission Records, Lancaster Reference Library.
164. West, *A Guide to the Lakes*, 23.
165. Gooderson, 'The Social and Economic History of Lancaster', 137.
166. William Stout in Marshall (ed.), *The Autobiography of William Stout*, entry for 1727, 196.
167. 'Cross Fleury', *Time Honoured Lancaster*, 42–4.
168. 'Cross Fleury', *Time Honoured Lancaster*, 41; Clark, *An Historical and Descriptive Account of the Town of Lancaster*, 48–9.
169. Gooderson, 'The Social and Economic History of Lancaster', 120.
170. Hughes, *Notes on the County Town of Lancaster*, 20.
171. Clark, *An Historical and Descriptive Account of the Town of Lancaster*, 46–7.
172. 'Gleanings in Local History', Scrapbook 2, Lancaster Reference Library, 3.
173. William Stout in Marshall (ed.), *The Autobiography of William Stout*, entry for 1725, 194.
174. Gooderson, 'The Social and Economic History of Lancaster', 138.
175. Clark, *An Historical and Descriptive Account of the Town of Lancaster*, 47.
176. 'Gleanings in Local History', Scrapbook 2. Lancaster Reference Library, 9; 'Cross Fleury', *Time Honoured Lancaster*, 376.
177. Gooderson, 'The Social and Economic History of Lancaster', footnote 11 and page 138; Corfield, *The Impact of English Towns*, 119–23.
178. Gooderson, 'The Social and Economic History of Lancaster', 138, 145; 'Cross Fleury', *Time Honoured Lancaster*, 376.
179. Murray, *The Royal Grammar School Lancaster*, 55, 63, 85, 87, 93.
180. Quoted in A. L. Murray, 'The school on Castle Hill', in J. L. Spencer (ed.), *The Royal Grammar School Lancaster – Quincentenary Commemorative Volume 1469–1969*, Neill & Co., 1969, 5.
181. Gooderson, 'The Social and Economic History of Lancaster', 137–8; Hughes, *Notes on the County Town of Lancaster*, 8.
182. 'Cross Fleury', *Time Honoured Lancaster*, 83.
183. Gooderson, 'The Social and Economic History of Lancaster', 141.
184. Clark, *An Historical and Descriptive Account of the Town of Lancaster*, 51.
185. Gooderson, 'The Social and Economic History of Lancaster', 130.
186. Clark, *An Historical and Descriptive Account of the Town of Lancaster*, 52.
187. Gooderson, 'The Social and Economic History of Lancaster', 121.
188. Fandrey, *The Craggs of Greenbank*, 37.
189. Kennerley, *The Brockbanks of Lancaster*, 15; C. R. Dobson, *Masters and Journeymen. A Prehistory of Industrial Relations 1717–1800*, 1980, 147.
190. Schofield, *Economic History of Lancaster*, I, 51.
191. Gooderson, 'The Social and Economic History of Lancaster', 43.
192. Schofield, *Economic History of Lancaster*, II, 14–5.
193. *Ibid.*, 22–3, 122–33.
194. *Ibid.*, 25–6.
195. Gooderson, 'The Social and Economic History of Lancaster', 38.

196. *Ibid.*, 42.
197. Schofield, *Economic History of Lancaster*, II, 22.
198. Quoted in Schofield, *Economic History of Lancaster*, II, 18.
199. Gooderson, 'The Social and Economic History of Lancaster', 40.
200. Schofield, *Economic History of Lancaster*, II, 21.
201. *Ibid.*, 121.
202. Gooderson, 'The Social and Economic History of Lancaster', 54–5, 60.
203. *Ibid.*, 102–3.
204. *Ibid.*, 109.
205. *Ibid.*, 71.

CHAPTER FIVE

The Town Transformed, 1815–1914[1]

Michael Winstanley

By 1914, although many of Lancaster's Georgian buildings survived, little remained of the trade and society which they represented. The port, once the hub of its economic life, had long since ceased to be of any importance and most of the industries which it had spawned had withered and died along with influential families which they and overseas trade had supported. The town's wealth and population were now dependent not on commerce, but on a new manufacturing empire providing work for thousands which specialised in the production of table baize, oilcloth and linoleum. A small but extremely wealthy group of local entrepreneurs had replaced the merchants and local gentry as the local social and political elite.

Population had quadrupled over the century, most of the increase taking place after 1870 in response to industrial growth and the expansion of massive institutions dedicated to caring for the sick, the poor and the mentally retarded. The built-up area and the borough's jurisdiction now extended into what had previously been separate rural townships: Skerton to the north, Bulk to the east and Scotforth to the south. The town's retail facilities had been dramatically restructured. No longer did they cater primarily for the relatively affluent and the surrounding rural areas. The working-class market was now much more important.

Transformations in provision of institutional services had been equally dramatic. In 1815, apart from the safety net provided by parish poor relief and the housing of prisoners in the castle, town and county authorities had been responsible for very little. Education, medical care, transport, basic urban amenities and cultural facilities were largely the domain of the churches, voluntary associations, public spirited individuals and charities or were only available to those able to pay for them. By 1914, although charitable and voluntary activity remained important – indeed, it had expanded – the increasing size and complexity of town life meant that local authorities were now much more involved in the provision of a wide range of services. The town's significant number of gentlemanly legal and medical practitioners who had relied heavily on the custom of wealthy merchant families and local gentry had given way to new class of salaried professionals, hired to provide what were increasingly seen as services for the benefit of society at large, not the exclusive privilege of rich individuals. Political control of the town, and representation in parliament, had been transferred from the rich Tory merchants and county gentry to the new Liberal manufacturing and retailing classes.

Much of the scale and general nature of this transformation reflected the patterns of development elsewhere in the country. But the timing and speed of many of the changes were peculiar to Lancaster. In the half century after Waterloo, while much of the North West boomed, the town stagnated. Unlike Liverpool it did not participate in the growth of overseas trade. Unlike south east Lancashire, it did not experience a dramatic growth in textile manufacturing. As the rest of the country gained in confidence and prosperity in the 1850s in the wake of the Great Exhibition, the town seemed poised to descend into terminal decline. Paradoxically, as national optimism waned and population growth slowed in the last quarter of the century, Lancaster's fortunes revived and confidence waxed, reflected in the extensive redevelopment of the town centre which is still clearly evident today.[2] Only during the Edwardian period did much of this buoyancy evaporate.

Trade and Transport

To understand this peculiar pattern of development we need to return first to the continuing collapse of Lancaster's maritime trade in the decades after 1815.[3] The depression which hit Britain in the immediate post-war years was amongst the worst in the century. Lancaster's underlying problems made it particularly vulnerable. As unemployment rocketed after 1817, poor rates reached record levels. In 1822 and 1826 respectively Thomas Worswick, Sons & Co. and Dilworth, Arthington and Birkett, the town's only banks, both privately owned, collapsed, taking with them thousands of pounds of accrued savings.

From the mid 1820s, however, there were hopeful signs of a trade recovery. Local capitalists pooled their resources to establish the Lancaster Banking Company in 1826, one of the first joint stock banks in the country. In the same year the canal spur from Galgate to Glasson Dock was completed and the number and tonnage of ships engaged in overseas and coastal trade and paying harbour dues at Lancaster began to show signs of revival. Unfortunately this did not herald a return to former glory. The reasons for this are various. In the first place the rich, exotic produce of the eighteenth century had been displaced by bulky; relatively low value cargoes of timber from the Baltic and Canada, and, to a lesser extent, grain from the Mediterranean and, subsequently, North America. Although some of the timber was used in local building work and the grain helped to fuel the development of animal feedstuffs processing in the town, trade no longer generated significant port

View of Lancaster from the Moor, 1854, published by Thomas Edmondson of Market Place. The distinctive skyline is still recognisable today although the factory chimneys and the fields which separated the town from Morecambe have long since disappeared. Soon after this print was published, parts of the Moor were laid out as a cemetery while the old council-owned quarries were landscaped to create Williamson Park in the late 1870s.

related industries as it had in the eighteenth century. Shipbuilding on the Lune had ceased by the early 1830s and was never successfully re-established despite an attempt to revive it in the 1860s by the Lune Shipbuilding Company.[4] Such activity as existed was confined to Glasson where the Liverpool-trained Daniel and Matthew Simpson, partnered initially by their relative, James Penny Nicholson, a Lancaster draper, opened a shipbuilding and repair yard in 1837 on Port Commission land.[5] Sailcloth manufacture, rope making, soap boiling, sugar refining and other industries directly dependent on overseas trade also disappeared or substantially contracted. Although Gillows retained its reputation for fine furniture, the family itself ceased to be actively involved with the firm. Richard Gillow, grandson of the originator of the business, effectively retired sometime between 1811 and 1814, withdrawing completely by the early 1830s after he had bought Leighton Hall near Carnforth in 1823 from his bankrupt cousins, the Worswicks.[6] From this time on it was increasingly obliged to import most of its hardwoods through Liverpool and to rely rather more on the competitive domestic market, rather than on the more lucrative export trade.

Cargo handling itself was also increasingly distanced from the town. It was Preston, then without adequate port facilities of its own, and land-locked Kendal, which the canal had finally reached in 1819, which benefited most from the canal's direct connection to the sea at Glasson. Although sales of timber continued to take place on Green Ayre into the 1840s, much of the cargo bypassed Lancaster entirely as local importers like John Stamp Burrell established their main handling procedures and storage at Glasson. Unlike the eighteenth century, many of the ships which visited the port and the cargoes they carried were not owned by local men. Apart from the income directly derived from trans-shipping, therefore, profits from trade increasingly lined the pockets of outsiders.

Many of these qualifications apply equally to the apparent revival in coastal trade from the mid-1820s. This, too, was largely confined to the carriage of bulk produce like grain, ore, coal and timber. The geographical area these cargoes originated from had changed little from the previous century. Despite a marked increase in imports from Irish east coast ports in the 1830s the majority of trade was with other north west ports, especially Liverpool and Ulverston. Much of this coastal trade contracted from the 1840s. Imports of Irish grain declined dramatically during and after the Great Famine of 1845–51 as Irish farmers shifted to dairy and meat products which were shipped in via the Mersey. The loss of this trade coincided with increasing competition from better placed ports and, even more significantly, the expansion of the rail network. Improvements in port facilities at Preston after 1846 largely circumvented that town's need to rely on Glasson. Railway companies also actively promoted Fleetwood and Morecambe around the same time the latter successfully creaming off most of Ulverston 's iron ore trade from Glasson, at least before the rail link from Carnforth to Barrow in 1857 killed it off entirely. Lancaster and Glasson in contrast received no such boost from railway capital. The locally owned canal company, which actually leased the troubled Lancaster and Preston Junction railway between 1842 and 1849, had no incentive to divert Glasson's trade off its waterway. When this bizarre situation ended, the line passed into the hands of the Lancaster and Carlisle and was subsequently leased (1859) and then taken over (1871) by the London and North Western, a company which had already invested heavily in promoting ports elsewhere. Despite the efforts of Edmund Sharpe, the prominent local engineer, architect and mayor of Lancaster in 1848–49, plans to revive St George's Quay itself by connecting it directly to the (Little) North Western Railway down the Lune valley to Yorkshire and, via a new canal, to Morecambe jetty, also foundered. The majority of the railway company's shareholders were not local and saw no point in building a canal to an obsolete port when a direct rail link to a new harbour at Morecambe was both feasible and cheaper.[7] Not until 1883 were Glasson and St George's Quay belatedly linked to the major railway network which had passed within sight and earshot for over half a century. Any revival this connection brought was curtailed by the Midland Railway Company's massive promotion of Heysham harbour, opened in 1904. Long before then, however, rail had largely supplanted coastal shipping as the major haulier of bulk produce and Lancaster's dependency on waterborne trade had long since evaporated.

As in many other Victorian towns, however, there were high hopes that

The North Western Railway Viaduct over the Lune (*Illustrated London News*), November 1849. The distinctive elegant curve is still evident on the road bridge which replaced this when the line to Morecambe was closed in 1965.

the coming of the railway would create new economic opportunities. With early connections to Preston (1840), Carlisle (1846), Morecambe (1848) and the Yorkshire textile towns (1850), Lancaster seemed well placed to benefit from the expansion of the network.[8] But these lines failed to generate significant commercial or industrial development in the town, at least before the 1860s; most of the jobs they created related directly to operational activities. None of the companies involved made Lancaster its main servicing centre: the Midland, which took control of the Little North Western Railway after 1852, formally leased it in 1858 and bought it out in 1871, concentrated its efforts on Carnforth and Derby; the Lancaster and Carlisle and the London & North Western, which absorbed it in 1879, focused on Carlisle. The direct control of the rail link to the south by the canal company till 1849 and subsequent collusive agreements between water and rail operators meant that the town did not reap the benefits of significantly lower carriage charges for bulk cargoes like grain and coal for nearly twenty years. The absence of industrial and commercial premises along the main north-south trunk route bears witness to the limited impact the line had on the location and expansion of local business. Textile mills, coal merchants and grain dealers tended to remain clustered on the east side of town or around the quay.

It is difficult, too, to see how the railways improved Lancaster's position as a marketing and service centre for North and South Lonsdale. Much of the village trade continued to rely on road transport and in particular on the network of carriers who called at public houses in Lancaster on market days. Railway connections from Oxenholme to Kendal and Windermere

Castle Railway Station, late 1860s. The site from which this view was taken was occupied by the County Hotel after 1870. The origins and purpose of the caravan remain a mystery.

(1847) and from Carnforth to Ulverston (1857) and Wennington (1867) undermined rather than strengthened North Lonsdale's dependence on Lancaster and finally killed off the cross-sands route across Morecambe Bay. By destroying the lucrative coaching trade and enabling long distance travellers to avoid an overnight stay in the town, railways also contributed to the decline of Lancaster's central hotels and the town's reputation as a fashionable place of resort.

The major exception to this relatively gloomy picture was engineering and carriage building. Several local firms, especially two off St Leonardgate – Dunn's carriage and wagon building company and the Phoenix Foundry, the latter briefly owned by Edmund Sharpe – turned their hands in the 1840s and 1850s to manufacturing and repairing rolling stock.[9] However, it was not until local capital was subscribed to develop the Lancaster Carriage and Wagon Works on a virgin site to the east of Green Ayre station between 1863 and 1865 that significant expansion took place. Despite initial financial difficulties this firm gradually established an international reputation, manufacturing rolling stock for export all over the world. However, its workforce of over 1,000, large by local standards, was small by national standards, its profits fluctuated wildly and it was regularly and adversely affected by downturns in international trade and growing foreign competition. Eventually in 1902–3 it, too, like the railway companies before it, passed out of local control and was quickly run down before closing completely in 1909.[10]

The limited opportunities offered by Lancaster's economy for much of the nineteenth century meant that members of many local families left in search of alternative employment and investment openings elsewhere. Some, like Samuel Gregson, gravitated to London, but Merseyside was the most popular destination with Thomas Ripley (trade), Matthew Gregson (steam saw mills), James and Thomas Harrison from Cockerham (shipping), Thomas Higgin (salt at Frodsham) and the Bibby brothers (oilcake and animal feedstuffs) among those who were successful. In mid-century in particular, many joined those emigrating to the new antipodean colonies. Among them were William, elder brother of the town clerk, Thomas Swainson, who became New Zealand's first speaker of the legislative council and Attorney General, and James Penny Nicholson who abandoned Glasson shipbuilding for Australia. Many more left to pursue distinguished professional careers, especially in law, science and the church: the anatomists, Richard Owen and William Turner; Master of Trinity College, Cambridge, William Whewell; chemists Edward Frankland and Robert Galloway; the water engineer, Thomas Mansergh and the cleric Rev J. C. Bellew (né Higgin), being some of the more nationally renowned.[11]

Manufacturing: Textiles, Oilcloth and Linoleum

Among those who remained there were hopes that textile manufacturing might revive the town's fortunes in much the same way as it had transformed the economies of many south Lancashire towns, especially after the widespread application of steam power and the introduction of power-loom weaving in the 1820s. Experience north of the Ribble, however, was a very different story. Several local merchants had diversified into textiles in the late eighteenth century, building or converting small water-powered mills for worsted, cotton or silk spinning at Halton, Caton, Dolphinholme and Galgate, and other forms of industry, including hat making had also developed in Quernmore and Wray.[12] Within the town, however, developments were somewhat slower. Although the *Lancaster Gazette* enthused about the opportunity cotton presented as early as November 1802, few traders in the depressed mercantile community initially had much inclination, or appropriate training and contacts, to transform themselves into manufacturers. Although the courts and yards of the city centre housed a number of small 'manufactories', from the little we know of them the scale and nature of their organisation did not merit the description 'mill' or 'factory'. Prior to 1819 the only concern of any consequence was the purpose-built, steam-powered Canal Side mill (later White Cross) built by Thomas Mason with financial backing from Thomas Burrow, a member of a prominent West Indian trading family.

When textile investment picked up in the 1820s younger members of established local business and professional families made the early running. In 1819 Thomas Housman Higgin, son of the governor of the castle, grandson on his mother's side of Robert Housman of Lune Bank, Skerton, brother of the town clerk and a staunch Anglican, built a worsted mill on

Moor Lane. By 1828 he had converted this mill to cotton and, with Thomas Burrow's son George, had also taken over White Cross mill on Mason's death in 1827 and was operating the two premises as a combined spinning and weaving concern. By 1824–5 William Jackson, son of a local cooper, was operating as a cotton spinner at 'Canal Side', later Factory Hill or Albion Mill, off St Leonardgate and Jackson and Barber were listed as power-loom weavers in Bulk Road along with two other cotton manufacturers in town centre streets.

The most dramatic transformation, however, was brought about by the involvement of the Greg family, substantial, Unitarian textile manufacturers from Quarry Bank Mill, Styal, near Wilmslow. Their decision to expand into the town was largely fortuitous and owed nothing to Lancaster's possible advantages as a textile town. The founder of the dynasty, Samuel Greg, had been associated through West Indian trading ventures and marriage with the Hodgsons, a mercantile family who traded through Liverpool but who also had land and a small mill at Caton, built in 1784. In 1817 this had passed to Greg's company as payment for a business debt. Recognising that it was not viable as an enterprise on its own, Samuel bought a small sailcloth factory opposite Higgin's factory on the south of Moor Lane in 1822 and converted it to cotton. One of his sons, John, ran the two mills in tandem, Caton spinning the warp thread, the Lancaster mills producing the weft and weaving the final velveteen cloth. By 1832, after further expansion, it was the largest operation both in the Greg's extensive empire and in Lancaster itself where it employed 560 hands. John continued to run the business after his father's death in 1834 and inherited it when the company was dissolved in 1841.[13]

By 1837 three more mills were being erected alongside the canal, all of them by members of established local families.[14] In May 1836 two solicitors, Henry Gregson and Thomas Mason, paid the Daltons £1,600 for four acres of land just outside the borough boundary in the neighbouring township of Bulk and built Ridge Lane silk mill. Gregson was not simply a local solicitor: he was the youngest son of Samuel Gregson, Anglican landowner and a principal promoter of the Lancaster Canal company; Mason was the son of Thomas who had pioneered White Cross mill over thirty years earlier. After completion in December 1837 their mill was temporarily used for cotton spinning by John Greg, whose Low Mill at Caton had been gutted by fire, but by 1840 it was occupied by W. Hinde & Co., who operated it first as a worsted and later as a waste silk mill until the late 1870s.[15] William Satterthwaite and John Barrow built Queen Street cotton-spinning mill at the end of Aldcliffe Lane between 1837 and 1840. They were members of established local Quaker dynasties and successful businessmen in their own right, trading as a grocer and woollen draper respectively. Bath Mill, promoted by the Threlfalls, another family with a local retail background but connections with the West Riding and Blackburn, was the most ambitious of the schemes, envisaging the construction of a reservoir and 100 cottages.[16]

An early Victorian Mayor. Edmund Sharpe (Tory, 1848), architect, engineer, railway promoter, proprietor of the Athenaeum.

Collectively these mills provided much-needed employment in the town, for women and children as well as adult males. They were largely responsible for fuelling the increase in the borough's population from just over 10,000 in 1821 to in excess of 14,000 thirty years later. In comparison with textile towns to the south, however, such growth was modest and by the late 1840s it was increasingly clear that even this could not be sustained. Lancaster lacked many of the advantages of the cotton towns around Manchester. Coal supplies were both more expensive and less reliable than those which mills on the south Lancashire coalfield enjoyed. Locally sponsored geological surveys in the 1820s and 1830s failed to find substantial coal deposits in the district. [17] Despite Lancaster's port facilities, raw cotton had to be imported through Liverpool where exchange facilities were increasingly dominated by the needs of south-east Lancashire. Except for the Gregs, marketing of the final products through distant Manchester was also a problem.

Rather than attracting new entrants, therefore, cotton stagnated. The town suffered badly during the depressions of 1841–2 and 1847–9 and never really recovered. Bath Mill was particularly hard hit. Only seven of the projected cottages were built before John Threlfall, ironmonger-turned-manufacturer, who had returned to his home town from Blackburn to run the family business, died in September 1840. The premises apparently lay unoccupied for the rest of the decade before being taken over and expanded by John Cooper of Penwortham in the winter of 1851–52.[18] In March 1846 Burrow and Higgin's business collapsed. Their Moor Lane mills were taken over by John Greg, those at White Cross by Satterthwaite and Barrow. When the latter retired in 1855 the sale of their mills evoked little outside interest;

only one buyer attended the initial auction in June 1856 despite widespread advertising in the Manchester press. White Cross was subsequently sold to Storey Brothers who set about re-equipping it, while the Queen Street mill was bought by another Quaker partnership, cousins William and Richard Jackson, who ran cotton and paper mills at Calder Vale and Oakenclough near Garstang.[19]

Over the next two decades cotton manufacturing was largely subsumed into the integrated concerns of the Storeys and James Williamson whose oilcloth businesses came to dominate the town. John Greg retired during the cotton famine occasioned by the American Civil War, selling his Lancaster mills in 1861 and those at Caton three years later to Storeys. Bath Mill continued to operate sporadically until it was acquired in May 1870 by James Williamson.[20] Although the Jacksons had been declared insolvent in 1869, largely as a result of heavy losses incurred by their recently acquired Preston weaving factory, Richard expanded Queen Street Mill in the early 1870s in the wake of the dissolution of the family partnership. Ten years later, however, he left the town and the mill was acquired by Storeys for table baize production.[21] Only the smaller Albion and Ridge Lane Mills remained independent by then. After William Jackson's death in 1870 the former was bought initially by Richard Preston, a local Catholic grocer. It was then owned briefly by Richard Jackson before passing in 1875 into the hands of Joseph Sly, landlord of the King's Arms, whose son William converted it to coconut-matting production, running it successfully until the First World War. After 1879 Ridge Lane Mill was operated briefly by the Lancaster Oil Cloth and Varnish Company but, after Henry Gregson's death in 1885, the site was cleared and houses were erected on it between 1888 and 1891.[22]

The mass production of table baize, oilcloth and, later, window blinds and linoleum revitalised the town's flagging economy from the 1850s. Demand for such products grew particularly rapidly after the 1870s as a result of rising domestic working-class living standards and a thriving export trade, but the concentration of production in Lancaster was largely fortuitous and owed more to the town's links with painting and decorating than its struggling textile sector. Unlike the early cotton firms, it was also developed by men who were new to the area and who, initially at least, lacked both capital and social contacts: James Williamson and the Storey brothers, William, Thomas and, in an associated capacity, Joseph.

James Williamson (1813–79) originated from Keswick where his father was a small estate owner and woollen manufacturer. After arriving in Lancaster in 1827 and serving his apprenticeship under Richard Hutton, a master painter and decorator, he spent some time in London, where he is reported to have developed a passion to develop the mass production of oilcloth, then a labour intensive and expensive process. After spending some time in Liverpool he returned to Lancaster and in 1837 set up as a painter and decorator in Church Street in partnership with widowed Ellen Shrigley, whose late husband Joseph had run a successful business for many years. Over the next twenty years he diversified into a variety of businesses including slate-dressing, upholstery, wallpaper and pottery manufacture, but in 1844 he apparently perfected the formula to produce the cheap oilcloth which was to be the basis for his family's personal fortune. Within a few years he had established himself in premises on the quay and in the late 1850s and early 1860s erected St George's Works, just to the west of the Carlisle railway bridge. In 1863–4 he also built Greenfield Mill on Moor Lane to supply the necessary backing cloth, expanding the premises after only two years. Further expansion followed the acquisition of Bath Mill in 1870 and the purchase of the site of the bankrupt Lune Shipbuilding Company in 1871 where he proceeded to lay out a modern integrated factory in which he diversified into floorcoverings and, later, window blinds. After purchasing yet more land on the Marsh in 1889 and 1894, this time from Lancaster corporation, his son, James Williamson II, later Lord Ashton, further extended the firm's operations, especially in the late 1890s and the years immediately prior to outbreak of the First World War. By the early 1900s the firm was the largest of its kind in the world, controlling every stage of the industrial process and employing over 2,000 men and boys in Lune Mills alone, as well as considerable numbers of women and children in its two textile mills.[23]

The Storeys originated from Bardsea, Furness. Their father was village schoolmaster, their mother was descended from a local farming family. After a chance meeting with George Stephenson's railway surveying assistant, Charles Binns, who hailed from Lancaster, one of their sons, John, migrated to the town to work for him. The rest of the family followed in 1835 and two of John's brothers, Joseph and Thomas, joined him in railway-surveying. Another brother, William, served an apprenticeship with Hutton, Williamson's first master, and then worked under Williamson in the 1840s before setting up his own business on the quay in 1848. After a couple of shortlived partnerships, his brother Thomas joined him in 1851. This linked the firm with Edmund Sharpe for whom Thomas had worked as a railway surveyor and commercial manager for both the Little North Western and Phoenix Foundry. This undoubtedly assisted the business, with the foundry providing valuable early orders for railway carriage seat upholstery covers. After 1856 William and Thomas redeveloped White Cross Mills and were joined by Joseph, who set up Heron Chemical Works in 1860 alongside the Moor Lane mills which his brothers purchased from John Greg in 1861. From then on, Storey Brothers expanded rapidly to employ upwards of 1,000 workers by the end of the century.[24]

Institutions of Confinement and Care: a new service role

Lancaster's role as an administrative and service centre was also transformed during the century. Although the castle continued to dominate the town's Victorian skyline, its judicial importance had already declined before the queen ascended the throne. Until 1835 the wealthy and influential had descended on the town twice a year to witness the spectacle and theatrical drama of criminal and civil cases heard before the Northern circuit judges and grand juries at the Assizes and to participate in the array of social occasions and balls laid on for the occasion. When Edward Baines, son of the famous Leeds newspaper proprietor, called at Lancaster with friends in September 1827 on their way to a tour of the Lakes he found the town full to capacity, the criminal court thronged with ladies anxious to witness the fate of the infamous Jane Scott, accused of murdering her parents, and the Nisi Prius court crowded with admirers of Henry Brougham, the renowned Liberal lawyer.[25] From occupying little more than a week in the late eighteenth century, the Assizes by then required two to three weeks to cope with the increased number of cases. In 1824 the county authorities had purchased the large house at the top of Church Street to accommodate the judges during their stay. One hundred and sixteen barristers were required to deal with the ninety-two criminal and 242 civil cases at the sessions which Baines attended.[26]

While the season associated with the Assizes appealed to leisured county society, however, for many of the businessmen from south Lancashire the experience was far less appealing. 'I saw there', remarked Baines,

> a great number of friends, some of them jurors, some witnesses, some professional men. All were unanimous in their outcry against the extremely slow progress of the business ... and each had a particular reason for wishing to get away from Lancaster.[27]

After years of complaints, Lancaster's monopoly of the county assizes was finally removed in 1835, south Lancashire cases being transferred to Liverpool. The town council's energetic lobbying for the restoration of the town's monopoly, based on the premise that the new railway connection in 1840 overcame the problem of Lancaster's inaccessibility, came to nought.

From the mid-1830s the Assizes were but a pale reflection of their former glory and Lancaster's reputation as a fashionable resort went into terminal decline. A series of damning reports on the town's inadequate sanitary provision and polluted water supply in the 1840s added to the malaise. The annual horseracing, which had been revived by the building of a new stand and racecourse on Lancaster Moor in 1809, had already been dealt a blow as early as 1819 by the death of the 9th Duke of Hamilton of Ashton Hall, chief patron of the sport in the area. Moral reformers' attacks on the drunkenness, ribaldry and cock-fighting associated with the event led to more problems by the late 1830s and, after riots in 1840, there were strident demands for the races to be discontinued. From then on despite continuing financial support from the corporation, they were poorly attended and finally petered out in 1857, the racecourse grounds and stand subsequently being incorporated into the county asylum.[28] Rowing regattas and the Lune Hunt were formally revived in 1842 but petered out by the end of the decade.[29]

Audiences at the Theatre Royal in St Leonardgate also dwindled in the late 1830s and the premises were increasingly used for meetings of the Temperance Society and for formal lectures. In 1843 they were purchased by Edmund Sharpe who converted them into a music hall (for serious concerts) and museum, operated after 1849 by a private company which he founded, the Lancaster Athenaeum.[30] Only the exclusive John O'Gaunt Bowmen's annual gala day and ball continued to survive relatively unscathed.[31]

The Castle also experienced mixed fortunes in its other role as a prison. In the first half of the century it was the recipient of much county investment. Additional accommodation in the form of a female penitentiary was erected between 1818 and 1821 and new single cells were built in the years around 1850 in an attempt to meet the requirements of the regime of solitary confinement which Home Office prison inspectors first recommended and then required. But difficulties inherent in the ancient fabric of the buildings and the physical layout of the site meant that attempts to upgrade its facilities proved both expensive and only partially successful. Until the reform of the bankruptcy laws in 1869, the presence of large numbers of debtors detained in the county gaol further impeded reforms since it was deemed unjust and imprudent to inflict increasingly severe penal discipline on men who had not necessarily committed any criminal offence. It was, therefore, both cheaper and more convenient for the county authorities to erect purpose-built accommodation nearer the major centres of population from which most of the criminal prisoners came. The number of serious male offenders housed at Lancaster consequently declined dramatically after 1850 when the prison was downgraded to north Lancashire's female prison for nearly twenty years. After the Home Office took over control from the county in 1877 numbers declined still further, 115 cells being summarily condemned as 'unsuitable' in April 1879. As the national prison population continued to fall into the present century the prison became surplus to requirements and was eventually closed in 1916 and only re-opened after the Second World War.[32]

In stark contrast, there was a dramatic development of residential institutions providing care and treatment for the unfortunate, the destitute and the mentally retarded from all over the north of England. By 1911, despite the growth of employment in local manufacturing, ten per cent of the borough's population were inmates or resident staff in five substantial institutions: the County Lunatic Asylum, Ripley Orphanage, the Royal Albert Asylum, the workhouse and the military barracks.[33] The construction, maintenance and day-to-day running of these provided considerable employment in the town while their food and clothing contracts were eagerly sought after by local retailers.

The lunatic asylum was by far the largest of these establishments. The original building was erected between 1811 and 1816 on a site high on the moor to the east of the town which had been donated to the county by a town council anxious to ensure that the facility was not developed elsewhere.

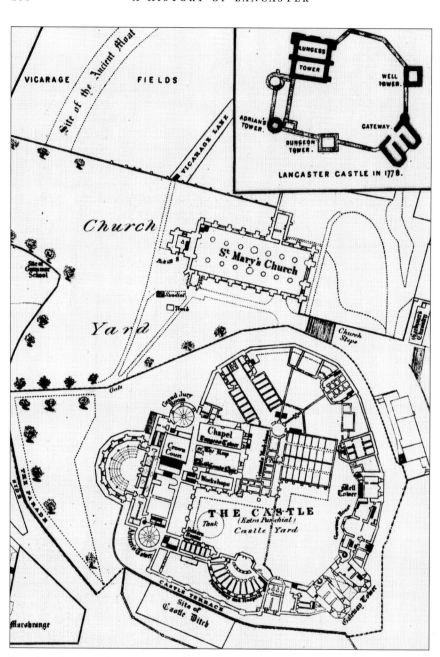

Plan of the Castle, c.1885, with inset 1778. These two plans clearly show the massive rebuilding of both the courts and the prison between the late eighteenth and mid-nineteenth century. Debtors' rooms are in the gatehouse and adjacent to the courts; the new male tower blocks, one of them now converted to single cell accommodation, to the north; the female penitentiary in the south wall and the governor's house beside the gateway.

Debtors' Quarters, Lancaster Prison, c.1836: the Quakers and the Smugglers. Conditions for debtors were very different from those of other prisoners and were largely self-regulated. Entry charges for the different, usually named, communal living rooms mirrored social distinctions within the prison population. The Quakers was regarded as one of the better rooms: the Smugglers was less well appointed: note the folding hammock style beds. Debtors were allowed to pursue their occupations while in prison as the man working by the light of the window is evidently doing. Edward Slack passed the time by drawing, and his sketches were subsequently published.

It was initially intended solely for the county's pauper lunatics who had previously been housed with other inmates in parish workhouses, or, if they had committed crimes, in the castle, but an Act of 1815 allowed the admission of non-pauper patients. From the time of its opening in 1816 it was subject to almost continuous expansion. In 1824 it housed 280, eight years later the figure had risen to 354, by 1841 it was 611, by 1877 over 1,000. By 1911 there were 2,327 inmates and 268 resident officials and their families. Equally dramatic changes occurred in the nature of patient care. In the 1840s under the direction of a new superintendent, Samuel Gaskell, and the consulting physician, Edward De Vitre, a new regime of 'moral treatment' and 'non restraint' displaced the original emphasis on mechanical restraint and physical purges. The legacy of these enlightened men ensured that life in Lancaster's asylum remained superior to many institutions elsewhere for the rest of the century. Even so, by the 1870s the difficulties of maintaining morale and recruiting committed trained staff combined with the sheer size of the institution meant that custodial care was gradually displacing treatment as the major priority of its regime.[34]

Unlike the asylum, which enjoyed rate support from the county, both the Ripley Orphanage (or hospital) and Royal Albert Asylum relied on voluntary donations, many of them from outside the town. Thomas Ripley was a local man who had moved to Liverpool in the early nineteenth century after his family had been declared bankrupt in 1817. In the more auspicious Merseyside environment he made a fortune as a successful merchant. Just before his death in 1852 he expressed a desire to endow an institution in his home town on the lines of the Blue Coat School in Liverpool. His wife, Julia, now resident at Springfield Hall, Lancaster, dedicated the rest of her life to

The Medical Superintendent's House at the Lancaster County Asylum, c.1910. The exterior of the building remains virtually unchanged. It was later the Moor Hospital's children's unit, Red Oak House, but has now been converted to a private residence.

Springfield Hall, 1846. Built in the early 1790s, this stood on the site of what is now the Royal Lancaster Infirmary. In the early nineteenth century it was home to a succession of retired merchants and gentry before being occupied by Julia Ripley, who erected Ripley Orphanage in the grounds, and oilcloth manufacturer and MP, Norval Helme, who bequeathed it to the Royal Lancaster Infirmary. It was pulled down in 1962.

fulfilling his wishes, laying the foundation stone of the orphanage in 1856. Finally opened in 1864, this had as its mission the care, education and indoctrination in the principles of the established church of children of poor respectable parents who, prior to the death of their father, had resided for two years within fifteen miles of Lancaster or seven miles of Liverpool. On Mrs Ripley's death in 1881 she bequeathed her entire fortune, some £250,000, to the hospital. Not surprisingly this was used to extend and upgrade facilities in the 1880s and 1890s. By the turn of the century it was home to some 330 children.

The euphoria and public spiritedness which surrounded the opening of the Ripley hospital on 3 November 1864 undoubtedly prompted the initiative eleven days later to raise funds to found what became known in 1866, after Queen Victoria had given it her blessing, as the 'Royal Albert Asylum for Idiots and Imbeciles in the Northern Counties'. Although local men took a prominent role in the early promotion and the continuing management of this, the vast majority of the funding, in the form of gifts, legacies and subscriptions, came from all over northern England. By 1867 building work had commenced. Three years later the first patients were admitted although construction was not completed until 1873. From then on there was a steady stream of improvements and additions largely paid for by prominent bene-factors or subscriptions: an infirmary (1882), a residence for private pupils (1887), Thomas Storey's home for forty girls (1898), the Ashton wing housing 100 patients (1901), the Herbert Storey industrial schools and workshops (1904), a reception house dedicated to the memory of the first secretary of the institution, James Diggens (1907), and a farm colony and buildings (1912). Like the county asyium, the regime in the Royal Albert was influenced by changes in national ideas about treatment and custodial care. In the 1870s it had optimistically been envisaged as a place of education and training for the young who, it was hoped, would then be able to support themselves independently in society; by the 1900s the emphasis on reform had dwindled, largely superseded by a more pessimistic view which implied the need for long-term custodial segregation. As the age profile of its patients changed, the asylum gradually developed as a self-contained community complete with its own farm, workshops, sport and recreational activities. By 1911, 679 patients and 110 officials and their families were resident on the site.[35]

In addition to these three massive institutions, the town also housed considerable numbers of paupers and military personnel. The Poor Law Amendment Act of 1834 required individual parishes to combine into unions administered by boards of guardians who were to determine poor relief and manage purpose-built workhouses. It was only in 1840, however, that a Lancaster Union encompassing twenty-one previously independent town-ships was established.[36] Over the next two years the old parish workhouse on Quernmore Road was substantially rebuilt. Originally intended to deter the able-bodied from applying for relief, in practice it tended, like most workhouses, to cater for the aged, invalid and orphaned. Further extensions and modernisations were carried out in 1889–90, and in 1908 a separate children's home was erected. By 1911 the workhouse housed 320 inmates and fifteen resident staff.

Lancaster had a long military tradition. Until the last quarter of the century, however, its physical presence in the town was largely limited to providing facilities for a part-time volunteer force, the militia. The barracks at the top of Penny Street were built in the mid-1850s at the time of the Crimea War as a training depot and stores for the Lancashire Militia and from 1864 there was an officers' mess on Dalton Square. This tradition of voluntary service continued into the twentieth century with various territorial headquarters in Dallas Road, Phoenix Street and Castle Park. It was not until 1873, however, in the wake of Cardwell's army reforms, that work on permanent barracks at Bowerham for the King's Own Royal Regiment (4th Foot) began and not until 1880 that they were fully open. These also provided accommodation for the local militia, Storeys taking over the Penny Street site. The barracks were comparable in scale to the workhouse with some 300 residents on the site in 1911, roughly two-thirds of whom were military personnel.[37]

Population and Housing

The growth of these institutions and of manufacturing not only rescued Lancaster from economic oblivion; the prosperity they created reshaped the size, appearance and structure of the town. The borough's population, which

Population Trends: Lancaster and District, 1801–1911

	Lancaster Township	Lancaster Castle	Skerton Township	Scotforth Township	Bulk Township	Lancaster Borough & Castle	Lancaster District		Borough & Castle Decennial % Change	District Decennial % Change
1801	9030	*	1278	462	190	9030	10960			
1811	9247	*	1254	466	113	9247	11080	1801–11	2.40	1.09
1821	10144	*	1283	579	111	10144	12117	1811–21	9.70	9.36
1831	12167	446	1351	557	102	12613	14623	1821–31	24.35	20.68
1841	13531	558	1665	643	113	14089	16510	1831–41	11.70	12.90
1851	14378	226	1586	693	124	14604	17007	1841–51	3.66	3.01
1861	14324	163	1556	955	109	14487	17107	1851–61	−0.80	0.59
1871	17034	211	1817	1139	116	17245	20317	1861–71	19.04	18.76
1881	20558	105	2838	2263	117	20663	25881	1871–81	19.82	27.39
1891	26380	61	3757 (311)	2749 (1598)	671	31038	33618	1881–91	50.21	29.89
1901	31224	64	6340 (−)	1847 (401)	1255 (−)	40329	40730	1891–01	29.93	21.16
1911	†	†	† (−)	† (304)	† (−)	41410	41714	1901–11	2.68	2.42

Sources

Published Census Tables

Victoria County History, vol. 3, 1907, Appendix II.

Notes and Definitions

* The population of the Castle was not separately returned 1801–21 and is included in the township figure for these years.

† Data not available.

( ) these figures refer to the area remaining outside the borough boundaries after the extensions of 1888 and 1900.

Townships   The figures refer to the area of each township as it existed in 1801, as far as possible.

Lancaster   Until 1888 township and borough boundaries were the same.

Skerton   This township was largely incorporated into Lancaster Borough in 1888 and 1900; the remainder was added to Halton, Slyne with Hest and Morecambe.

Bulk   The figure for 1801 includes Aldcliffe; Bulk was largely merged with Lancaster in 1900; the remaining rural area was attached to Quernmore.

Scotforth   The bulk of this township was merged with Lancaster in 1888 and 1900.

The part of Scotforth added by 1888 Lancaster Corporation Act cannot be distinguished in 1901, and so is included in Lancaster.

Borough   The figures refer to the area under the jurisdiction of corporation at the time of each census PLUS the inhabitants of the Castle.

Borough jurisdiction strictly did not extend to the Castle which was the property of the County and, after 1877, of the Home Office.

District   This is the total of the Castle and Townships.

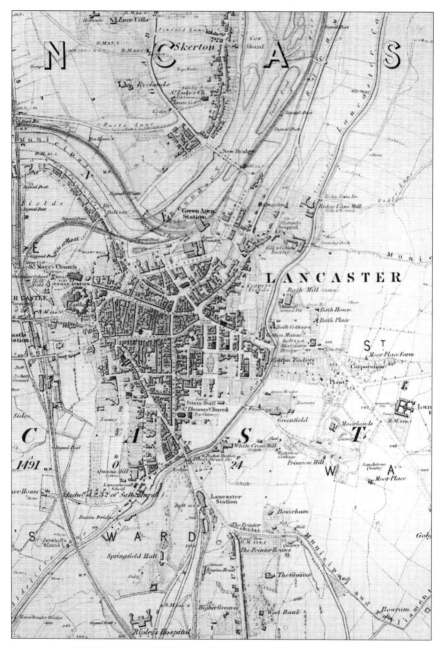

Lancaster in c. 1845 (*above*) and c. 1895 (*opposite*). Despite the expansion of the population Lancaster still retained a compact built-up area. The Freehold estate (to the east), Primrose and Bowerham (to the south), Skerton (to the north) and Regent Street/Lindow Square (to the west) are the most prominent additions. Apart from Williamsons' Luneside industrial complex and the Wagon Works on Caton Road, industry remained clustered alongside the canal.

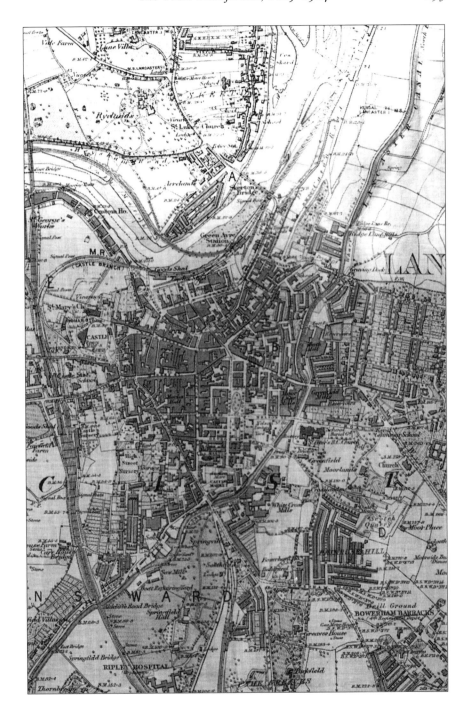

had risen only modestly before 1851 and had actually fallen in the 1850s, virtually trebled between 1861 and 1901. Growth was actually rather steadier than the raw figures for the 'borough' in the decennial census suggest, the huge leaps in the 1880s and 1890s reflecting boundary extensions in 1888 and 1900 to incorporate housing developments in parts of Skerton, Scotforth and, to a lesser extent, Bulk, all of which had been returned as separate townships in previous censuses. Numbers in these contiguous townships had in fact been increasing since the 1860s, Skerton's population rising from 1,556 in 1861 to 2,838 in 1881, Scotforth's from 955 to 2,263, boosted to some extent by the inmates of the Royal Albert. These qualifications, however, do not detract from the overwhelming impression of massive expansion.

The most obvious physical manifestation of this cumulative growth was the rapid expansion of the housing stock, especially from the 1870s. In stark contrast with the grandeur of the late eighteenth century, residential building in the first sixty years of the nineteenth century had been largely confined to piecemeal, low quality infill in the town centre, especially in the St Leonardgate area.[38] Most of this was carried out by small-scale speculators; only Albion and Bath mills provided accommodation for more than a handful of their workers with some eighteen cramped back-to-back houses and seven substantial properties alongside the canal respectively.[39] Although the Freehold estate on the hill to the east of the canal was laid out in 1852 by the National Freehold Land Society, a forerunner of the Abbey National Building Society, its initial purpose had been to expand landownership rather than provide new residences. The unusually large plots and strict building regulations reflected not just a more enlightened attitude towards public health issues but also the need of the national Liberal political promoters to ensure that the properties which would be erected would be sufficiently valuable to enable their owners and occupiers to vote in county and borough elections, hopefully to unseat the Tories. Although building commenced in 1853, most of the properties were erected in the 1860s and 1870s and many of the plots at the top of Borrowdale and Rydal Roads and along Derwent Road, where regulations stipulated that only semi-detached or detached houses could be built, remained undeveloped until the 1890s when there was an expansion in the white-collar and commercial class in the town. Most of the early development consisted of substantial terraced houses occupied, if not owned, by better paid artisans, railway workers or shopkeepers who were anxious to escape from the unsavoury city centre, and the varied appearance reflected the fragmented nature of landownership and the piecemeal way in which the estate developed.[40]

Private speculative builders, many of them relatively small scale, provided virtually all of the accommodation needed to house the armies of workers employed in the town's expanding industrial and service sectors. The council laid down increasingly stringent bye-laws after 1859 but took no further role, despite Radicals' calls to do so in the early 1890s when a temporary housing shortage was created by the surge in employment at Williamson's. The

Co-operative Society dabbled in the market, building eleven houses on Park Road in 1872–3, twenty-eight in Wolseley Street in 1876 and a small number of lower quality terraces twenty years later, but it preferred to use its resources to promote expanded ownership through loans to members.[41] The vast majority of properties occupied by the working classes were rented, the local building societies which emerged in the town catering primarily for the middle class, either as owner-occupiers or landlords of property to let.

Despite some isolated examples of impressive detached residences, notably on Cannon Hill and the Haverbreaks estate (the latter laid out as early as 1875 but only developed around the turn of the century), the majority of the new houses in the town were terraced. Superficially, many of these were, and are, very similar in appearance, but variations in style and size reflected not just different dates of construction, but gradations of wealth and status within the community. There were superior terraces with single or double storey bay windows for Lancaster's burgeoning clerical, supervisory and commercial classes on South Road, Greaves Road, Regent Street, Lindow Square, Thornfield on Ashton Road, Dale Street, Dallas Road, Blades Street and the Westbourne Road area. The working classes were accommodated in smaller terraces with small back yards to ensure maximum density, but conformity to increasingly stringent housing bye-laws ensured that they were far superior to the cramped, insanitary courts which they superseded. Prior to the 1880s much of this development was piecemeal: De Vitre, Denis and Shaw Streets in the early 1870s to the west of the canal; Dry Dock or Nuns' Field to the east from 1876; Park (or Quarry) Road on the fringes of the Freehold, Lune Street on the Marsh. From the 1880s, however, new estates, laid out in rigid grid patterns, were developed on the edge of town comprising mainly of small, straight fronted terraces but with more substantial bay fronted properties set back from the pavements on the perimeter roads. The Marsh to the west and Primrose to the east were the first to emerge in the mid-1880s and early 1890s. Houses were erected on the site of the old Ridge Lane silk mill after it had been demolished in 1888–9. In the following decade the Moorlands estate was quickly developed on the grounds of the late Henry Gregson's family estate. In the early years of the following century, activity shifted to Bowerham and the Greaves area of Scotforth, assisted in no small way by the coming of the trams.[42]

All these developments meant a significant decline in the relative importance of the town centre for residential purposes. Many of the town centre tradesmen and artisans had already abandoned residential premises above or adjacent to their places of work by the 1870s. Although there was no substantial slum-clearance there was an absolute decline in the number of people living in central wards between 1901 and 1911, suggesting that some of the residents of the chronically overcrowded courts and yards were also leaving. While Scotforth's residents rose by just over 2,800 over the decade, those living in the central wards of Castle, St Anne's and John O'Gaunt fell by over 1,700.

The most obvious beneficiaries of this building boom were Lancaster's building and decorating trades. These had, in fact, remained fairly buoyant even in the dark, depressed mid-century decades largely as a consequence of major restructuring and extensions at the castle and asylum, municipal sanitary improvements, church building and a variety of private commissions for the local gentry. Lancaster also boasted a number of architects of regional fame, notably Edmund Sharpe and his successor E. G. Paley, joined in 1868 by Hubert Austin, who brought in major commissions.[43] By 1901, even with the massive increase in the numbers employed in oilcloth manufacture and at the wagon works, fourteen per cent of males over ten years old were still involved in building and associated trades.

The Service Trades: Professions and Retailing

Population expansion, however, affected other elements of Lancaster's private service sector in fundamental ways. From being primarily concerned with meeting the demands of the local elite and the town's rural hinterland, Lancaster's professional class, shopkeepers and craftsmen became increasingly attuned to the requirements of a mass working-class and institutional market.

In the first half of the nineteenth century, lawyers, doctors, surveyors and architects were essentially drawn from the ranks of landed or mercantile families whom they served. For younger sons in particular, a training in medicine or law was viewed as a refined accomplishment, and a passport to a prestigious career which did not necessarily impinge too much on a leisured lifestyle. Not surprisingly Lancaster's population until the 1860s contained a much higher proportion of professional men than almost any other Lancashire town.[44] Most of these lived in elegant town houses or in detached villas just beyond the built-up area, and their lifestyles mirrored those of the people they served. The surgeon, Christopher Johnson (d. 1866), for example, enjoyed the friendship of intellectuals like the historian Dr Lingard of Hornby, had time to pursue his own biological and chemical research, to translate learned works from Italian, to participate in local politics, as both alderman and mayor, and to give support to the Mechanics Institute. One of his sons, James, retired as a physician early in life and devoted himself to scientific pursuits. Another son, Thomas, although practising as a solicitor, devoted much of his time to promoting outdoor activities for young men and regularly visited the Hebridean island of Iona, where he was buried in 1892, the town honouring his memory with a public drinking fountain in Dalton Square, later removed to Stonewell when the new town hall was built.[45]

Early and mid-Victorian Lancaster was very much dominated by men in this mould. From the 1860s, however, their relative importance, numerically and socially, declined while the professional demands made upon them

Queen Victoria's Diamond Jubilee celebrations, Market Street, 1897. Many local businesses participated in the grand procession. As the float shown above implies, James Hatch's business was renowned for church woodwork and was closely associated with the famous architectural practice run by members of the Sharpe, Paley and Austin families. Electricity had only recently been introduced into the town by the corporation and was a great novelty (*below*).

A Society Wedding Party: Dr William Wingate-Saul, MD and Miss Marion Storey (*centre*) in the grounds of William Storey's residence, Fairfield House, 4 June 1872. Marriage consolidated the Storeys' links with members of local professional, Conservative families. Mr and Mrs Edmund (Alice Storey) Sharpe are fourth and sixth from the left respectively; Ada Jane Storey, fifth from right, was later married to William Roper, notary and solicitor in the firm of Swainson, Son & Roper, and subsequently town clerk; also in the photograph is Herbert Storey (*far right*). Wingate Saul practised in Fenton Cawthorne House, now the site of the Post Office.

significantly increased. Many of the new recruits were outsiders, dedicated careerists with little or no unearned income to fall back on. More were to be found in what would now be regarded as lower-middle-class residential quarters and fewer kept household servants. Doctors were either increasingly full-time, salaried officials in one of the town's institutions, or endured increased workloads brought about by the rise in population.[46] Lawyers were drawn into servicing the expanding local government sector. Those who possessed sufficient independent resources and social connections increasingly resided out of town.

Shopping facilities were similarly transformed. Even in the depths of depression in 1818, the anonymous compiler of Pigot's Commercial Directory had remarked that Lancaster's shopkeepers were numerous and opulent and the retail trade greater than could be expected from the number of inhabitants'.[47] Twenty-six years later, however, the equally anonymous author of *The Pictorial History of the County of Lancaster* remarked on the 'deserted and sombre appearance of the streets after quitting the manufacturing towns of the county'.[48] The latter description in fact provides the answer to the conundrum posed by the former. Until the last quarter of the century many of Lancaster's retailers were not heavily dependent on working-class trade. Like the professional class, they served the urban rich and Lancaster's extensive rural hinterland.

J. & W. Bell, Penny Street, c. 1899. The window display betrays how the grocers' trade had been transformed in the late nineteenth century with the appearance of branded products, many of which – Huntley & Palmer's and Carr's biscuits, Quaker oats and Bovril – remain household names. Mazawattee Tea, a leading brand of the time, has not proved so enduring.

Widespread changes in retail practice were slow to materialise but, as in other towns, tea and drapery trades were the pacemakers in promoting both advertising and low prices for ready money. Thomas Atkinson established his successful 'Grasshopper Tea Warehouse' in Cheapside as early as 1837, trading under the slogan 'Ready Money, Extensive Business and Small Profits' and Hinde's drapery business in the same street was the first shop to install plate glass windows seven years later.[49] But there is also evidence to suggest that collusive practices continued to characterise much mid-century retailing and that competition was restricted to quality and service rather than aggressive price cutting. When the young T. D. Smith opened his shop in Penny Street in November 1858 he found he 'had the greatest fight to get into the best markets for buying the various articles of stock' since 'certain firms sought to monopolize over me, by preventing the representatives of the best London or Liverpool business houses from calling on me'. Smith, however, preferred to trade on quality rather than price and expressed no respect or sympathy in his memoirs for a competitor in St Nicholas Street who 'made a great push and cut [in price] some articles' with the result that he 'disgusted respectable customers'.[50]

In the later nineteenth century, however, the growth in working-class spending power outstripped that of Lancaster's shopkeepers' traditional clientele, spawning new types of shops and radically different trading practices. The growth of the Co-operative Society was the most visible and, for many shopkeepers, the most disturbing manifestation of this change since the movement represented not just a threat to trade but a challenge to their

Lancaster Co-operative Society's central premises, New Street, prior to rebuilding, c.1900. Co-op membership expanded rapidly from the 1880s and the society opened branches throughout the district but its sales per member remained much lower than in textile towns of south Lancashire, possibly because of the fierce competition posed by grocers like Bell and T. D. Smith.

belief in the superiority of economic individualism and private enterprise. Founded in 1860 its first shop in Penny Street relied initially, like societies elsewhere, on the custom of relatively well-paid craftsmen, in Lancaster's case the engineers at the Phoenix Foundry and silk workers at the Ridge Lane mill. By 1875 it had 2,238 members, by 1900 – 8,738, by 1914 – 12,192. Sales of just over £5,500 in the first year rose to over £269,500 over the same period. By 1914 it employed a staff of 240, boasted a modern department store on the corner of New Street and Church Street, and operated twenty branches throughout town, in neighbouring Morecambe, Bare, Heysham, Caton, Halton and Galgate.[51] An entirely new breed of shop, the multiples, owned and controlled by national or regional companies, also appeared in the town. Tea firms like the National Tea Company and London & Counties Tea Company were the first to appear in the 1870s but most expansion occurred in the 1890s with the arrival of Freeman, Hardy & Willis's shoe shops, Liptons grocers, Maypole Dairy, Eastman's butchers, Boot's Cash Chemists, Singer's Sewing Machines and several drapers and outfitters including Hepworth's.[52]

From the 1880s, however, town centre retailers, grocers in particular, faced an even more serious threat: an expansion in the number of small shopkeepers. These quickly established themselves in the new working-class suburbs where they benefited from residents' preference to purchase their basic weekly requirements within easy walking distance of their homes. By 1886, even without venturing down on to nearby Moorgate, the residents of the Freehold Estate could choose from two boot-and-shoe makers, a butcher, a chemist, two drapers, four grocers, three pubs and beerhouses, two dressmakers and six general shopkeepers. Although delivery services to the middle-class quarters remained economically viable, centrally situated retailers could only compete with these local shopkeepers in the working-class market by opening branch shops. Some, like T. D. Smith, did just that and greatly increased their business as a result, but most continued to rely on their single outlet.[53]

In the increasingly prosperous climate of the late nineteenth century, however, there was sufficient demand for many family businesses to thrive without adopting radically new methods. The boom in consumer spending led to significant expansions in the number of specialist outlets and spawned several new trades. Bakers, butchers, chemists and newsagents all more than doubled their numbers between the 1850s and 1912 by which time fish-friers, cycle shops, music professors and coffee taverns had all appeared in significant numbers. Within the central trading area there was also substantial investment in the redevelopment of retail premises. In 1880 the council rebuilt the covered market which it had first erected in 1846, expanding the accommodation for purveyors of perishable produce – meat, fish, dairy produce and greengrocery.[54] Many shop fronts were redesigned and their interiors gutted and restyled to reflect the latest fashions.

Leisure: Commercialism and 'Rational Recreation'

The restructuring and upgrading of retailing was parallelled by an extensive redevelopment of the town's major hotels. As the premier coaching inn, the King's Arms had accommodated many illustrious travellers, among them members of European royal families and noted literati of the day. Charles Dickens had a particular affection for it, describing it as a

> genuine old house of a very quaint description, teeming with old carvings, and beams, and panels, and having an excellent old staircase with a gallery or upper staircase, cut off from it by a curious fence-work of old oak, or of the old Honduras Mahogany wood.

He corresponded regularly with Joseph Sly, its landlord between 1856 and 1877. After Sly's retirement, however, its exotic contents – including Gobelin tapestries, Hogarth prints and such antique furniture as a fifteenth-century bed – were auctioned off and the lease was acquired by Samuel Ducksbury, proprietor of the fashionable County Hotel on Station Road which had been built in 1870. In 1879 the old coaching inn was demolished; three years later the present building was opened.[55] A pair of imposing new hotels, the White Cross (now the Farmers Arms) and the Alexandra, graced the southern approaches to the town over the rebuilt Penny Street Bridge after 1901.

A vigorous temperance lobby, however, ensured that despite the surge in

Yates & Jacksons' dray at the Park Hotel, Bowerham Terrace, c.1900. William Yates, landlord of the Slip Inn, and William Jackson of the Boot and Shoe, Scotforth, opened a modern brewery in January 1879. They and William Mitchell (1880) rapidly expanded their network of tied houses throughout the district. The business ceased trading in 1984, Thwaites of Blackburn purchasing the pubs, and Mitchells moving into the brewery premises from where it operated until 1999.

population there was no increase in the number of working-class pubs and beerhouses in the town. The latter's numbers ceased to rise after the repeal in 1869 of the Beer Act of 1830 which had established the simple mechanism by which they could be set up. Some were successful in obtaining full licences, but others disappeared with the death of their proprietors in the later nineteenth century. The demolition and redevelopment of old property on the castle approaches in the mid-1870s and on China Lane in the 1890s further reduced numbers. Unlike retailing, there was no marked expansion in the new working-class suburbs. In contrast to the slightly earlier Freehold area, provision on the estates laid out from the 1880s was restricted to solitary, modern, and intentionally respectable 'hotels': the Victoria (Marsh), Moorlands (Gregson estate), Park (Primrose), Bowerham and Greaves, the majority under the control of William Mitchell who had rapidly established himself as a major brewer in the town since 1880.

The pub's monopoly of many popular leisure activities was, in any case, being eroded in the late Victorian period by a variety of other factors. The temperance lobby, dating back to the 1830s, not only vigorously opposed the granting of new licences, it actively promoted alternative 'rational recreations'. The most commercial of these was the Lancaster Coffee Tavern Company which operated a chain of premises in Penny Street, Market Street and the Gregson memorial on Moor Lane.[56] Churches were also regular sponsors of uplifting pastimes for the young. The Pleasant Sunday Afternoon or Brotherhood movement, for example, offered 'Brief, bright and brotherly meetings' and was originated by the minister of Congregational church on Rosemary Lane in 1893. By 1901 it had moved into the neighbouring Cromwell Hall on the corner of North Road and was advertising a variety of evening and Sunday entertainments. By 1914 it boasted 1,000 members.[57]

The Mechanics Institute, founded as early as 1824 in Mary Street, had initially functioned solely as a library, but gradually acquired additional functions, especially in the 1850s, running a school of art, penny bank and newsroom and offering a variety of evening lectures and socials. Its expansion necessitated a number of moves before it found a permanent home in 1856 in a large Georgian house on the corner of Meeting House Lane and Castle Hill. Demolished, rebuilt and renamed the Storey Institute between 1887 and 1891 it was handed over to the council in 1893 as a free library and venue for educational and cultural activities.[58] True to its ideals, the Co-operative Society also dedicated funds to the provision of social facilities for its members. By 1867 it had opened a library; by 1913 it boasted seven reading rooms throughout the district. From the 1870s it organised regular lectures and outings; after 1886 it supported a cricket club, from 1890 a Women's Guild and after 1900 a choral and orchestral class.[59] The intellectual and spiritual impact of such efforts, however, remains questionable.

These organisations were supplemented by a proliferation of voluntary associations and societies catering for musical, scientific, cultural and sporting interests. In the first half of the century such organisations had been the domain of the wealthy middle class or local gentry. Some, like the Amicable Society's library (1768), Philippi Club (1797) and Agricultural Society (c. 1799) dated back to the previous century. Many more were founded in the 1820s and 1830s: the Society of Arts (1820), Choral Society (1836), Literary, Scientific and Natural History Society (1835), Literary & Philosophical Society (1833) and Law Library (1837). Admission to the John O'Gaunt Bowmen (reformed 1788) was by nomination only, while cricket and rowing clubs of the early 1840s appealed primarily to local professionals and county men. Membership was kept deliberately small by high subscription fees. Working-class organisations tended to be concerned with more practical considerations like the provision of friendly society benefits.

By 1900 both the range of interests and memberships of such societies had been considerably expanded. Although the bowmen remained totally unaffected, and cricket, together with the new pursuits of golf and tennis, retained elements of social exclusivity, other sports appealed to a broader social spectrum. After 1867, the elitist, essentially Tory, rowing club faced a challenge from the more open, Liberal John O'Gaunt Rowing Club which subsequently attracted the backing of Lord Ashton. Football operated at a variety of levels ranging from the town's own club (1888) to local leagues supported by works, school, church and shop teams. Swimming, athletics, rugby football, water polo, bowls, wrestling and angling all established formal organisations and participated in competitions. Outdoor activities were run by the Public Footpath Protection and Preservation Society (1878) and various cycling clubs, the latter attracting a fair number of women members. Membership of artistic and scientific societies also increased as subscriptions fell: Lunesdale Field Naturalists' Club (1869); Amateur Dramatic & Operatic Society (1869); Entomological Society (c. 1881); Orchestral Society (1881); Philosophical Society (1885); Photographic Society (1889); Art Union (active 1890s); Chess Club (1895); Dickens Fellowship and the Astronomical & Scientific Association (1903).[60]

The commercialisation of leisure, made possible by the rise in living standards, was arguably even more significant for the majority of the towns workers. This was reflected not just in the enhanced attraction of home and family-based pastimes such as reading, board-games or piano playing but in the development of a rapidly expanding menu of public attractions. Prominent amongst these was neighbouring Morecambe, a short tram or train ride away, with its seasonal entertainments and year-round menu of theatrical and musical performances. Music halls also emerged in Lancaster itself. Even before the promoters of the Athenaeum went into liquidation in 1882 they had been obliged to temper their refined and uplifting programme of 'public entertainment and instruction' with occasional 'musical and theatrical entertainments'. When the theatre reopened under new proprietors in 1884 it concentrated unashamedly on popular melodrama and comic opera, with a sprinkling of amateur concerts and visits from touring companies. In 1898 the Oddfellows' Hall on Brock Street was converted to the 'Palace of Varieties', offering popular musical and variety shows. After 1906 it was joined by the Hippodrome on Dalton Square in premises which had originally been erected as a Catholic chapel in 1798 but had been used after 1859 by the local temperance society. The conversion of the Victoria Hall on Lower Church Street to the Picturedrome in 1911 heralded the dawn of yet another mass leisure pursuit.[61]

Church and Chapel

Commercial enterprise and voluntary associations, however, were less able to provide spiritual succour or basic education. As in the rest of the country, church building was a physical reflection of a competition for souls and minds. The Church of England's influential patrons and accumulated funds allowed it to steal a march on the less well-endowed Nonconformists and Catholics until well into the century. Eighteenth-century provision was supplemented by the erection of St Luke's, Skerton in 1833 and seven years later by St Thomas's, Penny Street on land given by George Marton, MP for the town 1837–47. Samuel Gregson, who represented the town as Liberal MP in 1847–8 and 1852–65, donated the site and the money to build Christchurch (1857), which was intended to cater for the emerging Freehold estate, inmates of the workhouse and pupils at the grammar school. St Paul's, Scotforth was erected in 1876 to serve the new parish created for this township's growing population. In the closing decades of the century, the church directed its attention to the new working-class suburbs, providing mission halls in Marsh, Bulk and Primrose in the 1890s. Existing buildings were also upgraded and extended. St Mary's received a new peal of bells in 1886, courtesy of James Williamson, a new porch designed by Austin & Paley in 1902, a commemorative chapel on the north side of the nave dedicated in 1903 to members of the King's Own Regiment who fell in the Boer War and a number of memorial windows financed by local families. St Anne's was restored in 1878 and 1894, St Luke's in 1882 and 1896, Christchurch and St John's in 1889, and St Thomas's in 1894 and 1909.

Anglican performance in the second half of the century, however, in Lancaster as in the rest of the country, was matched by other denominations most of whom were able to erect impressive new places of worship. Roman Catholics, their confidence boosted by the reinstatement of Catholic bishoprics in Britain, erected St Peter's on East Road between 1857 and 1859 to replace their much smaller chapel on Dalton Square. In 1900 they built St Joseph's, with almost as many seats as the Anglican St Luke's to serve the increasing population of Skerton, and in 1902 Margaret Coulston provided the Sisters of Mercy with land for Nazereth House at Scotforth.[62]

Apart from the beleaguered Quakers who lost wealthier adherents to Anglicanism without being able, or even willing, to expand their popular appeal, Old Dissent exhibited considerable resilience.[63] Baptist numbers recovered sufficiently froim a mid-century slough for them to open a new chapel on White Cross in 1872 and to erect the present building on Nelson Street between 1894 and 1897. Congregationalists, or Independents, expanded beyond their High Street base in 1872 when they opened a mission on the east side of town and followed this seven years later with the imposing 'Centenary' church on the corner of St Leonardgate.[64] During the 1880s they established missions in Bowerham, Hest Bank, Carnforth and Halton and after 1889 they were heavily involved in managing the Jubilee Town Mission in the old British School premises on Aldcliffe Road.

But it was New Dissent in the form of Methodism which exhibited most vitality. Primitive Methodists erected a chapel on Moor Lane in 1857, renovated it twelve years later and replaced it altogether in 1895. Eight years later they totally rebuilt their premises in Skerton. The United Methodists, a sect which first met in rooms in Mary Street in 1861, erected a chapel in Brock Street in 1869 and a mission room in Wolseley Street. Wesleyans, boosted by the growing affluence of their staunchest supporters, the town centre shopkeepers, and by the backing of men like Norval Helme, the Halton-based oilcloth manufacturer, exhibited even more impressive growth. Their original premises in Sulyard Street, dating back to 1806, were rebuilt and extended in 1877–8 to provide additional premises for day and Sunday schools and further enlarged in 1893. They also enhanced their physical presence in the suburbs with imposing new chapels in Skerton (Main Street 1869, rebuilt Owen Road 1910) and Greaves (1909) as well as mission rooms and Sunday schools on the Marsh (1882) and Primrose (Westham Street 1888).[65]

The Expansion of Education

Nonconformists failed, however, to dislodge Anglican and, to a lesser extent, Catholic dominance of elementary education. For most of the century they simply lacked sufficient funds and were obliged to concentrate their efforts on Sunday school provision. After the Education Act of 1902 had given local education authorities power to build and maintain schools they placed their hopes in provision of rate-supported, non-sectarian schooling. The Wesleyan schools in Sulyard Street, by far and away the largest of the Nonconformist efforts with a capacity of nearly 500 by 1902, were handed over to the council's education committee in 1904 where they were apparently in the safe hands of the growing number of Nonconformist councillors.

Subscriptions from wealthy local individuals, supplemented by financial help from the National Society, meant that Anglicans were able to raise sufficient funds on their own or, after 1833, to qualify for supplementary grants from central government to finance an extensive school network. In 1817 the foundation stone of the Boys' National School was laid by the Rev John Manby, incumbent of St Mary's church, on a site on Green Ayre donated by the exclusively Anglican corporation. When this site was re-developed as part of Little North Western's railway terminus it was replaced in 1850 by a larger building on St Leonardgate capable of holding 500 pupils. The Girls' National School, built on land in Fenton Street donated by the town's Anglican Tory MP John Fenton Cawthorne, opened in 1820. 'The children', observed Edward Baines four years later, 'are instructed in reading, writing and household work, to fit them for useful domestic servants.'[66] By the 1880s every Anglican church in town had a school attached to it: St Luke's (1836, enlarged 1839 and 1887–9), St Thomas's (1843), St Anne's (1853), St John's (1868), Christchurch (infants 1873, expanded 1875 and 1882), St Paul's, Scotforth (1879) and St Mary's, the last belatedly built in 1880 to serve the resident population of St George's Quay. Until new premises were built on East Road in 1851, the Catholics were catered for in a small school on Friar's Passage, opened in 1820. In 1896 they expanded north of the river, erecting St Joseph's, Skerton in 1896.

This impressive record meant that the Education Act of 1870, which set up rate-supported School Boards to 'fill the gaps' in elementary schooling provision, remained inoperative in Lancaster until 1893. By then the progressively impoverished and embattled Anglican establishment, increasingly short of funds and unable to rely on fees after legislation of 1891 had abolished them for elementary schooling, was progressively unable to meet the demands made upon it by the burgeoning suburban population. A new local School Board stepped in, building schools in Bowerham (1895) and Marsh (1896) and purchasing and enlarging the struggling Skerton British School in 1900–2. After 1902, when the board's powers had passed to the town council, Bowerham was extended (1904) and new schools were opened at Greaves (1906) and Dallas Road (1912), the latter replacing the Methodists' old premises on Sulyard Street. Denominational influence was bolstered, however, much to the annoyance of Nonconformists, by a clause in the 1902 Education Act which permitted surviving religious schools to be subsidized from the rates.[67]

None of these establishments purported to offer anything beyond basic elementary schooling, primarily intended for the working-class population. An array of private 'academies' pandered to those who could afford to pay for more appropriate, or appropriately select, education. Comparatively little is known about most of these schools which were often based in substantial converted houses in streets like Regent Street, Rydal Road, Ullswater Road and Dalton Square. Some of them appear to have been well patronised and offered boarding facilities. Many more, however, were clearly ephemeral organisations disappearing with the death or retirement of the proprietor. A significant number were female-run establishments catering for 'young ladies'. Only after 1902 was there substantial investment in girls' secondary education with the old charity school in Middle Street being converted into a Higher Grade School which was, in turn, superseded by the grammar school on Dallas Road, opened in 1914.

The Lancaster Royal Grammar School and, to a lesser extent, the Quakers' Friends' School and Castle Howell School on Queen's Square, supplied further education for boys on a fee-paying basis. Castle Howell was founded in 1850 by Rev W. Herford, Unitarian minister of St Nicholas's chapel, and was subsequently continued by his brothers-in-law, Revs D. and R. Davis, until it closed in 1889. It offered an unorthodox curriculum and a humane regime which contrasted markedly with those commonly found in public schools of the day and attracted a significant following in the area which extended beyond the small Unitarian community.[68]

The Anglican Grammar School's development, however, was fraught with controversy, largely because it was partially financed and controlled by the town council. After 1824, although the corporation continued to provide some capital funding and assistance with the masters' salaries, the sons of freemen lost their traditional right to free education. In the gloomy decades of the 1830s and 1840s the dilapidated old school on the hill below St Mary's church fell into disrepair and was lucky to survive. Only after the corporation had completely rebuilt it on a site on the new East Road in 1851–53 did its fortunes revive. The corporation continued to provide some funding in return for reduced fees for a small number of local students, but essentially it was transformed into a fee-paying establishment, taking boarders to subsidize the education of local boys. This was not how many councillors perceived it, however. In their eyes ratepayers were subsidizing an Anglican education for outsiders. New buildings in the late 1870s had to be funded primarily by subscriptions. The dilemma was only partially resolved by further gifts which established scholarships for talented boys from humbler backgrounds and a large legacy from an ex-pupil in the early 1890s. After 1902 the county council agreed to take over additional responsibility, enabling further building work to be undertaken. This state support led to diminution in fees, the first since 1824, and a marked increase in the number of places allocated for local pupils, many of them on free scholarships. 'Since then', remarked A. L. Murray, the school's youthful historian, 'its usefulness in the town and neighbourhood has notably increased.'[69]

The Politics of Local Government

Local government's increasing role in education was part of a wider gradual, hesitant expansion of municipal activity which was occurring everywhere in the nineteenth century. In 1815, apart from maritime affairs which were the responsibility of the Port Commission and the poor whose relief was the responsibility of the parish, the town was still largely governed, if that is the right word, by the corporation. This relied primarily on market and road tolls and on rent from property for its income. It had no power to levy rates, no legal concept of responsibility to the wider community and only a handful of paid officials. By the end of the second decade of the nineteenth century, its financial affairs were in disarray, partly due to maladministration, partly as a consequence of the collapse of trade in the town. In 1817 it discontinued its policy of providing street lighting for the town.

As a result of this unsatisfactory state of affairs, a group of wealthy residents applied for legislation to establish an entirely new body, the Police or Improvement Commission, which first met in June 1824. This received a small sum from the corporation but more significantly it enjoyed powers to levy rates and provide a range of services: lighting, paving, street naming, scavenging (street cleaning and night soil removal), policing (or watching), and fire fighting. Before 1835 it was this body's monthly meeting, not the town council, which was largely responsible for the limited range of basic urban amenities in the town and for the opening up of new thoroughfares like Ffrances Passage (1829).

The Municipal Corporations Act of 1835 swept away the privileges of all the old corporations and sought to establish more democratically accountable local government. Under this act the council was only obliged to take over responsibility for policing, which it did with extreme reluctance. Beyond that it was required to do little else. New councillors were elected largely to ensure that rates were kept as low as possible and that is precisely what they did. For the next fourteen years, a dual system of local administration existed with the undemocratic Police Commission continuing to be responsible for many services, including the laying out of new streets such as North Road (1840), subsequently renamed as the northern extension to Cheapside, and East Road (1848).[70]

In the 1840s, however, the pace of improvement was forced by Lancaster's professional men, especially the physicians. Possibly they were worried about the damage poor sanitary conditions were inflicting on the trade they enjoyed from wealthy visitors and undoubtedly they were concerned about its effects on the health of the local population, rich and poor alike. In 1842, 1844 and 1848 a series of reports by Dr Edward De Vitre, chief physician at the county asylum, ex-Lancastrian Sir Richard Owen of the Health of Towns Association and Sir Robert Rawlinson of the government Health of Towns Commission, drew unhappy councillors' attention to the dire state of the town. There was no public water supply, not even a private water company as in many other towns. The wells were polluted, the rainwater sooty and undrinkable. Drainage was totally inadequate. The few surface sewers all drained directly into the old mill race alongside Danside Street which was regularly blocked and flooded at high tides, backing up into the cellars of houses built near, and in some cases, over it. Despite this, the council did nothing and the Police Commission virtually nothing. Even when the market was resited from Market Square to its present site in 1846, the council ruled out the possibility of removing the slaughterhouses, a major public health hazard, from the neighbouring Shambles in Marketgate.[71]

Sanitary reformers on the council were dismayed at the cost of the remedies proposed by Rawlinson in 1848 and his colleague James Smith the following year; their opponents were appalled. The Public Health Act of 1848, however, required Lancaster to set up a Board of Health because of its high death rate. After cholera had visited the town again, affecting ten per cent of the population, councillors were reluctantly persuaded to act, gratefully accepting the assurances of Edmund Sharpe that his scheme for tapping water on the fells behind Clougha would be much cheaper than the schemes proposed by government inspectors. Permission to go ahead was granted by the Lancaster Waterworks Act of 1852, and work on piping, a compensation reservoir at Abbeystead and a service reservoir on Wyresdale Road was completed in 1855. Further government directives led in 1854 to the formation of a Burial Board which closed the overcrowded denominational cemeteries in town and laid out a new twenty-one-acre site on Lancaster Moor with separate chapels for Anglicans, Catholics and Dissenters.

This did not herald the dawn of further major municipal improvements. Rather, the huge cost of draining and watering the town, considerably more than the initial estimates, provoked a furious reaction from many ratepayers who were by then being seriously affected by the town's declining economic fortunes. Apart from an agreement to extend the water supply to neighbouring Morecambe, no major capital expenditure occurred again for over twenty years. During this period spending on labour-intensive services like policing continued to be closely monitored and kept to the minimum standards to qualify for central government support. As in other towns, ratepayers were reluctant to part with their money, and the limited democracy which existed often checked, rather than promoted, the growth of local services.

Between the late 1870s and the early 1900s, however, growing prosperity and expansion tripled the rateable value of property in the town and gradually overcame this reluctance to spend. Major Improvement Acts granting new powers were obtained by the council in 1876,1880,1888 and 1900, the last two also extending the boundaries of the old borough to encompass suburbs in the neighbouring townships of Skerton, Bulk and Scotforth. Coupled with this there was national legislation, especially on public health and education, which first encouraged and then increasingly obliged local authorities to appoint inspectors or to support specific services, while offering financial inducements to do so in the form of central government subsidies.

Public health again dominated the agenda. Under the Act of 1876 the Abbeystead reservoir was enlarged in 1881 and new ones built over the next fifteen years at Damas Gill and Blea Tarn. When the market was rebuilt in 1880 new municipal slaughterhouses for the butchers were erected alongside the canal opposite White Cross Mills. In 1878 the first Medical Officer of Health was appointed, followed in 1894 by an Inspector of Common Lodging Houses – premises which had long been regarded as a risk to both health and morals – and, in 1903, the first Lady Health Visitor. In 1891 a new sanatorium for fever and isolation cases and convalescent patients was opened on a site near Freeman's Wood to replace an earlier smaller building which was demolished to make way for an extension to Williamson's industrial premises. The baths on Cable Street, which Samuel Gregson MP had presented to the town in 1863, were refurbished in 1880 and new Turkish baths added fourteen years later.

Since 1826 gas had been supplied by a private company on St George's Quay. The Lancaster Gas Act of 1879 empowered the council to purchase the company to ensure quality and control pricing; this it duly did the following year at the cost of £80,000. In 1894 it introduced electricity into the town, initially for street lighting, public buildings and commercial and manufacturing premises. The council also undertook considerable street widening at this time, demolishing the entire west side of the narrow China Lane and widening Nicholas Street in the 1890s, and building a new bridge over the canal at the top of Penny Street in 1900. In 1902-3 it constructed electric tramways with lines running from Dalton Square via Bowerham to Williamson Park, to Scotforth and, after 1905, to Castle railway station. By this time it had also taken over responsibility for elementary education, the Storey Institute, a new public library and Williamson Park, including a new observatory erected at council expense in 1892 to house the astronomical telescope donated by John Greg's son, Albert. Another public cemetery was laid out in Skerton in 1904 and the small one provided by Scotforth township in 1890, prior to being incorporated into the borough, was significantly enlarged in 1908.[72]

Although this expansion of local government responsibility was impressive, we should beware of exaggerating it or of assuming that it was motivated purely by notions of public service. Rather than embracing the extra responsibilities thrust upon it by central government, the council tended to view many of them as unwelcome burdens. It took most satisfaction from the construction of prestigious tangible assets like the market, street improvements and civic buildings or from the purchase of private utilities like gas and electricity whose profits could be used to subsidize rates. Municipal enterprise was a far cry from the 'municipal socialism' which some radicals in the country dreamed of. All this meant that there was still significant scope for voluntary or private provision of services. The council's public health measures, for example, were overwhelmingly preventive not curative. When the Royal Lancaster Infirmary was built between 1888 and 1896 to replace the increasingly inadequate premises on Thurnham Street which the dispensary had occupied since 1833, it was funded by voluntary subscriptions. Medical care received here or from the town's general practitioners had to be paid for unless patients were sponsored by a subscriber or could claim from a friendly society. Despite occasional pleas from radical councillors, especially in the early 1890s when the housing shortage was particularly acute, the provision of municipal housing for the poor was never put on the agenda. Bye-laws controlled the type of housing which could be erected but, with the majority of the council benefiting from the expanding demand for accommodation, either as private landlords or as builders, interference did not stretch beyond that. Proposed extensions to the public tramway system, including the purchase of Lancaster & District Tramways Company which operated a horse-drawn service from Stonewell to Morecambe, were shelved after 1905. Even in education, the most rapidly expanding area in the 1890s, there was still considerable private involvement at secondary level and denominational influence in elementary schools.

To some extent, such policies were imposed upon councillors by an economically-minded electorate whose sullen resentment about paying rates tended to erupt into organised ratepayer rebellions after every major increase in public expenditure. Such protests were particularly evident during the early 1880s after heavy expenditure on waterworks, and they resurfaced in the mid-1900s as the town ceased to expand and the rate in the pound rocketed to finance the labour and capital intensive education services. But town councillors were far from being mere pawns in the hands of an electorate which, despite changes to the franchise, was still dominated by propertied and business interests; they were themselves representatives of those interests.

Prior to 1835 the corporation had been dominated by merchants, wealthy professionals and members of the local county gentry. These were exclusively Tory Anglicans elected by and from the freemen of the town. Only after the repeal of the Test and Corporation Acts in 1828 were non-Anglicans free to hold public office. Before the reform of 1835 few did. Excluded from

Astronomical telescope, Greg Observatory, Williamson Park. The Gregs were keen amateur scientists and astronomers and this instrument was originally situated in John Greg's observatory at Caton. It was presented to the town after his death by his son Albert. The ruins of the observatory built to house it can still be detected on a knoll to the west of the Ashton Memorial. It also housed telescopes for viewing Morecambe Bay, and the district meteorological record station. The building was pulled down after the Second World War.

Royal Lancaster Infirmary, erected by public subscription and opened by the Duke and Duchess of York, 24 March 1896. The exterior view above shows doctors' carriages waiting; the photograph below is the matron's sitting room.

Lancaster Corporation tramshed, Thurnham Street. Trams were among the last of the council's municipal enterprises and one of their least successful, arousing considerable opposition from ratepayers in early years when they failed to return profits. The site is now used as a garage.

corporate office, Nonconformists and non-freemen channelled their political energies into the Police Commission. This was not an elected body; membership was open to all owners of property valued at £70 per annum or tenants of premises valued at £40 for poor rate purposes, except those running licensed premises.[73] Nationally, the Liberal challenge to Anglican, Tory-dominated institutions peaked in the 1830s and led to the passing of the Municipal Corporations Act of 1835 which swept away all the privileges of old corporations such as Lancaster, and introduced a limited form of democracy, based on a property qualification. Resident male ratepayers now elected eighteen councillors representing three wards – Queen's, Castle and St Anne's – who in turn elected two aldermen for each ward and the mayor. As its promoters intended, the act upset existing patterns of control, the initial elections returning an alliance of Whig (moderate Liberal) manufacturers, led by Greg, Burrow, Higgin and Gregson, and Radical tradesmen who were anxious to rid the corporation of alleged corruption and to effect further reductions in expenditure.

By the early 1840s, however, their force had been dissipated and the political heat had evaporated allowing the Tories to regain control. For the next decade and a half, professional men, especially lawyers, physicians and the architect Edmund Sharpe, took a leading role, supported by leading members of the business community. Professionals' involvement declined markedly after the mid-1850s, however, after the full cost of the sanitary improvements became clear and as the demands of their careers increased. Their place was filled from the 1860s by a loose alliance of Liberal small property owners, businessmen and retailers, under the watchful eyes of the Storeys and Williamsons on whose prosperity they were largely dependent. The ending of Anglican dominance of religion and education in the town by the 1890s was mirrored in the council chamber where an increasing proportion of new entrants were Nonconformists. Although Wesleyans had to wait until 1896 when Norval Helme occupied the chair, the mayoralty ceased to be the monopoly of Anglicanism and Old Dissent when the first Catholic mayor, Thomas Preston, was elected in 1875. The complete absence of women and working men from local politics, however, continued to symbolise their relative powerlessness in a town essentially dominated by propertied interests.[74]

Parliamentary Politics

There was a similar transformation in the social and political backgrounds of the men elected to represent Lancaster in parliament. Prior to 1832, only freemen of the borough were entitled to elect the town's two MPs. The vast majority of resident freemen had interests in trade, as too had those who had migrated to Liverpool but had retained their rights to vote in their home town. Agricultural interests were bolstered by the large number of farming 'outvoters' in the surrounding district. Lancaster's parliamentary representatives in the early nineteenth century invariably reflected this mix of economic interests, being drawn exclusively from mercantile and landed families. Before the 1830s, party labels were largely immaterial and it was well nigh impossible for less privileged outsiders to mount any form of challenge to this arrangement. Elections were often uncontested and tended to take the form of public celebrations and carousing. Liverpool men's interests in the dwindling merchant community in Lancaster declined after the contested election of 1818 when William Gladstone's father, John, a Liverpool merchant, and Gabriel Doveton, an officer in the East India company, were both returned. Thereafter, local Tory gentry re-asserted their influence in the persons of John Fenton Cawthorne and Thomas Greene of Whittington Hall.

The Reform Act of 1832, which nationally gave the vote in boroughs to men occupying property rated at £10 per annum, only marginally affected Lancaster since freemen and their sons, however poor, were allowed to retain their right to vote and continued to comprise the majority of the electorate. In 1832 and 1835 Greene and Patrick Stewart, a Whig and nephew of the Duke of Hamilton, were returned unopposed. The small band of Liberal manufacturers in the town, their confidence boosted by success in the municipal elections after 1835, ran John Greg's brother, William Rathbone

SIR THOMAS STOREY.

By the end of the nineteenth century, the town's major employers were in opposing political camps and in the election of 1892 the Conservative (or Unionist) Thomas Storey stood unsuccessfully against James Williamson, the incumbent Liberal. Not surprisingly in view of his opposition to Irish Home Rule, his appeal was distinctively nationalistic.

Despite his elevation to the peerage, Lord Ashton continued to be actively involved in the local political arena. His open telegram supporting the Liberal Norval Helme in 1906 (*facing page*) made it crystal clear how he wanted his workers to vote, as well as indicating what might happen to their jobs if the Tories triumphed.

Greg, in the election of 1837 and John Armstrong, proprietor of Galgate silk mill, four years later, but the Tories were again successful on both occasions, Greene and George Marton of Capernwray Hall, patron of the vicarage of Lancaster, being returned with handsome majorities.

From the late 1840s, however, landed Tories' fortunes were on the wane and successes became conditional upon them espousing Liberal causes. Greene's success in 1847 and 1853 was due in large part to his support for the cause of freer trade; William Garnett of Quernmore Park and Bleasdale Hall, returned in 1857 and 1859, had manufacturing connections and was also a free trader who even claimed to support further, if limited, electoral reform. After 1847, however, the local gentry were obliged to share representation with wealthy urban Liberals like Samuel Gregson (1847–8 and 1852–65) and John Armstrong's son, Robert (1848–53), who could claim to represent the manufacturing interests of the town.

Unfortunately for Lancaster, diehard Tories refused to accept defeat graciously. They cried foul, successfully petitioning against Gregson's election in 1847 and Armstrong's five years later on the grounds that the electorate had been illegally bribed. Evidence from the poll books, publications which

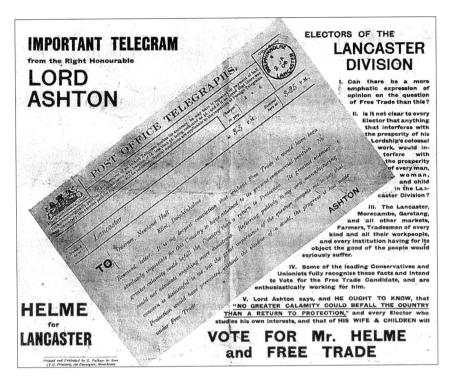

IMPORTANT TELEGRAM
from the Right Honourable
LORD
ASHTON

POST OFFICE TELEGRAPHS.

HELME
for
LANCASTER

ELECTORS OF THE
LANCASTER
DIVISION

I. Can there be a more emphatic expression of opinion on the question of Free Trade than this?

II. Is it not clear to every Elector that anything that interferes with the prosperity of his Lordship's colossal work, would interfere with the prosperity of every man, woman, and child in the Lancaster Division?

III. The Lancaster, Morecambe, Garstang, and all other markets, Farmers, Tradesmen of every kind and all their workpeople, and every institution having for its object the good of the people would seriously suffer.

IV. Some of the leading Conservatives and Unionists fully recognise these facts and intend to Vote for the Free Trade Candidate, and are enthusiastically working for him.

V. Lord Ashton says, and HE OUGHT TO KNOW, that "NO GREATER CALAMITY COULD BEFALL THE COUNTRY THAN A RETURN TO PROTECTION," and every Elector who studies his own interests, and that of HIS WIFE & CHILDREN will

VOTE FOR Mr. HELME
and FREE TRADE

Printed and Published by C. Falkner & Sons (T.U. Printers), 170 Deansgate, Manchester

recorded each individual's open vote, does not suggest that any bribery which may have occurred had much effect since, here as elsewhere, an elector's occupational status was the major determinant of voting behaviour. Farming, professional and mercantile groups tended to support the Tories, shopkeepers and craftsmen the Liberals.[75] The borough nevertheless acquired a reputation for corruption. When the Tories were defeated in 1865 they again resorted to petitioning against the result. The Liberal government, anxious to root out abuses and to establish a case for further political reform, seized on the opportunity to establish a Royal Commission to enquire into the matter. As a result of its highly critical report, Lancaster was disenfranchised, losing its ancient right to return its own MPs to parliament.[76] The Second Reform Act of 1867 consequently had no impact on the town despite its growing manufacturing prosperity and importance. Until 1885 Lancaster's parliamentary representation was subsumed within the larger county constituency of North Lancashire where more restrictive voting qualifications favoured dominant agricultural, Conservative interests. Only once, in 1880, when Thomas Storey presented himself as a Liberal candidate for this constituency, did the town attempt to challenge the might of the dominant county aristocracy, but to no avail; he was crushed by the combined forces of General Randle Joseph Feilden of Witton Park, Blackburn and the Right Honourable Frederick Arthur Stanley, later the 16th Earl of Derby.

In 1885, however, as a result of the Redistribution of Seats Act, the town's separate representation was restored, but only as a single member constituency and with extended boundaries which took in some surrounding districts. Local Tory, landed influence briefly reasserted itself in 1885–6 and 1895–1900 when George Marton and Yorkshire industrialist and owner of Hornby Castle, Colonel W. H. Foster, respectively headed the polls, but in both cases they benefited from being portrayed as local candidates against unknown Liberals brought in at short notice from outside. With the exception of these two short interludes, the town was represented until 1918 by just two men, both of them local oilcloth producers, both of them Liberals: James Williamson (1886–95) and Norval Helme (1900–18). In 1892 Williamson faced a challenge when Thomas Storey, who had defected from the Liberal party in protest against Gladstone's decision of 1886 to support Home Rule for Ireland, stood against him as a 'Liberal Unionist'. Despite obtaining Conservative backing he was soundly beaten, but only after a bruising, bitter contest.[77] Thereafter, despite continuing to support many of the town's charities and institutions, the Storeys effectively withdrew from active participation in national and local politics. Thomas died in 1898 in his town house, Westfield House, but his son Herbert withdrew to the country, concentrating on rebuilding the Bailrigg estate which his father had bought in 1887, while Isaac chose to reside in Caton where the firm still retained a significant manufacturing presence. James Williamson, or Lord Ashton as he was called after his elevation to the peerage in 1895, also purchased the country estates of Ashton Hall in 1884 and Ellel Hall in

Facing page Civic Opening of Penny Street Bridge, Thursday 24 May 1900, Queen Victoria's birthday. The flags and bunting were re-used from Mafeking celebrations of the weekend before. The new bridge was just one of many 'improvements' made in the two decades before the First World War. Demolition of the council-owned Corporation Arms and Prince William Henry Inn just to the north commenced the same week to make way for commercial hotels more in keeping with Lancaster's prosperous and progressive image. Commemorative plaques on the bridge were not approved of by the *Lancaster Guardian:* 'If the designers wish them to serve as reminder that at some time we shall be reposing calmly with coffin plates above us, well and good. But if they are intended as ornaments, they can only be described as miserable failures.'

Above The Ashton Memorial, Williamson Park, photographed by Ian Beesley.

1898 but unlike the Storeys he remained firmly rooted in his town house, Ryelands, overlooking the main road from the north. From here he gave his unreserved backing to Helme who, despite his business interests in Halton, resided at Springfield Hall overlooking the road from the south. Although he never held office after his peerage, Ashton used his purse, patronage and control of employment to wield considerable political influence in the town.[78]

Philanthropy and Power

In the late 1880s, as their wealth accumulated while their political differences widened, the Storeys and Williamsons, fathers and sons, vied to outdo each other in public generosity, dispensing donations to a wide variety of benevolent, medical, educational institutions and social clubs while supplying the capital to expand major civic amenities. Between 1887 and 1891, in commemoration of the jubilee of Queen Victoria, for which he, as mayor, had organised the local celebrations, Thomas Storey financed the rebuilding of the Mechanics Institute on Meeting House Lane. Renaming it the Storey Institute in 1891, he subsequently donated it to the town in 1893 as a technical and science school, newsroom, library, art school and gallery, and venue for musical recitals. In 1904 his son, Herbert Storey, donated another £10,000 to extend the premises up Castle Hill, providing more rooms for teaching science, domestic economy, art and commerce.

Lord Ashton supported local societies and council amenities on an even grander scale, and was largely responsible for two major landmarks in the urban landscape: Williamson Park and the Town Hall. Proposals to convert the corporation's old stone quarries on the Moor into a park had first surfaced during the Cotton Famine of the early 1860s when public works schemes for the unemployed were being widely used elsewhere in textile Lancashire for this purpose. In the end, however, the council did nothing beyond improving access to the site by building a road across it. Landscaping was only undertaken from the late 1870s when James Williamson I offered to meet the cost, later estimated to be in the region of £13,250. Given the intractable nature of the land, work proved to be protracted but, in 1881, two years after his death, his son finally handed the completed grounds over to the corporation, endowing them with a bequest of £10,000 to provide an income to maintain them. After 1904 he financed additional improvements: a new stone bridge over the lake, stone shelters, a bandstand, a fountain, a 'temple' and palm-house. In 1907–8 he spent a further £87,000 on what is now considered to be the park's centrepiece, the Ashton Memorial, or 'The Structure' as it was often known, opened, however, without public ceremony in October 1909. By this time he had also come to the rescue of the hard-pressed council with a substantial subsidy towards the £155,000 needed to construct the magnificent Baroque-style town hall on Dalton Square which

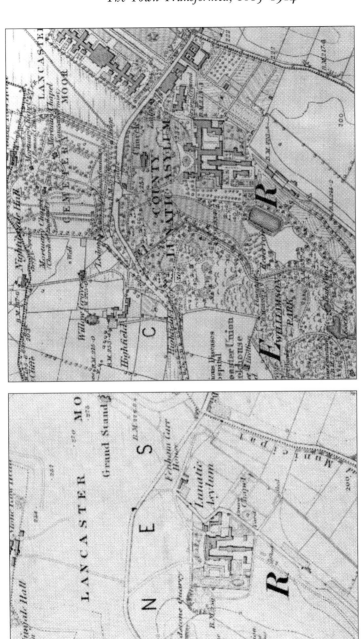

Lancaster Moor 1845–95. Over the half century the old stone quarries had been converted to Williamson Park, the rough pasture to the north end laid out as a municipal cemetery and the County Lunatic Asylum had been considerably expanded, incorporating land once used as a racecourse.

he, rather than the mayor, opened with appropriate public ceremony and
celebrations in December 1909. This boasted a full range of civic offices, a
new police headquarters, courts, banqueting rooms and hall capable of seating
2,800 people. Dalton Square was also redesigned, and the monument to
Queen Victoria and eminent personalities of her reign, including James
Williamson senior, was erected in 1907, also at Ashton's expense.[79]

Despite the shift from mercantile and landed to industrial wealth over the
century, therefore, money, status and power still seemed inextricably linked
in the local community as the new century outgrew its infancy. Despite some
erosion of local ownership of manufacturing industry, most noticeably and
disastrously in the case of the Wagon Works, and the emergence of national
multiples in the shopping district, the town's economy continued to be
dominated by local capitalists. Their involvement in municipal government
legitimised their power, power which, despite some erosion of autonomy
brought about by directives from Westminster, still granted the council
considerable freedom to manage its affairs as it wished. The town's tradesmen,
shopkeepers and many of his employees, also publicly acknowledged, though
not always willingly, the influence which Williamson and his factories had
over the town. Despite the existence of Storeys, firms with international
reputations such as Gillows and, until 1909, the Wagon Works, Lancaster
was very much Williamson's town. Even those who did not work for him and
those who sought in the closing years of the Edwardian era to challenge his
political dominance could hardly pretend it was otherwise when the skyline
was dominated by his mills, his town hall and his memorial.

Notes

1. References for this chapter are primarily intended to guide the interested reader
to published works, theses and collections which can be consulted in Lancaster
Central (LCL) and Lancaster University (LUL) libraries rather than to provide
a complete list of sources. Primary sources are only specifically cited for
quotations or when details they contain provide corrections to published
accounts. The most important original sources in the Central Library include
local newspapers especially *Lancaster Gazette* (1801–94), *Lancaster Guardian*
(from 1837), *Lancaster Observer* (1860–1944), *Lancaster Standard* (1893–1909)
as well as the shortlived *Lancaster Times* (1892–7), *Lancaster Mail* (1909–11)
and *Lancaster Herald* (1831–3); trade directories, maps, census enumerators'
books, electoral lists, poll books, Port and Police Commission records and a
wide variety of miscellaneous business, political and social records. The university holds unpublished theses, British Parliamentary Papers, census material,
some poll books, trade directories and a limited selection of newspapers. Among
the more significant collections in Lancashire Record Office (LRO) in Preston
are borough rate books, accounts and minutes, county records dealing with
the prison, asylum, poor law and education, and parish and church records.
Lancaster City Museums also hold some primary material which may be seen
upon request.

2. There are several published collections of old postcards which provide a rich visual panorama, particularly of the late Victorian and Edwardian period: A. White, *Lancaster: a Pictorial History*, Phillimore, 1990; S. Ashworth and N. Dalziel, *Lancaster and District in Old Photographs*, Alan Sutton, 1993; R. Alston, *Lancaster and the Lune Valley*, Alan Sutton, 1994; A. Duckworth, *Light on Old Lancaster*, Ashleigh Barrow Books, 1993.

3. M. M. Schofield, *Outlines of an Economic History of Lancaster, Part II: Lancaster from 1800 to 1860*, Lancaster Branch of Historical Association, 1951, provides the basis of much of the analysis of the port which follows.

4. A. White, *The Lune Shipbuilding Company*, Lancaster City Museums, Local Studies, no. 2, n.d.

5. N. Dalziel, *Shipbuilding at Glasson Dock*, Lancaster City Museums, Local Studies Series, no. 6, n.d.; J. Hayhurst, 'An economic and social history of Glasson Dock', unpublished M. Phil. thesis, Lancaster University, 1985, now edited by K. Soothill and published as J. Hayhurst, *Glasson Dock: The Survival of a Village*, Lancaster University, Centre for North-West Regional Studies, 1995.

6. M. E. Burkett, E. Tyson, D. How and R. Hasted, *A History of Gillow of Lancaster*, Lancashire County Council, 1984; *Lancaster Records, 1801–1850*, Lancaster Gazette, 1869, 144 (2 October 1823); L. Boynton, *Gillow Furniture Designs, 1760–1800*, The Bloomfield Press, 1995.

7. R. Fawthorp, 'Financing a provincial railway in the mid-1840s', *Centre for North-West Regional Studies, Regional Bulletin*, n.s., no. 5, Summer 1991, 15–20, estimates that Lancaster accounted for only 18 per cent of capital subscribed.

8. K. Nuttall and T. Rawlings, *Railways around Lancaster*, Dalesman, 1980, chapters 1–5 provide basic details. See also D. Joy, *Main Line over Shap*, Dalesman, 1975, and M. D. Greville and G. O. Holt, *Lancaster and Preston Junction Railway*, David & Charles, 1961; D. Binns, *Midland Lines around Morecambe, Heysham and Lancaster*, Trackside Publications, 1995.

9. Schofield, *Economic History*, 119–20; K. H. Docton, 'Phoenix Foundry', in *On Lancaster*, typed monograph, *c.*1971, 40–1.

10. G. Woodhouse, 'The Lancaster Railway Carriage and Wagon Company', *Contrebis*, vol. 1, no. 2, 1974, 21–3.

11. Obituaries in the local press often provided details of these individuals' careers. See also Cross Fleury, *Time-Honoured Lancaster*, Eaton & Bulfield, 1891, chapter XI; C. A. Russell, *Lancastrian Chemist: the early years of Sir Edward Frankland*, Open University Press, 1986; J. H. Brooke, *Inventing Science: Lancaster's Forgotten Sons*, Lancaster University, 1977; M. Farr, *Thomas Edmondson and his Tickets*, the author, 1991. Bibby's originally traded in Fleet Square, but transferred to Liverpool 1885–8 as its scale of operations grew, although local production was continued by W. & J. Pye. See J. B. & C. L. Bibby, *A Miller's Tale: a history of J. Bibby &Sons Ltd., Liverpool*, Bibby's, 1978, 3–14; J. A. Pye & A. P. Bathgate, *From Century to Century: the story of Pye Farm Feeds*, Pye Farm Feeds, 1997.

12. M. Winstanley (ed.), *Rural Industries of the Lune Valley*, Lancaster University, Centre for North-West Regional Studies, 2000.

13. M. B. Rose, *The Gregs of Quarry Bank Mill: the rise and decline of a family firm, 1750–1914*, Cambridge University Press, 1986, 38–9, 62–7.

14. *Lancaster Guardian*, 25 March 1837.

15. *Lancaster Guardian*, 10 December 1837, *Lancaster Gazette*, 21 April 1838; Tithe

Commutation Map and Apportionment, Township of Bulk, 1843 (LCL); O.S. 60" map, 1849 (surveyed 1845).

16. LCL, MS 5279-90 for background to the Threlfalls' business interests. The rate books for the 1840s (LRO) list the firm as Hardy, Threlfall and Co.

17. P. J. Hudson, *Coal Mining in Lunesdale*, Hudson History, 1998, 26–39.

18. *Lancaster Guardian*, 12 September 1840, 10 January 1852, 5 March 1853; Lancaster Poor Rate Books (LRO) 1841 and 1849.

19. *Lancaster Guardian*, 21 June, 12 July, 23 August 1856; for the Jacksons' background see J. M. Beeden, 'The origins of Calder Vale and Oakenclough', *Contrebis*, vol. 8, 1980, 63–7.

20. *Lancaster Guardian*, 8 February 1868, 21 May 1870. Most sources follow Schofield in dating this purchase to 1864.

21. *Lancaster Guardian*, 10 February 1899 (obituary of Richard Jackson); Lancaster Poor Rate Books 1871 and 1875; G. Sealey, 'The Quaker Community in Lancaster, 1850–1890', unpublished Diploma in Local History Dissertation, Lancaster University, 1992, 27 reproduces the Quakers' November meeting report on Jackson which discussed his insolvency.

22. For fuller descriptions of these mills and their remains see J. Price, *Industrial Lancaster*, Lancaster City Museums, Local Studies no. 12, n.d. and A. S. Mousdale, 'Textile mill architecture in Lancaster and its hinterland – a preliminary survey', unpublished Dissertation for the Diploma in Industrial Archaeology, Birmingham University, 1988 (copy in LCL).

23. P. J. Gooderson, *Lord Linoleum: Lord Ashton, Lancaster and the Rise of the British Oilcloth and Linoleum Industry*, Keele University Press, 1996. See also obituary of James Williamson in *Lancaster Guardian*, 11 January 1879; *Williamson's of Lancaster, 1844–1944*, Centenary History, 1944; Price, *Industrial Lancaster*; S. Ashworth, *The Lino King: the life and times of Lord Ashton*, 1989.

24. G. Christie, *Storeys of Lancaster, 1848–1964*, Collins, 1964, *passim*.

25. E. Baines, *A Companion to the Lakes*, 1829, 7–45.

26. *Lancaster Records*, 30 October 1824, 29 August 1827. Jane Scott was subsequently tried and executed for the murder of her mother in March 1828.

27. Baines, *Companion*, 7.

28. K. H. Docton, 'The Lancaster Races', in *On Lancaster*, 68–78 and *Lancashire and Cheshire Historian*, vol. 2 (LCL); *Lancaster Guardian*, July 1840, 20 June 1857; *Lancaster Gazette*, 10 July 1858.

29. N. Wigglesworth, *A History of Rowing in Lancaster*, Lancaster City Museums, Local Studies, no. 17, 1992.

30. A. G. Betjemann, *The Grand Theatre. Lancaster: two centuries of entertainment*, Lancaster University, Centre for North-West Regional Studies, 1982, 14–25.

31. Cross Fleury, *Time Honoured Lancaster*, 457–66; the society's records are in Lancaster Central Library.

32. M. de Lacy, *Prison Reform in Lancashire, 1700–1850: a study in local administration*, Chetham Society, vol. 33, 1986; J. M. Somekh, 'Lancaster Castle, 1774–1865: a case study in prison reform', unpublished MA dissertation Lancaster University, 1981; *Lancaster Guardian*, 12 April 1879; *Cross Fleury's Journal*, 1899–1900, *passim*; M. Winstanley (ed.), *Lancaster Castle as a 19th-century Prison*, Lancaster City Museums, Local Studies, no. 20, 1993; D. Sailor, *The County 'Hanging Town': trials, executions and imprisonment at Lancaster Castle*, Lancaster, Challenge Publishing, n.d.

33. Census of Population, 1911.

34. P. Williamson, *From Confinement to Community: the moving story of 'The Moor',
    Lancaster's County Lunatic Asylum*, Bay Community NHS Trust, 1999; *Lancaster
    Moor Hospital, 150th Anniversary Souvenir, 1816–1966*, North Lancashire and
    South Westmorland Hospital Management Committee, 1966; J. K. Walton,
    'The treatment of pauper lunatics in Victorian England: the case of the
    Lancaster Asylum, 1816–1870', in A. Scull (ed.), *Madhouses, Mad-Doctors and
    Madmen: the social history of psychiatry in the Victorian era*, Athlone Press, 1981,
    166–97; J. K. Walton, A. Hogg and L. Hurley, 'Lancaster Asylum in the 1850s
    and 1860s: patients and treatment', *Lancaster and Westmorland Medical Journal*,
    vol. 1, no. 3, Sept. 1990, 74–7; J. K. Walton, 'Lunacy in the Industrial Revol-
    ution: a study of asylum admissions in Lancashire, 1848–50', *Journal of Social
    History*, vol. 13, no. 1, 1979–80, 1–22.

35. J. Alston (with E. Roberts and O. Wangermann), *The Royal Albert: chronicles of
    an era*, Lancaster University, Centre for North-West Regional Studies, 1992;
    H. R. Hutton 'The Royal Albert Asylum and its work', in D. Davis (ed.), *The
    Castle Howell School Record*, Lancaster, 1889, 241–51; M. Elder, *Celebrating a
    Century of Service*, Lancaster Acute Hospitals Trust, 1996; P. Lavington, 'Lan-
    caster's Hospitals', typescript, Manpower Services Commission, n.d. provides
    a brief, illustrated history of all the institutions (LCL).

36. M. Macdonald, 'The introduction of the New Poor Law in Lancaster', unpub-
    lished MA dissertation, Lancaster University, 1994.

37. S. A. Eastwood, *Lions of England: a pictorial history of the King's Own Royal
    Regiment (Lancaster), 1680–1980*, Silver Link Publishing, 1991 provides a full
    history of the regiment.

38. A. G. Boulton, 'Lancaster, 1801–1881: a geographical study of a town in
    transition', unpublished MA thesis, University of Liverpool, 1976, provides a
    detailed survey of housing development within the old borough boundary.

39. Lancaster Borough Rate Books (LRO) and census returns can be used to
    provide a detailed picture of the growth of the town and social gradations
    within in it; see for example, A. Hogg, S. Kelly, C. Price and K. Smith, *St
    George's Quay and Bridge Lane, Lancaster*, Lancaster City Museums, Local
    Studies, no. 15.

40. J. D. Marshall, 'The Story of the Freehold', *Centre for North-West Regional
    Studies, Bulletin*, n.s. no. 4, Summer 1990, 19–22. For the national society see
    G. Elkington, *The National Building Society, 1849–1934*, Heffer, 1935, chapters
    1 and 2.

41. W. A. Smith, *A History of the Origin and Progress of the Lancaster and Skerton
    Equitable Co-operative Society Limited*, Milner, 1891, 46–7.

42. A. White and M. Winstanley, *Victorian Terraced Houses in Lancaster*, Lancaster
    University, Centre for North-West Regional Studies, 1996, provides a full
    history and gazetteer.

43. J. W. A. Price, *Sharpe, Paley and Austin: a Lancaster Architectural Practice, 1836–
    1942*, Lancaster University, Centre for North-West Regional Studies, 1998;
    R. Jolley, *Edmund Sharpe, 1809–1877: a Lancaster architect*, Lancaster Univer-
    sity, Visual Arts Centre, pamphlet, 1977.

44. P. J. Gooderson, 'The Social and Economic History of Lancaster, 1780–1914',
    unpublished Ph.D. thesis, Lancaster University, 1975, 192–224 provides an
    analysis of census returns.

45. Obituaries, three volumes of press cuttings, LCL.

46. J. K. Walton, 'The medical profession in mid-Victorian Lancaster', *Lancaster and Westmorland Medical Journal*, vol. 1, no. 6, September 1991, 164–7.

47. *The Commercial Directory for 1818–19–20*, J. Pigot, 1818.

48. Anon, *The Pictorial History of the County of Lancaster*, 1844, 300.

49. *Lancaster Guardian*, 21 October 1837; *Lancaster Records*, 5 August 1844.

50. M. J. Winstanley (ed.), *A Traditional Grocer: T. D. Smith of Lancaster, 1858–1981*, Lancaster University, Centre for North-West Regional Studies, 1991.

51. W. A. Smith, *Co-operative Society; Co-operative Congress Souvenir: Lancaster, 1916*, C. W. S., 1916; *Lancaster and District Co-operative Society Ltd: seventy five years of Co-operative service, 1861–1936*, 1937.

52. Trade directories, despite their inconsistencies, provide the best overview of changes in the number and location of retail outlets. For most of the nineteenth century, Lancaster was included in county or regional series published by firms such as Kelly, Slater and Pigot. Only selected trades and private individuals were listed. These continued to be produced into the present century but more detailed information was included in town or district directories published between 1881 and 1912: P. Mannex & Co., *Topography and Directory of Lancaster Sixteen Miles Round*, 1881; P. Barrett and Co., *Topography and Directory of Preston, the Fylde, Lancaster and District*, 1886; Well's *Lancaster and District Directory* 1889; W. J. Cook and Co., *Lancaster, Morecambe and District Directory*, 1896, 1899 and 1901; W. Watson & Co., *History, Topography, General and Commercial Directory of Lancaster, Morecambe etc.*, 1899; T. Bulmer & Co., *History, Topography and Directory of Lancaster and District*, 1912.

53. White and Winstanley, *Terraced Houses*, 43–8.

54. J. Catt, *A History of Lancaster's Markets*, Lancaster City Museums, Local Studies, no. 7, 1988.

55. Local newspapers regularly listed arrivals at the King's Arms in the early nineteenth century. Dickens's account of his visit to the hotel in 1857 with Wilkie Collins can be found in *The Lazy Tour of Two Idle Apprentices*, chapter IV. For the context see D. Steel, 'Charles Dickens, John Ruskin and the old King's Arms Royal Hotel, Lancaster with seven letters to its landlord, Mr Joseph Sly' in K. Hanley and A. Milbank (eds), *From Lancaster to the Lakes – the region in literature*, Lancaster University, Centre for North-West Regional Studies, 1992, 41–58.

56. File containing press reports and Articles of Association 31 October 1878, LCL.

57. LCL, Pamphlets, PT 808, 809, 957, 960.

58. Mechanics Institute Catalogues and Minutes, LCL; the local press also contained regular reports of its proceedings.

59. Smith, *Co-operative Society*, 32–40.

60. There are few published studies of these societies and clubs. See, however, P. Wade, 'Astronomy in 19th century Lancaster, IV; a wider view', *Reflections* (Journal of the Lancaster & Morecambe Astronomical Society), vol. VIII, no. 3, July 1985; Wigglesworth, *Rowing*; T. Alderson, *Cricket by the Lune*, Lancaster, *c.*1984; 'Cross Fleury', *Time Honoured Lancaster*, chapter XV (bowmen and Philippi Club) and appendix (societies); J. N. Stanley, 'Freemasonry and the middle class in Lancaster, 1789–1914', unpublished MA dissertation, Lancaster University, 1997; C. Haines, 'Libraries and Newsrooms in Lancaster prior to

the adoption of the Public Libraries Act in 1892', unpublished Diploma in Library Studies dissertation, University College, London, 1981, copy in LCL; G. Vidler, 'A Study of Libraries in Lancaster from 1695 to 1964', unpublished BA dissertation, Manchester Polytechnic, 1981, copy in LCL. Lancaster Central Library contains files on many of the societies but many records remain in private hands or have been lost.

61. A. Betjemann, *The Grand Theatre*, chapter 3; R. Bingham, *Lost Resort? the flow and ebb of Morecambe*, Cicerone Press, 1990; local trade directories and press advertisements.

62. R. N. Billington and J. Brownbill, *St Peter's Lancaster: a history*, Sands & Co., 1920, and N. Gardner, 'The Coulstons of Lonsdale and Lancaster: merchants, bankers and Catholic benefactors', *North West Catholic History*, vol. XXV, 1998, 10–27.

63. For the changing composition and problems of the Quakers G. Sealy, 'Quaker community'.

64. J. W. A. Price, '200 Years of Congregationalism in Lancaster', typescript, 1972, copy in LCL.

65. Methodist activities were regularly reported in the *Lancaster Guardian*, owned by the Milner family, but there are few published histories of them.

66. E. Baines, *History, Directory and Gazetteer of the County Palatine of Lancaster*, 1825, vol. II, 21.

67. G. R. Gregg, *Schools and Education in Lancaster*, Lancaster City Museums, 1982; W. French, *Education in Lancaster: N.U.T. Conference Handbook, Morecambe 1909*, 1909.

68. *The Castle Howell School Record*, 1888, contains an excellent description of the school and a full list of pupils, many of whom wrote articles for the volume.

69. A. L. Murray, *The Royal Grammar School: a history*, Heffer, 1952. This impressive piece of scholarship was begun while the author was still a pupil at the school.

70. P. J. Gooderson, 'Social and Economic History', 66–113, 234–85; T. J. Cooper, 'Police, Politics, Parsimony and Public Opinion at (sic) Lancaster in the second quarter of the nineteenth century', unpublished MA dissertation, Lancaster University, 1982; K. H. Docton 'The Lancaster "Police" Commissioners', *On Lancaster*, 99–114. Police Commission records are held in LCL.

71. Gooderson 'Social and Economic History', 286–315 provides an excellent history of the public health crisis and the subsequent backlash after the mid-1850s; E. D. De Vitre, 'The Sanitary Condition of the Town of Lancaster', *Local Reports on the Sanitary Condition of the Labouring Population of England*, 1842, 341–8; R. Owen, 'Report on the Sanitary Condition of the Town of Lancaster', *Health of Towns Commission*, 1845; J. Smith, *Report to the General Board of Health on the sanitary condition of the inhabitants of the town of Lancaster*, 1849; E. Sharpe, A *History of the progress of Sanitary Reform in the town of Lancaster, 1845–1875*, 1876.

72. The local press carried full details of all these activities and trade directories summarised the provision of council services. There are only a few published studies of specific provisions: S. Shuttleworth, *The Lancaster and Morecambe Tramways*, Oakwood Press, 1976; R. Wade, 'Astronomy in 19th.-century Lancaster, Part 3; the Greg observatories', *Reflections*, vol. VIII, no. 1, 1985.

73. Gooderson, 'Social and Economic History', 66–117; Cooper, 'Police, Politics',

83–4; and Royal Commission on Muncipal Corporations: report on the borough of Lancaster, 1833, copy in LCL.

74. Gooderson 'Social and Economic History', 234–85, 432–531 for full analysis of council membership. The first working man was elected in 1907.

75. Poll books have survived for most Lancaster elections up to and including 1865; M. A. Manai, 'Influence, corruption, and electoral behaviour in the mid-nineteenth century: a case study, Lancaster, 1847–65', *Northern History*, vol. XXIX, 1993, 154–64.

76. J. D. Marshall, 'Corrupt practices at the Lancaster election of 1865', *Transactions of the Lancashire and Cheshire Antiquarian Society*, Vol. LXIII, 1952–3, 117–30; Parliamentary Papers, 1867, XXVII, Royal Commission on the 1865 Lancaster Election Petition.

77. For detailed results of parliamentary elections see *MacAlmont's Parliamentary Poll Book, 1832–1918*, 8th edn, 1971, edited by J. Vincent and M. Stenton; for brief biographical details of successful candidates, see M. Stenton & S. Lees, *Who's Who of British Members of Parliament* vols 1 and 2, Harvester 1976 and 1978. The admittedly partisan local press remains the best source for election proceedings. Electioneering ephemera (posters etc) can be found in LCL and LRO.

78. Gooderson, *Lord Linoleum*, Part II.

79. The local press carried full details of all these activities. For the wider significance of the town hall see C. Cunningham, *Victorian and Edwardian Town Halls*, Routledge, 1981.

CHAPTER SIX

Challenge and Change
in a New Century

Stephen Constantine and Alan Warde

By the beginning of the twentieth century Lancaster had become a substantial community and a major industrial, commercial and service centre.
Its people, more numerous than ever before, were experiencing by their
own standards unprecedented prosperity. More and better housing was
being built even for some working people, and the quality of the environment
had been raised, for example by investment in improved sanitation, with
subsequent benefits to public health. Most of the architectural features
which still grace the urban landscape were already in place or were under
construction during the first decade, many owing to the munificence of
Lord Ashton, the Storeys and other members of the manufacturing and
commercial elite. The *Blue Guide to England* of 1920, based largely on
pre-war data, might devote only one short paragraph to a description of
Lancaster – a 'quiet county town' – but notice was taken of the Storey
Institute (erected 1887–91, extension 1906), the new Town Hall and the
Ashton Memorial (both constructed 1906–9) and not just of the ancient
priory and castle (admission sixpence). Its account also revealed to the visitor
how intimately Lancaster appeared to be connected to the outside world.
Naturally, most emphasis was placed upon its position on the main railway
line (230 miles from London on the route to Glasgow), but rail links east
to Yorkshire, west to Morecambe and south-west to Glasson Dock were
also noted, and references to road and tramway routes were given. Such
networks, of course, explain the contacts firmly established between the
town and the wider world outside. Lancaster served not only the communities of north Lancashire. Manufacturing and commerce connected it
intimately with the national and indeed with the international economy.

This involvement provides us with one interpretive guide to Lancaster's
twentieth-century experiences. Earlier chapters have shown that the town's
physical growth, character and economic fortunes had been frequently
affected by external opportunities, by outside competition and by the course
of national and international politics. Lancaster people had taken their
chances or been forced to respond to these external circumstances, with

greater or lesser degree of success. Nevertheless, much initiative had remained in local hands. At the beginning of the twentieth century the political and economic elite of the town were from well-established local families with largely local loyalties. Their labour force was also mainly recruited locally. Their patronage sustained local philanthropy and even many of the high cultural activities in the town, and the rest were still often locally devised and certainly locally managed. Moreover, the business decisions of their private companies were swayed largely by their local judgements. Sovereignty, though never absolute, was local. Not for nothing was Lord Ashton described as Lancaster's 'Lino King'.

Economic, cultural and political autonomy became more difficult to sustain in the modern period. The twentieth century witnessed still greater changes in the speed of communications, by road, if not invariably by rail, and more recently through telecommunications. The movement of goods and the sale of services became easier and accordingly more national and indeed international in organisation. Investment capital also became more fluid and could be raised and moved with increasing ease, across the country, eventually internationally, and both into and out of local societies. Such flexibility might make local economies more dependent upon outside support. Since the costs of modernising or equipping new businesses also tended to rise in real terms, small towns like Lancaster became more reliant upon external investment rather than upon locally-raised capital, and therefore more dependent upon outside decision-makers. Notoriously, the formation of public liability companies in Britain was followed by mergers, both national and international, and by the expansion of chain stores and branch offices and their penetration of local communities.

It might also be suspected that the twentieth century saw the erosion of local cultural activities. Of course, during the nineteenth century better communications (especially the railways), mass literacy and some improvement in living standards had accelerated the formation of a national market for books, newspapers and magazines and had encouraged enterprising theatre companies to tour the provinces. Professional sport, not least the formation of the national Football League in 1888, had linked major centres in England one with another. But the scale of cultural penetration from outside and the tendency towards a more homogeneous national culture were undoubtedly further assisted by modern communications, notably the cinema, radio and television. It may be asked how Lancaster people responded to these influences and how far, if at all, distinctive cultural practices and values were preserved.

We need to consider the impact upon the town of one other development in modern British society, the growth in the authority of central government. As previous chapters have demonstrated, particularly in the nineteenth century much of the quality of urban life – environmental, social, cultural and educational – had depended upon the decisions of local patrons, local charities and locally-elected town councillors. Of course, by the later nineteenth century many local council initiatives were driven by national legislation, increasingly mandatory and less permissive in character. Standards were being imposed from outside. However, during the twentieth century still more substantial changes were to be required locally as a result of national legislation and central government administration. The range of public services was to be considerably extended in scope. On the one hand local authorities increased their duties but more often as agents of central government rather than as independent actors, and on the other hand certain responsibilities were largely taken out of the hands of local town councils and even of local voluntary bodies, to be made the duties of enlarged county authorities, nationalised industries or central government agencies. Increasing and perhaps improving public services may have required a loss of local autonomy, or at least a loss of control may have been one result of their extension.

If such economic and administrative developments were among the conspicuous features of national British history, can their impact be discerned in Lancaster? To what extent were the town's fortunes increasingly subjected to outside forces and with what effect upon the life experiences of its citizens?

Before and After the First World War

In 1901 the population of the municipal borough was recorded as 40,329. At that time prosperity was being sustained by a broad economic spread, largely under local ownership and management, providing a wide range of employment, at least for men. Lancaster was an important regional service centre, and there were jobs on the railways, in the administration of justice, in the large local hospitals, in education, in retailing and in the provision of professional services to an extensive area of north Lancashire. Signs of local prosperity at the turn of the century can be seen in the flourishing building trade, constructing new housing especially to the east and south of the town centre. But above all the local economy depended on manufacturing. Industrial occupations were dominated by the linoleum, oilcloth and table baize businesses of Williamsons and Storeys. Gillows had merged successfully with Waring in 1897 and remained a major employer at their factory and showroom on North Road, opened in 1881. Breweries provided further opportunities, and the Phoenix Foundry turned out castings, steam engines and other engineering products for local and external markets. Then there was the Lancaster Wagon Company on Caton Road, a major engineering enterprise, first established in 1863, employing over 1,000 workers by 1901 and serving a national and particularly an international railway market. There were fewer openings for the paid employment of women outside textiles and the clothing trades, except in domestic service. Proportionately more homes in Lancaster contained a resident domestic servant in 1901 than the average for the county; indicative perhaps of the size and prosperity of Lancaster's middle class as well as of the lowness of domestic servants' wages. The economic activity rate, which measures the proportion of adults in or seeking paid employment, stood at 79.6 per cent for men and 30.5 per cent for women: these figures were a little below national averages because of the high proportion of Lancaster's population in institutional care in its large hospitals.[1]

Scarcely had the new century opened than Lancaster's vulnerability to outside forces was exposed. As noted in the previous chapter, the local Wagon Works were taken over in 1902 and incorporated into the Metropolitan Amalgamated Railway Carriage and Wagon Company, centred on Birmingham, which promptly began to run down the Lancaster business, virtually closing the plant by 1909 with substantial job losses. The local impact was severe, probably exacerbated by a national economic recession. The exodus from the local community of many skilled and formerly high earning engineers necessarily hit the local retailing and housing markets. About 500 houses stood empty in the town by 1913, rents had fallen, and building workers found themselves laid off. Hard times were even experienced in the oil cloth business.[2] The results were evident in the 1911 census. The population had only risen to 41,410, a mere 2.5 per cent increase over the previous decade compared with an 8.9 per cent increase in the administrative county and a very substantial 10.9 per cent in England and Wales. By contrast with the huge population increases in Lancaster recorded after almost all the previous censuses, this was a disturbing result. Even the percentage of households with a resident domestic servant had fallen, probably indicative of some tightening in the circumstances of Lancaster's middle class. The economic activity rate had fallen to 76.6 per cent for males and 29.1 per cent for females. These rates were not only lower than the county and national figures but had moved in the opposite direction. Already the new century had shown how the perhaps inescapable reduction in local control over the economy had left the town vulnerable to outside decision-makers.[3]

Depression had not lifted before other external events commanded local attention. Lancaster people would have followed the reports leading to the outbreak of the First World War in the columns of the national newspapers. *The Daily Mail* (founded 1896) and the *Daily Express* (launched in imitation in 1900) had already intruded into local popular culture. But in those days even local newspapers like the *Lancaster Guardian* and the *Lancaster Observer* carried a considerable volume of national and international news, and they described for readers their versions of the road to war. The declaration of war on Germany on 4 August 1914 was greeted locally, as elsewhere in the United Kingdom, with what to postwar eyes seems bewildering approval.[4] Years of political and social conditioning had led Lancaster people to accept war not just stoically but with enthusiasm. This, of course, was a garrison town with barracks at Bowerham and a long military tradition going back, for the romantically inclined, to defensive actions against the Scots and even to the Romans. More recently, soldiers of the King's Own Royal Lancaster

Civilian Soldiers. A contingent of 200 men, recruited into a 'Pals' company of the King's Own Royal Lancaster Regiment following the Mayor's appeal for volunteers, marching down Castle Park after a church parade, prior to departing for training, 11 September 1914.

Regiment had fought in the South African War of 1899–1902 and their dead had been magnificently honoured in 1903 with a Memorial Chapel in the Priory church. Eagerness to participate in the expected short, sharp and, of course, successful adventure ensured an early and plentiful supply of young men to the new armies which Lord Kitchener set about recruiting. For example, 297 men working at Storeys had already volunteered by January 1915.[5]

Neither the duration nor character of the war matched expectations. This proved to be total war, hard and bitter. National commitments exacted their price from all parts of the country, perhaps more severely felt the smaller and more intimate the community. Military conscription was imposed early in 1916; local casualty lists, printed in the local papers, lengthened. The dead of this war also were granted their memorials, many of them, for example in the roll of honour in the Priory's Memorial Chapel, in the Memorial Library at the Royal Grammar School, opened in March 1930, with its inscription *dulce et decorum est pro patria mori*, on the staircase in Waring and Gillow's showrooms, which proudly recorded the names of those employees 'who nobly responded to the call of duty during the Great War', and in particular on the ten bronze panels bearing 1,010 names in the Garden of Remembrance alongside the Town Hall, dedicated on 3 December 1924. The poet Laurence Binyon (1869–1943), born in High Street, Lancaster, immortalised them all in 'For the Fallen': 'They shall grow not old, as we that are left grow old ...'

But the most vital memorial was created out of the home and estate of the late Sir Thomas Storey at Westfield. Thomas Mawson (1861–1933), the internationally famous Lancaster architect, garden designer and town planning specialist, had been campaigning nationally to establish village settlements for disabled ex-servicemen. Herbert Storey offered his father's estate as a gift, a gesture of posthumous benevolence, and upon its grounds were built initially thirty-five cottages and bungalows in a garden village setting. Further donations from the Storeys and others subsequently expanded the facilities. Westfield Memorial Village was opened on 27 November 1924, fittingly by Field-Marshal Earl Haig whose military skills on the Western Front had been responsible for so many British casualties.[6]

Total war was a commitment of economic resources as much as of military manpower. As such, the First World War affected directly the home front in Lancaster as in other manufacturing towns. The appetite for armaments demanded a substantial increase in output, and largely under the vigorous direction of Lloyd George, as Minister of Munitions, later as Minister of War and ultimately as Prime Minister, the national government stumbled towards state economic mobilisation. The impact upon Lancaster's economy was felt in the redirection of several Lancaster firms towards war production: for example, aircraft wings and propellors were made by the craftsmen at Waring and Gillows, and Storeys made shells at White Cross. The Wagon Works site on Caton Road was first used as a prison camp for interned German aliens (guarded for a while by a detachment of the Royal Welch Fusiliers under the command of the poet Robert Graves), but during 1915 it was developed alongside a new state-owned National Projectile Factory and made munitions in conjunction with a National Filling Factory at White Lund.

War Work. Capping the filled shells at the National Projectile Factory, Caton Road. Two-thirds of the workers in this picture are women.

Women's Emancipation? Mollie and Maggie, two munitions workers, in overalls with trousers, 7 September 1918.

(Tragically, the casualties of war included ten workers killed in an explosion at White Lund in October 1917.) Over 8,000 people were being employed by these government factories at their peak. Such became the shortage of (literally) manpower during the war that many of these workers were women.[7] Here we might seem to see the transforming power of an outside force, lifting Lancaster's economy out of depression and enhancing (we are sometimes told) the status, earnings and aspirations of working people in general and of women in particular. It is doubtful if the First World War deserves even that credit. The ending of hostilities was greeted by understandably emotional scenes,[8] but even this relief was the prelude to greater difficulties in the town.

The munitions factories ceased production, and once again unemployment rose when returning ex-servicemen remained out of work or displaced others, particularly women, who had temporarily taken their places. The local Labour Exchange run by the Ministry of Labour, first established in Lancaster after national legislation in 1909 and occupying the former Assembly Rooms on King Street, was distressingly crowded. Local like national trade had been disrupted by war and postwar inflation, and Lancaster's international markets were difficult to restore. Moreover, postwar government policy was severely deflationary, making recovery difficult. Storeys, for example, felt obliged to reduce wages and cut prices in 1921–2.[9]

The census of 1921 provides a bleak picture. The recorded population of 40,212 was actually lower than in 1911, a fall of 2.9 per cent. In the administrative county and in England and Wales increases of 3.6 per cent and 5.0 per cent respectively had occurred. Over the decade, births in Lancaster had exceeded deaths by 2,263: many people, obviously discouraged by local economic dislocation and unattractive prospects, had left the town: an estimated 3,461. The female population had risen by just two over the ten years, but the number of males had dropped by a huge 1,200, the carnage of war adding to the losses caused by migrating workers. Such disruption largely explains a remarkable change in the sex ratios of the population: in 1911 there had been 1,049 females to every 1,000 males (below the national average for England and Wales of 1,068), but by 1921 the proportion of females had increased to 1,116, above the national figure of 1,096. (The still higher figures recorded thereafter, up to 1,134 in 1951, were probably affected by the composition of the hospital population.) Economic activity rates had also been disturbed by the postwar depression: figures of 78.3 per cent for men and 30.2 per cent for women were marginal improvements on 1911 but still below the levels of 1901. In later years, local people would look back on this period with grim memories.[10]

From the 1920s to the 1940s

These would seem inauspicious circumstances in which a Lancashire town should enter the 1920s and 1930s. Notoriously, these were years of exceptionally high unemployment nationally. Moreover, most of those out of work were concentrated in the north and west of the country where industrialisation had been heavily concentrated in the nineteenth century and where local prosperity had become hugely dependent upon exports. Foreign competition and changing patterns of domestic and international demand wreaked damage. Migration from the north-west, north-east and south Wales left several regions in distress and some towns devastated.[11] However, although Lancaster historically shared several features with other industrial communities, the town remarkably escaped the troubles of even near neighbours like Preston and Barrow. Those places were too exclusively committed to the staple export industries of cotton and shipbuilding respectively which were among the most severely savaged sectors, whereas Lancaster's economic mix proved to be more resilient and actually became more diversified. During the 1920s the local economy began a cycle of expansion which largely sustained the town until the 1960s.

The population figures are revealing, even allowing for some borough boundary changes. They record an increase to 43,383 by 1931, up by 7.9 per cent since the previous count, and to 51,270 by 1951, up by a further 18.2 per cent. (The outbreak of war prevented the holding of a national census in 1941.) Even faster increases occurred in the wider Lancaster region embracing also Morecambe, Heysham, Carnforth and adjacent rural districts: 10.1 per cent and then 28.5 per cent. By contrast the figures for England and Wales as a whole were only 5.5 per cent and 2.9 per cent and for the administrative county of Lancashire just 2.2 per cent and 1.5 per cent or virtual stagnation. Since the birth rate was also falling in this period in Lancaster (as elsewhere), from an average of 26.05 births per 1,000 of the population in 1900–9 to 16.61 births by 1920–30 and still lower thereafter, the rapidity of increase was due partly to a fall in the death rate and still more to inwards migration. Employment opportunities were growing. The economic activity rate reached a peak of 84.4 per cent for men in 1931 and was still over 80 per cent in 1951, while for women it touched 32.8 per cent in 1931 and climbed further to 33.6 per cent by 1951. Although unemployment was never eradicated between the wars, the rate recorded by the census even in the worst year of 1931 was much below national and especially county figures: just 6.5 per cent for men (compared to 11.5 per cent in England and Wales and a severe 17.2 per cent in Lancashire) and 7 per cent for women (10.4 per cent nationally and 16.3 per cent for the county).[12]

This reversal in Lancaster's previous economic experience owed something to the further expansion of its service sector. During these years Lancaster businesses benefited by responding to that growing demand for retail, administrative and professional services which more modernised economies create. The town's geographical position, comparatively free of competition in the large area of Lancashire and Cumbria north of Preston and south of Kendal, enabled it to expand its traditional service functions. The extension of local government responsibilities provided additional opportunities. About

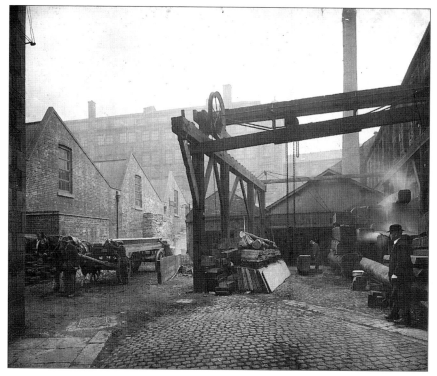

Fine Furniture. Waring and Gillows, about 1919. Selecting and moving timber from the yard behind the North Road site.

46 per cent of employed persons in Lancaster were in the service sector by 1931, increasing to 46.4 per cent by 1951, a figure slightly above the national average and nearly 5 per cent over the county's.[13]

Moreover, Williamsons and Storeys made the most out of the expanding national and international demand for their products. In spite of the high levels of unemployment in interwar Britain, the country as a whole probably grew economically at a faster rate than ever before. Much of this growth may have been generated in the midlands, the south and the south-east where, for example, motor car manufacturing, electrical engineering and the production of consumer goods were largely located. But the economy also benefited nationally from a remarkable boom in house building, some four million new homes being constructed in Britain between the wars.[14] Each of these homes needed furnishing, and it was to satisfy such domestic demands for oilcloths floor cloths, table baizes and later wallcoverings that Lancaster's principal industry responded. These businesses revealed a sensitivity to technical opportunities for improved production and later to new products like plastics which enabled them to respond to changes in market taste.[15]

However, the local economy was also strengthened during the 1920s by diversification. How this occurred remains obscure, but it is evident that the

Storeys Workers. A group of men and boys employed in the manufacturing of table baize and leathercloth, about 1920.

local council took some initiatives to persuade outside businesses to move some of their operations into the town. Morton's Ltd, trading as Sundour Fabrics, arrived from Carlisle in 1923 and occupied the former Wagon Works site to manufacture carpets and furnishing materials; later, under the name Standfast, they made dyes and bookcloths; James Nelson & Co. Ltd erected an artificial silk yarn factory in 1927; and the Cellulose Acetate Silk Co. Ltd, later renamed Lansils, began operations in 1928 and by 1931 were employing 1,600 people.[16] This investment from outside undoubtedly eased Lancaster's future, but it is obvious that the persuasive powers of local councillors were not alone responsible for it. This was in addition a town with good rail and reasonable road communications to national markets. But it was also a town whose labour force attracted outsiders in the 1920s. Many workers, it is true, were experienced in manufacturing, and efficient, hard-working and adaptable, according to the managing director of Cellulose Acetate Silk.[17] They were also, after the depressing experiences of the previous decade or so, comparatively poorly paid. Furthermore, this appeared to be a remarkably undemanding workforce, industrially subdued and politically quiescent.

Lancaster in the first half of the twentieth century was surprisingly free from industrial conflict. Elsewhere in Britain the opening of the century had seen a huge increase in trade unionism, growing from two millions in 1900 to a peak of nearly eight and a half millions in 1920, plus a veritable explosion of strike action by both skilled and unskilled unions, especially in clusters of years just before and after the First World War. By contrast in Lancaster there were few unionists, and still fewer signs of militancy. Ashton had perhaps set the tone of local industrial relations before the end of the previous century by refusing trade union recognition to all but a tiny elite of skilled craftsmen. Unions were largely confined to woodworkers, railway workers and skilled engineers. The principal employers undoubtedly co-operated then and thereafter in denying employment to workers who appeared troublesome. Their commanding position as major employers in a small town appeared to induce quiescence among most employees in self-protection. Depression in the town before and after the First World War further encouraged that response. Ashton had also acquired a reputation as a strict observer of local working-class behaviour, recording, for example, the names and activities of the disaffected in his 'black book' (now in the Lancashire Record Office). Though stories of his employment of spies may have been exaggerated, popular belief in these legends – and their perpetuation into the present – reveal their potency. Of course, it might be argued that such deterrents were at least matched by the reputation earned by Williamsons and Storeys as good employers. They provided job security and gold watches or similar rewards for long service and performed acts of benevolence to individual employees, often by stealth, in addition to their much more lavish philanthropic public gestures. Paternalism often combines both faces. The effect appears to have rendered the workforce docile, conscious of their powerlessness.[18]

This helps to explain why the Labour Party in Lancaster grew but slowly in comparison with other northern industrial towns. First attempts to establish Labour organisations in the early 1890s had rapidly folded, to revive insecurely in the new century: the Trades and Labour Council was recreated in 1900, a branch of the Independent Labour Party was restored in 1905, the first Labour town councillor, Henry Jemmison, was elected in 1907 and the Trades Hall was opened in 1908. But all these gains seemed to come to nothing after the notorious Skerton election in 1911 when the ILP candidate, William Wall, came within a whisker of defeating Lord Ashton's publicly endorsed candidate: his reaction, threatening a withdrawal of his patronage, reversing a promised wage increase and allegedly forcing the dismissal of dissidents from his workforce, effectively drove political and industrial radicals into disorganised retreat.[19]

It would be an exaggeration to say that Labour elsewhere in Britain invariably grew rapidly after its first trembling formation as a national parliamentary party in 1900, but certainly greater advances in organisation, competitiveness and achievements were being recorded in other northern towns during the 1920s and 1930s than occurred in Lancaster. It is true that the First World War had stimulated trade union development locally, and that unionists, surviving members of the ILP and representatives of the Co-operative Society succeeded at last in forming a constituency branch of the Labour Party in August 1918. But it made little headway against the Liberals and Conservatives. Labour was not ready to contest the election in November 1918 and failed to put forward a candidate in 1923. Fenner Brockway (1888–1988), early in his long career in socialist politics, brought credibility to the party at the election of 1922, drawing in such distinguished speakers as Ramsay MacDonald, Philip Snowden, Bernard Shaw and the young Clement Attlee. He won over 9,000 votes, 31.6 per cent of the poll. But Labour's share at later elections in the 1920s and 1930s actually fell, recovering from a low of 17.5 per cent in 1924 to 24.3 per cent in 1931 before falling again to 20 per cent in 1935.[20]

Perhaps Labour's most signal early achievement was to drive many former Liberal voters, fearful of socialism, into the arms of the Conservatives. Sir Norval Helme had held the seat for the Liberals in the four general elections held in 1900, 1906 and 1910 (twice), but after the war Lancaster soon ceased to be a Liberal parliamentary seat. It was held by the Liberals only in 1923–4, after the Conservative Prime Minister Stanley Baldwin had called an election on the divisive issue of tariff reform, and in 1928–9, after the by-election caused by the resignation of the remarkable Sir Gerald Strickland (1861–1940): born in Malta, he had served as a Colonial Governor in various parts of the British Empire before becoming not only MP for Lancaster from 1924 but in addition Prime Minister in Malta from 1927. After 1929 his former constituency became a safe seat for the Conservatives, whose majority in 1935 was 13,578.[21]

Meanwhile, Labour was making a poor showing even in local elections. Of the eighty-eight councillors who served the community from 1913 to 1938, only thirteen represented the Labour Party. Only three were elected in 1918–24, three in 1925–31 and a rather more creditable seven in 1932–8. The political apathy which derives from powerlessness was exemplified in the scarcity of political contests. Between 1918 and 1938, when the regular November elections or by-elections were held, local wards were only contested on sixty-one occasions out of a possible 191, and Labour was involved in only fifty-one: on all other occasions the sitting member was returned unopposed. It is true that the first Labour mayor, James Hodkinson, was appointed in 1930, but Labour remained firmly the minority party.[22]

Liberals and Conservatives, increasingly calling themselves Independents, therefore continued to run the local town council. The social character of this governing body had not much changed since the close of the previous century, except in some further withdrawal of the formerly dominant employers. Ashton, as noted in the previous chapter, had avoided all overt local political responsibility since the 1890s; when he died in 1930 his grandson and successor as chairman was Lord Clanfield whose interests were far more diverse and detached from the town. Likewise, the Storey family was moving away from its Lancaster roots and losing political interest, and the retirement of Sir Norval Helme from the council in 1919 began the decline of that dynasty's involvement long before his death in 1932. As a result, town councils were largely made up of small businessmen and shopkeepers. Nonconformists dominated, out of all proportion to their share of the population. These people had the virtues and sometimes the limitations of their class and background: proud of their independence, public-spirited

The Mayor and Ex-Mayors. Councillor Annie Helme, the first woman Mayor 1932–33, surrounded by the Beadle, Mr Ashcroft, and several of her male predecessors, including Alderman Till and Alderman Parr.

by their own lights, sympathetic to self-help and other liberal virtues, and irreproachable in their financial management of the town's affairs. Their probity, their negotiating abilities and more than likely the low level of local rates which their financial control of the town had ensured probably further explain the attraction of Lancaster to those important investors who came in from outside during the 1920s.[23]

One consequence of their values was a cautious attitude to collectivist action, a commitment to limited public expenditure and a reluctance to extend public services. This did not mean that local government responsibilities did not increase, but it is instructive to note where and why. The priority lay in improving those aspects of the town's economic infrastructure which supported business activities. Their encouragement of inward investment by new companies has been noted and may stand to their credit. Likewise the council was also involved in the improvement of roads and local transport. For example, the new road between Lancaster and Morecambe was completed in 1923, and the upper part of King Street was widened in 1937. Investment in motor buses (and a shift away from the trams which had rattled around Lancaster from 1903 to 1930) and the opening of a bus

Lancaster Slums. St Mary's Place, off the top end of Church Street just below the Priory Church, 16 May 1927. This is one of many photographs recording the Lancaster of the 1920s taken by the local photographer Sam Thompson.

station on Cable Street and in 1939 a depot at Kingsway are similarly indicative of a commitment to aid the daily movement of labour. Power, too, was a matter of economic importance, and the council evidently saw advantages to local businesses as well as potential profits to ratepayers when in 1922 it bought the electricity generating station from the former National Projectile Factory on Caton Road, and hugely increased local consumption (823,000 units in 1915: 32,600,000 by 1936). Likewise the council reconstructed its gas supply system in 1927 and built a new gasholder (and blot on the landscape) in 1933. Of similar economic and domestic value was the opening of a new reservoir at Langthwaite in 1935 and an improved sewerage scheme in 1937 to limit pollution of the Lune.[24]

Economic as well as social gains were also expected from Lancaster's commitment to municipal council house building in the 1920s and 1930s. A housing shortage was evident in Lancaster as in most towns of Britain after the war. The first council estate, built to generous standards between Bowerham Road and Scotforth Road, consisted initially of fifty houses, each costing £938 and to be let at rents (plus rates) ranging from 9s. 3d. (46p) for a two-bedroomed house to 12s. 3d. (61p) for one of four bedrooms. The quality of the houses, however, owed much to the terms of the Addison Housing Act passed by Lloyd George's Coalition Government in 1919: it limited the local cost to the product of a penny on the rates, the rest to be borne by central government. Later legislation, beginning in 1923, was less generous, and the extension of the Bowerham council estate and those constructed thereafter at Newton, Beaumont, Ryelands, Greaves, Skerton and Marsh were not so well-endowed. Altogether 1,748 council houses were erected between 1920 and 1938, making the council by 1939 the owners of thirteen per cent of the 12,700 houses in Lancaster. This substantial achievement was partly due to obligations imposed from outside by national legislation, both Conservative and Labour. A rise in recorded levels of overcrowding during the 1920s unequivocally demonstrated a local housing shortage, and the law demanded responses and set the standards. Similarly in the 1930s, national slum clearance legislation obliged the local council to quantify and clear substandard housing, and to rehouse the occupants in council housing. Over 600 unfit houses, many lurking in insanitary courts in the city centre, were closed or demolished between the wars, although much elsewhere remained to be tackled after 1945. There was perhaps one other incentive for local council action. It seems to have been one of the conditions demanded in 1923 by Morton's Ltd that housing would have to be constructed for the skilled workers they deemed it necessary to bring into the town, and the council seems to have accepted that obligation. Evidently private builders were thought unable to provide such accommodation at the right price. Since several councillors had business interests in the building trade, it is likely that all municipal housebuilding programmes were studied with exceptional care. One councillor, Thomas Till, who served without a break from 1916 to 1937, was a builder and contractor who also

Municipal Improvement. The formal opening of the Kingsway Public Baths by the Rt Hon. Walter Elliott MP, Minister of Health, 1 July 1939.

founded and became the first President of the Lancaster Property Owners Association, a body hostile to slum clearance proposals. Alderman Parr, a self-employed painter and decorator by profession, revealed a popular local priority in 1932: 'Lancaster is in the favourable position that the cost of its housing scheme is one of the lowest in the country.'[25]

More restricted were the council's commitments to welfare services between the wars. Perhaps exceptionally, the local authority constructed the splendid Kingsway Baths, opened in July 1939, at a cost of £59,000. (The National Swimming Championships were staged there in 1950 and 1951.) The Royal Lancaster Infirmary (opened 1896, extended 1929 and 1934) was a voluntary hospital dependent substantially upon charitable donations (recorded still in the entrance foyer and in some cases by wards and even beds named after benefactors). Its existence and status seemed to excuse the local authority from developing a municipal hospital. Although Morecambe Corporation had proposed a joint Hospital for Infectious Diseases in 1922, discussions were desultory. Even though the Lune overflowed its banks after a severe storm in 1927 and drowned three patients in the Lunesdale Isolation Hospital on Marsh Point, seven more years elapsed before the new hospital at Beaumont was ready for opening in 1934. Likewise, the council was slow to develop other services like child welfare clinics (three by 1938) and maternity clinics (two by 1938) whose establishment was by permissive, not mandatory, national legislation. It seems indeed that those services regarded by progressive opinion in the country as most valuable for women were least

'Follow the light, uphold the right.' The new Lancaster Girls' Grammar School was formally opened on 1 October 1914 by the Mayor in the presence of the Corporation and the Vice-Chancellor of Manchester University. The current school motto was adopted in 1919.

likely to be advanced in Lancaster. Expenditure per head in interwar Lancaster on such services (and on education and leisure facilities) rose but nevertheless remained lower than in, for example, Preston and substantially below that in Nelson. Priorities were in fact typical of those many other towns in Britain in which women's employment was comparatively low and in which the political energies of women were least organised. There were only three women councillors in the long period from 1913 to 1938 (although in turn they all became mayors, beginning with Annie Helme in 1932).[26]

Several of the other local services developed in these interwar years owed more to Lancashire County Council funding than to the town council. Since the passage of the Education Act of 1902, the county had been responsible for secondary education in Lancaster, leaving the town council (as a so-called Part III authority) in charge of elementary schools. County money and the county architect were therefore principally involved in the design and building of the new Lancaster Girls' Grammar School, previously and inadequately established in the Storey Institute in 1907, but transferred to its outwardly grand new quarters in Regent Street in 1914: additional buildings and the acquisition of sports fields followed between the wars. Responsibility for extensions to the Lancaster Royal Grammar School for boys also lay outside the town council (although town councillors were members of the governing body): an endowed school of some repute, it was able to tap private local wealth as well as county funds. The foundation stone of the New Building, designed and funded by the county authorities

Chain Stores. The original Marks & Spencer store, opened 3 November 1933. The original five bays upstairs became six when the store was extended in 1956 to incorporate premises next door to the right: the join is almost undetectable from the outside but can be identified inside from the pattern on the ceiling above the ground-floor showroom.

and costing £40,000, was laid in 1927 by one old boy and governor, Sir Norval Helme, and the building was opened in 1929 by another, Herbert Storey. Meanwhile, after delays caused by financial stringency in the 1920s, the town council constructed Skerton Central School in 1933 on severely utilitarian lines at a cost of £17,500, and later built two more junior schools at Marsh in 1936 and at Ryelands in 1939 to serve the expanding population on the new housing estates.[27]

Perhaps most radical was the reduction in the town's responsibility for its own poor. Not for the last time a Conservative government was suspicious of the operations of local authorities: Baldwin's administration in 1929 passed the Local Government Act which among other matters provided block grants on strict terms for the running of selected local services, and, more visibly abolished local Boards of Guardians. Their former duties for the administration of the Poor Law were transferred to Public Assistance Committees of county councils: Lancaster was left only with a subordinate committee presiding over local administration. Later, in 1934, the National Government, distrusting even county councils, passed the Unemployment Act which shifted responsibility for the able-bodied poor to Unemployment Assistance

Suburbia. Aerial photograph of Lancaster from the south in the late 1920s, showing private housing under construction off Greaves Road and council houses on Dorrington Road, to the right of the Royal Albert Hospital (*bottom left*). Also visible are Ripley Orphanage (*centre left*) and Storeys White Cross Mill with tall chimney (*centre top*).

Boards. Local offices appeared, as in Lancaster, to administer means-tested benefits but they were responsible not to the local town council, nor even to the county council, but to the Ministry of Labour in London (and more recently to the Benefits Agency). Discretion was being deliberately removed from local bodies.[28]

However, some of the other interwar developments in Lancaster were matters of private initiative, sometimes local. The town's comparative prosperity both attracted and was a consequence of local retailing changes. Some of these were undoubtedly due to local energies: Lancaster remained a town rich with family businesses. But already outside involvement was strengthening. W H. Smith's opened its first Lancaster shop in 1906. Boots, established in Nottingham in 1877, extended its branch on the corner of Common Garden Street and Penny Street in 1912. Marks and Spencer, founded as a limited company in 1903, opened a store next door on Penny Street in October 1933, to be followed later and lower down the street by Woolworths.[29]

Also arriving, in choking numbers, were motor cars and buses. Petrol stations and garages and AA-approved hotels became new business features of urban Lancaster. The joys of seaside holidays and the more tranquil

An Affluent Society? New buses, motor cars and the County Cinema in Dalton Square, originally a Catholic Chapel (1798) and latterly the Hippodrome variety hall and opera house – and now Council offices. Next door, to the left, stands the former home of Dr Buck Ruxton who in 1935 murdered his wife and servant. More cheerfully, the flags and the monument outside the cinema celebrate the granting of the city charter in May 1937.

delights of the Lake District had been discovered long before the interwar years, but on the whole in this period more people had more money for such enjoyments and they also discovered new ways of reaching their targets. As yet Lancaster was rarely a tourist destination itself: for many it was but a notorious bottleneck on the road to Morecambe or the Lakes where the A6 crossed the Lune via Skerton Bridge's single carriageway. Local traffic too was clogging up the city centre, as more buses, private cars and motor bicycles brought workers and consumers into town in larger numbers.

Such transport also encouraged the drift to the suburbs which was another common characteristic of British towns between the wars. Common too was the design of most of these new houses, making portions of urban Britain indistinguishable one from the other. They were usually squared semis with gardens front and back, the better owner-occupied versions often sporting bay windows and stained glass panels in their doors. These designs did not evolve from Lancaster's existing styles but were derived from the ideals of nationally respected housing reformers or even from the manuals issued by the Ministry of Health. Moreover, they were constructed largely from imported red bricks, sometimes stuccoed with grey pebbledash, discordant, some might say, with Lancaster's traditional (but expensive) stone. The rate of expansion was considerable: the 3,353 private houses built after 1920,

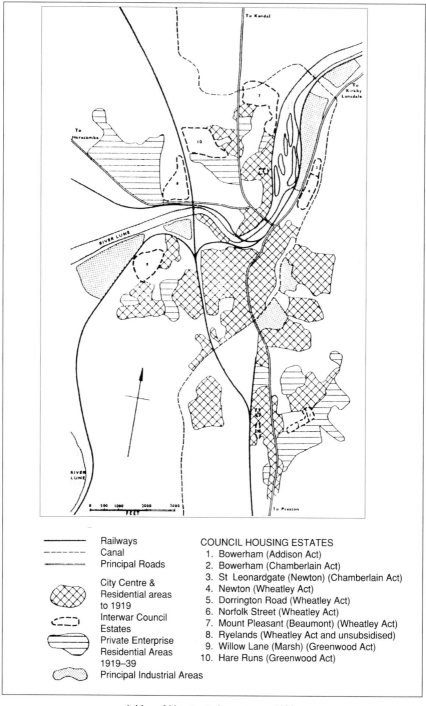

Railways
Canal
Principal Roads

City Centre &
Residential areas
to 1919

Interwar Council
Estates

Private Enterprise
Residential Areas
1919–39

Principal Industrial Areas

COUNCIL HOUSING ESTATES
1. Bowerham (Addison Act)
2. Bowerham (Chamberlain Act)
3. St Leonardgate (Newton) (Chamberlain Act)
4. Newton (Wheatley Act)
5. Dorrington Road (Wheatley Act)
6. Norfolk Street (Wheatley Act)
7. Mount Pleasant (Beaumont) (Wheatley Act)
8. Ryelands (Wheatley Act and unsubsidised)
9. Willow Lane (Marsh) (Greenwood Act)
10. Hare Runs (Greenwood Act)

A Map of Housing in Lancaster to 1939.

together with 1,748 council houses, meant that by 1939 some forty per cent of Lancaster homes had been built between the wars, compared to an average of around twenty-five per cent for England and Wales as a whole. But most new estates on green field sites were fairly small in scale, and much new building merely occupied vacant plots between existing houses on the roads leading out to Morecambe, Bare, Caton and south through Scotforth.[30]

These housing styles, brought in from outside, probably modified local culture. Some houses had been built with gardens before the First World War, as on the Freehold estate, but such properties were not as common as they now became. Gardening as a national preoccupation, even obsession, grew strongly between the wars, and no doubt in Lancaster too.[31] Other new (or newish) cultural activities in Lancaster also conformed to national patterns. All new houses, and very soon all of the old, were wired for electricity; most homes soon contained a wireless, tuned to the BBC, which began its services as a company in 1922 and as a public corporation in 1926. Lancaster, literally, became plugged into a national culture. Many homes, even of working people, also began to invest in gramophones, whose cultural reverberations were as much transatlantic as national. That was certainly true of the cinema. Lancaster's first picture house had opened in 1911; by 1938 there were seven. Lancaster people, especially the young, were as addicted as any other community to what A.J.P.Taylor described as the 'essential social habit of the age'.[32] But Lancaster people were not just passive recipients of the modern media: the Lancaster Amateur Dramatic and Operatic Society (LADOS), founded in 1891, continued its illustrious career (opening the interwar years in 1919 with 'Cingalee' and closing in 1939 with

Lancaster at Play (1): Skerton Athletic, football champions 1923–4.

Lancaster at Play (2):
Sir Lancelot Sanderson, a
member of the John O'Gaunt
Bowmen – founded 1788,
field day about 1930.

'Tulip Time'), the Footlights began its equally active tradition of amateur dramatics in 1920, WEA classes had been held since 1910, and the numbers participating in sport, including rowing, cycling, archery, cricket and particularly football, appeared to increase. Meanwhile, in 1923 the museum opened in the former town hall in Market Street, and in 1932 the public library moved to new quarters next door.[33]

Perhaps impressed by such signs of cultural as well as physical change, leading councillors felt some satisfaction by the mid 1930s with local achievements. In so far as the town was economically more prosperous than depressed Lancashire to the south, there were grounds for pride or at least relief. However funded, services for the local community had been increased. Though not lavishly endowed, the town was better equipped with educational, health and leisure facilities than before, and the quality of housing had been raised by some slum clearance and municipal and private building. Public health had generally improved, the death rate dropping from an average of 15.3 per 1,000 during 1900–9 to 12.1 per 1,000 by 1920–30; infant mortality, still shockingly high by modern standards, had at least fallen from 135 deaths per 1,000 live births in 1900–9 to seventy-three by 1920–30.[34] In these circumstances, councillors readily warmed to the

A City Celebrates. The formal announcement of the city charter, on the steps of the Town Hall, 14 May 1937.

suggestion, reputedly floated by Alderman Parr, that the town should be raised to the status of a city. This was accomplished with predictable pomp in 1937 when King George VI on the morning of his coronation (14 May) granted a new charter.[35]

It seems characteristic of the twentieth century that opportunities for celebration were brief. During 1938 all local authorities were receiving instructions from central government on the preparation of air raid precautions. Once again outside events were severely to disturb the community's activities. This time, however, the declaration of war against Germany on 3 September 1939, was received with stubborn resignation, perhaps with relief, but not with exhilaration.[36] This time, from the beginning, military recruitment was planned and ordered via conscription. Reservists were called up first, to Bowerham Barracks, and others followed in their age-cohorts, except for the unfit and for those men in reserved occupations in militarily important industries. Lancaster servicemen fought in Europe and in the Far East. One local regiment, sent to Singapore in 1941, disembarked straight into captivity: the Japanese set them to labour on the notorious Burma Railway. Many did not return. The city's dead were linked to the victims of the previous 'War to End All Wars', by adding 300 more names to the memorial in the Garden of Remembrance. Lancaster Royal Grammar School recorded the loss of 114 old boys.[37]

Evacuees. Children, whose luggage includes gasmasks in boxes, arrive with escorts at Greaves School, probably from Salford, September 1939. Near the junction of Greaves Road and Cheltenham Road.

The impact of the war was also experienced on the home front. The city had its air raid wardens and fire watchers. The Royal Observer Corps took over the castle. Brick air raid shelters were built for self-defence, and trench shelters dug in parks and playing fields. But only a few stray bombs fell locally, probably jettisoned by aircraft heading to or from such major targets as the shipyards at Barrow. Ripley Orphanage was taken over by the Auxiliary Territorial Service (ATS) and later by the Army as a training centre. Scrap metal collections deprived the city of, amongst other things, the Crimean War cannons which had stood outside the Shire Hall behind the castle and the railings and gates around Williamson Park. Council and community participated in the 'Dig for Victory' campaign, including the creation of more allotments and the coaxing of fresh vegetables out of school playing fields. Other local duties, particularly involving women, included work for the Red Cross, running a WVS Spitfire Shop in Market Street and the provision of aid for troops in transit – endless cups of tea and, judging by a rise in illegitimate births, more warming comforts. (Illegitimate births rose from 5.6 per cent in 1938 to 10 per cent of births by 1945: the national figure rose to 14.9 per cent.) The city was also designated a reception area for evacuees, and the council's billeting officers and the school authorities had to find homes and arrange schooling for working-class children, initially mainly from Salford. During the first week, 4,000 children arrived and were sent to Dallas Road School before distribution. By reputation these

Comforts for Soldiers. A fully-equipped WVS mobile canteen, presented by Lady Ashton at Ashton Hall, October 1940.

were slum kids from a rough city, and offers of billets came in slowly. Later evacuees came from Barrow, South Shields and London. Educational premises had to be shared and in some schools classes were taught in a two-shift system. Boys from Salford Grammar School were squeezed into Lancaster Royal Grammar School, and girls from Broughton and later Pendleton High Schools (also in Salford) were educated at Lancaster Girls' Grammar School.[38]

The city's other duty was once again to reorientate its economy for war purposes. The Royal Canadian Army Pay Corps was stationed in the city and employed large numbers of Lancaster women, and many others were drawn into industry. Joinery skills and equipment at Waring and Gillows were directed first towards making aircraft and later utility furniture particularly for the nation's blitz victims. Employees also sewed tents and camouflage netting. Storeys began turning out blackout fabric, gas capes and waterproofs, Williamsons also produced munitions, Standfast turned out tropical uniforms, camouflage materials and even bullet-proof vests, while other Lancaster businesses manufactured shoes for the ATS, insecticides and military clothing. Armstrong-Siddeley moved in from bomb-vulnerable Coventry to make aircraft components in Queen's Mill on Queen Street (now the site of B&Q). Many other Lancaster women had to travel out of Lancaster to work for English Electric in Preston or ICI in Heysham.[39]

VE Day (8 May 1945) was greeted in Lancaster with the enthusiasm typical of the country as a whole, undoubtedly to the distress of those with family or friends still locked in combat in the Far East or in Japanese prison camps.[40] Their war ended on 14 August. By then the domestic political scene in Britain had been transformed by the election of the first majority Labour government, committed to the creation of the Welfare State, the provision of housing and the nationalisation of the principal industries and services. The result was announced on 26 July. Lancaster's contribution had been to re-elect its sitting Conservative MP, Brigadier Fitzroy Maclean, just back from fighting alongside the partisans in Yugoslavia. He won a majority over Labour of 7,723 votes.[41] To what extent the war would be followed in Lancaster by economic depression, as after 1918, or by radical transformation, as promised by the government in London, remained to be seen.

Post-war to the Present

Hardships there undoubtedly were during the later 1940s as a punished British economy struggled to reinvest and to regain international markets while the population coped with shortages and substitutes. Lancaster's experience appears to have been no worse than elsewhere, and as already noted the population had risen to 51,270 by 1951. Thereafter, population figures for the municipal borough alone are misleading – they show a marked fall to 48,253 by 1961 and further decline thereafter to 47,888 by 1991 – because many people, encouraged by slum clearance and suburban housing developments and by public or more commonly private transport, were moving out of the city proper into surrounding areas. However, statistics for a Lancaster District, eventually created formally by local government reorganisation in 1974 and combining the city with adjacent Morecambe, Heysham, Carnforth and the villages of Lancaster and Lunesdale Rural Districts, show a combined population of 110,540 in 1951, rising by 3.9 per cent to 114,818 by 1961, and by a further 7.7 per cent to reach 123,619 by 1971. Growth then temporarily faltered, and by 1981 the total was down to 120,900. However, over the next decade the district's population grew by 4.8 per cent to reach 126,682 by 1991. It continued to rise. The estimated resident population in 1996 was 136,948. Moreover, economic activity rates for men were 76.9 per cent by 1981 and a significantly increased 57.1 per cent for women. Incomers since the war, compared with many other urban centres in Britain, have included only a small number of overseas immigrants, initially mainly from Poland and later, but a mere 1380 by 1991, from India and other parts of the New Commonwealth.[42]

This population expansion was greatly stimulated by the growth in the local economy's service sector. Service employment in the Lancaster 'travel-to-work-area' rose from less than 51 per cent of the total in 1961 to over 67 per cent, 29,200 jobs, by 1981. (The figure for Great Britain as a whole

Public Service. Two nurses at the
Garnet Clinic, 1965.

was by then only 62 per cent.) By 1995 the Lancaster District figure was
nearly 79 per cent, 32,400 jobs. More specifically, one consequence of more
public ownership and the extension of public services by the central government – begun by Labour after 1945 and sustained by most subsequent
administrations – was the growth of health, educational and other public
services with which Lancaster was already well-endowed. Local public service
employment therefore greatly increased, to provide nearly 25 per cent of
local jobs in 1971 and over 29 per cent, totalling 12,683, by 1981.[43]

However, it is plain that this expansion was coupled with a reduction in
the specific responsibilities of the city council. For example, nationalisation
transferred the ownership and management of the municipal gas and electricity supplies to nationalised companies in 1947–8 and eventually of the
city's water to the Lune Valley Water Board in 1961 and later to the North
West Water Authority. Privatisations in the 1980s did not, of course, return
these to council control. Similarly, the creation of the National Health
Service in 1948 involved welcome extensions to local health services, including more child welfare, ante-natal and later family planning clinics, plus in
due course a considerable expansion in the size and range of facilities of the
Royal Lancaster Infirmary and of the Beaumont, Royal Albert and Moor
hospitals (although later health policy changes caused the actual or virtual

Last Orders. The Lancaster City Police, photographed outside the Town Hall, on the occasion of the merger of the force into Lancashire County Police, March 1947. William Thompson, Chief Constable, Alderman Robertson, Chairman of the Watch Committee.

closure of the last three during the 1990s). But the city council lost, and was to continue to lose, such responsibilities as it had once shouldered either to Lancashire County Council or to the Regional Hospital Board, and later the Area Health Authority (reorganised in 1998). Likewise the borough police force was taken over by the county in 1947 (Lancaster was to gain in return a prestigious new police station in 1966), and the fire service was similarly absorbed by the county through the Fire Brigades Act, also in 1947 (and again Lancaster eventually acquired a new building, the fire station on Cable Street in 1972). Even local control over the castle was lost when it reverted in 1955 to use as a prison under Home Office control. Similarly, national policy launched by the Conservative government in 1980 to en-courage council tenants to purchase their homes had reduced the city council's housing stock by 1992 to 4,611 properties, less than nine per cent of the district's housing stock, and to just 4,469 by 1997.[44]

Meanwhile, the 1944 Education Act and the expansion of the child population of the area led to the building of more schools in Lancaster, the extension and improvement of facilities, and an increase in both teaching staff and the bureaucracy to support them. Local education became highly complex since schooling was divided between special, nursery, primary and secondary schools. The last were also subdivided after 1944 into grammar schools and secondary modern schools of different purpose but supposedly equivalent status. Moreover, account had to be taken of what became 'voluntary-aided' schools with their Anglican, Roman Catholic or, in the case of the boys' grammar school, non-denominational characters. New schools appeared, in particular following the merger which created Ripley St Thomas Church of England School in 1966 on the former Ripley

Orphanage site on Ashton Road, the opening of Our Lady's Roman Catholic High School north of the river in 1964, the construction in 1965–6 of Castle School (now known as Central High) to serve the population to the east of the city, and the building of new primary schools, such as Moorside in 1952. Proposals for the reorganisation of Lancaster's educational system along the principles of comprehensive education, once favoured by all national political parties in the 1960s and early 1970s, foundered, at least south of the river, on the objections in particular of the district's aided schools. All these schools, however, whatever their status, were largely (though with aided schools not entirely) financed and managed by Lancashire County Council as the Local Education Authority, albeit with central government support. When educational reforms were being planned nationally in 1944, Lancaster had fought and lost a battle with the Ministry of Education to secure 'Excepted District Status' which would have allowed it to retain control over its own primary schools. The city thereafter was represented on governing bodies only as a 'minor authority'. Subsequently, encouraged by the 1988 Education Reform Act, the two grammar schools chose to opt-out of county control and place themselves directly under the Department of Education in London. This choice may have increased the influence of local teachers, some parents and interest groups represented on their governing bodies: it was never intended, of course, to restore control to the locally elected city council. Jamea-Al-Kauthar Islamic College, an independently funded residential school for Muslim girls, which opened in the premises of the former Royal Albert Hospital in 1996, was similarly outside local authority care.[45]

The central government's decision to expand post-war education required an appropriate increase in teacher training education. For a short period after the war an Emergency Training College for ex-servicemen was established in the Ripley Orphanage, but more lasting was the opening of S. Martin's College in 1964 as a Church of England teacher training college in the grounds of the former Bowerham Barracks, funded by central government.[46] Further and adult education locally was also given some encouragement, this time by the county, especially by the opening in four phases between 1953 and 1974 of the Lancaster and Morecambe College on Morecambe Road, although county control was supplanted in 1993 by the central government's Further Education Funding Council. The county, not the city, also became responsible for adult education, initially centred in St Leonardgate but since 1990 located as the Adult College in the former mill buildings at White Cross.[47] Much was accomplished in often difficult circumstances, and any detected inadequacies of financing and status reflected a British disease and not just a Lancaster disorder.

Post-war political enthusiasm for the expansion of educational opportunity also encouraged the establishment of new universities. Here at least the city council seems to have played a vigorous lobbying role to ensure that the university to be sited in North Lancashire came to Lancaster (rather than

Quality Products. Williamsons' Lancaster Showroom, 1948. Rolls of printed and patterned linoleum.

Blackpool). Appropriately, the site chosen at Bailrigg had not only been the estate of Herbert Storey but much earlier that of John Gardyner, the fifteenth-century benefactor of the boys' grammar school. It has been argued that the siting of these new institutions in comparatively small cities on rural sites, rather than in major industrial areas amid teeming populations, reflected a characteristic malaise in British culture and policy-making.[48] The economic benefits accruing to the city of Lancaster from the foundation of the University of Lancaster in 1964 must, however, be accounted positive. University staff, like those in other educational establishments and in the health service, were mainly paid according to nationally negotiated salaries which were generally above local norms, and their presence may have obliged other employers needing support staff to raise their pay levels, with important effects upon overall local incomes. Expenditure in the first year of operations was a mere £355,641, but had risen to £72 million by 1998–9. Already, by 1991–2, University expenditure plus that by students and the Student Union, totalling £66 million, prompted £47 million of gross local output, generated £24 million in local disposable income, and created the equivalent of 2,045 full-time jobs.[49]

   The expansion of the public service sector therefore had a discernible effect upon the local economy and boosted population growth. But to it must be added the consequences of manufacturing prosperity during the 1950s and early 1960s. The industrial structure established between the wars proved well suited to meet national and international markets in the so-called age of affluence. Citizens in wealthy societies spend an increasing proportion of their incomes on furnishing and equipping their homes. The ideology of

Industrial Dereliction. Formerly Williamsons', Bath Mill closed 1972. Photographed 13 June 1974 from Alfred Street, and subsequently demolished.

the home-centred society, nourished by women's magazines, Sunday news-paper colour supplements, television advertising and other agencies, encouraged the creation of 'ideal homes', and Williamsons and Storeys succeeded in persuading consumers to buy Lancaster-made wallpapers, floor-coverings, fabrics and other products.[50] Moreover, sophisticated indus-tries at home and abroad absorbed the chemicals and artificial silks which Nelsons and Lansil produced. If we include the activities of ICI at Heysham, some spin-offs from the harbour, the summer holiday trade at Morecambe and – a classic instance of a central government decision impacting on the local community – the very considerable expenditure on the construction of two nuclear power stations at Heysham from the 1960s (the second employ-ing 6,500 workers during the early 1980s), we have additional explanations for the apparent buoyancy of the local economy at least until the later 1960s. Up to this time the city even experienced a shortage of labour.

However, the viability of the manufacturing industries in Lancaster was being compromised. From the early 1960s some production facilities began to close down or were reduced in scope, partly because of changes in demand for products, partly because rationalisation accompanied changes in owner-ship. Waring and Gillow was acquired by Universal Stores in 1961, who closed the workshops the following year with the loss of 300 jobs. Sub-sequently the trading name alone was sold to front a retail outlet store, with a head office in West Bromwich, only to close finally in 1996. (Much of the building was converted into a bar and night club in 1998–9.) K Shoes, who first expanded into Lancaster from their Kendal base in 1920, were bought by Clarks in 1981, and staff cuts followed. Then in April 1992 the company

decided to concentrate its production in Somerset. The factory on Bulk
Road was closed entirely, with the further loss of 85 jobs, and the factory
building was subsequently demolished. The local chemical industry was also
squeezed and more jobs shed, over 400 between 1951 and 1964 and a further
600 between then and 1977. Artificial fibre production was reorganised.
James Nelson & Co. was bought up by Courtaulds in 1963. Lansil suffered
terminal change. First purchased in 1962 by Monsanto, a Canadian multinational, this site was also taken over by Courtaulds in 1974, who introduced
new technology and reduced the size of the labour force during the 1970s,
and then closed down its Lancaster operations entirely in 1980, claiming
overcapacity in the industry and greater efficiency at one of the company's
other plants in Derby. By the mid-1980s the Lansil site had been cleared
for a new industrial park. Even more significant was the sharp decline of
the oilcloth, floorcovering and coated fabric businesses, around 2,000 jobs
being lost during the 1960s. The fate of Williamsons is illustrative. On the
collapse of demand for linoleum the firm amalgamated in 1963 with their
old rivals, Nairns of Kirkcaldy, and a series of redundancies ensued, reducing
the labour force from 3,000 to about 1,200. The Lancaster plant then
concentrated primarily on producing vinyl-coated wallpapers and plastic floor
coverings. However, further rationalisation, following acquisition by
Unilever in 1975, had reduced the labour force to 550 by May 1985 when
the company was sold to Forbo, a Swiss-based chemicals multinational. At
least the plant at Lune Mills continued to operate, as Forbo-CP, at the start
of the new millennium, but with a workforce of only 200. Storeys, passing
through a rather similar process of takeover by the Manchester-based
company Turner and Newall in 1977, was disposed of as an unprofitable

Revival. The offices of Lancashire Enterprises Ltd in 1986, on the former site of Storeys' White
Cross Mills (and originally Springfield Barracks).

All Change. May 1956, city centre looking south, with the Great John Street and St Nicholas Street area in the centre foreground shortly before redevelopment.

subsidiary to Wardles, a firm producing similar products in Earby, who quickly closed down the Lancaster factory at White Cross. Since 1982 Lancashire Enterprises Ltd, funded by Lancashire County Council, has nurtured new businesses in the reconditioned buildings on that historic site. Manufacturing which in 1961 had provided 16,700 jobs in the Lancaster district, about 37 per cent of the total, was reduced to employing only about 5,000, or 12 per cent, by 1995.[51] This de-industrialisation of the city was part of a process occurring in the British economy more generally, though the impact was felt early in Lancaster. The effect was to make the community more dependent on its large public sector, particularly in education and health. This concentration may prove to be something of a liability if and when national government policies reduce the size or at least restrict the growth of the public sector. However, general prosperity since the war and the development of a consumer culture also encouraged the further expansion of the city as a retail, service, tourist and, more recently, residential centre. Increased car ownership widened Lancaster's potential market area. Changes to the physical appearance of the town followed. First, the traffic problem became such a burden that drastic measures had to be taken. The extension around Lancaster in 1960 of the M6, which had begun in 1957 as the Preston by-pass (the first motorway in Britain), may have done something to ease the passage of through traffic north or south, but it required the pedestrianisation of the city centre from 1973 and the establishment of a remarkably successful one-way system to restore something like pleasure to shopping.

Those convinced that Lancaster still had a traffic problem continued to press for a further expensive by-pass around the city and across the Lune.

A second visible change was the increased prominence in the city centre of local branches of national businesses. In particular, premises on Market Street, Cheapside and Penny Street in these years were taken over by the offices of most national banks, building societies and latterly estate agents, or by retail chains like Littlewood's (1957), British Home Stores (1971), Sainsbury's (1985) and enlarged branches of Boots (1969), Marks and Spencer (1956, 1972 and 1992) and W. H. Smith (1981, on the site of the former Palladium cinema). On the city's perimeter new additions included E. H. Booth's (1982) and B&Q (1984). Sadly, the cost was often the disappearance of several of the older Lancaster-owned family shops. These included T. D. Smith Ltd, the grocer, whose local shops employed over 80 staff in 1958 but which was finally driven out of business in 1981 by the competition of the supermarkets. Similarly, Kenneth Gardner Ltd, founded 1921, whose music and electrical goods shops had employed over 60 staff at their height in the late 1980s, succumbed to the competition early in 2000.[52]

A third change to the city's appearance was still less warmly received. Town planning legislation had increased the responsibility of the city council for development planning and land use. To their credit, local councillors and officials wished to build up Lancaster's prosperity by extending its attractiveness as a commercial centre. But the first results were not without their critics. During the 1960s development companies were allowed to

Rehousing. Demolition and new flats, Lune Street, Skerton, looking south over Skerton Bridge, about 1959.

demolish several city centre structures, especially on St Nicholas Street, Common Garden Street and King Street, and to replace them with what then passed for modern architecture, invariably discordant, dull, and rapidly tacky in appearance (St Nicholas Arcade, Arndale House). At the same time, municipal energy and local prosperity led to more slum clearance, especially in Skerton, and to further house-building, initially mainly of council houses and flats, but predominantly from the 1960s of private owner-occupied houses on suburban estates such as that on Hala Hill.[53] Much later, attempts were made, with architecturally more attractive results, to recolonise derelict land and property in the city centre, especially by the canal, on St George's Quay, and in the grounds of redundant hospital buildings to the east and south. Post-war housing, not only graced in the main with gardens but also increasingly containing televisions (like the majority of homes in Britain by the 1960s), broadened access to national cultural tastes and standards and perhaps nurtured home-centred values.

However, although difficult to quantify and compare with the practices in similar-sized cities elsewhere, it seems probable that certain distinctive cultural activities also survived and may even have grown. The community and the region seemed to contain enough activists prepared to leave their domestic hearths to sustain amateur theatre and music, for example, LADOS, the Footlights, the Lancaster and District Choral Society and the Haffner Orchestra, as well as to support professional companies performing at the Duke's Playhouse, which opened in 1971. Scanning the local paper and the notice boards in the local library reveals a rich variety of other local societies, including a branch of the Historical Association (first founded in 1939 but reformed in 1962). Art exhibitions and concerts, both classical and popular, at the University, S. Martin's College, in town, and more recently at the splendidly renovated Ashton Memorial, also added to cultural opportunities, and the Lancaster Literature Festival, first launched in 1978, became an established tradition. The churches retained their role, though surely not their central status, in the community. Sports continued to flourish, though Lancaster never made it into the Football League. But perhaps just as vibrant was pub culture, enhanced for *aficionados* by Quiz League competitions, and a recent remarkable rash of nightclubs aimed at the youth market.[54]

Cultural activities drew upon the interests and energies of old and new Lancastrians after the war. Undoubtedly the expansion of the public services, of manufacturing and of retailing introduced more outsiders into Lancaster. It has been argued that in urban Britain one may distinguish among the middle classes between 'burgesses' and 'spiralists'.[55] The former are typically from local families, probably born and educated locally, carving out careers within the community and perhaps advancing to positions of local influence and maybe of political power. Lancaster, traditionally, had been a society run by 'burgesses'. 'Spiralists', on the other hand, were usually professional people working in the public or private service sector or industrial managers and technicians. Their careers commonly required migration from town to

Culture. The Duke's Playhouse in 1986, containing a theatre, cinema, restaurant and bar. Opened in 1971 in the former St Anne's Church on Moor Lane.

town, with luck moving upwards in their career ladders, so that they spiralled through the communities in which they temporarily settled. Observation of post-war Lancaster shows many 'spiralists' in full flight. Their trajectories drew them into the city in pursuit of expanding opportunities, for example, in the health service, at the University, in the management of banks, as technicians at Storeys and with other businesses; and then, often, they whirled off elsewhere. However, recession and the reduction in professional opportunities in recent years restricted geographical mobility, and rather more came to ground in Lancaster and became bedded in as first generation 'burgesses'. Several (or their spouses) became active in local cultural life, for example in local theatres, in the Civic Society, on parent-teacher associations, or as school governors. Some also became engaged politically, not invariably tolerant in their response to local practices, not by any means in agreement among themselves, but perhaps bringing in ideals and aspirations from the outside and offering challenge and change. The effect of this might be seen in local politics, where councillors were more often people in professional occupations rather than running small local businesses.

The political world they entered altered during the 1960s. Until then political expectations deduced from the city's class composition suggest that Lancaster was exceptionally pro-Conservative in its political preferences. But thereafter a discernible shift took place. Indeed, it was boundary revisions taking in Conservative rural hinterlands which largely preserved the Lancaster constituency as a usually secure Conservative seat: Fitzroy Maclean held it until 1959, Humphrey Berkeley thereafter until 1966, and Elaine Kellett-Bowman from 1970 to 1997. This Conservative sequence was interrupted briefly when Stanley Henig, then a lecturer in politics at the University, won the seat for Labour at the general election of 1966. To repeat the trick it took national politics and a massive national swing against the Conservatives in 1997 to break again the Conservative hold and allow Hilton Dawson, a graduate of the University of Warwick and of Lancaster and professionally employed in social services, to become Lancaster's second Labour MP.[56]

However, Labour's successes also owed much to political changes which had a more obvious effect on local city elections. It was suggested earlier that for various reasons Lancaster's working-class electorate between the wars was politically quiescent and that that characteristic helped explain the scarcity of electoral contests and the success of Conservative (or Independent) candidates. However, this was challenged by the economic restructuring of Lancaster underway by the 1960s. The growth of the service sector was rapidly changing the social composition of the city. Middle-class professionals and white-collar workers became proportionately more numerous, and these were more inclined to vote Labour, especially those in education and welfare. At the same time, the city's manual workers were also finding more jobs in public sector employment, where trade unionism was better organised and more tolerated by management. Moreover, many of the city's remaining industrial employees had been shaken out of old habits and allegiances by the threat or experience of redundancy.[57]

As a result largely of these processes, Labour gained fleeting majorities on the council in 1958-9 and 1963-4, and a substantial majority in 1972 – just before local government reorganisation in 1974, imposed by national legislation, merged Lancaster, Morecambe and surrounding rural areas into a single local government district. Initially Labour's political advance was thereby checked, although in Lancaster's city wards its appeal continued to grow. Labour has so far attracted the largest share of the vote inside the boundaries of the old borough in every election since reorganisation and, except in 1976, most seats. Indeed, by 1991 it had become the largest single party on the council, holding 24 of the 60 seats. Moreover, in 1995 Labour gained an absolute majority, winning all 21 seats in the old borough wards, ten in Morecambe and three in the rural areas. Remarkably, the Conservatives were largely driven out to the rural wards, and won no Lancaster city seats in any of the three local elections of the 1990s.

However, the 1974 merger had a further significant impact on local politics, for it brought together into a single administrative area the populations of an old and struggling seaside resort, a large rural hinterland and de-industrialising Lancaster. The interests of these communities did not always coincide. For instance, plans to reinvent Lancaster as a service centre but with an appeal to tourists, which became a council strategy in the 1980s, implied investment in improving the built environment of the city, but at the perceived expense of Morecambe whose tourist industry was clamouring for support. Indeed, one expression of political division was candidates

Labour Politics. May Day rally on the steps of the Old Town Hall, 1980.

running for office as Morecambe Bay Independents, committed to removing the seaside town from an unacceptable political union or at least of ensuring that resources were also directed to servicing Morecambe's perceived needs. They did well in the 1991 local elections, winning 12 seats, mainly from the Conservatives. Efforts were indeed made by the council, including the dominant Labour group, to stimulate Morecambe tourism, but these included some unsuccessful and very expensive investments (including a 'Mr Blobby' theme park) which led to a backlash by council tax payers. The principal political victims in the 1999 council elections of this botched effort to help Morecambe were the governing Labour Party, which suffered at the hands of the Green Party, representing disgruntled Lancaster voters, who won five seats, and ironically of the Morecambe Bay Independents who found them- selves marginally the largest single party, with 18 councillors, all from Morecambe, to Labour's 17, largely from Lancaster.[58]

For Lancaster city residents the most significant recent council debates have concerned the role of shopping and tourism in the city. A distressing fire in 1984, which burnt down the centrally located Victorian market, stimulated proposals for ambitious redevelopment schemes for the city. These culminated in March 1986 in the first draft of a Plan, subsequently frequently revised, and the holding of a public inquiry. There were proposals for a controversial new road and for substantial city centre changes, involving moving the market from its central position to the bus station site and building new shopping arcades running from south to north. The council's

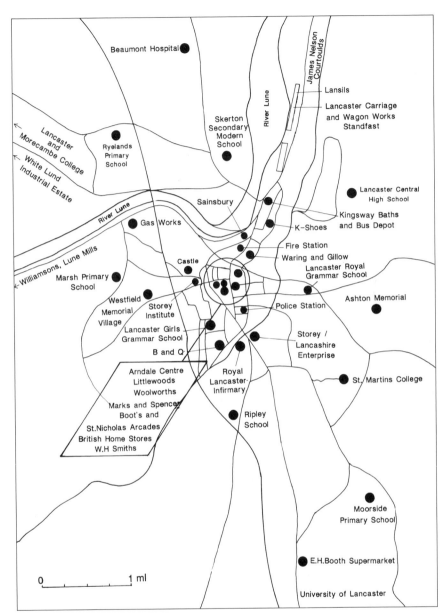

The modern topography of Lancaster.

economic rationale was to consolidate and improve retailing facilities so as to enhance Lancaster's position in the hierarchy of service centres in the north-west. This necessitated partnership with outside private investors, inducements to large national retail companies to open new or larger branches in the city, more car park space for visitors and additional roads to avoid traffic congestion. The Plan also contained artists' drawings of the kind of postmodern architectural buildings and façades that would make the new centre supposedly appealing to the eye of the new phalanx of expected shoppers. Over 1,400 individual and institutional objections to the draft were received, many from local residents concerned about the generation of more traffic, the need for local control, the enforcement of standards for the new buildings and the loss of the traditional market site. But bodies outside the city also objected, such as the retailers of Morecambe and Kendal who feared the competition from an enormous expansion of shopping space concentrated in Lancaster.

One bone of contention concerned issues of preservation and heritage, for Lancaster also sought to take advantage of its relatively unspoiled and little exploited Georgian buildings both to attract tourists and generally to enhance the local built environment. Hence some other groups of people were most concerned that the historic ambience of the town should not be destroyed by unsympathetic new constructions. The findings of the public inquiry in some ways vindicated this last group, though it was economic recession and the inability to secure the required levels of investment rather than the advice of the inspector that initially restricted reconstruction to an area facing Stonewell and to the reconstruction of St Nicholas Arcades. Here, interestingly, the principal alteration was to modify the most jarring of the concrete creations of the 1960s, by lowering its height and adding a playful mock medieval façade.[59] Subsequently, in the early 1990s and learning from experience, Arndale House was demolished and the market, alongside new department stores, was reconstructed on its historic site, its roof-top car park hidden within an amusing, stone-faced, postmodern design. These recent constructions suggest that the city planners had managed to accommodate adroitly the contradictory pressures of the demand for up-to-date commercial and retailing facilities with the preservation of the historic aura that appeals to the nostalgia of many tourists and residents.

The recent history of Lancaster, then, might be seen in terms of the competing imperatives of retaining local controls and distinctiveness in circumstances where external pressures, increasingly of a global kind, impinge on local autonomy. The economic agents primarily influencing Lancaster's prosperity are no longer locally owned or controlled. The state, the banks and the chain stores operate policies national in scope and with little consideration for local sentiment. The most profitable industrial corporations are multi- or trans-national in provenance, and hence their strategies for the location of new businesses and the closure of old ones pay no regard to consequences for local populations. Equally, the culture industries – television, music, publishing, advertising – have become increasingly global operations, both in terms of targeting audiences and of determining popular taste. Add to these forces a post-war tendency to reduce the autonomy of local political authorities and it would seem that the scope for control and independence at the local level is in sharp decline.

Yet there are counter-tendencies. Now that big businesses can locate almost anywhere, the particular features of individual places become more rather than less influential in decision-making. For personal as well as business reasons, low levels of congestion, an attractive residential environment and a rich local culture may make towns like Lancaster appealing to entrepreneurs, managers and professionals with mobile capital and movable skills. Likewise, tourists wish to visit, and re-visit, those scenes that are distinctive, different and memorable. The preservation of Lancaster's distinctiveness, including selected features of its past, may be the necessary clue to the city's future.

Notes

1. *Census of England and Wales 1901*; A. Warde, *Changes in the Occupational Structure of Lancaster 1901–1951*, Lancaster Regionalism Group, University of Lancaster, 1982, 2–7, 16–18; J. Price, *Industrial Lancaster*, Lancaster City Museum, 1978; J. Price (ed.), *Lancaster a Century Ago*, Landy, 1990; P. J. Gooderson, 'The Economic and Social History of Lancaster 1780–1914', unpublished PhD thesis, University of Lancaster, 1975, 373–80; N. Todd, 'A History of Labour in Lancaster and Barrow-in-Furness', unpublished MLitt. thesis, University of Lancaster, 1976, 7–10.

2. Warde, *Occupational Structure*, 7; Gooderson, 'Economic and Social History', 380–2; Todd, 'Labour in Lancaster', 100–1; R. Irving, *More Lancaster Past and Present*, Neil Richardson, 1988, 11–12; J. G. Cullingworth, *Housing in Transition: a Case Study in the City of Lancaster 1958–62*, Heinemann, 1963, 19.

3. *Census of England and Wales 1911*; Warde, *Occupational Structure*, 2–7, 19–24.

4. *Lancaster Guardian*, 8 and 15 August 1914.

5. S. Eastwood, *Lions of England: A Pictorial History of the King's Own Royal Regiment (Lancaster), 1680–1980*, Silver Link Publishing, 1991; G. Christie, *Storeys of Lancaster: 1848–1964*, Collins, 1964, 171.

6. *Lancaster Guardian*, 30 November 1918, 15 and 29 November 1924; T. H. Mawson, *Life and Work of an English Landscape Architect*, Richards Press, 1927, 259–70, 297–302; Christie, *Storeys*, 235–6; Visual Arts Centre, *Thomas H. Mawson: a Northern Landscape Architect*, University of Lancaster, 1978, 35–6.

7. Todd, 'Labour in Lancaster', 153–4; Warde, *Occupational Structure*, 9; Christie, *Storeys*, 164, 174; Irving, *More Lancaster*, 12; R. Graves, *Goodbye To All That*, Cape, 1929, 103–7; *Lancaster Guardian*, 13 October 1917.

8. *Lancaster Guardian*, 16 November 1918.

9. Irving, *More Lancaster*, 25; Christie, *Storeys*, 176; Warde, *Occupational Structure*, 9, 24–35; Todd, 'Labour in Lancaster', 164; E. Roberts, 'The Working-Class Family in Barrow and Lancaster, 1890–1930', unpublished PhD thesis, University of Lancaster, 1978, 199.

10. *Census of England and Wales 1921*; Warde, *Occupational Structure*, 2; A. E. Myall, 'Changes in Social Control in Lancaster between 1913 and 1938', unpublished MA thesis, University of Lancaster, 1976, 1, 6.

11. S. Constantine, *Unemployment in Britain between the Wars*, Longman, 1980.

12. *Censuses of England and Wales 1931 and 1951*; Warde, *Occupational Structure*,

2–3; E. Roberts, *Working-Class Barrow and Lancaster 1890–1930*, Centre for North-West Regional Studies, University of Lancaster, 1976, 78–9.

13. Warde, *Occupational Structure*, 10–12.

14. S. Constantine, *Social Conditions in Britain 1918–1939*, Methuen, 1983.

15. Christie, *Storeys*, 109–13, 119–28.

16. *Lancaster Guardian*, 16 December 1922, 13 January 1923, 23 July 1927 and 9 January 1931; Irving, *More Lancaster*, 12.

17. *Lancaster Observer*, 3 February 1933.

18. A. Warde, *Conditions of Dependence: Working-Class Quiescence in Lancaster in the 20th Century*, Lancaster Regionalism Group, University of Lancaster, 1989, 1–13, and 'Working-Class Quiescence in Lancaster in the 20th Century', *International Review of Social History*, vol. 35, no. 1, 1990, 71–105; Myall, 'Social Control'; Gooderson, 'Social and Economic History', 420–8, 532–54; Todd, 'Labour in Lancaster', 59–60; Roberts, 'Barrow and Lancaster', 26–8; Christie, *Storeys*, 158–73.

19. Gooderson, 'Economic and Social History', 571–94; Todd, 'Labour in Lancaster', 36–61, 95–126.

20. F. Brockway, *Inside the Left*, Allen and Unwin, 1942, 135–7; F. W. S. Craig, *British Parliamentary Election Results 1918–1949*, Political Reference Publications, 1969. It is pleasing to record that in 1982 the University of Lancaster awarded Lord Brockway an honorary degree: *Lancaster Guardian*, 10 December 1982.

21. F. W. S. Craig, *British Parliamentary Election Results 1885–1918*, Macmillan, 1974, and *British Parliamentary Election Results 1918–1949*; L. G. Wickham Legg (ed.), *Dictionary of National Biography 1931–1940*, Oxford University Press, 1949.

22. Myall, 'Social Control', 45.

23. Myall, 'Social Control', 24–37.

24. *Lancaster Guardian Supplement*, 24 March 1933; Myall, 'Social Control', 17; Price, *Industrial Lancaster*, section 12.

25. *Lancaster Observer*, 24 March 1932, quoted in Myall, 'Social Control', 10; D. Beattie, 'The Origins, Implementation and Legacy of the Addison Housing Act 1919, with special reference to Lancashire', unpublished PhD thesis, University of Lancaster, 1986, 398, 435–7, 488; Cullingworth, *Housing in Transition*, 20–34; J. H. Jennings, 'Geographical Implications of the Housing Programme in England and Wales', *Urban Studies*, vol. 8, 1971, 121–38 (includes a study of Lancaster).

26. *Lancaster Observer*, 4 November 1927; *Lancaster Guardian*, 7 July 1939; J. Mark-Lawson, M. Savage and A. Warde, 'Gender and Local Politics: Struggles over Welfare Policies 1918–1939' in L. Murgatroyd *et al.*, *Localities, Class and Gender*, Pion, 1985, 195–215; Myall, 'Social Control', 19–20; Irving, *More Lancaster*, 23–4.

27. J. D. Marshall, *The History of Lancashire County Council 1889 to 1974*, Martin Robertson, 1977, 76–85, 245–91; J. M. Skinner *et al.*, *Lancaster Girls' Grammar School: the History 1907–87*, Lancaster Girls' Grammar School, Lancaster, 1987, 4; A. L. Murray, *The Royal Grammar School Lancaster: A History*, Heffer, 1952, 213–15, 222–3; J. L. Spencer (ed.), *The Royal Grammar School, Lancaster*, Neill, 1969, 17–26; *Lancaster Guardian*, 2 February 1934; Myall, 'Social Control', 18–19.

28. Constantine, *Unemployment*, 72–3.
29. R. Irving, *Lancaster Past and Present*, Neil Richardson, 1987, 21; *Lancaster Guardian*, 27 October 1933.
30. Cullingworth, *Housing in Transition*, 24, 26, 33–4; Jennings, 'Municipal Housing', 134–7.
31. S. Constantine, 'Amateur Gardening and Popular Recreation in the 19th and 20th Centuries', *Journal of Social History*, vol. 14, no. 3, 1981, 387–406.
32. A. J. P. Taylor, *English History 1914–1945*, Clarendon Press, 1965, 313.
33. *Lancaster Guardian*, 27 May 1938, 15 March 1991; LADOS Centenary Programme for 'The Merry Widow', 1991; A. G. Betjemann, *The Grand Theatre, Lancaster: Two Centuries of Entertainment*, Centre for North-West Regional Studies, University of Lancaster, 1982; Irving, *More Lancaster*, 28.
34. Roberts, *Barrow and Lancaster*, 80.
35. Myall, 'Social Control', 23; *Lancaster Guardian Anniversary Supplement*, 1987, 8–9; *The City of Lancaster*, Lancaster City Museum Service, 1987, 1.
36. *Lancaster Guardian*, 8 September 1939.
37. J. Kent, 'Women in Wartime Lancaster: a View of the Changing Experience of Women in Lancaster 1939–1945', unpublished MA thesis, University of Lancaster, 1986, 1, 17; Murray, *Royal Grammar School*, 224.
38. Kent, 'Women in Wartime', 17–22; Y. Wareham, 'The Dig for Victory Campaign in the Second World War, with special reference to Lancashire', unpublished MA thesis, University of Lancaster, 1992; Irving, *More Lancaster*, 3, 5, 39, 42; Murray, Royal Grammar School, 224; Spencer, *Royal Grammar School*, 28; R. R. Timberlake, *Memories: Lancaster Royal Grammar School 1939–1961*, privately printed, 1991, 24–7; Skinner, *Lancaster Girls' Grammar School*, 6–7.
39. Kent, 'Women in Wartime', 27–33; Irving, *More Lancaster*, 12; Christie, *Storeys*, 181.
40. *Lancaster Guardian*, 11 and 18 May 1945.
41. *Lancaster Guardian*, 27 July 1945; Craig, *Parliamentary Election Results 1918–1949*.
42. *Census of England and Wales 1951, 1961, 1971, 1981, 1991*; *The Lancaster District Profile*, Lancaster City Council, 1998; L. Murgatroyd, *Deindustrialisation in Lancaster*, Lancaster Regionalism Group, University of Lancaster, 1981, 8; P. Bagguley *et al.*, *Restructuring: Place, Class, and Gender*, Sage, 1990, 93, 96.
43. P. Bagguley, *Service Employment and Economic Restructuring in Lancaster, 1971–81*, Lancaster Regionalism Group, University of Lancaster, 1986, 16–17, 69; *Lancaster District Profile*.
44. Bagguley *et al.*, *Restructuring*, 70–7; Marshall, *Lancashire County Council*, 128, 132, 292–305; Irving, *More Lancaster*, 10, 33; M. Elder, *The Royal Lancaster Infirmary: Celebrating a Century of Service 1896–1996*, Lancaster Acute Hospitals NHS Trust, 1996, 18–20; J. Alston *et al.*, *The Royal Albert: Chronicles of an Era*, Lancaster University, Centre for North-West Regional Studies, 1992; P. Williamson, *From Confinement to Community: The Moving Story of 'The Moor', Lancaster's County Lunatic Asylum*, Bay Community NHS Trust, 1999, 25–34; Lancaster City Council, *Council Housing Services Annual Report 1991–92*, Lancaster City Council, 1992, 2; *Lancaster District Profile*.
45. Irving, *More Lancaster*, 3, 5; Marshall, *Lancashire County Council*, 245–78; G. Phythian, *The Ripley Legacy, Ripley St Thomas Church of England High School*,

Lancaster, 1999; Timberlake, *Memories*, 52–3, 59; Spencer, *Royal Grammar School*, 33–4; J. W. Fidler, *Lancaster Royal Grammar School*, Friends of LRGS, 1998, 11. The vote by parents for opting-out at the boys' school in June 1989 was carried by 58 per cent to 42 per cent on a turn-out of only 68 per cent, and at the girls' grammar school in June 1990 by 54 per cent to 46 per cent on a turn-out of 67 per cent: *Lancaster Guardian* published extensive reports and correspondence.

46. Irving, *More Lancaster*, 5; Phythian, *Ripley Legacy*; P. Gedge and L. Louden, *S. Martin's College Lancaster 1964–89*, University of Lancaster, Centre for North West Regional Studies, 1993.

47. H. Gregson, *A Century and a Half of Further Education*, Lancaster and More-cambe College, 1974, 11; Marshall, *Lancashire County Council*, 279–90; Irving, *More Lancaster*, 28; *Lancaster Guardian Commemorative Edition*, 1 January 2000, 23, 28.

48. M. J. Wiener, *English Culture and the Decline of the Industrial Spirit 1850–1980*, Cambridge University Press, 1981, 133–4.

49. M. E. McClintock, *University of Lancaster: Quest for Innovation*, University of Lancaster, 1974, 6–17, 418; Marshall, *Lancashire County Council*, 290; Irving, *More Lancaster*, 39–40; H. Armstrong *et al.*, *Building Lancaster's Future: The Economic and Environmental Impacts of Lancaster University Expansion to 2001*, Department of Economics and the Centre for the Study of Environmental Change, Lancaster University, 1994; *Report and Accounts 1999*, Lancaster University, 2000, 36.

50. Christie, *Storeys*, 188–213.

51. Murgatroyd *et al.*, *Localities, Class and Gender*, 30–53; Bagguley *et al.*, *Restructuring*, 35–47, 178; J. Urry, *Economic Planning and Policy in the Lancaster District*, Lancaster Regionalism Group, University of Lancaster, 1987, 17–21; P. Bagguley, *Economic Restructuring and Employment Change in Lancaster 1971–1981: Manufacturing Industries*, Lancaster Regionalism Group, University of Lancaster, 1986, 13, 15; *Lancaster District Profile*; Irving, *Lancaster*, 27, 55; M. E. Burkett and R. Hasted, *A History of Gillow at Lancaster*, Lancashire County Museum Service, 1984, 23; R. Martin and R. H. Fryer, *Redundancy and Paternalist Capitalism*, Allen and Unwin, 1973 – a study of Lancaster; *Lancaster Guardian Commemorative Edition*, 13. For the history of K Shoes see S. Crookenden, *K Shoes: the First 150 years 1842–1992*, K Shoes, 1992; but see also *Lancaster Guardian*, 2 September 1972, 9 January 1981, 30 April 1982, 21 February and 17 April 1992.

52. *E. H. Booth & Company Ltd, 1847–1985*, E. H. Booth & Co, 1985; M. J. Winstanley *et al.*, *A Traditional Grocer: T. D. Smith of Lancaster, 1858–1981*, University of Lancaster, Centre for North-West Regional Studies, 1991, 32, 46–7; *Lancaster Guardian Commemorative Edition*, 21; *Lancaster Guardian*, 17 March 2000, 12.

53. Cullingworth, *Housing in Transition*, 37–58.

54. Betjemann, *Grand Theatre*; *Lancaster Guardian*, 15 March 1991; *Lancaster Guardian Commemorative Edition*, 17, 37, 43–4.

55. The terms are discussed in W. Watson, 'Social Mobility and Social Class in Industrial Communities' in M. Gluckmann (ed.), *Closed Systems and Open Minds*, Oliver and Boyd, 1964; and also in R. Frankenberg, *Communities in Britain: Social Life in Town and Country*, Penguin, 1966.

56. F. W. S. Craig, *British Parliamentary Election Results 1950–1973*, Parliamentary Research Services, 1983; F. W. S. Craig, *British Parliamentary Election Results 1974–1983*, Parliamentary Research Services, 1984; *Lancaster Guardian*, 17 April 1992, 9, and 9 May 1997, 13. Prior to the 1997 election the constituency had been redefined as Lancaster and Wyre, excluding areas north of the Lune and including more to the south.

57. J. Mark-Lawson and A. Warde, *Industrial Restructuring and the Transformation of a Local Political Environment*, Lancaster Regionalism Group, University of Lancaster, 1987; Warde, *Conditions of Dependence*, 13–25; Bagguley *et al*, *Restructuring*, 194–209.

58. *Lancaster Guardian*, 10 May 1991, 12 May 1995, 14 May 1999.

59. Bagguley *et al.*, *Restructuring*, 146–72.

Select Bibliography

J. Alston (with E. Roberts and O. Wangermann), *The Royal Albert: Chronicle of an Era*, University of Lancaster, Centre for North-West Regional Studies, 1992.

R. Alston, *The Old Photographs Series: Lancaster and the Lune Valley*, Alan Sutton, 1994.

Anon, *Lancaster Records 1801–50*, Lancaster Gazette, 1869.

Anon, *Lancaster & District Co-operative Society Ltd: Seventy-five years of Co-operative Service 1861–1936*, Lancaster & District Co-operative Society, 1937.

Anon, *Williamsons of Lancaster 1844–1944: Centenary Memoir*, Williamsons, 1944.

H. Armstrong *et al.*, *Building Lancaster's Future: The Economic and Environmental Impacts of Lancaster University Expansion to 2001*, Department of Economics and the Centre for the Study of Environmental Change, Lancaster University, 1994.

S. Ashworth, *The Lino King: the Life and Times of Lord Ashton*, Lancaster City Museums/Village, 1989.

S. Ashworth and N. Dalziel, *Lancaster and District in Old Photographs*, Alan Sutton, 1993.

P. Bagguley, *Economic Restructuring and Employment Changes in Lancaster 1971–1981: Manufacturing industries*, University of Lancaster, Lancaster Regionalism Group, 1986.

P. Bagguley, *Service Employment and Economic Restructuring in Lancaster 1971–1981*, University of Lancaster, Lancaster Regionalism Group, 1986.

P. Bagguley *et al.*, *Restructuring: Place, Class and Gender*, Sage, 1990.

E. Baines, *The History of the County Palatine and Duchy of Lancaster*, 3rd edn, 1892.

W. Beamont, *A Discourse of the Warr in Lancashire*, Chetham Society, vol. 62, 1864.

D. Beattie, 'The Origins, Implementation and Legacy of the Addison Housing Act 1919, with special reference to Lancashire', unpublished PhD thesis, University of Lancaster, 1986.

A. G. Betjemann, *The Grand Theatre, Lancaster: Two Centuries of Entertainment*, University of Lancaster, Centre for North-West Regional Studies, 1982.

R. N. Billington and J. Brownbill, *St Peter's, Lancaster: A History*, Sands & Co., 1910.

A. G. Boulton, 'Lancaster 1801–1881: a geographical study of a town in transition', unpublished MA thesis, Dept. of Geography, University of Liverpool, 1976.

E. Brockbank, 'The Story of Quakerism in the Lancaster District', *Journal of the Friends Historical Society*, vol. 35, 1939, 3–20.

R. A. Brown, H. M. Colvin and A. J. Taylor, *The History of the King's Works. 2, The Middle Ages*, HMSO, 1963.

J. Brownbill and J. R. Nuttall, *A Calendar of Charters and Records Belonging to the Corporation of Lancaster*, Lancaster Corporation, 1929.

J. Catt, *A History of Lancaster's Markets*, Lancaster City Museums, Local Studies, 7, 1988.

C. Chalklin, *English Counties and Public Building, 1650–1830*, The Hambledon Press, 1998.

J. Champness, *Lancaster Castle: A Brief History*, Lancashire County Books, 1993.

G. Christie, *Storeys of Lancaster: 1848–1964*, Collins, 1964.

C. Clark, *An Historical and Descriptive Account of the Town of Lancaster*, C. Clark, 1807.

D. M. Clark, 'The Economic and Social Geography of Rural Lonsdale 1801–1861', unpublished MA dissertation, Dept. of Geography, University of Liverpool, 1968.

T. J. Cooper, 'Police, Politics, Parsimony and Public Opinion in Lancaster in the second quarter of the 19th century', unpublished MA dissertation, University of Lancaster, 1982.

S. Crookenden, *K Shoes: The First 150 Years, 1842–1992*, K Shoes, 1992.

'Cross Fleury', *Time-Honoured Lancaster. Historic Notes on the Ancient Borough of Lancaster*, Eaton and Bulfield, 1891.

J. G. Cullingworth, *Housing in Transition: A Case Study in the City of Lancaster 1958–62*, Heinemann, 1963.

R. Cunliffe Shaw, *The Royal Forest of Lancaster*, Guardian Press, 1956.

N. Dalziel, *Lancaster Maritime Museum, a Companion Guide to Lancaster's Maritime Heritage*, Lancaster City Museums, 1992.

D. Davis (ed.), *The Castle Howell School Record*, n. p., 1888.

M. De Lacy, *Prison Reform in Lancashire, 1700–1850*, Chetham Society, vol. 33, 1986.

K. Docton, 'Lancaster 1684', *Transactions of the Historic Society of Lancashire and Cheshire*, vol. 109, 1957, 125–42.

S. Eastwood, *Lions of England: A Pictorial History of the King's Own Royal Regiment (Lancaster), 1680–1980*, Silver Link, 1991.

M. Elder, *Lancaster and the African Slave Trade*, Lancaster City Museums, Local Studies, 14, 1991.

M. Elder, *The Slave Trade and the Economic Development of 18th Century Lancaster*, Ryburn, 1992.

M. Elder, *The Royal Lancaster Infirmary: Celebrating a Century of Service 1896–1996*, Lancaster Acute Hospitals NHS Trust, 1996.

W. Farrer and J. Brownbill, *The Victoria County History: Lancashire*, Constable, vols 2, 1908, and 8, 1914.

J. W. Fidler, *Lancaster Royal Grammar School*, Friends of the LRGS, 1998.

P. Gedge and L. Louden, *S. Martin's College Lancaster 1964–89*, University of Lancaster, Centre for North-West Regional Studies, 1993.

P. Gooderson, 'The Social and Economic History of Lancaster 1780–1914', unpublished PhD thesis, Dept. of History, University of Lancaster, 1975.

P. J. Gooderson, *Lord Linoleum: Lord Ashton, Lancaster and the Rise of the British Oilcloth and Linoleum Industry*, Keele University Press, 1996.

H. Gregson, *A Century and a Half of Further Education*, Lancaster & Morecambe College, 1974.

M. D. Greville and G. O. Holt, *The Lancaster and Preston Junction Railway*, David & Charles, 1961.

C. Haigh, *The Last Days of the Lancashire Monasteries and the Pilgrimage of Grace*, Chetham Society, 3rd ser., vol. 17, 1969.

C. Haigh, *Reformation and Resistance in Tudor Lancashire*, Cambridge University Press, 1975.

R. Halley, *Lancashire: its Puritanism and Nonconformity*, Tubbs & Brook, 2 vols, 1882.

G. B. Harrison (ed.), [*Thomas Potts*] *The Trial of the Lancaster Witches, A.D. 1612*, Peter Davies, 1929.

J. Hayhurst, 'An economic and social history of Glasson Dock', unpublished MPhil. thesis, University of Lancaster, 1985.

A. Hewitson, *Northward Between Preston and Lancaster*, George Toulmin & Sons, 1900.

D. C. Janes, *Lancaster*, Dalesman Books, 1974.

R. C. Jarvis, 'Some records of the port of Lancaster', *Transactions of the Lancashire and Cheshire Antiquarian Society*, 58, 1945–6, 117–58.

J. H. Jennings, 'Geographical Implications of the Municipal Housing Programme in England and Wales', *Urban Studies*, vol. 8, 1971, 121–38.

G. D. B. Jones, 'The Romans in the North-West', *Northern History*, 3, 1968, 1–26.

G. D. B. Jones and D. C. A. Shotter (eds), *Roman Lancaster: Rescue Archaeology in an Historic City 1970–75*, Brigantia Monograph no. 1, 1988.

E. Kennerley, *William Penny and Penny's Almshouses*, Lancaster City Museums, Local Studies, 3, [1987].

J. Kent, 'Women in Wartime Lancaster: a view of the Changing Experience of Women in Lancaster 1939–1945', unpublished MA thesis, University of Lancaster, 1986.

D. Kenyon, *The Origins of Lancashire*, Manchester University Press, 1991.

J. Mark-Lawson and A. Warde, *Industrial Restructuring and the Transformation of a Local Political Environment: a Case Study of Lancaster*, University of Lancaster, Lancaster Regionalism Group, 1987.

J. D. Marshall, 'Corrupt practices at the Lancaster election of 1865', *Transactions of the Lancashire and Cheshire Antiquarian Society*, vol. 43, 1952–3, 117–30.

J. D. Marshall (ed.), *The Autobiography of William Stout of Lancaster 1665–1752*, Chetham Society, 3rd ser., vol. 14, 1967.

J. D. Marshall (ed.), *The History of Lancashire County Council 1889 to 1974*, Martin Robertson, 1977.

T. H. Mawson, *Life and Work of an English Landscape Architect*, Richards Press, 1927.

M. F. McClintock, *University of Lancaster: Quest for Innovation*, University of Lancaster, 1974.

N. J. Morgan, *Lancashire Quakers and the Establishment, 1660–1730*, Ryburn Academic Publishing, 1993.

A. S. Mousdale, 'Textile mill architecture in Lancaster and its hinterland – a preliminary survey', unpublished dissertation for Diploma in Industrial Archaeology, University of Birmingham, 1988.

M. A. Mullett, *Early Lancaster Friends*, University of Lancaster, Centre for North-West Regional Studies, 1978.

M. A. Mullett, 'Conflict, Politics and Elections in Lancaster, 1660–1688', *Northern History*, vol. 19, 1983, 61–86.

M. A. Mullett, *Catholics in Britain and Ireland, 1558–1829*, Macmillan, 1998.

L. Murgatroyd, *Deindustrialisation in Lancaster*, University of Lancaster; Lancaster Regionalism Group, 1981.

A. L. Murray, *The Royal Grammar School Lancaster; A History*, Heffer, 1952.

A. E. Myall, 'Changes in Social Control in Lancaster between 1913 and 1938', unpublished MA thesis, University of Lancaster, 1976.

R. Newman, *The Archaeology of Lancashire; Present State and Future Priorities*, Lancaster University Archaeological Unit, 1996.

J. L. Nickalls (ed.), *The Journal of George Fox*, Cambridge University Press, 1952.

K. Nuttall and T. Rawlings, *Railways around Lancaster*, Dalesman Books, 1980.

T. Pape, *The Charters of the City of Lancaster*, Lancaster City Council, 1952.

S. H. Penney, *Lancaster: the Evolution of its Townscape to 1800*, University of Lancaster, Centre for North-West Regional Studies, 1981.

N. Pevsner, *The Buildings of England: Lancashire 2: the Rural North*, Penguin Books, 1969.

J. W. A. Price, *The Industrial Archaeology of the Lune Valley*, University of Lancaster, Centre for North-West Regional Studies, 1983.

J. Price, *Industrial Lancaster*, Lancaster City Museums, Local Studies, 12, 1989.

J. Price, *Lancaster a Century Ago*, Landy, 1990.

J. Price, *Sharpe, Paley and Austin: A Lancaster Architectural Practice 1836–1942*, University of Lancaster, Centre for North-West Regional Studies, 1998.

R. H. S. Randles, *The History of the Friends' School Lancaster*, privately printed, 1982.

E. Roberts, *Working-Class Barrow and Lancaster 1890 to 1930*, University of Lancaster, Centre for North-West Regional Studies, 1976.

E. Roberts, 'The Working-Class Family in Barrow and Lancaster 1890–1930', unpublished PhD thesis, University of Lancaster, 1978.

W. O. Roper, *Materials for the History of the Church of Lancaster*, 4 vols, Chetham Society, 1892–1906.

W. O. Roper, *Materials for a History of Lancaster*, James Stewart, 1907.

D. Ross and A. White, *The Lancaster Custom House*, Lancaster City Museums, Local Studies, 9, 1988.

M. M. Schofield, *Outlines of an Economic History of Lancaster from 1680 to 1860*, Lancaster Branch of the Historical Association, 2 vols, 1946 and 1951.

M. M. Schofield, 'The Letter Book of Benjamin Satterthwaite, 1737–1744', *Transactions of the Historic Society of Lancashire and Cheshire*, vol. 113, 1960, 125–67.

D. Shotter and A. White, *Roman Fort and Town of Lancaster*, University of Lancaster, Centre for North-West Regional Studies, 1990.

D. Shotter & A. White, *The Romans in Lunesdale*, University of Lancaster, Centre for North-West Regional Studies, 1995.

D. Shotter, *Romans and Britons in North-West England*, 2nd edn, University of Lancaster, 1997.

D. Shotter, 'The Roman Conquest of the North-West', forthcoming.

S. Shuttleworth, *The Lancaster and Morecambe Tramways*, Oakwood Press, 1976.

R. Simpson, *The History and Antiquities of the Town of Lancaster*, T. Edmondson, 1852.

J. M. Skinner *et al.*, *Lancaster Girls' Grammar School: The History 1907–87*, Lancaster Girls' Grammar School, 1987.

J. Somekh, 'Lancaster castle 1774–1865: a case study in prison reform', unpublished MA dissertation, University of Lancaster, 1981.

J. L. Spencer (ed.), *The Royal Grammar School, Lancaster: Quincentenary Commemorative Volume 1469–1969*, Neill & Co., 1969.

R. R. Timberlake, *Memories: Lancaster Royal Grammar School 1939–1961*, privately printed, 1991.

N. Todd, 'A History of Labour in Lancaster and Barrow-in-Furness: 1890–1920', unpublished MLitt. thesis, University of Lancaster, 1976.

J. Urry, *Economic Planning and Policy in the Lancaster District*, University of Lancaster, Lancaster Regionalism Group, 1987.

(Visual Arts Centre), *Thomas H. Mawson: A Northern Landscape Architect*, University of Lancaster, 1978.

J. K. Walton, *Lancashire. A Social History 1558–1939*, Manchester University Press, 1987.

J. K. Walton, 'The treatment of pauper lunatics in Victorian England: the case of the Lancaster Asylum, 1816–70', in A. T. Scull (ed.), *Madhouses, Mad-Doctors and Madmen: the social history of psychiatry in the Victorian era*, Athlone Press, 1981.

A. Warde, *Changes in the Occupational Structure of Lancaster 1901–1951*, University of Lancaster, Lancaster Regionalism Group, 1982.

A. Warde, *Conditions of Dependence: Working-Class Quiescence in Lancaster in the 20th Century*, University of Lancaster, Lancaster Regionalism Group, 1989.

A. Warde, 'Working-Class Quiescence in Lancaster in the 20th Century', *International Review of Social History*, vol. 35, 1, 1990, 71–105.

Y. Wareham, 'The Dig for Victory Campaign in the Second World War with special reference to Lancashire', unpublished MA thesis, University of Lancaster, 1992.

W. T. Watkin, *Roman Lancashire*, privately printed, 1883.

A. Whincop and A. White, *Lancaster's Maritime Heritage*, Lancaster City Museums, 1986.

A. White (ed.), *The Beauties of the North: Lancaster in 1820* (reprinted from the Lonsdale Magazine, vol. 1, 1820), Lancaster City Museums, 1989.

A. White, *Lancaster: A Pictorial History*, Phillimore & Co. Ltd, 1990.

A. White and M. Winstanley, *Victorian Terraced Houses in Lancaster*, University of Lancaster, Centre for North-West Regional Studies, 1996.

A. White, 'Gentlemen's Houses in Lancaster', *Georgian Group Journal*, VI, 1996, 120–30.

A. White, *The Buildings of Georgian Lancaster*, University of Lancaster, Centre for North-West Regional Studies, 2nd edn, 2000.

P. Williamson, *From Confinement to Community: The Moving Story of 'The Moor': Lancaster's County Lunatic Asylum*, Bay Community NHS Trust, 1999.

M. J. Winstanley et al., *A Traditional Grocer T. D. Smiths of Lancaster 1858–1981*, University of Lancaster, Centre for North-West Regional Studies, 1991.

Index

(Illustrations in **bold**)

Agricultural Society 118
Almshouses 76
  Gardyner's 76
  Gillison's 154, **155**
  Penny's 138, 154
Archaeological sites
  Bollihope Common 14
  Bolton-le-Sands 14
  Burrow Heights 20–1, **21**
  Carlisle 7
  Cockersand Moss 27
  Ingleborough 4
  Market Hall 33
  Mitre Yard 10
  Old Vicarage 7
  Ribchester 9, 20
  Skelmore Heads 4
  Vicarage Field 7, 10, 14,
    56
  Vindolanda 9
  Warton Crag 4, 15
Architects
  Hubert Austin 196
  Joseph Gandy 150
  Richard Gillow 129, 151
  Thomas Harrison 145,
    146, 149–51, **150**
  Major Thomas Jarrat **146**
  Thomas Mawson 233–4
  E. G. Paley 196
  Edmund Sharpe *see also*
    People **181**, 196
Armada 92
Ashton, Lord *see* James
  Williamson II
Assizes 78–80, 138, 162, 184
Atlantic trade 103–4, 117

Bailiffs 39, 102
Banks
  Dilworth & Hargreaves
    137
  Dilworth, Arthington &

Birkett 174
  Lancaster Banking
    Company 174
  Worswicks 137, 174
Barracks 190
Black Death 67–8
Boundaries 40–1
Bridges 47–9, **48**, 123–4,
  129, **138**, 145, **161**,
  177, 249
Brigantes (Iron Age/Roman
  tribe) 4, 5
Buildings
  Ashton Memorial **219**,
    220, 229, 265
  Assembly Room 138, 236
  Custom House 129, **129**,
    150
  Dispensary 156
  Judges Lodging 50
  Kingsway Baths 245, **245**
  Queen Victoria
    monument 222
  Storey Institute 210, 220,
    229, 246
  (Old) Town Hall 35, 118,
    146, **146**, 151, **268**
  Town Hall 220, 229, 233,
    253, **258**
Buoy Masters 128
Burgage plots 53, 66
Burgesses 36, 38–9, 40, 102
Burning by Earl of Derby
  96–7
Burning by Scots 35, 41, 45,
  49, 64, 66–7
Businesses, merchants etc.
  Backbarrow Company 127
  Bulman, Helme & Co.
    153
  Burrows 124, 162
  Gillows 120, 126, 135,
    162, 175, 222, 231

Halton Iron Company 127
Heron Chemical Works
  183
Thomas Hinde & Sons
  124
Lancaster Carriage &
  Wagon Works 178,
  222, 231, 232, 234
Lansils 239, 261, 262
James Nelson & Co. Ltd
  239, 261, 262
Noble 126
Phoenix Foundry 178, 183
Rawlinsons 120, 122, 124,
  125, 128, 162
Edward Salisbury & Co.
  124
Standfast 239
Storeys 182, 183, 222,
  231, 233, 234, 236,
  238, 255, 261, 262–3,
  239
Suarts 124, 135
Waring & Gillow 231,
  233, 234, **238**, 255, 261
Williamsons 182, 194,
  222, 231, 238, 255,
  260, 261, **261**, 262

Cabinet-making 126, 131
Canal 138, 147, 159, 174, 175
Carvetii (Iron Age/Roman
  tribe) 4
Castle 41, 42–6, **47**, 66, 73,
  87, 92, **93**, 95–8, 119,
  134, 138, 147–51, **150**,
  155, 159, 162, 185,
  186, 258
  Adrian's Tower 45, 46
  Debtors 119, 149, 185,
    186, **187**
De-militerisation after
  Civil War 98

Dungeon Tower 46
Former names of towers
    46
Gatehouse 44, 45
Garrison 95–8
John O'Gaunt gateway 45
Keep (Lungess Tower)
    44, 46
Prison regime 149–50,
    155, 185, 258
Shire Hall 46, 150
Well Tower 46
Castles **42**
Chantries 54, 57, 62–3, 74, 76
Charters 33, 35–6, **37**, 38,
    38, 39, 40, 50, 57–9,
    58, 78, 80, 107, 108,
'Chercaloncastre' 34, 57
Churches and chapels (other
    than Priory church)
    Christchurch 204
    High St (Independent) 156
    St Anne 156, 205, **266**
    St John 146, 205
    St Luke, Skerton 204, 205
    St Peter (Catholic) 205
    St Thomas 204, 205
    Sulyard St (Methodist)
        156, 205
Cinema **249**, 251
City Council *see* Corporation
City status 253, **253**
Civil War 92–9
Coaching 144–5
Coastal trade 122–3, 160,
    174, 175
Cockersand Abbey 50, 55, 60
Coffee-houses 142
Corporation (City Council)
    38–9, **109**, 130–1, 146,
    155, 157, 162, **163**,
    164–5, 208–15, 241–6,
    267–70
    Buses 242
    Council Housing 244–5,
        248, **250**, 258, 265
    Gas 244
    Drainage 164, 209, 244
    Electricity 244
    Slum clearance **243**, 244,
        265,
    Street lighting 164
    Tramways 210, 211, **214**,
        229, 242
    Water supply 209, 244,
        257
Cotton 122, 127, 179–82

Cotton Famine 220
Crosses, stone 34, 43, 55, 57

Domesday Book 34, 43, 57
Duchy of Lancaster 45–6,
    48, 54, 77, 79, 81, 82,
    93

Evacuees 254, **254**
Executions 36, 85–7, 88–91,
    134, 150

Fee Farm Rent 80, 102
Fishing 61–2, 112
Friary, Black (Dominican)
    41, 53, 62, 63–4, 74, 84
Furness Abbey 48, 49, 59,
    60–1

Glasson Dock 130, 159, 175,
    176

Halton 43, **43**
Hamilton estate 118
Health care 156, 173,
    185–90, 196, 252,
    257–8, **257**
    County Lunatic Asylum
        (Moor Hospital) 185–6,
        188
    Dispensary 156
    Isolation Hospitals 245
    Ripley Orphanage 185,
        188–9, **189**
    Royal Lancaster Infirmary
        189, 211, **213**, 245
    Royal Albert Asylum 185,
        188–90, 194, 259
Herber House 62–3
Historians
    Camden 35, 41, 102
    'Cross Fleury' 73
    Leland 56, 73
    Tacitus, Cornelius 4, 5
Hornby Castle 73, 77, 81,
    218
Horse fair 103
Horse racing 140, **141**, 184
Housing *see also* Corporation
    49–50, 135–7, 147,
    194–6, 232, 244–5,
    249–51
Houses
    Ashton Hall 218, **255**
    Fairfield **198**
    Moorlands 195
    Ryelands 220

Springfield Hall 188, **189**,
    220
Westfield 218, 233

Immigration 256
Imports 121, 160
Industries 126–7
Inns 142, 144, **144**, 201–2,
    202

Jacobite Rebellion 1715
    133–4
Jacobite Rebellion 1745
    134–5, **135**

King's Own Royal Regiment
    190, 232–3, **233**

Labour Exchange 236
Labour Party 240, **268**
Lancaster & Morecambe
    College 259
Lancaster University 259–60
Lancashire County Council
    258, 263
Leprosy 65
Libraries 142, 210, 252
'Lino King' *see* James
    Williamson II
Linoleum **260**
Livery and maintenance
    39–40, 77–9
Livestock 103
Localities in and around
    Lancaster
    Aldcliffe 40–1, 59
    Beaumont 61, 112
    Bowerham 40
    Dalton Dam 61
    Edenbreck 63
    Freehold Estate 194, 201,
        251
    Greaves 40, 154
    Haverbreaks 40, 195
    Ladies Walk 138, **138**
    'Mabildancote' 61
    Marsh 39, 41, 42, 118,
        141
    Moor 39, 40, 84, 134,
        150, **175**, **221**
    New Quay 129
    Newton 41, 59
    'Nuns' Fields' 65, 195
    Pothouse 124
    Scotforth 173, 194, 195,
        210
    Skerton 48, 65, 66, 140,

173, 194, 210, **264**
White Lund 234, 236
'Loncastre' 34
Lune, river 4, 5, 7, 8, 10, 14,
  16, 40, 47, 117, 130,
  138, **138**, 245
Lune valley 4, 7, 15, 22, 43

Mahogany 126
Maps
  Binns' 64
  Docton's **34**, 154
  Mackreth's **48**, 49, 53, 154
  Speed 50, **79**
Markets **34**, 35, **39**, 50, 118,
  268, 270
Mayor 38–9, 40, 101, 102,
  130–1, 140, **242**, 246,
  246
Mercia 34
Mills, corn etc. 35–6, 54–5,
  65, 76
Mills, textile etc 127, 162,
  179–82
  Albion 180, 182, 194
  Bath 180, 181, 182, 194,
    261
  Greenfield 183
  Moor Lane 180, 181
  Queen St 180, 182
  Ridge Lane 180, 182
  St George's Works 183
  White Cross 179–80,
    181–2, 183, **262**
Monasteries **60**
Morecambe 176, **177**, 204,
  267–8
Morecambe Bay 13
MPs 81–2, 94, 132, 215–8,
  240–1, 266–7
Museum 252
Music 140–2, 203–4, 265
Music Hall 185, 204

National Filling Factory 234,
  236
National Projectile Factory
  234, **234**
Newspapers 232
Northumbria 34

'Old Lancaster' 35, 41

Parliament 81–2, 94–8,
  131–2, 215–8, 240–1,
  266–7
Pendle Witches *see also*

Witchcraft
People
  Lady Ashton **255**
  Hubert Austin 55
  Laurence Binyon 233
  Fenner Brockway 240–1
  Henry Burton 91
  Randall Carter 112
  Cartimandua 4
  John Dalton 147
  Robert Dalton 55, 76
  Agnes de Baldreston 66
  John de Bolron 68
  Hubert de Burgh 45
  John de Catherton 68
  Hulle de Ellel 36
  Robert de Holand 49
  Derby, Earl of 84, 95–7,
    101
  Dodshon Foster **122**
  George Fox 99–101
  John Gardyner 54–5, 76,
    112, 260
  Godfrey (the Sheriff) 59
  Robert Graves 234
  Sir John Harrison 112
  Annie Helme **242**, 246
  Sir Norval Helme **216**,
    241, 247
  Giles Heysham 112
  William Heysham 154
  John Hodgson 104, 119
  Thomas Holcroft 84
  Thomas Holme 157
  Christopher Johnson 196
  Lancaster, Thomas Earl
    of 49, 65
  John Lawson 100, 101,
    104
  Robert Lawson 119
  Stephen Lemeyngs 50
  George Marsh 84–5
  Mollie and Maggie **235**
  William of Mortain 44
  Robert of Normandy 43
  Roger of Poitou 42, 44,
    57
  William Penny 154
  (Rev) Joseph Rowley 150
  Edmund Sharpe 176, 178,
    183, 185, 209, 214
  Thomas Shires 153
  Lambert Simnel 73
  Edward Stanley, Lord
    Monteagle 63, 81
  Storey Brothers 183, 229,
    241

Sir Thomas Storey 233,
    216
  William Stout **103, 106**,
    108, 119, 123, 133
  Tosti 43
  Brian Tunstall 63
  William Tunstall 61–2
  Venutius 4
  Thomas Weeton 125
  James Williamson I 182–3
  James Williamson II
    (Lord Ashton) 183,
    216, 217, 218, 220,
    229, 230, 239–40, 241
  Gideon Yates **129, 153**,
    161
Persecution 85–7
  Catholic Martyrs 86–7
Pilgrimage of Grace 83–4
Policing 159, 208, **258**
Poor relief 154–5, 173, 190,
  247–8
  Workhouse 190
Popish Plot 107–8
Population 151–3, 173, 190,
  191, 194–5, 231, 232,
  236–8, 256–7
Port Commission 128–30,
  153, 175
Poulton-le-Sands
  (Morecambe) 139
Preservation 270–1
Preston 78
Priory church 10, 33, 34, 47,
  50, 55–9, **58**, 60–2, 73,
  74–6, 83, 84, 100, 146,
  205
  Bells 205
  Chantries 62
  Choir-stalls 55
  King's Own chapel 55,
    56, 205, 233
  Precinct walls 56
  Tithe barn 57
Privateering 124–6, 160

Quarter Sessions 79, 80
Quernmore 12, 20, 21, 36,
  40, 45, 63, 75, 78, 80,
  81, 108

Railways 176–8, **178**
  Lancaster & Carlisle 176,
    177
  Lancaster & Preston
    Junction 176
  Little North Western

177, **177**, 183
London & North
   Western 176, 177
Midland 176, 177
Reeve 38
Religion 82–5, 204–6, 215
   Anglicanism 204–5
   Catholicism 83–4, 85,
     111–2, 205
   Methodism 205–6
   Presbyterianism 99, 108
   Protestantism 84–5, 111
   Puritanism 99
   Quakers 99–101, **103**,
     108, 119, 128, 143, 205
Roman archaeology
   Altar 13, 14, 16
   Barcae (barges) 13
   Barracks 8
   Basilica 11, **12**
   Bastion 25
   Bath-house 11, **12**, 18,
     18, 20,
   Brick and tile 20–1
   Bridge 10, 15, 47
   Burial 15, 18
   Cavalry 12
   Coins 11, 21, **24**, 27, 41
   'Courtyard House' **18**
   Farms 22–3
   Fort 3, **3**, **6**, 7, 8, **8**, 9, **9**,
     10, **10**, 14, 15, 19, 20,
     23–7, 33, 44, 50, 59
   Garrison 15, 19
   Gate 8
   Inscriptions 11
   'King Street' 5, 7
   Mansio (rest-house) 14
   Milestones 20
   Pottery 20, 27
   Public buildings 18
   Rampart **8**, 10
   Roads 20–1
   Ruins 33, 55
   'Saxon Shore' 23, 26
   Sculpture 17
   Temples 16, 17
   Tombstone 11
   Vicus (civilian settlement)
     3, 15–20, 27
   Well 8, 12, **23**
   Wery Wall 23–5, **25**, **26**
Roman emperors
   Aurelius, Marcus 12
   Constans 26
   Constantine 26
   Postumus 11

Severus, Septimius 12
   Trajan **10**
   Vespasian 7
Roman governors
   Agricola, Gnaeus Julius 7,
     12
   Bolanus, Marcus Vettius 5
   Cerialis, Quintus Petillius
     5, 7, 12
Roman gods
   Apollo 17
   Dionysus (Bacchus) 17
   Jalonus Contrebis 14, **16**,
     17
   Mars 13, **13**
   Mars Cocidius 14, 16, **17**
   Mars Nodens 27
   Mercury 17
   Mithras 17, **21**
   Silvanus 14
   Vulcan 17
Roman military units
   Ala Augusta 11, 12
   Ala Gallorum Sebosiana
     12, **13**, 14, 15
   Legio XX 7
   Legio II Adiutrix 7
   Numerus Barcariorum 13,
     13, 15, 27
Roman persons
   Ammausius, Flavius 14
   Apollinaris, Lucius Julius
     11, 13
   Januarius, Julius 14, 17, 22
   Micianus, Gaius Tetius
     Veturius 14
   Sabinus 14
   Tritus 20
   Vibenius, Lucius 14, 16,
     17
Royal Forest 36, 42, 50
Royalty
   David, King of Scotland
     44
   Edward I 36
   Edward IV 40, 54
   Henry IV 45
   Henry V 45, 56
   Henry VII 78
   James II 111
   John of Mortain (later
     King John) 35, 44, 54,
     65
   Richard I 44
   Stephen of Blois 43, 61

St Leonard's Hospital 41, 54,

64–5, 74
S. Martin's College 259
St. Wilfrid 34
Schools 158, 206–8, 258–9
   Castle Howell 207
   Castle (Central High) 259
   Free (Lancaster Royal
     Grammar) 54, 76, 112,
     156–7, 207–8, 233,
     246, 253, 255, **77**
   Friends' 157, 207
   Girls' Grammar 246, **246**,
     255
   Islamic College 259
   Our Lady's 259
   Ripley 258–9
   Skerton Central 247
Seez, Normandy 57
Setantii (Iron Age/Roman
   tribe) 4
Seton nunnery 65
Shipbuilding and
   shipbuilders 123–4, 175
   Edward Barrow 123
   Richard Brekell 123
   George Brockbank 123
   John Brockbank 159, 160,
     161
   Lune Shipbuilding
     Company 175
   James Nicholson 175, 179
   James Smith 124, **129**
   Daniel & Matthew
     Simpson 175
   Thomas Wakefield 123
   Worthington &
     Ashburner 124, 160
Ships and shipping 120–6,
   120, 129, 145, 159–61,
   174
   Bonaparte 125
   Cato 121
   Clarendon 124
   Imployment 120
   Kidnapper 125
   Lambe 119
   Love 135
   Minerva 124
   Olive Branch 123
   Paragon 125
   Prince Frederick 121
   Robert 133
   Sunderland 127
   Thetis 125
Shops 118–9, 198–201, **199**,
   200, **247**, 248, 264, 268
Silk 126

Slave trade 121–2, **122**, 161
Societies, Friendly 158–9
Solemn League and
    Covenant 99, **110**
Sport 203, 230, **251**, 252,
    252, 265
Stallenge Rolls **106**
Street names 41, 50–3, **52**
Streets and places in
    Lancaster
  Bridge Lane 48, 53
  Bus Station 48, 242–3
  Cable St 146
  Calkeld Lane 53
  Castle Hill 3, **3**, 7, **8**, **9**,
    11, 24, **24**, **25**, **26**, 27,
    35, 53, **135**, 138–9, 153
  Castle Park 147, **233**
  Caton Rd 231
  Cheapside 11, 33, 53,
    118, 199
  China St 50, 53
  Church St 3, 8, 16, 17,
    20, 27, 33, 50, 53, 118,
    125, 147, 153, **243**
  Cock Pit 118, 140
  Common Garden St **155**,
    265
  Dalton Square 64, 147,
    148, 222, **249**
  Damside St 54
  Green Ayre 53, 54, 138,
    161, **163**, 178
  High St 147
  King St (Back Lane,
    Chennell Lane) 53,
    118, 154, 242, 265
  Market Square 35, 118,
    145
  Market St 35, 50, 53,
    153, **197**
  Moor Lane 33
  New St 145
  New Rd 145

North Rd 231, **238**
Parliament St 146
Penny St 3, 8, 16, 20, 33,
    49, 53, 96, 102, 200
Pudding Lane 50
'Priestford' (Priest Wath)
    47, 59
Queen Square 147
St George's Quay 24, 47,
    129, **129**, 145, 153,
    161, 176
St Leonardgate 65, 139,
    194
St Mary's Place **243**
St Mary's St (St
    Marygate) 50
St Nicholas St 50, 199,
    265
Salt Ayre 47, 59
Scale Ford 47, 59
Shambles 118, 153
Stonewell 15, **153**
Sulyard St 64
Vicarage Fields 59
Westfield Memorial
    Village 16
'Stycas' (Northumbrian
    coins) 34
Sugar refinery 101, 126
Sunderland Point 123, 139
Syon Abbey 54, 55, 56, 74–6

Temperance 201–2
Theatre 139, 185, 204, **266**
Thornbush 130, 159
Tobacco 119, 126
Tokens **105**
Tolls 80, 145
Tory Reaction 108
Trade guilds 104
Trade Unions 239–40

Vicars of Lancaster
    Richard Burton 75

Richard Chester 74–5
James Fenton 108, 134,
    143
William Green 75
William Marshall 99, 100
Augustus Wildbore **135**
Virginia 104, 119, 120
Visitors
    Anonymous (1764) 118,
      123
    Capt Thomas Bellingham
      104
    Rev Thomas Coxe 119
    David Cragg 124, 149
    John Crofts 118, 121,
      126, 129, 138–9, 151
    Daniel Defoe 119
    Charles Dickens 201
    Celia Fiennes 104, 117,
      118, 145
    John Harden 138
    J. Holt 151
    James Mackenzie 145
    Rev MacRitchie 139, 149
    Thomas Pennant 126
    Robert Southey 139
    James Ray 119
    Arthur Young 121, 126,
      136

War, First World 232–6
War, Second World 253–6
Wars of the Roses 73
Westfield Memorial Village
    234
West Indies 120, 121, 124,
    160
    Barbados 121, 125, 135
    Jamaica 124
Whalley Abbey 84
Witchcraft 88–91, **89**
Williamson Park 210, **212**,
    220, **221**
    Greg Observatory **212**